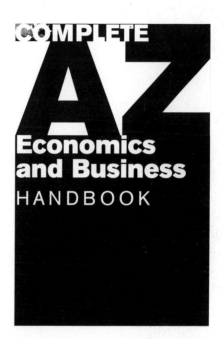

# COMPLETE

# A-Z

## Economics
## and Business

## HANDBOOK

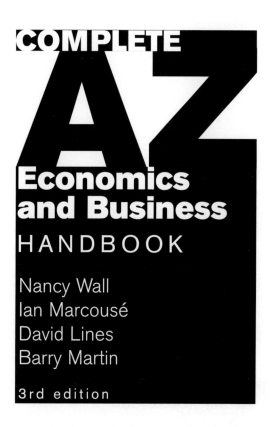

# COMPLETE A Z

## Economics and Business

### HANDBOOK

Nancy Wall
Ian Marcousé
David Lines
Barry Martin

3rd edition

Hodder & Stoughton

A MEMBER OF THE HODDER HEADLINE GROUP

A B C D E F G H I J K L M N O P Q R S T U V W X Y Z

*British Library Cataloguing in Publication Data*
A catalogue record for this title is available from The British Library

ISBN 0 340 87276 4

First published 1996
Second edition 2000
Third edition 2003

Impression number 10 9 8 7 6 5 4 3 2
Year 2007 2006 2005 2004

Cover photograph: PhotoDisc/Getty Images

Typeset by GreenGate Publishing Services, Tonbridge, Kent.
Printed and bound in Great Britain for Hodder and Stoughton Educational,
a division of Hodder Headline plc, 338 Euston Road, London NW1 3BH,
by CPI Bath

# CONTENTS

A
B
C
D
E
F
G
H
I
J
K
L
M
N
O
P
Q
R
S
T
U
V
W
X
Y
Z

# HOW TO USE THIS BOOK

The *A–Z Economics and Business Studies Handbook* is an alphabetical textbook designed for ease of use. Each entry begins with a one-sentence definition. This helps the user to add precision to the completion of reports or case studies.

Entries are developed in line with the relative importance of the concept covered. *Job sharing* is covered in a few lines, whereas a central issue such as *change* or *productivity* receives half a page. The latter would provide sufficient material to enrich an essay. Numerate topics are developed through the use of worked examples. All formulae are set out explicitly.

The study of economics and business can be developed further by making use of the cross-referenced entries. For example the entry for *unemployment* refers the reader to *demand deficiency* and *structural unemployment*. Cross-referenced entries are identified through the use of italics. Therefore essay or project writing should benefit from following the logical pathway indicated by italicised entries.

Economics and business students have always had difficulties with the language of the subject. This stems from several factors:

- both economics and business have their own jargon
- different firms have their own terminology, and their own ways of using words
- the media use or invent phrases (such as 'white knight'), some of which prove temporary, while others need assimilating into course content
- textbooks recommended by the exam boards use technical terms in different ways.

The *A–Z Economics and Business Studies Handbook* is a glossary providing a single solution to these problems. Where terms have more than one meaning, both are explained. In addition, the entries have enough detail to make the book a valuable reference/revision companion. It provides full coverage of the GCE A level and joint subject syllabuses.

To aid the revision process, carefully selected lists are provided at the back of the book, such as the 'Top 30 terms in marketing'. Those facing examinations can use the lists to make the best use of the *Handbook* during their revision time. The revision recommendations are split into modules, for ease of use. The section on examiners' terms provides an explanation of the trigger words used on exam papers, such as 'analyse', 'discuss' and 'evaluate'.

This *Handbook* will help anyone who wants to understand current events in business and the economy. Many terms that are used in the financial media are fully explained so that their significance will become clearer. We hope that, as well as providing an invaluable resource for A level Economics and Business Studies, this *Handbook* will be used more widely by people with an interest in the general field.

Nancy Wall, Ian Marcousé, David Lines and Barry Martin.

# ACKNOWLEDGEMENTS

The book took a year to research and write. The authors were fortunate to have the assistance of a number of people and organisations. Among the organisations were the Banking Insurance and Finance Union (BIFU), the City Business Library, the Advisory Conciliation and Arbitration Service (ACAS) and the Advertising Association.

The individuals fell into two groups. First, the family aides. Maureen Marcousé did much of the research into employment practices and laws; Fiona Martin proved a hawk-eyed proofreader; Jill Turner provided ideas and support throughout; David Wall provided vital assistance with material on the financial markets. The other people to be thanked are the team at Hodder Arnold, especially the late Tim Gregson-Williams.

Researching, writing and editing a book of this size requires the occasional willingness to sacrifice technical accuracy in favour of clarity. A considerable amount of time went into checking the entries, but if any mistakes have slipped through, the authors apologise and accept full responsibility.

Nancy Wall, Ian Marcousé, David Lines and Barry Martin.

**abnormal profit:** see *supernormal profit*

**absenteeism** measures the rate of deliberate workforce absence as a proportion of the employee total. Ideally this statistic would exclude absence due to ill health, though it may be impossible to distinguish between genuine absences and truancy.

FORMULA: $\dfrac{\text{number of staff absent}}{\text{staff total}} \times 100$

Main causes of absenteeism include: *alienation*, poor staff welfare systems, stress, poor working conditions.

Remedies include: pay systems linked to attendance, *job enrichment*, better *human relations*, better working conditions.

**absolute advantage:** a country has an absolute advantage in trade in a particular good with another country if it can produce that good using fewer real resources. This means that its costs will usually be lower in money terms. For example, Jamaica has an absolute advantage over the UK in the production of bananas because its climate is suited to banana production.

**absolute poverty:** a standard of living which fails to provide basic necessities of life. Poverty may also be relative, in the sense that some people have very much less income than others, and may therefore be unable to buy the things which are regarded as necessary in that society. Poverty can therefore be defined in different ways in different societies: a poor person in the UK will usually have a higher standard of living than a poor person in India. (See also *poverty*.)

**absorption costing** calculates the unit cost of an item after allocating a proportion of the estimated fixed *overheads*, i.e. each unit must absorb its fair share of the overheads.

Pros:
- ensures that prices are set after all costs have been considered
- requires thought about the most accurate method for allocating overheads.

Cons:
- ignores the problem that *fixed costs per unit* can only be estimated accurately if demand/output can be predicted
- often undermined by imprecise methods of *overhead allocation*.

**ACAS:** see *Advisory Conciliation and Arbitration Service*

**accelerator:** the theory that *investment* spending by firms is a function of the rate of change in consumer *demand* or *output*. Therefore if demand is rising, firms' requirements for more capital equipment will accelerate. The extra investment is an injection into the circular flow of money, which will generate a larger increase in output. The economic growth that is already taking place will in turn accelerate.

**accelerator/multiplier model:** the theory that the *accelerator* and the *multiplier* interact to bring about cyclical changes in the economy. An increase in investment during the upswing of the *business cycle* will have a multiplier effect, generating a larger increase in income. As the economy approaches full capacity and real growth slows, the accelerator theory predicts that investment needs will fall, leading to a downturn. The fall in injections will have a downward multiplier effect, until such time as the need for replacement investment again causes investment to grow. At that point the cycle repeats itself.

**accountability** is the extent to which a named individual is held responsible for the success or failure of a policy or a piece of administration. When a company's management structure is clear, staff will know what authority has been given to them, and by whom. If that authority is exercised poorly, the employee should be held to account for his or her mistakes.

Pros: • clear accountability is the basis for providing two of Professor *Herzberg*'s 'motivators' – achievement and recognition for achievement

• in order to correct mistakes it is essential to know how they came about – usually a function of people's decision-making or communication failures.

Cons: • if a firm operates in an atmosphere of mistrust, accountability can be seen as a threat; managers may fear that overambitious sales targets have been set with a view to proving their incompetence.

Accountability is also important when discussing how organisations or people in the public sector may be answerable to a higher authority such as a Minister or the House of Commons. The government is ultimately accountable to the electorate.

**accounting principles:** a chosen set of accounting conventions that must be applied consistently if company accounts are to be useful to observers. These include: matching costs to related revenues; valuing assets with prudence; making the assumption that the firm is a going concern; and establishing accounting rules to ensure objectivity, i.e. minimising personal judgement in the drawing up of accounts.

**accounting ratios:** see *ratio analysis*

**Accounting Standards Board:** the body which lays down the accounting standards that firms should follow and checks on whether the standards are being met. If concerned about an issue, the Accounting Standards Board may review the Statement of Standard Accounting Practice (SSAP) that governs the problem, or may issue a new *Financial Reporting Standard (FRS)* to cover it.

**accounts:** a systematic way of recording the financial history of an organisation over a certain time period. The principal accounts kept are the *balance sheet*, *profit and loss account*, and *cash-flow statement*.

**accruals:** according to the matching principle, expenses (and revenues) are to be allocated in the accounts to the time period in which the cost (or benefit) to the organisation is felt. An invoice may not yet have been paid for a benefit already received, e.g. a gas bill. If so, the expense must still be shown in the accounts despite the fact that no cash has been paid. It would appear as an accrued expense under *current liabilities* in the *balance sheet*.

**accumulated profit** is the total retained profit a firm achieves over its lifetime. Also known as *reserves*, accumulated profit forms part of the *shareholders' funds*. A common mistake is to assume that accumulated profit represents an asset that can be used or liquidated. It is a source of long-term finance that has already been invested in *fixed assets* or *working capital*. If a firm needs cash today, it must look at its assets not its past profits.

**acid test ratio** measures a firm's ability to meet its short-term debts, i.e. to pay its bills. The firm's total *current liabilities* are compared with *current assets* excluding *stock*. This is because it can be hard to turn stock into cash, such as for a clothing company when fashion turns against it.

FORMULA: $\dfrac{\text{current assets} - \text{stock}}{\text{current liabilities}}$

Accountants recommend that this figure should be about 1, i.e. that there should be about £1 of liquid assets for every £1 of short-term debt.

**Worked example: extract from the Rochelle Clothing Ltd balance sheet**

|  |  | £000 | £000 |
|---|---|---|---|
| Current assets | Stock | 160 |  |
|  | Debtors | 80 |  |
|  | Cash | 60 | 300 |
| Current liabilities | Creditors | 180 |  |
|  | Tax due | 45 |  |
|  | Overdraft | 55 | 280 |
| Net current assets |  |  | 20 |

$$\text{Acid test ratio} = \frac{300 - 160}{280} = 0.5$$

This means that the firm has only 50p of highly liquid assets for each £1 of short-term debt: very low liquidity.

**ACP states** are the African, Caribbean and Pacific states which had colonial links with member countries of the European Union. To some extent they have been able to negotiate favourable trading arrangements with the EU. India is not included despite its ex-colonial status.

**acquisitions:** a term used to refer to businesses which have been or are being taken over.

**activity rates:** see *participation rates*

**added value** refers to the value added to an input by a business, as it creates its final output. (See also *value added*.) It can be calculated by subtracting the cost of all the material inputs from the value of output. It reflects the value of the services of land, labour, capital and entrepreneurship which have been used in the process of production.

**administration:** when a company in severe financial difficulties brings in an administrator whose task is to protect the best interests of the shareholders by keeping the business going. The administrator may need to sell off some *assets*, but is most unlikely to close down the whole firm. If the financial problems cannot be resolved a *receiver* might be called in. He/she would act in the best interests of *creditors*, possibly by liquidating all the firm's assets.

**ad-valorem tax:** a tax which is charged as a proportion of the price. The tax will be set as a percentage of the price charged by the retailer, and then included in the final price to the customer. A good example is *VAT (value added tax)*.

**advances:** banks use the term 'advances to customers' to describe their loans and over-drafts.

**advertising** is paid-for communication through media such as television, newspapers or radio. Most advertising can be categorised as either *informative* or persuasive, or a combination of the two.

**advertising agency:** a firm specialising in creating, planning and executing a client's advertising strategy. Agencies are usually divided into three main departments, all of which draw upon the work of market research:

● Planning: decides which type of consumer to target the advertising at, and the strategy for doing so

● Creative: designs and writes the advertisements and commercials, including the *slogans* and catch-phrases

● Media: plans and buys the media time or space to reach the *target market* as cost-effectively as possible.

**advertising campaign:** the complete realisation of the client firm's strategy, i.e. all the advertisements appearing for a certain product within a specified time period.

**advertising elasticity** measures the extent to which changes in advertising spending affect *demand*. If a relatively small change in spending caused a major shift in demand, the product would be termed advertising elastic.

FORMULA:  $\dfrac{\text{percentage change in demand}}{\text{percentage change in advertising spending}}$

**Worked example: if a firm doubled its advertising spending and demand rose from 20 000 to 28 000 units as a result, its advertising elasticity is:**

percentage change in demand $= (8\,000 \div 20\,000) \times 100 = +40\%$
percentage change in advertising spending $= +100\%$
advertising elasticity $= \dfrac{+40\%}{+100\%} = 0.4$

**advertising ethics** are the moral issues raised by the persuasive power of *advertising*. Laws prevent advertisements from containing untruths, but do not force firms to state the whole truth. This allows companies to use advertising images that exaggerate or mislead. An ethical company should reject such an approach. In recent years a further ethical issue has arisen because of the way in which firms incite children to use 'pester power' on their parents.

**Advertising Standards Authority (ASA)** is a self-regulatory organisation set up to ensure that advertisements are kept socially acceptable. It administers the *Code of Advertising Practice*. Critics suggest that because it is financed by advertisers, the ASA is not harsh enough on advertisements that appear to break the code.

**advertising strategy** is the plan for meeting advertising objectives. Frequently, these objectives consist of targets that are not directly linked with sales volume, such as improving consumers' awareness of a brand name. The strategy will set out the *target market*, the preferred media for reaching these potential customers, and the overall style of the advertising. The *advertising agency* puts the strategy into practice.

**Advisory Conciliation and Arbitration Service (ACAS)** was set up in 1975 as an independent source of expertise in preventing or settling industrial disputes. It is the organisation companies, unions or individuals turn to when seeking an expert, unbiased conciliator or mediator. Upwards of 110 000 individual conciliation cases are handled each year. ACAS has a reputation for unbiased advice that has been helped by its policy of not commenting publicly on the strength of the case of either side to a dispute. (See *conciliation* and *arbitration*.)

**AER** see *annual equivalent rate*

**after-sales service** is the appreciation that customer needs do not end when a sale has been made. Spare parts and maintenance may have to be provided, and friendly, supportive advice should always be available. Efficient after-sales service may be a vital factor in encouraging a high level of repeat purchase.

**aged creditors analysis** means listing your unpaid bills from suppliers in age order, with the most overdue account at the top of the list. By paying the oldest account first, you hope to maintain good relations with your creditors.

**aged debtors analysis** means listing the unpaid bills of your customers in age order, with the most overdue account at the top of the list.

**ageing population** occurs where people are living longer and therefore the average age of the population is rising. Japan and a number of European countries have rapidly ageing populations. The UK population is ageing more slowly. The economic implications include the necessity of providing more health care and pensions.

**ageism** is discrimination based on a person's age. Currently this is legal in the UK, but the 1988 Human Rights Act forces the government to make age discrimination illegal by 2006.

**agenda:** the notification to those attending a meeting of the topics to be discussed and the order in which each will be tackled.

**agent:** an independent person or company appointed to handle sales and distribution within a specified area. An agent's income comes from the commission or *mark-up* they make on each sale.

Pros:
- for a small firm the appointment of agents removes the need for the high set-up and overhead costs of a distribution network
- as agents work solely for a percentage of the *sales revenue* they may work harder than a salaried *salesforce*.

Cons:
- if the agent sells many different products, he or she may not give yours enough attention.

**aggregate demand** is the total level of demand in the economy. It consists of consumer spending on goods and services, the investment expenditure of firms, government spending, and net revenue from abroad (export earnings less spending on imports). An increase in aggregate demand may lead to an increase in output provided there is under-utilised productive capacity in the economy. If there is no spare capacity, rising demand is likely to lead to inflation. See the graph on page 6. (See *circular flow of national income*.)

**aggregate demand curve:** aggregate demand can be graphed by plotting output on the horizontal axis and the price level on the vertical axis. It will be downward-sloping because lower prices will allow higher levels of output demanded for any given income level. In combination with the *aggregate supply* curve, it can be used to analyse macroeconomic events.

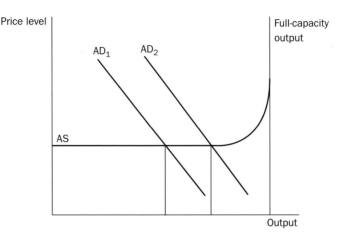

*An increase in aggregate demand leads to increased output if there is underutilised productive capacity in the economy*

**aggregate demand shock:** any sudden change in a component of aggregate demand which has a noticeable effect on the economy. For example a change in interest rates may rapidly affect both consumer and investment demand, so that there is a shift in the aggregate demand curve.

**aggregate supply:** the total of all goods and services produced in the economy. In the short run, aggregate supply may increase in response to rising *aggregate demand*. In the long run, it can increase only if more resources become available (e.g. oil), or if there are improvements in technology, or if efficiency is increased in some other way. (See also *full capacity output*.)

**aggregate supply shock:** a sharp change in the capacity of the economy to supply goods and services. This may occur if there is a natural disaster, or a war, or a sudden change in the price of an important commodity such as oil. These kinds of events will cause the aggregate supply curve to shift.

**AGM:** see *annual general meeting*

**aid** is provided by wealthier developed countries to countries with low per capita incomes. It includes payments made by charities. However the political aspects of foreign aid can be extremely complex. It may be given as a grant or a loan, and loans may be at market or at concessional rates of interest. Some kinds of aid are more effective in meeting poor countries' needs than others. Much depends on how the money is spent. Spending on some major construction projects such as dams has attracted criticism because it has been unsuited to the long-term needs of the country concerned. There are serious controversies surrounding much aid spending. Some of the money which is classed as aid is spent on defence. Many developing countries have tried to negotiate larger aid donations.

**aims** are the long-term intentions that provide a focus for setting *objectives*. They are usually expressed qualitatively, sometimes in the form of a *mission statement*. A typical corporate aim might be 'to produce the finest chocolate in Europe'. From this starting point a firm can build a series of quantifiable targets, such as to increase its consumer quality rating from fifth in Europe to third within three years.

**alienation** is the state of mind that results from a boring, unpleasant meaningless job. It is most likely to occur in a situation of high *division of labour*, or when the workforce rejects the approach or objectives of senior management. Once established, alienation is very hard to dispel. Improved *human relations* or *job enrichment* could only work after the apathy and mistrust have been overcome.

**allocation of resources:** economic decisions about the uses which should be made of land, labour and capital leading to an overall allocation of resources, which generally matches the pattern of consumer demand. Consumer demand creates profitable opportunities for entrepreneurs to organise inputs of factors of production so as to meet that demand. In this way the allocation of resources responds to the pattern of demand exhibited by consumers. This is known as *consumer sovereignty*. However the idea of the allocation of resources can be applied much more widely to a range of decisions which may be taken by individuals or by governments. People decide how to allocate their own resources when they choose between work and leisure, or whether to save more or consume more. Governments make resource allocation decisions when they consider making changes to different categories of spending: they may consider whether to allocate more towards defence or education, or towards health care or unemployment benefit.

**allocative efficiency** is the extent to which resources are allocated effectively between competing market wants or needs. The most efficient *allocation of resources* will be the one which matches the genuine needs of consumers most closely. An economy can move closer to allocative efficiency when ways are found to help businesses to respond effectively to consumer demand. For example, in a *centrally planned economy* such as North Korea's, some producers may be bound by administrative decisions and will not necessarily be able to produce the type of goods which consumers want most. The *transitional economies*, such as Russia and Poland which have moved a long way towards being market economies, have become more allocatively efficient because enterprises producing items which consumers do not want have gone out of business. Government controls of any kind are liable to reduce the responsiveness of markets to consumer demand. However they may be able to protect consumers from the *market power* of large businesses.

**Alternative Investment Market (AIM):** a market for buying and selling shares in firms which are too small or too young to be quoted on the full London Stock Exchange. AIM became the successor to the *Unlisted Securities Market* (USM) in 1995.

**amalgamation:** the merging of two or more divisions of a business, perhaps as part of a *rationalisation* process.

**amortisation:** the *depreciation* of *intangible assets* such as *goodwill*.

**Annual Abstract of Statistics** is published once a year by the Office of National Statistics. It contains key economic and social statistics such as the rate of capital investment and the level of unemployment, and some industry-specific data.

**annual equivalent rate** is the effective annual interest rate paid on credit purchases or received on bank accounts. It shows the compound interest rate and is considered more accurate than its legal predecessor, APR (annual percentage rate).

**annual general meeting (AGM):** a meeting held by *public limited companies* to which all shareholders are invited in order to:

- approve the year's accounts
- vote on resolutions and the election or re-election of board directors
- have the opportunity to put questions to the company chairman.

**annualised hours agreement:** the acceptance by an employee of working hours that are measured per year instead of per week. As a result, the company is able to obtain higher working hours at seasonally busy periods of the year without needing to offer overtime payments. This is an example of flexible working.

**annualised percentage rate (APR)** measures the interest charges on a loan or credit as a percentage of the loan amount outstanding. This is an attempt to ensure that borrowers can compare the true cost of credit from different lenders. APR contrasts with the highly misleading flat rate method of interest calculation, which makes the interest charge appear much lower than it really is. Lenders are legally required to quote the APR on loans so that the necessary consistency is achieved.

**annual report and accounts:** at the end of each accounting year a company must produce a set of accounts to be sent to every shareholder and to *Companies House* (for public scrutiny). For public limited companies (plcs), the annual report must include: a *balance sheet*, a *profit and loss account*, a *cash-flow statement*, a *directors' report* and an *auditor's report*.

**Ansoff, Igor** (b.1918) developed the notion of corporate strategic planning, arguing that a business needs to look at its resources and in a formal way, match them against its competitive environment. He attempted to formalise this process into a series of 'rules' that managers could apply, but this has been criticised for ignoring the dynamics of the business environment, which require strategies to be evaluated and altered as necessary.

**Ansoff's matrix:** a diagram indicating the risks and rewards involved in launching new products. Staying with an existing product in an existing market is the lowest risk/reward strategy. More risky is to launch either a new product into an existing market or an existing product into a new market. The most radical approach is to launch a new product into a new market. Here, the chances of success are low, but the reward from success may be very high. Ansoff, in his 1965 book 'Corporate Strategy' suggested that firms should analyse their own approach to ensure a suitable mix of risk and potential reward.

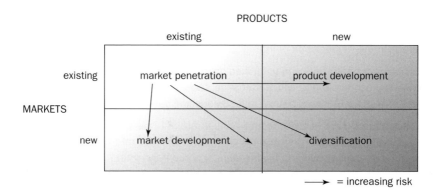

**anticipated inflation:** expected inflation, which has rather different consequences from unanticipated inflation. People will build their inflation expectations into their wage demands. In this way anticipated inflation may become self-perpetuating.

**anti-competitive activities:** where a firm in a dominant market position uses its powers to restrict or eliminate competition. Such actions undermine free competition within a market-place and may therefore lead to poorer customer service or higher prices. For example, in 1995 British Airways apologised for actions taken by employees which could have threatened the survival of the rival Virgin Atlantic airline. In other cases, firms as prestigious as ICI have been fined by the European Commission for price fixing.

Anti-competitive activities can take many forms:

- exclusive dealing, i.e. forcing suppliers to deal exclusively with the dominant firm
- refusing to supply distributors who handle competitors' products
- *full line forcing,* i.e. where the dominant firm requires distributors to stock all of its product line, thus preventing a rival from getting a toehold even in a niche
- tie-in sales, where the dominant firm requires the purchaser to buy a package which not only includes the good of primary interest but others as well, for example a consumer may be offered a guarantee only on the understanding that the product is serviced by the supplying firm
- aggregated discounts, i.e. where a distributor is given a discount for the total sales over a year or any other lengthy period. This encourages the distributor to stay with the dominant firm and discourages competitors.

Such activities come under the Competition Act 1998, and are therefore subject to review by the *Office of Fair Trading* and the *Competition Commission.*

**anti-trust laws** are the laws in the USA which control the growth of large businesses in order to prevent monopoly power from developing.

**apportioned costs** are *overheads* that have been allocated in an arbitrary way to cost or *profit centres*. An example would be allocation of *corporate advertising* expenditure as a pro-portion of the *sales volume* of each brand held by a firm.

**appraisal** is the process of assessing the effectiveness of a process or an employee. It is usually conducted by comparing goals with outcomes. An employee appraisal might be conducted through a questionnaire but is more commonly a one-to-one discussion between employee and manager. The conversation will focus on the employee's performance, perhaps in relation to pre-set indicators such as timekeeping, customer sales levels, and contribution to teamwork. The appraisal interview may take place annually or more fre-quently; it will usually end with discussion of career prospects and training needs.

**appreciation** occurs when the value of an *exchange rate* rises. This means that export prices will be higher and import prices will be lower. Companies which are competing with foreign producers will lose some competitiveness. They may have to consider how they can become more efficient and some may in time be forced out of business.

**apprenticeship:** a form of training for young people, focused upon learning the skills and methods required to carry out a single job. It usually consisted of three or more years of on-the-job training plus some practical and written tests. Apprenticeships faded out in the 1970s and 1980s as new technology reduced the need for craft skills and modern employment practices emphasised multi-skilling and job flexibility. There has recently been an attempt to revise this approach using *modern apprenticeships*.

**appropriation account:** the section of the *profit and loss account* that shows how the firm has used its after-tax profits (its *earnings*). Part may be paid to *ordinary shareholders* as dividends, part to *preference shareholders*, and the remainder will be retained within the company as investment capital. The part of the appropriation account that is retained adds to the balance sheet *reserves*.

**APR:** see *annualised percentage rate*

**arbitrage** is trading between two or more markets when profitable opportunities arise. For example, if the pound equals 2 000 lira on the Italian foreign exchange market and 2 050 lira in London, a profitable arbitrage deal can be made by buying pounds in Italy and selling them in London. In this way currency dealers' actions ensure that different market rates keep in line with each other.

**arbitration** is resolving a dispute by appointing an independent person or panel to judge the appropriate outcome. The arbitrator will listen to both sides to the dispute then make his or her decision. If both sides have agreed it in advance, this decision can be legally binding. Otherwise, either side could reject the arbitrator's decision. (See also *conciliation*, *Advisory Conciliation and Arbitration Service* and *pendulum arbitration*.)

**arithmetic average (mean):** the arithmetic mean or average of a distribution is a *measure of central tendency* which is calculated by dividing the total value by the number of occurrences.

FORMULA: $\dfrac{\text{sum of (variable} \times \text{frequency)}}{\text{sum of frequencies}}$

The mean is a useful measure and can be subject to further calculations but it is distorted by extreme values and may not be a whole number or the same as one of the items in the distribution.

**ARR:** see *average rate of return*

**articles of association:** one of two documents required by law to establish a limited company. It sets out the internal rules under which the company will operate and its relationship with its shareholders. Examples include: the way meetings are conducted, the types of shares and the rights attached to each type, and the powers of the directors. Together with the *memorandum of association*, the articles are submitted to the *Registrar of Companies*. They can be viewed by anyone on payment of a fee.

**ASA:** see *Advertising Standards Authority*

**Asian Development Bank** exists to provide development finance for developing countries in Asia and the Pacific. Its affiliate, the Asian Development Fund, provides loans at concessional rates of interest to poorer countries in the region.

**Asian financial crisis:** in 1997, Thailand and Korea encountered serious problems with loss of confidence in their banking systems. There followed very rapid selling of their currencies and sharp falls on their stock exchanges. This led quickly to depressed trading conditions and similar problems in other countries including Japan and Indonesia. The fall in Asian exchange rates generally made UK exports uncompetitive and the loss of a large part of their export markets affected some UK businesses quite seriously. Confidence was gradually restored and by 1999 the problems were much reduced, but the crisis interrupted the usually high growth rates in the affected countries.

**assembly line** is the final stage in the manufacturing process, where components and *sub-assemblies* are fitted together to make the finished product. The assembly line usually works on the basis of high *division of labour*, with the use of conveyor belts to move the parts from one stage to the next.

**asset:** anything providing a flow of benefits to an organisation over a certain time period. Those reported as assets on a *balance sheet* are the ones which can be given a monetary value, usually because they have been bought and a value thus obtained. Assets show how an organisation has deployed the funding available. Assets represent what is owned by an organisation or what is owed to it.

**asset-led marketing** bases the firm's marketing strategy on its strengths (instead of purely on what the customer wants). An example of this was the use of the Mars Bar as the starting point for Mars to move into the ice-cream market.

**assets employed:** the book value of all the firm's assets minus *current liabilities*. It is calculated by adding fixed (long-term) assets to (short-term) working capital.

**asset stripping** occurs when a *predator* takes over a target company because it feels that the market price of the target's assets is higher than its *stock market* value suggests. Thus the stock market is undervaluing the target company whose assets can be stripped out individually and sold in total for more than the price the predator pays. The sum of the parts is greater than the whole (the opposite of *synergy*).

**asset structure:** the way a firm balances its holdings of assets broadly between fixed (long-term) and current (short-term).

**asset turnover:** a measurement of a firm's ability to generate *sales turnover* from its asset base. Its importance is that unless the assets owned by a business can produce income, they must represent a drain on its resources and/or efficiency. Businesspeople like to use the phrase 'making the assets sweat'; by this they mean working all the firm's assets hard enough to generate high sales. For example, a fast-food chain might decide to close down its 10 worst performing outlets because even though they are profitable, the firm's capital could be employed more effectively in branches with a higher asset turnover.

FORMULA: $\dfrac{\text{sales}}{\text{net assets}} = \text{asset turnover}$

**assisted areas:** carefully defined parts of the UK in which government grants may be given to persuade firms to locate there (see the map on page 12). These grants are available for production and service businesses. They represent an element of the government's *regional policy*. The objective of this policy is to reduce the unemployment which has been caused by the decline of many traditional industries such as coal and steel. Tier one qualifies the highest levels of help. Other areas are in Tier two, which gets some help but not as much.

**auction** is a method of selling based on gathering buyers together to bid for the item being sold. Buyers compete openly, with the highest bid being the winner.

**audit:** an independent check on the financial accounts of an organisation. It is conducted by auditors who are professional accountants. In the wake of a series of unexpected company failures in 2001 and 2002, auditors came under repeated criticism for their failure to clarify accounting irregularities to the shareholders. It was pointed out that although the process should be independent, the fact that the client firm was selecting and paying the auditor might undermine that independence.

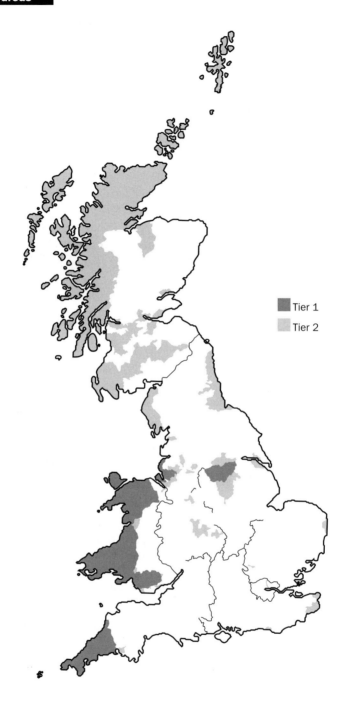

*Assisted areas*

**auditor's report** is part of an organisation's annual accounts and will be read carefully by shareholders, *creditors*, tax authorities, employee organisations and others to check for indications of concern. If satisfied, auditors will report that the accounts reveal a *true and fair view* of the organisation's affairs for the period. If the auditors qualify their remarks, there may be cause for concern.

**Austrian School:** Austrian economists have been associated since the nineteenth century with a strong commitment to a free market determined allocation of resources. In this century these ideas have been associated particularly with the work of Friedrich von Hayek, who left Austria in the 1930s to work at the London School of Economics and later at the University of Chicago. His view was that governments could not make decisions which would lead to an efficient allocation of resources because they would always lack the necessary information. Further, in a planned economy, people would lack the incentive to take risks. It is the prospect of large personal gains that stimulates entrepreneurs to make decisions which lead to efficient use of scarce resources.

**authorised share capital:** the value of *share capital* which a company may issue, i.e. sell, to raise funds. This is found in the *memorandum of association*. A company may choose not to issue all its authorised share capital, ensuring the ability to raise new funds from existing and new shareholders at any time in the future.

**authoritarian leadership style** assumes that information and decision-making are best kept at the top of the organisation. This may be because the senior managers lack trust in the competence or good faith of their staff, or it may reflect acute pressures on the firm that force the directors to make rapid, difficult decisions. (see also *leadership style*.)

**autocratic leadership style:** see *authoritarian leadership style*

**automatic stabiliser:** part of the economic system which helps to iron out fluctuations in the *trade cycle*. The most common example is social security expenditure and, in particular, unemployment benefit. As the economy goes into *recession* more people become unemployed, and so government expenditure rises to pay benefits to those out of work. This maintains demand at a higher level than would otherwise be the case were the unemployed simply left with no money at all. The other important automatic stabiliser is income tax. As incomes rise in the *boom* phase of the business cycle, income tax receipts rise more than proportionately because income tax is progressive. Similarly, if incomes are falling during a recession, tax receipts will fall more than proportionately. In this way the tax system takes more spending power out of the economy in a boom than it does in a recession, so helping to counteract the fluctuations in aggregate demand and diminish their impact.

**automation** uses machinery to replace human labour. This may reduce total costs, but could result in a more inflexible production process. This makes a firm more vulnerable to changes in consumer taste or increases in competition. Modern, *lean production* techniques emphasise the need for flexible automation, using computer-controlled machines that can quickly be reprogrammed to perform different tasks.

**autonomous group working** is a term used to describe the delegation of set tasks to a team of workers. They are given the power to decide how best to complete the task; to decide if there should be a team leader and if so, who; and to decide who should do what. It is a process of decentralised teamworking.

**average cost** is the total cost divided by the number of units produced. It is also known as unit cost.

FORMULA:   average costs = $\dfrac{\text{total cost}}{\text{total output}}$

**Worked example: a firm buys materials at 50p per unit and spends £1 000 on weekly overheads; the production rate is 4 000 per week:**

So average costs are:   $\dfrac{(\pounds 0.5 \times 4\,000) + \pounds 1\,000}{4\,000} = 75\text{p}$

This figure must be treated with great caution as it is highly deceptive. It gives the impression of being a constant figure per unit. In fact it varies at different levels of output because if more units are produced, the fixed cost element per unit falls. This can be seen in the diagram below.

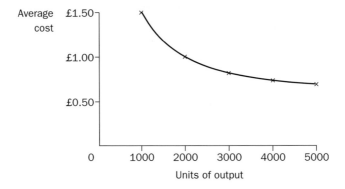

*Average costs falling as output rises*

**average fixed costs** are the costs of the fixed factors of production, land and capital, per unit of output. They fall in the short run as output increases because the fixed costs are spread more thinly over the larger number of units produced.

FORMULA:   average fixed costs = $\dfrac{\text{total fixed costs}}{\text{units of output}}$

**average propensity to consume:** that proportion of income which people choose to allocate towards consumption spending.

**average rate of return (ARR):** a calculation of the average annual profit on an investment as a percentage of the sum invested.

FORMULA:   $\dfrac{\text{total profit over project life} \div \text{number of years}}{\text{capital outlay on project}} \times 100$

It provides the firm with a percentage figure that can be compared with the percentage rates of return on other uses of its capital. It can also be judged against the rate of interest to identify the rewards the firm is hoping to receive for the risks involved in its investment. The diagram on the following page shows a situation where a firm anticipates a 10 per cent ARR at a time when interest rates are 7 per cent. It must then make a judgement about whether a 3 per cent real return is sufficient given the risks involved. If the investment is by Marks and Spencer PLC in a new store opening, the risk may be low enough to justify going ahead. For the launch of a new computer software house, however, a 3 per cent *reward for risk* would be hopelessly inadequate.

**Worked example: a 4-colour printing press will cost Colour Co. £120 000. It is expected to generate the following net cash flows over its four years of useful life:**

| | |
|---|---|
| Year 1 | £38 000 |
| Year 2 | £60 000 |
| Year 3 | £60 000 |
| Year 4 | £34 000 |

Step 1  Calculate total cash contribution over lifetime:

$$£38\ 000 + £60\ 000 + £60\ 000 + £34\ 000\ =\ £192\ 000$$

Step 2  Deduct the investment outlay to find lifetime profit:

$$£192\ 000 - £120\ 000\ =\ £72\ 000$$

Step 3  Calculate average annual profit:

$$£72\ 000 \div 4\ =\ £18\ 000$$

Step 4  Take the annual profit as a percentage of the sum invested:

$$\frac{£18\ 000}{£120\ 000} \times 100\ =\ 15\%$$

See also *reward for risk.*

**average revenue** is the total revenue derived from sales divided by the number of units sold.

**average variable costs** are the costs of variable factors of production such as labour, raw materials and components. In the short run they may rise as output rises, because efforts to produce more without increasing the amount of capital (a fixed factor) may make production less efficient.

FORMULA:  $\text{average variable costs} = \dfrac{\text{total variable costs}}{\text{units of output}}$

**What other subjects are you studying?**

A–Zs cover 18 different subjects. See the inside back cover for a list of all the titles in the series and how to order.

**backdata** is past research information that can be used to interpret new findings. For example if a survey finds that 47 per cent of beer drinkers say they would buy a new American malt liquor, how could one translate that into a sales forecast? Only by comparing the result with backdata on the research and actual performance of past product launches. If a new German lager had, a year ago, received a 45 per cent result and, since then, had actual sales worth £40m. a sales forecast of more than £40m. could be made for the malt liquor.

**bad debt:** an unpaid customer's bill for goods or services sold on *credit* which is now thought unlikely to be settled, perhaps because the customer is in *liquidation*. As a credit sale has been already included as *revenue* in the organisation's books, the bad debt needs to be charged to the *profit and loss account* as well as to the *book value* of debtors.

**balance of invisibles** is the term used to describe that part of the *balance of payments* account which registers exports and imports of invisible payments and receipts. Exports and imports are categorised as either visible or invisible. Visible trade is that which involves goods, such as cars and machinery, i.e. those which you can clearly see and touch. Invisibles include services such as banking, insurance and tourism, which you cannot see and touch. Traditionally, the UK has run a surplus on invisibles thanks mainly to its finance sector.

**balance of payments:** a record of all transactions associated with imports and exports, together with all international capital movements. It consists of the *current account*, the *capital account* and the financial account. The current account shows trade in goods and services, income from employment and investments abroad, and transfers which may be made by governments or individuals.

It is not always possible to identify all payments: unrecorded transactions are shown as 'errors and omissions'. The capital account is of little significance, accounting for changes associated with immigration and emigration.

The financial account shows the capital outflow from the UK caused by investments overseas and the capital inflow resulting from foreign investment in the UK. These investments may consist of factories or offices built by foreign companies in the UK or they may be money flowing into or out of UK bank accounts (known as *portfolio investment*). Net UK investment overseas shows the balance between the two. See table on following page.

**balance of trade** is the term used to describe that part of the *balance of payments* account that registers exports and imports of visible goods. The UK has been importing more visible goods than exports since the last quarter of the nineteenth century, and this has been paid for by the surplus on *invisibles*.

| | Credits | Debits | Balance |
|---|---|---|---|
| *Current account* | | | |
| Total goods | 190.1 | 223.7 | −33.6 |
| Total services | 77.7 | 66.4 | 11.3 |
| Income | | | |
|   employment abroad | 1.1 | 1.0 | 0.1 |
|   investment income | 141.6 | 129.0 | 12.5 |
| Current transfers | 16.4 | 23.1 | −6.7 |
| Total current account | 426.8 | 443.2 | −16.4 |
| *Capital account* | | | |
| Totals | – | – | 1.5 |
| *Financial account* | | | |
| Net UK investment overseas | – | – | 13.3 |
| Net errors and omissions | – | – | 3.4 |

UK balance of payments, 2001, £billion.
Source: ONS, Annual Abstract of Statistics, 2002

**balance on current account:** this is the total of visible and invisible exports and imports.

**balance sheet:** a statement of an organisation's *assets* and *liabilities* at a precise point in time, usually the last day of the financial year. Liabilities must equal assets thanks to the accounting convention of *double-entry bookkeeping*. An alternative way of interpreting a balance sheet is that liabilities (capital employed) show where the capital came from and assets show how and where the capital is employed. So assets employed must equal capital employed, as shown below.

**Balance sheet for A–Z Ltd 31 December 200–**

| | £000s | £000s |
|---|---|---|
| Fixed assets | | 450 |
| Stocks | 125 | |
| Debtors | 160 | |
| Cash | 45 | |
| Less trade creditors | (260) | |
| Net current assets | | 70 |
| ASSETS EMPLOYED | | 520 |
| Long-term liabilities | 135 | |
| Share capital | 25 | |
| Reserves | 360 | |
| CAPITAL EMPLOYED | | 520 |

**balanced budget:** if the government exactly balances tax revenue and expenditure it is said to have a balanced budget. In fact on an annual basis this happens rather rarely. Most often there is a budget deficit, sometimes a budget surplus, and very occasionally the budget nearly balances. Over a period of time the annual budget deficits and surpluses may balance each other out. The current golden rule is that expenditure should not exceed tax revenues by more than the level of public investment. Borrowing to invest can be justified because of the expected future income which the investment will create.

**balanced growth** is *economic growth* which does not produce environmental degradation, or permanently reduce the resource base of the economy. This means that there must be measures which prevent businesses from causing environmental damage, and the use of *depletable resources* must be controlled. The emphasis will be on using resources in a sustainable way.

**balancing item:** a term used in the past to show the difference between the current balance and the capital balance. Since 1999 the accounts have been constructed differently and no longer use this term.

**ballots:** the process of voting for or against a course of action. Ballots authorising *industrial action* must meet the requirements of the *Trade Unions Act 1984* and the *Employment Act 1988*. These demand that ballots must be secret, must offer voters an alternative which stops short of strike action and must include a warning that strike action may lead to dismissal. Only if the industrial action receives more than 51 per cent support will the union be immune from being sued.

**bank:** a bank is a financial intermediary which takes deposits from people or businesses which wish to save, and lends money to people or businesses which wish to borrow. By doing this on a large scale, and by exploiting the fact that not all of its deposits will be withdrawn at any one time, a bank can expand its lending over and above the total of deposits which it receives from savers. This process is known as *credit creation*.

Banks supply a wide range of financial services. Some also specialise. *Merchant banks* exist to meet the needs of large businesses. *Retail banks* take deposits from all kinds of small and large customers. Investment banks specialise in funding large investment projects and in advising on finance. In recent years a number of *building societies* have become banks.

**bank advances** are the loans which banks make to individual or business customers.

**bank bills** are very short-term loans, usually for three months only. They can be bought and sold on the money market. There is no interest to pay on them but the maturity value will be larger than the loan, so giving a rate of return to the lender. This means that until maturity they are traded at a discount. They are sometimes known as bills of exchange.

**bank deposits** are the amounts deposited by customers with their banks.

**bankers' balances** are the accounts held by banks with the Bank of England, which they use to settle their accounts with each other, and which are a very *liquid asset*.

**banking covenants** are formal agreements between a firm borrowing money and its bank that set out the limits within which the company can operate. For example, a bank lending £200 000 to a firm may insist that no more than £100 000 be borrowed from any other source. If the firm breaks its covenant, the bank can insist that the loan be repaid. If the firm is not in a position to do this, it may be placed in the hands of a *receiver*.

**Bank of England:** the UK's *central bank*. It is responsible for the issue of notes and coins in the economy, and also, more importantly, for implementing *monetary policy* including interest rate and *exchange rate policy*. It is also responsible for ensuring that public sector net borrowing is funded through the sale of bills and bonds. Until 1997 the Bank of England acted as a watch-dog for all banking activities in the economy. This *bank supervision* is now carried out by the *Financial Services Authority*, an independent body whose other main objectives are to ensure that financial services such as insurance, accounting, stockbroking and investment advice operate honestly and competently.

There have been calls to make the Bank of England independent, to make monetary policy less political. There used to be close collaboration between the *Chancellor of the Exchequer* and the Governor of the Bank of England. This has changed since the *Monetary Policy Committee* was set up in 1997. This has given the Bank considerable independence in setting interest rates.

**bank rate** is the original name for the interest rate set by the *Bank of England*. It is still sometimes used (as in *base rate*) by the press when referring to the interest rate set monthly by the *Monetary Policy Committee*. The real name for this is the *repo rate*.

**bank supervision:** the process by which the Financial Services Authority aims to ensure that banks do not lend more than they ought to. If they do they will eventually be unable to meet the demands of their customers to withdraw their cash. This is known as bank failure. Supervision means making sure that the banks are holding a sufficient quantity of *liquid assets*, enough to balance the growth of their lending, so that they do not run out of cash.

**bankruptcy:** an individual or an *unincorporated* body may request (petition for) bankruptcy or be declared bankrupt when unable to settle its *liabilities* or if acting in such a way as to lead *creditors* to think that it is unable to settle, e.g. by refusing to communicate with them. Note that the term bankruptcy should not be applied to *limited liability* companies (see *insolvency* and *liquidation*).

**bar chart:** a diagram used to give a quick comparison between variables, e.g. monthly *sales revenue* of a company's three products. The values are plotted vertically and time horizontally. The heights of the bars represent the values. While good for impact, the bars lack precision and it may be difficult to ascertain actual values from the vertical axis. Also distortion can be created by selecting the width of bar inappropriately and by starting the vertical scale at above zero.

**bar coding** is the recording of data in a form that can be read instantly by a laser beam. When used on packaging it enables each sale to be recorded, thereby providing accurate stock records.

**barriers to communication** are physical or attitudinal reasons why messages fail to be received.

Physical reasons include:

* noisy environments making conversation impractical
* geographic distance, as when firms have their production in the North-East but their head office in London.

Attitudinal reasons include:

* *intermediaries* deciding not to pass a message on (a complaint, for example)
* the unwillingness of an alienated worker to listen.

**barriers to entry** occur when it is difficult for new firms to enter an industry. This most commonly arises because there are substantial technical *economies of scale* being reaped by existing firms, and a new entrant to the industry, starting up in a small way, would have higher costs. Many manufacturing industries have barriers to entry because the production process is very *capital-intensive*. Other economies of scale, marketing and financial, may be important too.

A second source of barriers to entry is legal and arises from *patents*. When an invention is patented, only the holder of the patent is allowed to produce it for a specified number of years. This means that no other company can copy the product until the patent expires. Other barriers include exclusive dealership arrangements, *full line forcing* and any kind of collusive agreement between existing firms in the industry.

**barriers to trade:** see *import controls*

**barter** is the swapping of goods or services to conduct a non-monetary transaction. It is likely to be needed when the deal is between different countries, one of which has a currency which cannot be converted freely.

**base rate:** a commonly used term for the interest rate at which the Bank of England lends money to the banks whenever they are short of cash. (The real name for this is the *repo rate*). This rate is set at the monthly meetings of the *Monetary Policy Committee* and is the basis for setting interest rates throughout the banking system.

**base year:** where *time series* data are put into *index number* form, the year chosen to have a value of 100 in the index series is called the base year.

**basic pay:** an agreed regular wage excluding any bonus, shiftwork, or profit-sharing supplements.

**basket of currencies:** when exchange rate changes are measured, an index number is created which shows the extent of the change for one currency against those of its main trading partners. The currencies selected for this are known collectively as a basket of currencies.

**batch production** is the manufacture of a limited number of identical products, usually to meet a specific order. Within each stage of the production process, work will be completed for the whole batch before the next stage is begun. This provides some *economies of scale* compared with *job production*, but nothing like as many as through *flow production*.

**bear market:** a period of pessimism and falling share prices on the *stock market*. Individuals who anticipate this happening sell shares in the expectation that they will be able to buy them back in the future at a lower price. To a certain extent it results in a self-fulfilling prophesy, in that if everyone sells, more shares will come onto the market, and their price will indeed fall. A bear market is the opposite of a *bull market*. The 2000–02 bear market saw share prices halve, following a long bull market.

**benchmarking** means setting competitive performance standards against which progress can be measured. These standards are based on the achievements of the most efficient producers within a market-place (if you can find out their figures). They ensure that production managers focus upon the competitive environment, instead of looking purely at this year's achievements compared with previous years'. Benchmarking is seen as a vital element in achieving *world-class manufacturing*.

**benefits in kind:** people receive many benefits from the welfare state which are not given in the form of money. Health care, education and other services provide benefits in kind which add to people's well-being but do not increase their money income in the short run.

**best practice benchmarking:** see *benchmarking*

**Beveridge Report:** in 1942 Lord Beveridge produced his report, Social Insurance and Allied Services, which provided much of the thinking which underlay the creation after 1945 of the *welfare state*. Some of the benefits of the welfare state have remained to the present, others were gradually eroded by the changes brought in by the Conservative governments in power since 1979.

**bias** is a factor that causes data or an argument to be weighted towards one side. Statistical bias occurs when a *sample* has – by chance or by mistake – an overweighting towards one subgroup (e.g. too many pensioners within a research sample). Personal bias occurs when a decision-maker consciously or subconsciously favours one side over another. *Scientific decision-making* methods such as *investment appraisal* or decision trees are supposed to avoid bias. In fact, the results they produce will depend upon the assumptions made, which may be biased.

**bilateral** talks or arrangements are those that occur between two parties. Therefore discussions on trade between the American and British governments could be termed bilateral trade negotiations.

**bilateral monopoly** occurs where there is a single seller and a single buyer. A trade union which represents all the workers in an industry and a dominant employer can create a bilateral monopoly, as in the case of the British Medical Association which negotiates doctors' pay, and the National Health Service which employs most of them.

**bilateral trade** occurs when two countries swap equal quantities of exports and imports. More often trade is multilateral, characterised by surpluses and deficits between pairs of countries, so that the UK might export engineers' services to Saudi Arabia, which might in turn export oil to Japan, which in turn exports cars to the UK.

**bill:** see *bank bills*

**binding arbitration:** see *arbitration* and *pendulum arbitration*

**biotechnology** is the attempt to harness nature for commercial purposes such as the manufacture of medicines. Whereas pharmaceutical drugs, food colourings and flavourings have traditionally been based scientifically on chemistry, the intention is that advanced biology will become more important in future. Biotechnology is best known for genetic engineering, but it is the vast worldwide market for medicines that most attracts investors into this high-risk, high-tech area.

**birthrate:** the average number of live births occurring in a year per 1000 population.

**black economy** is the term used to describe all those transactions which do not appear in the national accounts. Some of these are legal, others are not. The black economy includes the wages of people who are on *means-tested benefits* while actually working more than the few hours allowed. It also includes payments, e.g. to babysitters, which do not need to be recorded for tax purposes. It is estimated that 3–5 per cent of tax revenue is lost through illegal activities taking place on the black economy.

**black market:** when a market is controlled, e.g. by rationing, a black market develops, where people who have things to sell and people who want to buy them evade the controls. A black

A B C D E F G H I J K L M N O P Q R S T U V W X Y Z

market developed during World War II in the UK, and more recently countries with strict foreign exchange controls have experienced black markets in currencies.

**blacking** is the refusal to deal with goods or personnel of a firm, usually because they have been involved in strikebreaking.

**blacklist:** a list of names of people or companies that a firm or country will not deal with.

**blind product test** is a consumer test of the taste or smell of two or more rival products. What makes it a 'blind' test is that the brand name and therefore image of the product is hidden from the consumer.

**block release** is off-the-job training based on blocks of time at college (such as three months). It is an alternative to the more common system of *day release*.

**Blue Book:** a publication of the Office of National Statistics which contains the UK National Income Accounts.

**blue chip:** a company that is so large, well established and soundly financed that it can be regarded as a secure investment or employer.

**blue collar union:** a *trade union* that represents manual workers.

**body language** is the conscious or unconscious use of the body to convey unspoken messages. A shrug of the shoulders may convey indifference, while an aggressive stance may undermine a manager's attempt to apologise to a subordinate.

**bonds:** a borrower may issue a bond, which is a promise to repay a certain sum of money at a date some time in the future (from one to twenty years or so). In return for the loan which is the price of the bond, interest will be paid, usually at a fixed rate. Bonds may be traded on the Stock Exchange, and the price will reflect the attractiveness of the interest rate relative to current market rates. Bonds issued by the Bank of England to finance government spending are known as Treasury Bonds, also as gilts, because the government will always be able to repay on maturity, since it has the right to tax. (Hence, they are said to be 'as good as gold'). Bonds issued by companies are known as corporate bonds. Because the rate of interest and the maturity value are fixed, bonds are much less risky than shares, but are likely also to have a lower rate of return.

**bonus issue:** a free issue of shares to shareholders on a proportional basis, e.g. one for every five already held. For fuller information see *scrip issue*.

**bookkeeping:** recording a firm's transactions in a series of account books on the basis of *double-entry* accounting. From these books a trial balance can be arrived at, from which a full set of accounts can be drawn up.

**book value:** the *balance sheet* value of an asset. For *fixed assets* this is the *historic cost* minus accumulated depreciation. For stocks it is the lower of cost and *net realisable value*. In either case, the stated book value depends on assumptions made by the business, and is therefore only as reliable as the individuals concerned and the information they have available to them.

**boom:** the phase of the *business cycle* in which economic growth is at its most rapid. As recovery gathers pace, economic growth becomes faster until in a boom it is growing at a rate which cannot be sustained in the long run. The economy will be characterised by relatively low levels of unemployment and a tendency for inflation to accelerate.

**Boston Matrix:** a method of analysing the current position of the products within a firm's portfolio, in terms of their *market share* and growth within their market-place. Devised in America by the Boston Consulting Group, this system of product portfolio analysis is far more sophisticated than the *product life cycle*. The Boston Matrix points out not only the importance of market share, but also that firms want products that can support each other's development. Product life cycle theory implies that declining brands have no future other than to die, whereas the Boston Matrix shows that an ageing brand can be a *cash cow* to be milked for the benefit of a rising star or to finance the changes needed to a problem child. (See diagram below.)

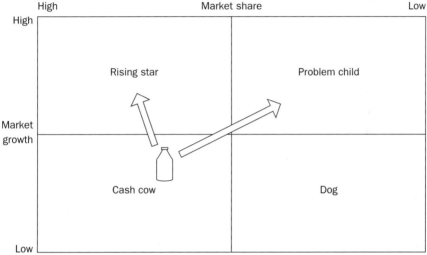

bottlenecks are hold-ups in the assembly lines of a firm, or supply constraints in the whole economy. Within an individual business, bottlenecks might be caused by poor management planning, or by trying to rush more output through the factory than is possible using the available labour, materials or capital resources.

Bottlenecks in the economy as a whole are caused by inability to increase supply to match an unexpected surge in demand. In boom years, for example, there have been shortages of microchips, forcing producers of a huge range of products to slow down their rate of output. There may also be shortages of skilled labour which make it difficult for businesses to hire the kind of people they need in order to expand. Bottlenecks can lead to prices of scarce resources being bid up as buyers compete for them. This can be the start of an acceleration in inflation during a *boom*.

**bottom line:** jargon for the bottom line of a *profit and loss account*, or the estimated *net profit* on a specific activity or project. Care must be exercised to see which version of profit is meant.

**brainstorming:** a group activity in which members are encouraged to say the first answer that strikes them about how to solve a problem, no matter how weird. Having obtained as many ideas as possible, the group will consider each one in more detail. It is a way of encouraging more creative solutions than the normal carefully considered, safety-first ideas that managers may put forward.

**branding:** establishing an identity for your product that distinguishes it from the competition. Marketing managers often talk about the personality of their brands as if referring to people. Successful branding adds value to an item and can ensure *brand loyalty*.

**brand leader:** the brand with the highest percentage share of a specific market or segment. This has become an increasingly valuable position as retailers have become more powerful over recent decades. Supermarkets such as Tesco have such strong *own-label* products that they do not have to stock every national brand within a sector. Usually, they stock the brand leader, their own label, and just one other brand. Therefore the second biggest selling brand often has to compete fiercely with the numbers three and four for shelf space, and that means cutting prices to the bone. Only the brand leader is able to negotiate on equal terms with the retail giants.

**brand loyalty** exists when consumers repeat-purchase your product on a regular basis. Such customers are unlikely to be price sensitive, therefore your product's *price elasticity* will be low. This enables you to increase the price level without much effect upon demand. Brand loyalty can be active or passive:

- active loyalty stems from a conscious decision on the part of your customers that they prefer the taste, look, quality, or image to that of the competition

- passive loyalty stems from consumer inertia, that is from people's tendency to become used to a purchasing pattern from which they do not bother to change; for new products, this is the hardest marketing problem to overcome

**brand mapping:** see *mapping*

**brand standing:** a measure (in effect an audit) of where one firm's brand stands in consumer affections compared with rivals. This is monitored regularly by the use of *market research* into the images, attitudes and usage of those within the *target market*.

**breach of contract:** breaking a term laid down in a legal contract and therefore being liable to be taken to court or to be sued.

**break-even chart:** a line graph showing total revenue and costs at all possible levels of *output* or *demand*, i.e. at every point from an output of zero through to maximum capacity. This enables the reader to see at a glance the profit at any output level that interests them (by looking at the vertical difference between revenue and costs). An example is shown below.

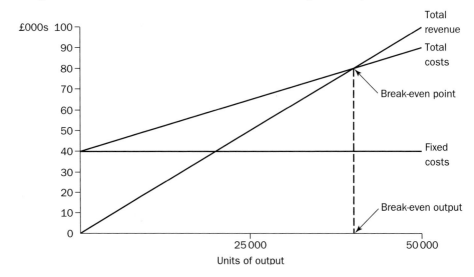

The chart comprises three lines: *fixed costs*, total costs and total revenue. They are plotted with pounds on the vertical axis and output on the horizontal axis.

Fixed costs: form a horizontal straight line

Total costs: line starts at fixed costs and rises as a diagonal straight line

Total revenue: line starts at 0 and rises as a diagonal straight line

To construct the chart, first set out a grid with the following headings:

| Quantity | Revenue | Variable costs | Fixed costs | Total cost |
|---|---|---|---|---|

In the quantity column should be no more than three figures:

**1**   0 units

**2**   Maximum output (which might have to be assumed)

**3**   A convenient point between them (probably halfway).

**Worked example: compile a table of data for a firm with fixed costs of £40 000, variable costs of £1, a selling price of £2, and a factory capable of producing 50 000 units:**

| Quantity | Revenue | Variable costs | Fixed costs | Total cost |
|---|---|---|---|---|
| 0 | £0 | £0 | £40 000 | £40 000 |
| 25 000 | £50 000 | £25 000 | £40 000 | £65 000 |
| 50 000 | £100 000 | £50 000 | £40 000 | £90 000 |

From this information the graph can be drawn as shown opposite, with pounds on the vertical axis and output on the horizontal.

**break-even point:** the intersection of total revenue and total cost on a *break-even* chart. It can be calculated without drawing the chart as shown below:

FORMULA:   break-even output $= \dfrac{\text{fixed costs}}{\text{contribution per unit}^*}$

* selling price − variable cost

**Worked example:**

$$\frac{£40\,000}{£2 - £1} = \textbf{40 000 units}$$

**breaking bulk:** see *wholesaling*

**Bretton Woods:** the name given to the post-Second-World-War economic system that sought freely convertible currencies within a worldwide *fixed exchange rate* system. Between 1945 and 1971 this was remarkably successful, helping world economic growth achieve its highest ever levels. The name Bretton Woods stems from the location of the wartime conference that set up this system.

**British Rate and Data (BRAD):** a monthly publication that lists all the advertising media available in the UK, from THE TIMES to THE GROCER. Each entry gives the address of each medium, together with the cost of buying advertising space. It is available at many local libraries and is ideal for discovering real advertising costs for projects or business plans.

**British Standard 5750** is the best known certification of quality management within the country. Its supporters believe that it ensures standards that can be relied on by purchasers. Critics consider it a bureaucratic nightmare: a triumph of paper over performance. What is not in doubt is that BS 5750 does not guarantee a quality standard. It is a system for ensuring that firms set quality targets and then monitor their actual performance in relation to those targets. By implication, then, a firm could hold a BS 5750 certificate for setting and achieving a relatively low quality target. Firms today tend to use the international equivalent term: *ISO 9000*.

**British Standard 7750** is a certification of environmental management standards. It is a tool by which an organisation can recognise whether it is achieving acceptable environmental standards. In the longer term, it is hoped that it will become as important a market differentiator as BS 5750.

**British Standard 7850** measures a firm's progress towards achieving TQM (*total quality management).*

**British Standards Institute (BSI):** the body responsible for setting quality and performance standards over a wide range of product fields. Seeing the BSI *kitemark* logo on a product should give consumers confidence that it has been manufactured to a high quality and safety standard.

**broker:** someone who acts as an intermediary between a buyer and a seller, helping to negotiate a sale. Brokers are usually found in the financial services sector, as in the case of stockbrokers or insurance brokers.

**brown goods:** a collective term for electrical household goods that were traditionally made with wood castings, such as televisions and hi-fis.

**BS 5750:** see *British Standard 5750*

**BS 7750:** see *British Standard 7750*

**BSI:** see *British Standards Institute*

**Budget (the):** sets out the government's income and expenditure plans for the forthcoming year. Government income is raised through *direct* and *indirect taxes* on firms and individuals, and spent on goods and services such as defence, education and social security benefits (e.g. unemployment benefit). Note that the budget does not have to balance; if expenditure is greater than income it is known as a budget deficit, and if income is greater than expenditure it is known as a budget surplus. The budget occurs in March each year. Each November the Chancellor of the Exchequer sets out the government's spending plans. Both occasions provide all-embracing statements of economic policy, including detailed forecasts of expected levels of economic activity.

The budget performs a macro-economic management function, as well as involving detailed adjustments to policies which affect the *allocation of resources*. An example of the latter occurs when there are changes in expenditure taxes on fuel which have environmental objectives. Changes in spending on benefits are also announced at this time.

**budget:** a forward financial plan usually involving a *cash-flow forecast*, forecast sales and forecast costs. The budget is a kind of route map that should have been set in the light of the company's objectives for the period. Divergences from a budget figure can be analysed by variance analysis. Budgets can be used as a discipline, a coordinator, a motivator, a monitoring and control device and a trigger for remedial action, as well as a test of forecasting ability.

**budgetary control:** progress throughout an accounting period can be checked by regularly comparing actual with budgeted figures for *revenues* and *expenses*. Variances can then be investigated. Regular monitoring may correct divergences to allow reallocations within the budget to cope with the unexpected.

### Worked example: budgetary control through variance analysis

| | All figures in £000s | | | | | | | | |
| | January | | | February | | | March | | |
| | Budg | Act | Var | Budg | Act | Var | Budg | Act | Var |
|---|---|---|---|---|---|---|---|---|---|
| **Revenue** | 85 | 80 | (5) | 95 | 86 | (9) | 110 | | |
| **Materials** | 36 | 34 | 2 | 42 | 39 | 3 | 46 | | |
| **Fixed costs** | 42 | 44 | (2) | 45 | 45 | – | 45 | | |
| **Profit** | 7 | 2 | (5) | 8 | 2 | (6) | 19 | | |

**budget deficit:** the result of government expenditure being greater than its income. The difference has to be made up by boosting the money supply, or by borrowing, which the government can do by selling *bonds* and *bills* or by attracting more savings into Premium Bonds or other *National Savings* products. Heavy government borrowing may, however, increase interest rates, making life hard for businesses and individuals with large loans.

A budget deficit may be caused by structural or cyclical factors:

- structural: a long-term tendency for spending to exceed revenue, perhaps because government spending is more popular politically than government taxation

- cyclical: in a recession, tax receipts inevitably fall because people are out of work, and firms are making less profit. In addition more people out of work means more spending on social security benefits such as unemployment benefit.

Cyclical causes should be self-correcting when the economy recovers. Structural causes will not disappear unless tackled directly.

Borrowing for investment makes sense when the income generated by the investment is likely to be sufficient to pay the interest on the debt.

The annual budget deficit is known as *public sector net borrowing*. The combined deficits from the past are called the *National Debt*.

**budget surplus:** when government revenue exceeds its spending. (See *budget* and *budget deficit*.) The surplus in any one year is called the Public Sector Debt Repayment.

**buffer stock:** the desired minimum stock level held by a firm just in case something goes wrong. Possible causes include a supplier's failure to deliver, the discovery of sub-standard supplies or an unexpected increase in demand. The more efficient the firm and its suppliers, the lower the buffer needed. Those aspiring to a *just in time* production system set their sights on removing the buffer stock completely. This would release capital to be put to more profitable use elsewhere in the business.

The term buffer stock is also used to refer to stocks of commodities, such as wheat, which are held in many countries and can be used in the event of shortages at some time in the future. Some are held by government bodies and some in the private sector.

**building society:** a financial intermediary which specialises in lending for house purchase, i.e. very long-term loans. In recent years building societies have diversified into offering retail banking services to customers, and several have changed their status to become banks.

**built-in obsolescence:** see *obsolescence*

**built-in stabilisers:** during different phases of the business cycle, the government will automatically be changing the level of spending on benefits, and will receive varying levels of tax revenue. These changes offset the changes in aggregate demand in the economy as a whole. As more people become unemployed, their benefit entitlement rises, and they are able to continue spending, albeit on a lower level even though they are no longer earning. Similarly they will pay little or no tax. The reverse happens as the economy recovers. So as demand falls in recession, it is offset by a rise in government expenditure, and a fall in taxation, which reduces leakages from the circular flow of money. This reduces the severity of the slump. The opposite happens as the economy recovers and so the boom is slowed.

**bulk buying** means purchasing in large enough quantities to secure a lower price per unit. This is an important *economy of scale* and is a reason why firms are attracted to *horizontal integration* (mergers). Traditionally, even small firms thought it sensible to buy in large quantities, gaining discounts but needing to hold stocks for a long time. This desire to buy in bulk has become unfashionable due to the focus on *just in time* production and *stock control*.

**bulk-decreasing good** is one which loses size and/or weight during its manufacturing process, e.g. steel and glass making. Because the reduction in bulk decreases transport costs, industries which do this tend to be located close to their supply of raw materials. (See *industrial location*.)

**bulk-increasing good** is one which increases in size and/or weight during its manufacturing process, e.g. car body shells and soft drinks. Because adding weight and/or size increases transport costs, industries which do this tend to be located close to their market and the consumers. (See *industrial location*.)

**bull market:** a period when prices on the *stock market* are on a rising trend. Individuals who anticipate this happening buy shares in the expectation that they will be able to sell them in the future at a higher price. Sometimes this can get out of hand, so that the speculation on a high rising market begins to develop a momentum of its own, which has no relationship to the real value of the companies themselves. Such a market can only be sustained by its own momentum, and once a hint of doubt sets in it collapses very rapidly. Exactly this happened in the 1929 *Wall Street Crash* and again in October 1987. A bull market is the opposite of a *bear market*. There was a bull market in the US for most of the mid to late 1990s.

**bureaucratic:** a process or management that is rooted in paper-based checks and counterchecks on decisions or actions. As a consequence, creativity is likely to be stifled and decision-making both slow and cautious.

**business confidence** is widely assumed to be a major factor in decisions regarding firms' manpower plans, investment plans and stock levels. It is measured regularly by many research groups, of which the best regarded is the *CBI*'s Quarterly Survey. Many believe that confidence can produce a self-fulfilling prophesy, with an optimistic outlook causing the investment spending and stockbuilding that makes the economy grow. This can lead governments to 'talk up' the economy in recessionary times.

**business cycle:** the regular pattern of upturns and downturns in demand and output within the economy that tend to repeat themselves every five years or so. The causes of this cyclical pattern to economic activity are not fully known, but are partly explained by:

- bunching of investment spending which, by definition, need not be repeated for some years
- government policies that aim for rapid growth just prior to election dates (leading to *inflation* and therefore the need to constrain the economy post-election).

For managers, the key point to remember about the business cycle is that it has existed for over 150 years. Therefore, even when economic prospects look especially rosy, they should remember that a recession may follow the current boom. So the company should always ensure that its liquidity is high enough and borrowings low enough to survive an unexpectedly bad year or two.

Sometimes recession can be a slowing down of growth rather than an actual fall in output.

The phases of the business cycle are as follows:

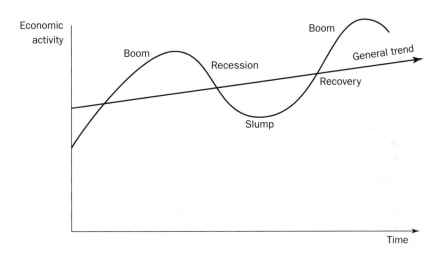

**business environment** is the combination of factors which lie outside an individual firm's control, but which have an effect on its performance. Such factors include economic circumstances, changing technology, government legislation and policy, the social environment, *pressure group* activity and the ethical climate.

**business ethics:** see *ethics* and *ethical code*

**Business Monitors** are government-produced statistics showing quarterly *output* within a series of manufacturing and construction sectors. For instance, if information was required on production trends for umbrellas, Business Monitors would provide this piece of *secondary data*. They are published by the Stationery Office and are available through subscription or in business-orientated public libraries.

**business objectives:** targets set by the board of directors that affect decision making throughout the organisation. Examples might include:

- to break even
- to make a 20 per cent return on the capital invested in the business
- to become known as the technological leader within a marketplace (for example, Sony in the audio and video markets).

A business plan will be devised to attempt to achieve the objectives set.

**business plan:** a report detailing the marketing strategy, production costings and financial implications of a business start-up. The plan is useful for helping the *entrepreneur* to think his or her idea through, though it is mainly drawn up to persuade investors or lenders to inject capital into the business. The main sections of a business plan are:

- a *marketing plan* showing the market gap, product positioning and competition within the chosen market-place
- an account of the entrepreneur's business experience and financial commitments
- a *cash-flow forecast*
- a projected *profit and loss account* and *balance sheet* for the end of the first year
- details of the finance needed from the investor, and the forecast rate of return on the investor's capital
- a brief account of the long-term forecasts and plans of the business.

**business responsibility:** some businesses recognise an obligation to consider and act on the interests of everyone that their activities affect. They will look at the needs of all of their *stakeholders*, be they customers, employees, suppliers, shareholders, creditors, the community in which the business is located or the wider community. Business responsibility might mean making changes in working conditions or product safety, or examining the environmental impact of the activities of the business.

**buyers' market:** if there are large numbers of sellers trying to sell to a relatively small number of buyers, then the buyers will be able to force a drop in price. This is sometimes used to describe the housing market when the number of houses for sale exceeds the number of potential buyers.

**by-product:** when a production process leads to the production of other goods which are not the main objective for the producer, these are known as by-products. The term is often used in relation to the chemical industry. Straw, however, is a by-product of wheat.

**CAD:** see *computer-aided design*

**Cadbury Committee:** set up to report on the financial aspects of *corporate governance*, it recommended a voluntary *code of practice* relying heavily on non-executive directors. Among its other proposals were:

- separation of the roles of *chairman* and *chief executive*
- firms should set up audit committees with a strong independent element

**called-up share capital** is the face value of all the shares that have been paid for by shareholders. A *share* has a *nominal value* written on the face of the share certificate, say £1. A share may be issued fully paid at par and so the buyer pays £1 in full for the share. Alternatively this share may be issued partly paid, say for 40p, so the called-up capital is 40p and the uncalled 60p. Future owners of this share will have to meet this 60p call at some time, or sell the share. Called-up share capital will be the same as actual *share capital* except when some shares are still partly paid.

**CAM:** see *computer-aided manufacture*

**cannibalisation** is the effect of a new product launch on sales of a firm's existing brands. If Mars launched a mint Mars Bar they would worry that its sales would eat away at sales of the standard Mars Bar. This would need to be taken into account when estimating the profitability of the new product.

**CAP:** see *Code of Advertising Practice* or *Common Agricultural Policy*

**capacity** is the maximum amount the organisation can produce in a given period in the short run, i.e. without extra *fixed assets* and/or fixed *overheads*. Capacity is often difficult to estimate as more output can often be produced by a more intensive use of *plant*, e.g. motivated workforce, better materials, better maintenance or *shift work*.

The term can also be used in relation to the whole economy.

**capacity utilisation** at the individual firm level is the extent to which the maximum capacity of the firm is being used, i.e. actual output as a percentage of maximum potential output. At the economy-wide level it is used to refer to the total capacity of all firms together.

FORMULA: $\dfrac{\text{actual output per period}}{\text{full capacity output per period}} \times 100$

A firm's capacity utilisation is of considerable financial importance, because of the impact of fixed *overheads* per unit on profit margins. If a 40 000 unit factory has fixed overheads of £400 000 a year, full capacity working carries *fixed costs per unit* of £10. Should demand halve to 20 000 units, fixed costs per unit double to £20. So high capacity utilisation keeps fixed costs per unit down, by spreading the overheads over many units of output. Low utilisation can push a firm into severe loss making, forcing it to consider a strategy of *rationalisation*.

Capacity utilisation for the economy as a whole is an important indicator. It shows how close the economy is to full-capacity output, and will help to show when the pressure of aggregate demand is likely to lead to accelerating inflation, because the amount of unused resources in the economy is diminishing. The CBI measures capacity utilisation for a representative sample of firms; the data will reflect the position of the economy within the business cycle. In a recession there will normally be substantial under-utilised capacity.

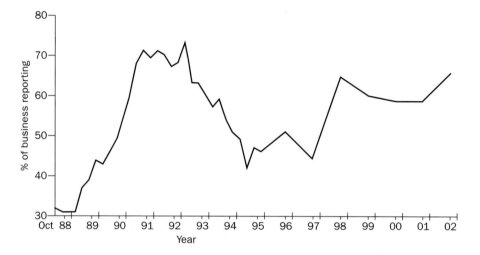

*Percentage of respondents working below capacity (in manufacturing). Source: CBI*

**capital:** to an economist, capital is one of the *factors of production*, the others being land, labour and entrepreneurship. It will mainly consist of buildings and plant and machinery. To the businessperson it means funds invested in the company, either from the shareholders (*share capital*) or from lenders (*loan capital*). Both, however, recognise that capital is stored-up wealth, which when combined with the other factors of production, can be used to make goods and services more efficiently.

The return to capital may be *interest*, *profits* or *rent*. These provide compensation to the owner of the capital for not having the use of it in the present for consumption purposes.

**capital account:** see *balance of payments*

**capital adequacy ratio** defines the amount of capital needed by banks to ensure that they do not run out of funds when customers ask to withdraw their deposits. The amount is fixed in relation to the amount and types of loans which the bank is providing to customers.

**capital consumption** measures the amount of capital needed to replace equipment which has worn out during the course of one year. The term is used in the national accounts to show how much of total (gross) investment can be attributed to normal wear and tear or depreciation, and how much reflects a net addition to the nation's stock of capital or productive capacity.

**capital deepening** occurs when more capital equipment is provided for each person employed. It will normally lead to an increase in productivity or output per person employed.

**capital deficiency:** many *developing countries* experience slow growth, or sometimes no growth at all, because there is a low level of investment in capital equipment and *infra-structure*. This is particularly prevalent in sub-Saharan Africa where the capital stock has in most countries remained small in relation to the population.

**capital employed:** the total of all the long-term finance of the business, consisting of loans, *share capital* and *reserves*. It provides the funds for obtaining the company's assets, therefore capital employed must equal assets employed.

**capital expenditure** is spending on new *fixed assets* such as machinery or new buildings. This affects the *balance sheet*, as a cash purchase would cause cash to fall while the fixed asset total rises. Capital spending does not, however, have any direct effect on the *profit and loss account*. This is because the cost of capital expenditure is only charged to the profit and loss account through *depreciation*, i.e. the cost is spread over the useful lifetime of the asset.

**capital gain:** a gain arising from the increase in value of an *asset*, which becomes apparent when the asset is sold for more than its *historic cost* or is subject to professional revalua-tion, e.g. property. A capital gain is accounted for in the *balance sheet* through an increase in *shareholders' funds*.

**capital gearing** measures the proportion of *capital employed* that is financed by long-term liabilities such as *debentures*. Capital gearing is, as a percentage:

FORMULA: $\dfrac{\text{long-term liabilities}}{\text{capital employed}} \times 100.$

A highly geared organisation is heavily reliant on borrowing and is therefore vulnerable as it must meet interest payments to lenders, whatever its earnings. A gearing level above 50 per cent is regarded as uncomfortably high.

**capital goods:** another term for a *fixed asset* such as *plant* or machinery.

**capital-intensive** means that the way a good or service is produced depends more heavily on capital than the other *factors of production*. Examples of production systems which are very capital intensive include steel production and oil refining. A capital intensive production process will require very high spending on *plant* and machinery, causing *fixed costs* to represent a high proportion of total costs. This will give it high *operational gearing*.

**capitalism** is the social and economic system which relies on the market mechanism to allocate *factors of production* in the most efficient way. Land and capital are owned by indi-viduals who will decide how they are used on the basis of the profit that can be obtained. Similarly they will pay employees according to the amount needed to attract them to undertake the required work. The extreme alternative to capitalism is a *centrally planned economy*. Most economies however fall between those extremes, being *mixed economies*, with market systems and some government involvement in economic activity.

**capital:labour ratio** measures the proportion of those two factor inputs in the production of a good. A good with a high capital:labour ratio is said to be *capital-intensive*, and *labour-intensive* when the reverse is true. Some economists have argued that a purely quantitative measure such as this is unhelpful. The quality of the capital and the labour (e.g. how well the workforce is trained) is more important.

**capital movements** are flows of capital from one currency to another. The location of the money may or may not change: it could be moved from a dollar account in New York to a sterling account in London, but it might equally be moved from a dollar to a sterling account in London. Money which is 'footloose' in this way and moves from one currency to another in search of the best rate of interest is sometimes called *hot money*.

**capital:output ratio** measures the amount of capital employed in producing an amount of output.

**capital rationing** is a situation in which tight financial constraints force a firm to choose between projects that are all attractive. Were there no capital shortage, all the projects would be adopted.

**capital stock:** the amount of capital currently available for use in the economy. Changes in the capital stock provide a guide as to the productive potential of the economy.

**capital structure** refers to the way an organisation has arranged its funding between *ordinary shares*, *preference shares* and *debentures*. Its importance, is that shares pay *dividends* which may be waived in bad trading years, whereas debentures pay interest which cannot be passed.

**capital widening** occurs if employment is increasing and there is investment in new plant and machinery to give them the capacity to produce. This contrasts with *capital deepening*, which enlarges the amount of capital available to a given number of people.

**captive market** is a group of potential customers who are virtually unable to obtain alternative supplies because one company has a *monopoly* position. Isolated villagers would represent a captive market for a small village shop and are likely to be charged high prices as a consequence.

**cartel:** this is the name given to a group of producers who make an agreement to limit output in order to keep prices high. In order to do this they must control a large proportion of the *output*, and they must agree on levels of production. The problems with cartels are:

- that if they do force a high price it will encourage other producers to enter the market
- the members of the cartel may cheat by secretly producing more than laid down in the cartel agreement in order to gain revenue.

In most countries cartels are illegal because of their potential to exploit customers.

**cascading** is the process of passing important information or training down the hierarchy. Each director holds a meeting with senior managers; each senior manager then passes on the knowledge to the managers below; each of them . . . and so on until the whole staff have been fully briefed. It is a more time-consuming but much more effective communication method than a huge meeting or lecture.

**cash** is the most liquid of *assets*. All other assets are measured against it in order to define *liquidity*. The speed with which assets can be turned into cash depends on how saleable they are. The disadvantage with holding cash is its *opportunity cost*, in other words the loss of potential interest or profit. Sometimes, notes and coins are described as the only forms of cash, but instant access bank accounts are so near cash as to be virtually indistinguishable from it.

**cash and carry:** a wholesale operation which offers rapid, local service to retailers, but without providing credit or delivery.

**cash balance:** a firm's net cash position at a point in time, as shown by the bank statement.

FORMULA:   cash at start + cash inflows − cash outflows = cash balance

**cash cow:** a brand that has a high share of a declining market. Firms use their cash cows to generate the cash to invest in newer products with greater growth prospects. The cash generation (or 'milking') is achieved by pushing prices up as high as possible while minimising expenditure on *research and development*, *market research* or *advertising*. (See *Boston Matrix*.)

**cash flow** is the sum of cash inflows to the organisation minus the sum of cash outflows, over a specific period. Inflows can arise from cash sales, *debtors* paying up, interest received or disposal of assets. Outflows can be caused by cash purchases, settling *creditors*, or asset purchases. As not all these items pass through the *profit and loss account*, cash flow and *profit* are different concepts. Profit may be affected by non-cash items such as credit given and taken, *depreciation* and stock valuation.

**cash-flow forecast:** a detailed estimate of a firm's future cash inflows and outflows per month. From this can be derived the monthly *cash flow* and, by adding together each month's figures, the cumulative cash position. As the worked example below demonstrates, a firm may face a period of negative cash flow that is purely temporary.

**Worked example: cash-flow forecast**

All figures in £000s

| | Jan | Feb | Mar | Apr |
|---|---|---|---|---|
| **Cash at start** | 45 | 30 | (20) | (5) |
| **Cash inflows** | 115 | 130 | 150 | 170 |
| **Cash outflows** | 130 | 180 | 135 | 145 |
| **Net cash flow** | (15) | (50) | 15 | 25 |
| **Cumulative cash** | 30 | (20) | (5) | 20 |

As long as it has been forecast, *overdraft* arrangements can be made with the bank to ensure that temporary finance is available.

**cash-flow statement:** an account that shows the sources and uses of cash within a firm over its financial year. Whereas a cash-flow forecast is based on estimates of the future, a cash-flow statement records what has happened in the past, i.e. it shows historic cash-flow. Following the Companies Act 1985, it succeeded the Sources and Application of Funds as one of the three financial documents that must be published each year by every public limited company.

**cash on delivery (COD):** if a seller wishes to speed up cash inflow, or where the purchaser's creditworthiness is uncertain, cash is demanded before goods are released on delivery.

**caveat emptor** means 'let the buyer beware'. In other words, however much consumer protection legislation there is, buyers always have a responsibility to take reasonable care over their purchases.

**CBI:** see *Confederation of British Industry*

**CD Rom** stands for 'compact disk read only memory'. It is a method of information storage and recall via a computer. Like a music CD, it can be played and information accessed, but no new material can be added to it. Data such as newspapers and encyclopaedia are increasingly being put on CD Rom.

**cell production** splits a continuous-flow production line into self-contained units. Each cell will produce a significant part of the finished article, enabling the cell workforce to feel committed to their complete unit of work. It is part of what the management consultant Schonberger calls 'building a chain of customers', which he believes to be a vital part of *just in time* (*JIT*) production.

**central bank:** all countries have a central bank whose main function is to issue notes and coins and to implement monetary policy. Britain's central bank is the *Bank of England* and in the United States it is the *Federal Reserve Bank*. Central banks act as *lenders of last resort*; they ensure that the banking system is kept as stable as possible by lending to banks which find themselves temporarily short of cash to meet their depositors' needs. Within the *euro-zone*, the central bank function has been taken over by the *European Central Bank*, the ECB.

**central government** means that part of the government which deals with the affairs of the nation as a whole. It contrasts with *local government*, which covers a relatively small area and is generally accountable to the local electorate.

**centralisation** is drawing decision-making powers from the local or lower-level parts of the organisation, and concentrating them within the head office or centre. Its opposite is *decentralisation*.

Pros:
- centralisation allows consistent policies to be applied throughout the firm
- it ensures that quick decisions can be made.

Cons:
- centralisation reduces the input of the day-to-day experts (the shop-floor staff) into the firm's decision-making
- it risks demoralising branch managers who may feel powerless or mis-trusted.

**centrally planned economies** are those in which the allocation of resources is determined by the planning process rather than by market forces. Many centrally planned economies (such as Russia and Poland) began the process of becoming market economies in 1989. China and Vietnam remain partly centrally planned, although market forces are operating in some sectors of their economies. Some economies have retained a measure of central planning within what is mainly a market economy. India falls into this category. Most developed countries have privatised most of their state enterprises, thus reducing the amount of central planning within individual economies.

**centring:** a technique used in the *moving averages* method of forecasting to ensure that the moving average trend data coincides directly with a time period. In a four quarter moving average, for example, two successive four quarter averages are added together, and the result divided by two. This establishes a centred average which shows the trend figure for the third quarter. Centring is needed whenever the moving average is based on an even number of pieces of data.

**Worked example: centred averages**

| YEAR 1 | Sales average | Four quarter average | Centred average |
|---|---|---|---|
| Quarter 1 | 900 | | |
| Quarter 2 | 1 200 | | |
| | | 1 150 | |
| Quarter 3 | 1 300 | | 1 175 |
| | | 1 200 | |
| Quarter 4 | 1 200 | | |
| YEAR 2 | | | |
| Quarter 1 | 1 100 | | |

**CEO:** see *chief executive officer*

**Certification of Incorporation:** issued by the *Registrar of Companies*, this gives a company its legal personality and enables it to trade.

**certificate of deposit** is a way of turning a bank deposit into a negotiable asset. A business may turn a bank balance into a certificate of deposit (CD) which it can then sell if it needs to get the cash. In the meantime it will yield a higher rate of interest than an ordinary bank account. It thus gives a good rate of return while retaining liquidity.

**ceteris paribus** is a Latin phrase meaning 'other things being equal'. This is an important assumption in much economic analysis, for it enables one to assume that no variables are influencing a situation other than those under consideration. An example would be that when measuring a product's sales following a price increase, one can only draw conclusions about the product's *price elasticity* if one assumes other things are equal, i.e. ceteris paribus. Effectively the assumption allows us to isolate the action of a single variable, so that its effects may be studied. While the assumption is useful in economic theory, it is important to remember that in the real world, many things are apt to change at the same time.

**chain of command** is a vertical line of authority within an organisation enabling orders to be passed down through the *layers of hierarchy*.

**chairman (or chairperson):** the elected chair of the meetings of an organisation. A company chairman will not only run the meetings of the board of directors, but may also take responsibility for the long-term aims and objectives of the business, leaving the managing director to determine and execute the strategy and to run the business day to day.

**Chambers of Commerce** are groups of businesspeople in a town or city who gather together as a *pressure group* to look after the interests of local firms. They provide information and help for small companies as well as promoting *trade fairs* and exhibitions.

**Chancellor of the Exchequer:** the person responsible for running the nation's economy. He (there has not yet been a woman Chancellor) sets out the government's tax and spending plans (*fiscal policy*) in *the Budget* each year, usually in March. The Chancellor, with the Treasury, must decide important aspects of *stabilisation policy* which can have a considerable impact on individuals and on business. The Chancellor's decisions may also have a substantial effect on *income distribution*. Until 1997 the Chancellor would decide *monetary policy* but that role has now been passed to the *Monetary Policy Committee*.

A B C D E F G H I J K L M N O P Q R S T U V W X Y Z

**change** is a constant feature of business activity. The key issues are whether it has been foreseen by the company – and therefore planned for – and whether it is within the company's control. Extensive change may come from sales growth: requiring new management structures, new *layers of hierarchy*, new divisions or *profit centres*. Such organisational change may be difficult, but one could say, fairly, that failure would be due to bad management. Yet there may be failure. Growth may lead the company to become stiflingly *bureaucratic*, causing bright, young people to leave. Or extensive delegation to profit centres may backfire, as managers struggle to live up to their new responsibilities.

More problematic is unforeseen change. A small business that has a product which suddenly becomes very popular has many serious threats. An overstretched management may let costs get out of control: overtime payments, company cars, expenses and so on. *Quality control* may slacken in the rush to meet orders, leading to high returns (and therefore refunds) and a poorer reputation. Capital spending on new, bigger capacity will drain cash from the company. Worse, it may prove wasted if demand falls away as rapidly as it came. This example combines two problems: unforeseen change and change that is outside the company's control. Yet the firm could have brought the change within its control by ensuring steady, moderately geared, liquid growth, rather than frenetic, risky expansion.

External change is usually the hardest to control or even influence. Changing tastes or fashions, new laws or taxes, increased competition, or changes in the economy – all are major external constraints. The firm will try to affect these areas (by advertising or through *pressure group* activity), but may not succeed. In which case it must ensure that it is prepared to respond quickly and appropriately to whatever change occurs. *Contingency plans* are formulated to succeed in this aim. These will cover the marketing tactics and production planning needed in the short term. Long-term health will often depend on the product range and degree of *diversification* in the business. A sharp tax increase on whisky will not damage a company with extensive beer, wine and soft drinks interests.

**change management:** the process of planning, preparing, implementing and evaluating changes in business strategies or working methods. The key underlying factor in change management is trust. For only if staff have faith in the motives and competence of the managers concerned will they help to implement the desired change. Successful management of change requires:

• people whose motivation and trust makes them willing to accept and even harness it

• brand names with the consumer loyalty to ensure continuing, high sales revenues

• knowledge and confidence in several different markets

• the financial resources to be able to invest in new products or methods.

**Chapter 7:** the section of the US Federal Bankruptcy Act 1978 that provides for the *liquidation* of a company that cannot reasonably be expected to return to a viable operating condition. Typically, a company in financial trouble will first turn to *Chapter 11* of this Act. If the company cannot be turned round it may end up in Chapter 7: liquidation.

**Chapter 11:** a section of US Federal Bankruptcy Act 1978 that allows a firm in financial difficulties to protect itself from its creditors for a period of time. Filing for Chapter 11 fends off the threat of *liquidation* while managers attempt to return the firm to financial health.

**charismatic leader:** one who motivates employees to strive to meet an objective through the force of his or her personality. Such leaders were treated as the heroes of the stock market and dot.com booms of 1993–2000. After the collapse of *Enron*, Worldcom and Marconi in 2001–02 there was much more reflection on whether charismatic leaders can become too powerful within their companies.

**charity:** a *non-profit organisation* established with the aim of collecting money from individuals and spending it on a cause, which is usually specified in their title. There are tax benefits to the givers who are also not liable for the debts of the organisation. Although charities are not established to make profits, they can earn surpluses. Some are large-scale organisations employing many people across the world, such as Oxfam, Friends of the Earth, Médecins sans Frontières and Save the Children.

**chartered accountant:** one who has achieved a publicly recognised qualification from a professional association and can therefore charge higher fees to reflect higher qualifications.

**Chicago School:** a group of economists who have either worked at or been associated with the University of Chicago, who have promoted the importance of market forces in creating efficient, growing economies. They have tended to criticise government interventions in the economy as being likely not to produce the desired effect. Their work on the consumption function, on regulation and on monetary theory has been important. In particular, Milton Friedman's thinking underlay much of the Conservative government's monetary policy in the early 1980s.

**chief executive officer (CEO):** the director in charge of all operations within a business. In Britain, the term 'managing director' has usually described this function, but the American version CEO seems to be gaining popularity. The CEO is answerable to the chairman of the board of directors, although some companies combine these functions. This results in an individual having a degree of power that concerns those with an interest in *corporate governance*.

**chinese wall:** the wall of silence that is supposed to exist in *merchant banks* between those advising firms on *take-over bids* and the bank employees who are *stock market* dealers. If the dealers hear of a bid in advance, they could make huge profits by buying shares that are about to rise in value, but will lay themselves open to accusations of *insider dealing*.

**chinese whispers:** the way in which a message passed orally along a chain of people becomes distorted.

**cif** stands for cost-insurance-freight. Exports and imports may be calculated cif, thus including transport costs, or fob (freight on board), thus excluding transport costs.

**circular flow of national income:** a *macroeconomic* concept referring to the interconnectedness of the economy. Firms need workers who are paid from the sales of goods which are bought by *consumers*. Payments to workers are income, which is spent on goods and services. Hence, the flow of money is circular. The model can be extended to take in savings and investment, taxes and government expenditure and imports and exports. These *withdrawals* and *injections* respectively reduce or increase the circular flow.

See diagram on following page.

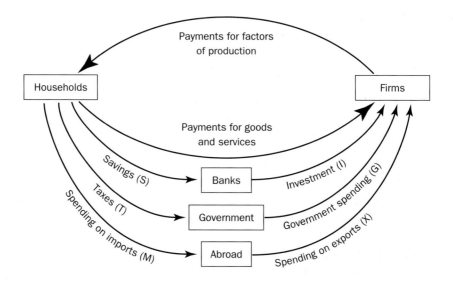

*Circular flow*

**circulating capital:** the funds flowing through a business enabling it to carry out its usual operations. Also known as *working capital* and defined as *current assets* minus *current liabilities*.

**The City** refers to the City of London and its financial services sector. These include the banking system, the money markets, the insurance industry, commodity exchanges, the Stock Exchange and all the advisers and analysts who market expertise in the ways of the markets.

**City Business Library:** located in Basinghall Street, London EC1, this is an exceptionally well-stocked and well-staffed public reference library for business. Its collection of *Mintel*, *EIU*, *Business Monitors*, trade magazines, *Extel cards* and innumerable other reports is invaluable for project work.

**civil law:** legislation which covers offences that are not automatically prosecuted by the police. The civil law gives the individual the right to pursue a grievance by taking another person or corporation to court.

**classical economics** was developed by, among others, *Adam Smith*, *David Ricardo* and J S Mill, between 1776 when Adam Smith's WEALTH OF NATIONS was published, and 1848 when J.S. Mill's PRINCIPLES OF POLITICAL ECONOMY was published. These economists laid down the general principles of the *market economy*, of *perfect competition* and of the theory of *comparative advantage*. They were concerned mainly with the principles of microeconomics, and the assumption of perfect competition was crucial to their analysis. They held that government intervention was mainly unhelpful and that the operation of self-interest would bring about efficient production in the long run. The classical economists continue to influence thinking right up to the present, being the forerunners of what is now known as *neo-classical economics*.

**classical management theory** was formulated by observing how large organisations worked, and concluded that the main management functions were: forecasting, planning, organising, commanding, coordinating and controlling. The main theorist, Henri *Fayol*, believed that a clear hierarchy and the specialisation of tasks were the keys to effective management.

**class intervals** are the dividing lines chosen in order to group data into categories for purposes of analysis, e.g. there might be 12 days in which sales volume was greater than 25 and no greater than 30. The class interval is five units. (See *frequency distribution*.)

**clearing bank** is the name given to the main high-street banks. They are so called because they developed by 'clearing' cheques, i.e. by paying cash for cheques drawn against them. (See also *commercial banks*.)

**clerical union:** an organisation designed to represent the interests of white-collar workers at their places of work. (See *trade union*.)

**client-server computing** means processing data on networks of computers, some of which provide computing or data services to the network, the rest serving as work stations.

**climate change levy:** a tax on the use of fossil fuels by businesses and public sector organisations. The objective is to reduce emissions of greenhouse gases that are thought to be causing global warming. Organisations are being given an incentive to economise on their use of electricity, gas, petrol and coal. This is inline with international commitments under the *Kyoto Agreement*.

**clocking-in** is a method of recording the exact arrival and leaving time of each employee. Abolishing this system has become a key element in the pursuit of *single-status* conditions in factories that once expected blue-collar workers to clock in while white-collar staff did not need to.

**closed economy:** one which does not trade with the rest of the world. The idea of a closed economy is used in economic theory simply so that the effects of certain changes on the macroeconomy can be studied in isolation. In contrast, an *open economy* is one in which trade is important.

**closed question:** a question to which a limited number of pre-set answers are offered, e.g. Do you buy a newspaper nowadays? Yes ☐ No ☐

| Pros: | • | ticking boxes is much quicker and easier for the respondent, so closed questions ensure a higher response rate |
| | • | a limited number of answers makes them easy to process and analyse. |
| Cons: | • | provides no scope for comment or qualitative input |
| | • | impossible to anticipate all the possible answers. |

**closed shop:** a workplace where employees must belong to a *trade union*. It can only occur by agreement between the employer and the union. The enforcement of 100 per cent union membership was made illegal in the *Employment Act 1988*. See *Employment Acts*.

**Club of Rome** an international group of academics and civil servants who have collectively advocated a greater degree of environmental awareness in the formation of government policies. They have shown that current rates of resource depletion may not be sustainable in the long run, and have researched ways in which environmentally desirable changes might be implemented.

**cluster sample:** respondents drawn from a relatively small area selected to represent a particular aspect of a product's *target market*. For example, the cluster may be a seaside town chosen by a producer of sun lotion.

A B C D E F G H I J K L M N O P Q R S T U V W X Y Z

**cobweb theorem:** a theory which analyses the changes which occur in markets over time when there are time lags between the decision to produce and the arrival of the output in the market-place. For example, farmers may decide to produce less lamb because the price is currently low (point A on the diagram). If they all make the same decision, there will in time be much less lamb on the market (B) and this will cause the price to rise sharply (C). This in turn will make farmers want to expand their flocks (D). The situation is thus inherently unstable, although it may eventually settle down (E).

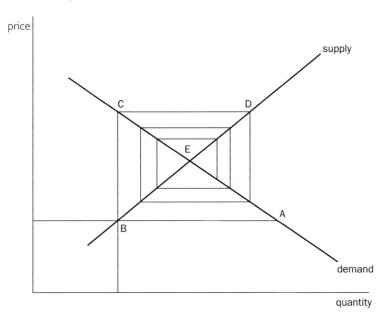

Whether or not the resulting diagram makes a nice-looking spidery cobweb like the one above depends upon what is assumed about the *elasticity* of the supply and demand curves. It is possible to show that the situation may be unstable and characterised by wide fluctuations in price over time. Sugar is one commodity with a tendency towards regular periods of unstable prices on world markets.

**COD:** see *cash on delivery*

**Code of Advertising Practice (CAP):** the document that sets out the boundaries of what is acceptable within an advertisement, as laid down by the *Advertising Standards Authority*. For example, the Code states that advertisements for alcoholic drinks should not feature people who are or who look under 25. If a member of the public complains about an advertisement to the Advertising Standards Authority, the test will be whether the advertisement breaks the Code.

**code of practice:** a form of *self-regulation* devised and run by an employers' organisation that lays down appropriate standards for firms operating within the industry. It is a way of improving the industry's public image and of avoiding government legislation and regulation. Although codes of practice are most obvious within industries with poor reputations such as time-share holidays, many conventional sectors also have them. Critics believe that rogue companies will always surface within a system of self-regulation. Advocates of codes of practice believe that industry experts can supervise their own industry more effectively and more economically than the State.

**co-determination** is the German system for *industrial democracy* within large firms. All companies with 2 000 or more staff must have an equal number of employer and employee representatives on a supervisory board of directors. This is to promote the idea that all those working for the company have a common interest in its success.

**coincident indicator:** a monthly economic statistic that can be taken as an indication of the health of the economy currently. A good example would be the demand for motor cars.

**collateral** is the security offered to back up a request for a loan. Usually the only acceptable form of collateral to a bank is property, since that tends to appreciate in value, whereas other business assets depreciate. For small business start-ups, the owners' personal property is often the only asset substantial enough to provide the security demanded by the banks.

**collective bargaining** is when one or more *trade unions* negotiate with management on behalf of a whole category of employees within an organisation or plant. Such negotiations usually cover pay, fringe benefits, working conditions and working practices. A benefit to the firm of collective bargaining is that a single negotiation can settle pay issues and potential disputes for a year. Less appealing to the employer is that the single negotiation gives the trade unions more power through solidarity.

**collusion** occurs when firms act in concert with each other, perhaps over *market sharing agreements* or price fixing. The word has strong implications of working together for reasons that are not in the public interest, though there is no reason why firms should not share marketing data or *research and development* effort.

**command economy:** an economic system controlled by the decisions of those at the centre of government. This contrasts with the Western model of free or social markets in which economic decisions are made by producers in response to demand from customers. The command economy rejects the notion of the *invisible hand* in favour of a system that hopes to distribute resources more fairly, but seems to be more *bureaucratic* and less able to supply goods of the right quality and quantity to meet consumer demand. The collapse of the command economies of the USSR (now Russia and a number of other states) and the Eastern bloc countries and the low living standards which prevailed before their collapse indicates the inefficiency which results from such a system.

**commercial banks** are those *banks* whose activities are directed at making a profit by borrowing from customers at an interest rate lower than that at which they lend. This makes them different from a *central bank*. Because customers who deposit their money with banks only ever need a small portion of that money in cash, commercial banks can engage in *credit creation*.

**commercial mortgages** are loans made by banks or building societies for the specific purpose of purchasing commercial property such as shop premises. The property serves as security on the loan.

**Commission for Racial Equality:** the government organisation given the responsibility to ensure the effective implementation of the *Race Relations Act 1976*. Among its key duties are to:

- work towards the elimination of discrimination

- promote equality of opportunity

- keep the workings of the Act under review, making suggestions for amendment when it considers they are necessary.

**commodity:** theoretically any good – as opposed to a service – which can be bought and sold. Often, however, commodities are referred to as those traded in commodity markets such as tea, sugar, rubber, wool and so on. In London there are specific commodity markets which deal in these goods, sometimes in a speculative fashion by effectively betting on their future prices. The term commodity is usually used when the good in question is homogeneous, so that no one producer's output is distinguishable from another's. For example, one load of iron ore is much the same as another of the same grade, irrespective of which firm mined it.

**commodity agreement:** a number of important commodities have fluctuating prices. Sometimes this seriously threatens producer incomes. There have been attempts to stabilise prices for individual commodities by establishing a system of buffer stocks. Stocks can be bought when the price is low and sold when it is high, thus compensating for changes in demand and reducing price fluctuations. However, it is very hard to make this work and in the period 1999–2002 no such agreements were in force.

**Common Agricultural Policy (CAP)** is the scheme by which agricultural production within the *European Union* is organised. It was set up by the Treaty of Rome as a way of helping small-scale and relatively inefficient European farmers to survive.

The CAP used to work on a system of price supports. This led to overproduction causing 'wine lakes' and 'butter mountains'. A reform package in 1992 changed the system in favour of direct income aids to farmers, including 'set-aside' premiums for the withdrawal of land from production. Further reforms in 1999 were hoped to reduce the huge cost of the CAP, which swallowed half the European Union's £55 billion budget in 1998.

Pros:
- it stabilises farm incomes
- it enables marginal producers to stay in business, e.g. sheep farmers on Welsh hills
- it has helped to make Europe self-sufficient in food production.

Cons:
- it is expensive to operate
- it is open to corruption
- it raises food prices above world levels; this hurts consumers, and it hurts poor consumers more than rich ones.

**common external tariff:** the set of *import duties* which are set by the European Union to cover certain imported goods for all member countries. The common external tariff favours producers within the EU and discriminates against producers outside the EU.

**common market:** a loose term which is often used to mean an area within which there is *free trade*, and in which regulations affecting producers are harmonised.

**communication** is the interaction between people, focusing primarily on the transfer of information. A communicator chooses an appropriate *transmission mechanism* in order to communicate with the intended receiver of the message. Communication can only be said to have succeeded once a response (*feedback*) has been achieved.

There is a tendency to believe that businesses need *more* internal communication, as if that would be beneficial in itself. This may not be the case, because people can feel swamped by too much communication – especially if it is passive, such as memos to all members of staff. *Herzberg* and others have emphasised the importance of direct communication in the psychology of motivation.

**communication channels** are routes through which communication occurs. Examples include *team briefing* sessions, *works councils,* plus the *chain of command* within an organisation. Communication channels can be 'open' or 'closed'. The latter means that access to the information is restricted to a named few. The former "open" means that any staff member is welcome to see, read or hear the discussions and conclusions.

**communication net** (or network) is a diagram representing the actual communication structure within an organisation. The most common types are the wheel and the circle. As the diagram below indicates, the circle gives strong, team-based communication whereas the wheel gives control to the person at the hub.

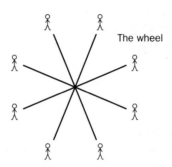

The circle

The wheel

*Communication networks*

**Companies Act 1985:** the main piece of legislation governing modern company law in England, Scotland and Wales. It sets out the legal procedures for forming a company, running a company and winding it up:

- to form a company, the founders must present two documents to the *Registrar of Companies*: the *memorandum of association* and the *articles of association*
- to run a company, directors must ensure that accounting information is presented to shareholders in a form that complies with the Companies Act 1985, and that the accounts must be available for public scrutiny at *Companies House*
- winding up a company can be done via compulsory or voluntary *liquidation.*

**Companies Act 1989:** a conscious attempt to bring UK company law into line with EU law. Among its provisions is to allow a firm to start up with a *memorandum of association* that places little restriction on a firm's trading freedom.

**Companies House** is where the *Registrar of Companies* holds the financial and ownership details on all the limited companies in the country. As laid down in the *Companies Act 1985*, all these records have to be available to the public. Students working on a project requiring the latest accounts for a company will find that the Cardiff and London bases for Companies House can provide the information required (for a fee of around £9).

**company objectives:** see *corporate objectives*

**company secretary:** appointed directly by the board of directors, the company secretary is the chief administrative officer of a business, usually responsible for the company's legal affairs.

**company union** is a Japanese approach whereby all workers within a firm are automatically represented by a trade union structure that is employed by the firm itself. Critics regard the lack of independence as a fundamental flaw.

**comparative advantage:** the idea that countries can benefit from specialising in the production of goods at which they are relatively more efficient. In this way consumers within each country gain the maximum benefit from international trade. At first, this may seem strange, because a country like the United States would seem to have an advantage at producing most goods when compared with a less developed country such as Jamaica. However, it is easy to see that while the US may be twice as efficient as Jamaica in the production of sugar, it is probably three times as efficient at the production of cars. It therefore benefits everyone if the US produces cars, and Jamaica sugar, and then they trade. The crucial factor relates to opportunity cost. The country with the comparative advantage is the one with the lowest opportunity cost in terms of real resources.

**comparability:** a yardstick for determining wage levels in negotiations between employers and trade unions. Unions may use wage rates in other comparable occupations as part of their argument for a pay increase. There is economic logic in this as a comparable wage could be seen as the opportunity cost of continuing to work for the current employer.

**compensation principle** shows that society gains from a certain change if the gainers gain more than the losers lose. In other words, the gainers could compensate the losers and still be better off. It is actually rather difficult to use the compensation principle in practical situations, because it is often hard to quantify gains and losses in money terms.

**competence-based qualifications** are those based on identified achievements such as writing a letter or operating a word-processing package.

**competition:** the process by which businesses strive against one another to capture a larger market. In price competition they may try undercutting each other's prices. This is also known as *competitive pricing*. In non-price competition they may seek to improve product quality, or increase demand through advertising and other marketing strategies. *Perfect competition* refers to a situation in which there are many sellers of identical products. *Imperfect competition* may still be very strong competition but involves fewer sellers.

**Competition Act 1980:** an Act which allowed anti-competitive practices such as the refusal to supply to be investigated by the *Competition Commission*. It was designed to extend *competition policy* to cover existing – especially public-sector – monopolies. Under the Act, a complaint about a nationalised industry would go to the *Office of Fair Trading (OFT)* which could decide whether the matter deserved a full Competition Commission investigation.

**Competition Act 1998:** this reformed and strengthened UK competition law by prohibiting anti-competitive behaviour and raising substantially the fines that can be imposed upon offending companies. The Act came into force on March 1st 2000. It brought UK competition law into line with *European Union* law. The responsibility for applying and enforcing the Act rests with the Director General of Fair Trading.

Key features of the Competition Act 1998 include:

- it prohibits anti-competitive agreements such as *cartels*
- it prohibits abuse of a dominant market position (e.g. abuse by limiting production, refusing supply, restricting technical development or *full-line forcing*)
- it allows for fines of up to 10 per cent of UK turnover
- it introduces a *Competition Commission* to take over the powers of the Monopolies and Mergers Commission
- the Competition Commission can investigate proposed mergers or takeovers that are too small, or too local, to be investigated by the European Commission.

The OFT has got stricter with the companies it investigates since the 1998 Act came into force in 2000. It does use its increased powers. Early in 2003, Argos and Littlewoods were fined £22.5 million for fixing the prices of toys and games. This sent a very strong message about how the OFT would use its powers in future.

**Competition Commission:** the government-funded organisation that oversees and enforces laws that attempt to eliminate anti-competitive business practices in the UK. Established in 1999 under the Competition Act 1998, the Competition Commission replaced the Monopolies and Mergers Commission (MMC). To be effective, the Commission must work in full cooperation with the Office of Fair Trading, the Department of Trade and Industry and the European Commission.

As a general rule, any merger which is likely to lead to a 25 per cent or greater share of the market will be investigated by the Commission. The Commission itself cannot take legal action; it can only advise the Office of Fair Trading that action is necessary. Increasingly, UK merger policy is influenced by EU directives.

**competition policy:** monopolies are generally considered to be against the interests of consumers and the public and governments legislate to restrict them. In the UK, the *Competition Commission* has the job of policing monopolies under the guidance of the *Office of Fair Trading (OFT)*. Any merger which creates a market share of 25 per cent or more is likely to be referred by the OFT to the Competition Commission, who will investigate whether the merger is thought to be in the public interest. Increasingly the power of the EU has come into play in this area under Article 86 of the Treaty of Rome. As well as controlling the development of monopolies, competition policy works to reduce *restrictive practices*. These include market-sharing agreements, and any other restriction on supply. They are covered by Article 85 of the Treaty of Rome.

**competitive advantage** describes the quality needed by a business which can flourish when there are many other businesses with competing products. It may be that the business has lower costs and prices, better quality or design skills, or it may enjoy superior marketing skills. Investment in new technologies may sometimes yield a competitive advantage. In general, competitive advantage usually rests on the extent to which the business emphasises innovation, the way it exploits relationships with other businesses and its reputation with customers.

**competitiveness:** the degree to which the business succeeds in selling its product when there is competition in the market place. Its competitiveness may rest on a price advantage, which may reflect lower costs than those of competitors, or a willingness to accept lower profits. Alternatively, competitiveness may rest on an advantage in design, quality, reliability or customer service, or some other important product feature. Either way, it is likely to be related to customers' perceived value for money.

**competitive pricing** means setting a price for a product or service based on the prices charged by competitors. This can be subdivided into two types:

1   In a market with low *product differentiation*, where all the producers are price takers, no one has the market power to set a price higher than the competition.

2   In a market dominated by a *price leader*, a less important brand would have to price at a discount in order to sell a significant sales volume.

**competitive tendering** is the practice of encouraging *private-sector* firms to compete to undertake tasks that were formerly done by council employees. This encourages those applying to find new, more efficient methods of carrying out the tasks, but often results in lower wages and/or poorer conditions of service for the employees.

**complaints procedure:** the process whereby a customer complaint is resolved to his or her satisfaction and the problem communicated to management to prevent its repetition. Some organisations have a special department for dealing with complaints. This is likely to be efficient, but may insulate other staff from hearing the causes of customer dissatisfaction. The ideal method is to ensure that all staff are trained to deal with – and resolve – complaints immediately. This is likely to achieve the desired effect: a contented customer who will return in future.

**complementary goods** are products which complement each other, such as bread and butter, cars and tyres, fish and chips. Because usage and demand are connected in this way, if the price of one product rises, demand for its complement is likely to fall. The amount by which these movements take place is determined by their *cross-price elasticity*.

**components** are manufactured parts used within production or assembly. They might be bought in from suppliers or produced within the factory.

**compound interest:** the way that the value of a lump sum can build up sharply if the interest is reinvested. For example, although intuition would suggest that savings earning 10 per cent a year would double in value every 10 years, the impact of compounding is:

|  | Apparent growth (10% uncompounded) | Actual growth (at 10% compound) |
|---|---|---|
| After 5 years | + 50% | + 61% |
| After 10 years | + 100% | + 159% |
| After 20 years | + 200% | + 575% |

Compound interest means that the capital sum will grow at an increasing rate as interest is earned on the interest. For example, with an interest rate of 10 per cent:

| Year 1 | £100 + £10.00 = £110.00 |
|---|---|
| Year 2 | £110 + £11.00 = £121.00 |
| Year 3 | £121 + £12.10 = £133.10 |

**computer-aided design (CAD)** enables designers and draughtsmen to store, retrieve and modify their work using multi-dimensional images.

**computer-aided manufacture (CAM)** involves the computer in a variety of manufacturing tasks beyond the use of robots on the *production line*. These include *stock control* and ordering goods.

**computer-integrated manufacture (CIM)** is the use of computers to coordinate every aspect of production, from product design through *stock control* to production scheduling and control.

**concentration ratio** measures the extent to which a market is dominated by a small number of large firms (at one extreme) or a large number of small firms (at the other). It expresses the percentage of the market accounted for by a given number of firms, for example, by five firms.

**conciliation** is the attempt to get both sides in a dispute to reconcile their differences. An independent conciliator might be found from ACAS, the *Advisory, Conciliation and Arbitration Service*. He or she would listen to the views of both sides, look for possible common ground, then encourage both sides to meet to discuss a compromise.

**conditions of employment** are the details of pay, working hours and holiday time that are set out in an *employment contract*.

**conditionality** refers to the practice of the IMF of offering loans on condition that the government complies with various requirements as to its economic policies.

**Confederation of British Industry (CBI):** the premier employers' association, listing most of the country's leading firms in its membership. The CBI's main functions are:

- to be a lobbying service for industry within the government and elsewhere, promoting the legislation and economic policies favoured by the *private sector*

- to promote the image of industry as a worthwhile career, especially among students

- to provide its membership with well-researched, nationally applicable research such as the CBI's Quarterly Survey of Economic Trends.

**confidence level:** a measurement of the degree of certainty to be attached to a conclusion drawn from a *sample* finding. For example, if a pre-election opinion poll puts the Conservatives 3 per cent ahead of Labour, how confident can one be of a Tory victory? Clearly, not 100 per cent certain since the research finding is not based on the whole population. Market researchers only feel happy to draw conclusions from findings that have a 95 per cent chance of being right (i.e. 19 times out of 20). The term given to that is a 95 per cent confidence level.

**conglomerate:** a firm which is comprised of a series of disconnected businesses. This provides the strength derived from *diversification* but has the potential weakness of a lack of focus. The modern approach to the management of a conglomerate is to delegate power very extensively to the different businesses within the group. This is to enable each business to act as its own core with its own strategy and focus.

**conglomerate mergers** occur between firms which have no clear connection with each other's business, either horizontally or vertically (see *horizontal* or *vertical integration*). The advantage to the firm of such a move is that it spreads risk, and may increase overall profit potential.

**consensus** is the area of agreement between people. It may be tacit rather than explicit. In other words it may not have been discussed and agreed formally. It is a key principle of

Japanese management that a strategy should not be implemented until a consensus has been arrived at.

**conservation** concerns the way in which depletable resources are used. When production involves the use of real resources which cannot be replaced, there will be a case for conserving those resources in such a way that they do not become excessively scarce too quickly. In this way conservation measures may apply to petrol, on which taxes are gradually rising so as to discourage consumption. Alternatively conservation may apply to a resource which is damaged by consumption; when new roads are built, countryside which could have been conserved will be destroyed.

**consistency** states that the accounting methods used to prepare firms' published financial data must be kept consistent so that proper conclusions can be drawn from the figures. This is an important accounting concept as it ensures that trends are a result of real changes in performance, not merely the consequence of an accounting change. For example the stated *profit* of a firm could be boosted by an accounting change that lengthens the assumed useful life of an *asset*, thereby reducing the annual *depreciation* charge. This would go against the principle of consistency.

**consolidated accounts** are the sum of the accounting data from all the divisions of a business, after allowance has been made for transactions within the group. They show the aggregate figures for all the sections of a group of companies consisting of a *holding company* and its *subsidiaries*. So the consolidated accounts show the *profit and loss account* and the *balance sheet* for the whole group.

**consortium:** a group of organisations which undertake to carry out a project in collaboration. For example the Channel Tunnel was built by a consortium of contractors.

**constant prices** are used when it is important to be able to measure a certain variable in a way that avoids distortion by inflation. For example, real income is measured in constant prices. This will involve the selection of a base year, so that the variable is expressed in, for example, 1995 prices.

**constant returns to scale:** when output can be increased in such a way that exactly the same quantities of inputs are required for each unit of output, there are said to be constant returns to scale.

**constraint:** a limitation on a firm's ability to meet its objectives. *Internal constraints* are those within the firm's control; *external constraints* are beyond it. Often, however, internal and external constraints interact, muddying the dividing line between them. For instance, a rise in interest rates (external) is primarily a problem for firms with high borrowings (internal).

**constructive dismissal** occurs when an employee resigns from a job because the employer has acted unlawfully, or broken the contract of employment. A black worker who has suffered racist abuse from a manager could take the company to an industrial tribunal on grounds of constructive dismissal.

**consultation:** asking for the views of those who will be affected by a decision. These views should then be taken into account by the executive responsible for taking the decision. It is important to distinguish between consultation and *delegation*. The latter means passing decision-making powers down the hierarchy, whereas consultation keeps power at the top.

**consumable:** any product that is not *durable*, i.e. can only be used or consumed once. Typical examples include food, detergent and petrol.

In addition, all services would be classified as consumables. From the business point of view, their significance is that:

- consumables do not share the *market saturation* problems of durables, therefore demand is more constant
- due to the possibility of regular purchasing it is easier to build strong *brand loyalty* towards consumables
- consumables are less subject to falling demand during *recessions* (whereas durables suffer as customers postpone replacement purchases).

**consumer:** a person who purchases or consumes a product. Manufacturers of children's products are aware that their consumers are often not the purchasers. This is why advertising for products such as breakfast cereals are often a strange combination of health information (for parents) wrapped up in jazzy, fun cartoon images (for children).

**consumer credit** is the means by which people buying goods can delay payment and so spread the cost. Purchasing in this way usually requires a deposit and carries a rate of interest. One of the most common types of consumer credit is *hire purchase (HP)*.

**Consumer Credit Act 1974** lays down the regulations covering the purchase of goods on *credit*. Its intention is to prevent consumers signing unfair contracts and also to ensure that purchasers know exactly what interest rate they are to be charged for the credit they receive. For the purposes of the Act, the term 'credit' includes any form of cash loan, including bank overdrafts and credit cards. Specific measures include: regulating the terms (especially the small print) allowable within a credit contract; the rule that all *advertising* or display materials quoting *credit terms* must also state the *annualised percentage rate (APR)* of interest.

**consumer durables** are goods which are owned by households but which are not immediately consumed by them. Examples include washing machines, dishwashers, cars and televisions. In effect, they are the *capital goods* of households.

**consumer expenditure** is the sum total of all spending by consumers in the whole economy over a period of time. It is a component part of *aggregate demand*. The level of consumer expenditure and its likely future growth are sometimes important variables for a business which is considering whether to expand.

**consumer goods** are the tangible products bought by consumers for imminent use. They contrast with investment or *intermediate goods* which are bought by firms as inputs for production.

**consumer panel:** a group of consumers within a firm's *target market* used on a regular basis for *market research* exercises. A typical use of a panel is for product testing, using the known tastes of the panellists to decide on the qualities of new product ideas, or of changes to the composition of existing products.

Pros:
- keeping the same sample saves the recruitment cost of finding new respondents every time
- avoids the problem of unmatched samples.

Cons:
- panels will become expert in the product field being tested and therefore become unrepresentative of the general public
- any bias within the sample chosen may not become evident because there may be no other comparative samples.

**consumer profile:** a quantified picture of a company's customers, showing the proportions of young to old, men to women, middle class to working class and so on. (See *demographic profile*.)

**consumer protection** legislation is that group of laws passed to control the worst excesses of past business practices towards their customers. Included within this legal grouping are:

- *Sale of Goods Act 1979*
- *Trades Descriptions Act 1968*
- *Consumer Credit Act 1974*
- *Competition Act 1980*
- *Food Safety Act 1990.*

**consumer resistance** is the term given for the factors that prevent potential customers from buying a particular product. The reasons for resistance may be active or passive. If people dislike the idea of whisky mixed with cream, they will actively resist trying or buying an Irish cream liqueur. An example of passive resistance would be a consumer who does not try a new brand of detergent because of loyalty to the Persil brand. Consumer resistance to a new product must be found out long before the product launch. Remedies may be to offer free samples in retail outlets, or to sell keenly priced trial packs. In 1999, the Rover 75 model was launched by offering a 24 hour test drive to help overcome executive car buyers' mistrust of the Rover brand.

**Consumers' Association (CA)** is an independent organisation that lobbies on behalf of its consumerist membership and produces the monthly magazine WHICH?

**consumer sovereignty** is the name for the process by which consumer demand determines the *allocation of resources*. An increase in demand will tend to make it more profitable to produce the item in question. This encourages firms to produce more. Similarly, if demand falls, losses may be made and these create an incentive for producers to move resources into some other line of production. In this way the *profit signalling mechanism* transmits the information given by consumer demand to producers so that the allocation of resources is kept in line with the pattern of demand. This theory underlies the competitive market model upon which much of microeconomics is based.

In practice, the existence of market friction such as imperfect information, as well as *market imperfections* like *monopolies* mean that the consumer is far from sovereign.

**consumer surplus:** a consumer good will be valued more highly by some consumers than by others. Yet they will all pay the same price for it. Some consumers would be willing to pay a price higher than the actual market price. The term consumer surplus refers to the value of the extra satisfaction which these consumers get from the item, over and above what they have had to pay for it. The consumer surplus is shown on a supply and demand diagram by the triangle enclosed by the demand curve and the price line. The demand curve shows how consumers value the product and all those who are prepared to pay a higher price get some extra satisfaction.

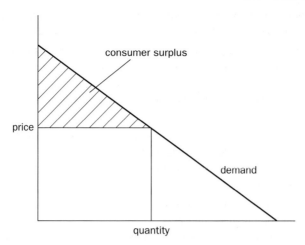

*Consumer surplus*

**consumption** means total consumption in the economy as a whole. (See *consumer expenditure*.)

**consumption function:** the proportion of income which is used for consumption is known as the consumption function. It can be measured in two ways, using the *average propensity to consume* or the *marginal propensity to consume*.

**consumption bundle:** a collection of consumer goods which a consumer might choose to purchase.

**contestable markets:** it may be comparatively easy for newcomers to the industry to break into a contestable market. This means that existing businesses, already in the field, face a constant threat of increasing competition. In the reverse case, where there are *barriers to entry*, existing businesses are protected from competition. We might expect that prices will be generally lower in contestable markets, merely because of the possibility of competition.

**contingency planning** means preparing for unwanted or unlikely possibilities. Since Perrier Water's setback when it was found to contain traces of benzine, firms include disaster planning as one contingency. Plans might also be prepared in case of:

- a severe *recession*
- *bankruptcy* of a major customer
- a sudden surge of demand.

Contingency plans can be prepared on computer models that provide the opportunity to ask and answer *what if? questions*.

**continuous improvement:**  see *kaizen*

**continuous research** consists of *surveys* that are carried out on a regular basis, such as every month. Firms might do this to monitor brand awareness and *brand standing*.

Pros:  • warns of any slippage in *brand loyalty* or image
       • helps measure the success of *advertising* campaigns.

Cons:  • regular research will be expensive over the year, therefore may not be economic for a small firm
       • accuracy relies on asking the same questions each month.

**contract:** an agreement between two parties, for example an employer and an employee. Contracts may be formal or informal, in which case they will be based on normal expectations.

**contracting out** means placing with independent suppliers a task that used to be done in-house, i.e. within the organisation. *Private-sector* firms, councils or nationalised industries might contract out services such as cleaning, refuse disposal, or even the production of components. Contracting out is a reversal of *vertical integration*. The term is now used less; *outsourcing* has taken its place.

Pros:
- might lead to lower costs as the contractor's wage rates do not have to be as high as those within the organisation
- putting the service out to *tender* invites new management thought on how to improve efficiency.

Cons:
- the subcontractor's employees may be less motivated towards providing the quality the organisation wants
- from the employees' viewpoint, working for a subcontractor may mean more intensive work for less pay.

**contractionary policy** is used by governments and the *Bank of England* when the economy appears to be growing unsustainably fast, or when *inflation* is becoming a problem. It consists of *monetary policy*, which would require high interest rates, and *fiscal policy*, in the form of either tax increases or government expenditure cuts, or both. The objective is to reduce the rate of growth of aggregate demand so that inflationary pressures are reduced. Reducing demand will slow down firms' attempts to recruit more labour, thus reducing the demand for scarce skills and making it harder for people to negotiate higher pay.

**contract of employment:** see *employment contract*

**contribution** is total *revenue* minus total *variable costs*. Therefore contribution minus *fixed cost* equals *profit*. The contribution of a product line or a department is its revenue minus the costs which would be avoided if it was discontinued. Contribution gives a clearer picture of the value of a product to a firm by removing general *overheads* or fixed costs which are difficult to allocate.

Revenue £150 000

| | |
|---|---|
| Minus £60 000 variable costs equals | |
| | Contribution £90 000 |
| Contribution of £90 000 | minus Fixed costs of £56 000 equals |
| | Profit of £34 000 |

### Worked example: calculating profit by use of contribution

**Question**: if a firm sells 20 000 units at £7.50, has £3 of variable costs and £56 000 of fixed costs, what is its profit?

**Answer**:

| | Total contribution | – | Fixed costs | = | Profit |
|---|---|---|---|---|---|
| | (£4.50 × 20 000) | – | £56 000 | = | |
| | £90 000 | – | £56 000 | = | £34 000 |

**contribution costing:** the valuation of a product's cost solely on the basis of *variable cost*, i.e. excluding *fixed costs* or *overheads* which are difficult to allocate (especially in multi-product companies).

**contribution per unit** is the amount each unit sold contributes towards covering the fixed *overheads* of the business. Once the *fixed costs* are covered, all extra contribution is profit. Contribution per unit is one of the most useful concepts in business studies. Among its applications are:

- for calculating profit: (contribution per unit × demand) – fixed costs
- for calculating break-even output: fixed costs ÷ contribution per unit
- for calculating appropriate minimum prices when considering a strategy of *price discrimination*.

**contribution pricing:** the setting of prices based on the principle that as long as an item is sold for more than the *variable cost*, it is making a contribution towards the *overheads* of the business. This notion may lead a firm towards one of two approaches to pricing: *price discrimination* and *loss leaders*. For exam purposes, the main consequence of contribution pricing is its effect on the acceptance of additional customer orders at cut prices. A standard exam question runs as follows:

### Worked example: contribution pricing

**Question**: the BG Co has sales of 2000 units at £5. Its fixed costs are £3000, variable costs are £3 and average costs are £4.50. BG's sales director has just phoned through with an extra order for 500 units at £4 each. Should it be accepted?

**Answer**: the immediate thought is that if average costs are £4.50, it must be unprofitable to accept an order at £4. That is wrong, however, because if fixed costs have already been covered and variable costs are £3, any price above £3 is profitable. The order will in fact generate an extra 500 × £1 = £500 profit (assuming BG Co has the capacity to produce the extra units).

**contribution statement:** a table of data setting out the contribution made by different departments or products to covering the company's fixed *overheads*.

In the example on page 56, all three brands make a positive contribution. However, if the total *fixed costs* were allocated equally to each of the three (£100 each), Brand X would show a loss of £50. This might encourage a manager to halt production of X. Yet without the £50 contribution made by Brand X, the fixed costs would not be covered so the firm would make a loss. So although a contribution statement is a useful way of presenting data, it must be treated with care.

A
B
C
D
E
F
G
H
I
J
K
L
M
N
O
P
Q
R
S
T
U
V
W
X
Y
Z

**Worked example**

| (All figures in £) | Brand X | Brand Y | Brand Z | Company total |
|---|---|---|---|---|
| Revenue | 100 | 200 | 300 | 600 |
| Variable costs | 50 | 75 | 150 | 275 |
| Contribution | 50 | 125 | 150 | 325 |
| Fixed costs | | | | 300 |
| Profit | | | | 25 |

**contributory negligence** occurs when an employee injured in a workplace accident is partly at fault and therefore has contributed to the occurrence. In such a case, if the employer is taken to court over the accident, any compensation payment will be reduced in line with the negligence. In other words if the accident is considered half the employee's fault, the award will be halved.

**control:** one of the two key factors involved in successful *delegation*; the other being trust.

**controlling interest** in a company is achieved when an individual or organisation owns one more than 50 per cent of the voting shares. A great deal of influence, if not effective control, can be exercised at lower levels of ownership: once an individual or an organisation such as a *pension fund* or *unit trust* gains a substantial block of shares, they may gain representation on the board of *directors*.

**Control of Substances Hazardous to Health (COSHH):** government regulations that lay down procedures for controlling unsafe substances. They are based on the provisions of the *Health and Safety at Work Act 1974*:

- the 1989 regulations require employers to prevent or control exposure to substances that are dangerous on contact, inhalation or ingestion

- the 1990 regulations require employers to apply appropriate measures for storing and handling dangerous substances, and coping with emergencies concerning them.

The COSHH regulations require all employers to carry out assessment, control, monitoring, health surveillance and training in relation to substances hazardous to health. Within individual workplaces, it will often be the safety representatives who work to ensure that employers pay proper regard to their COSHH obligations.

**convergence:** refers to the process of bringing the *European Union*'s economies and currencies into line with each other. This was an essential prerequisite for *economic and monetary union* (EMU) and the single currency. Unless all the member countries have similar levels of economic activity, rates of *inflation* and *interest rates*, being part of the *euro-zone* could cause major economic upheavals. The main focus for convergence is upon public sector borrowing and inflation rates. Convergence could present problems for some of the countries which will apply to join EMU in the future.

**convertible currency:** one which can be exchanged for another currency without limit. At its simplest level, this means if you go abroad you can take as much *sterling* out of the country as you like, or exchange it before you go. At another level it means that companies can move large sums out of and into currencies as they wish.

**cooperative** is an organisation run by a group of people, each of whom has a financial interest in its success and a say in how it is managed. That group might be the producers (as with agricultural cooperatives handling the packing and storage of several farmers' crops), the workers, or the customers (as with retail cooperatives).

**coordination** means ensuring that the work of many different people interlinks within a single plan. It is a major management function which can become hard to achieve when a great deal of decision-making power is delegated. The difficulty of coordinating the workings of a large organisation is a key *diseconomy of scale*.

**copyright** is the legal protection against copying for authors, composers and artists. Unlike *patents*, there is no requirement to register an author's copyright. The law on copyright is governed by the Copyright, Designs and Patents Act 1988.

**core activities** are the operating divisions that the firm sees as central to its corporate strategy. Other, more diversified functions may be seen as *peripheral* to the firm's purpose, and therefore sold off or closed down.

**core competencies** are the particular qualities that make the business effective in its main lines of business. Identification of core competencies can help the business to make good decisions about future developments. For example, a car company might identify its core competencies as design or technical innovation. This might lead it to use these qualities as a particular feature of its marketing strategies. There is a link between core competencies and the areas in which the business has a *competitive advantage*.

**corporate advertising:** an *advertising campaign* to boost the image of the company rather than to sell a particular brand.

Pros: • can increase sales of a whole range of products if, like Heinz, the company name is also the brand name

• can make the company more attractive to potential shareholders, suppliers and employees.

Cons: • can be regarded as a luxury, especially in times of recession

• has often been used to correct image problems caused by the company's own unethical behaviour (e.g. banks overcharging or oil companies polluting).

**corporate bonds** are loans to companies which carry a fixed rate of interest and have a fixed maturity value. They may be held by individuals or by banks or other financial intermediaries. They may be traded on the stock exchange, should the holder require liquidity. The price at which they are traded will vary according to interest rates and the comparative profitability of other investments.

**corporate culture:** see *culture*

**corporate governance** is an American term raising questions about who controls the boardrooms of public companies and whose interests they do and should serve. In theory, the shareholders have voting powers over company directors, but in practice these are rarely exercised. Practical power resides with institutional investors such as pension funds, but they rarely step in unless they see the company *dividend* or share price threatened. In Britain, issues of corporate governance became prominent after a series of City and company scandals revealed a moral vacuum at the top of many businesses. The *Cadbury*

A
B
**C**
D
E
F
G
H
I
J
K
L
M
N
O
P
Q
R
S
T
U
V
W
X
Y
Z

*Committee* was set up to address the issues raised. The Hempel Committee took this work further in 1997. In the US, corporate governance became a huge issue in 2001-02, due to the huge corporate collapses of *Enron* and Worldcom.

**corporate identity:** the design package that aims to create the company image desired by a firm. This may consist of a *logo*, a company uniform, the colour and style of the firm's stationery or even company cars and vans.

**corporate image:** the view of a company held by its customers, employees, and the public at large. For a bank, the ideal image might be: large, reputable, long-established yet innovative and approachable. *Market research* would aim to find the image characteristics desired by the customers, which would in turn influence decisions on *corporate advertising* and *corporate identity*.

**corporate objectives** are the goals of the whole enterprise. These are often based on the firm's mission or aims. The corporate objectives govern the targets for each division or department of the business. They provide a mechanism for ensuring that authority can be delegated without loss of *coordination*.

Among the most common corporate objectives are:

- to ensure long term, stable growth in real terms
- to spread risk and achieve growth through *diversification*
- to concentrate upon the firm's core skills
- to maximise *market standing*
- to add value through continuous technological *innovation*
- to achieve *profit maximisation* in the short to medium term.

corporate responsibility is the idea that organisations have to consider environmental and ethical factors in their decision making as much as those concerned with profit. The Cadbury Report (1992) spurred many companies into action, so that, for instance ICI now issues a separate environmental report; and many companies undertake *environmental audits* of their activities to examine the impact they are having.

**corporate saving** occurs when firms retain some of their profits, keeping them in reserve for the future. Often they will use their savings to replace capital equipment, or expand the business, in the future.

**corporation tax** is the tax which companies have to pay as a percentage of their profits. Although tax rates can be changed each year in the *Budget*, the level has usually been around 30 per cent. Smaller firms pay a lower tax proportion, currently 20 per cent.

**Worked example: Company A pays 30 per cent tax on profits while the smaller Company B pays 20 per cent**

|  | Company A | Company B |
|---|---|---|
|  | £000 | £000 |
| Revenue | 9 500 | 1 200 |
| Total costs | 7 300 | 840 |
| Pre-tax profit | 2 200 | 360 |
| Corporation tax | 660 | 72 |
| Profit after tax | 1,540 | 288 |

**correlation** is a measurement of how close a causal link there is between two or more sets of numerical data. Highly correlated data would form a predictable pattern, such as that for every £100 extra spent on advertising, sales rise £500. If the correlation is total, the data will form a straight line, as shown below.

*Correlation between advertising and sales*

A danger with statistical correlations is making assumptions about cause and effect. Perfume advertising is at its heaviest in the weeks prior to Christmas. Sales follow the same pattern. Yet it would be foolish to suppose that this proves the effectiveness of the advertising. Perfume companies advertise at Christmas because that is when the public is most receptive to their advertising. The sales and advertising data are correlated, but that does not in itself prove which factor is the cause and which is the effect.

**cost accountant:** one who is employed to decide how costs are to be allocated to different product lines. This is information on which key decisions may be based, such as the pricing or even the discontinuation of a product.

**cost accounting:** the aspect of *management accounting* that is concerned with the allocation of costs to different product lines. The techniques of cost accounting include *standard costing* and variance analysis. The cost accountant provides the detailed information to enable marketing and production managers to make pricing, promotional and new product decisions.

**cost-based pricing:** setting a price on the basis of production costs rather than market conditions. This can only be sensible for a firm with little or no direct competition. The two main cost-based pricing methods are *mark-up* and *cost-plus*.

**cost-benefit analysis** means weighing up the financial and social costs of an action or decision against the financial and social benefits. This requires a quantification of the *external costs* (such as pollution) and of the social benefits (such as jobs). This can be very difficult to achieve, which may undermine the analysis. For example, whereas it is known that taking a person off the dole queue saves the Treasury more than £10 000 per year, it may be impossible to calculate the cost of noise or air pollution.

Cost-benefit analysis is usually applied to *public-sector* projects where the benefits and costs cannot all be assessed on a commercial basis and where it is difficult to price or value them because of the absence of a market. *Private-sector* firms make their business decisions on the basis of their internal revenues and costs, i.e. those that affect their internal company accounts. A cost-benefit analysis of a second Channel Tunnel would consider the damage to the countryside, the advantages of a more efficient market as well as the excavation cost and future expected fares.

FORMULA:    social benefit − social costs = cost-benefit analysis

Within which:

social benefit    =    internal (company) revenues + external benefits

social costs    =    internal costs + external costs

**cost centre:** a department or section of an organisation to which specific costs can be allocated. If a large company splits itself up into cost centres, various benefits can result:

- team spirit is easier to generate among 20 people than among 2 000
- each individual knows that personal effort to cut costs can have an impact within a small *budget*, but not within a 2 000 strong workforce
- by identifying the costs generated by each department, the firm is better able to make decisions (especially if *benchmark* data is available from national sources or from elsewhere within the company).

(See also *profit centres* and *overhead allocation*.)

**cost curves:** see *average cost* and *marginal cost*

**cost of goods sold (COGS):** see *cost of sales*

**costing** is the process of determining the cost of producing or supplying a product or service to the customer. It may be based on historic information, or *standard costing* may be used to monitor the present and forecast the future.

**cost of living:** the money spent by the average household on necessities and luxuries over a period of time. This is difficult to determine precisely because each individual spends a different proportion of his or her income on different things. For example, a couple with two young children will probably spend a high proportion of their income on food and housing. In contrast, a middle-aged couple may spend a high proportion on holidays. If the mortgage rate goes up, the young couple will face a much larger rise in their cost of living than the middle-aged one. The government attempts to measure the cost of living using a 'basket of goods' which research has identified as the average household's expenditure. The best-known measure of the cost of living is the *retail price index (RPI)*.

**cost of sales** is the accountant's calculation of the *direct costs* that can be attributed to the *sales revenue* generated over a trading period. The cost of sales can then be deducted from revenue to show the *gross profit*. This is the first stage in constructing the trading account of a firm's *profit and loss account*.

The cost of sales is calculated as below:

FORMULA:   opening stock + purchases − closing stock = cost of sales

**Worked example: a firm's trading account**

|  | £ | £ |
|---|---|---|
| Sales revenue |  | 100 |
| Opening stock | 20 |  |
| Add purchases | 50 |  |
|  | 70 |  |
| less closing stock | (15) |  |
| Cost of sales | 55 | 55 |
| Trading or gross profit |  | 45 |

**cost-plus pricing** means adding a set profit percentage to the estimated total costs per unit.

**Worked example: a firm with fixed costs of £40 000 per month and variable costs of £1 per unit wants to price its product on the basis of 25 per cent cost plus. Monthly sales are estimated at 100 000**

| Total costs per unit | = fixed costs per unit | + variable costs per unit |
|---|---|---|
|  | = £40 000 ÷ 100 000 | + £1 |
|  | = £0.40 | + £1 |

$$\text{Total costs p.u.} + 25\% \quad = £1.40 \times \frac{125}{100} = £1.75$$

So the price is £1.75

Pros:
- cost-plus ensures that any cost increases will be passed onto the customer in the form of higher prices, thereby protecting the firm's profit margins
- it may be the only way of pricing a job for which the amount of work cannot be predicted, such as *research and development* into a supersonic military aircraft.

A B C D E F G H I J K L M N O P Q R S T U V W X Y Z

Cons: • cost-plus can only be applied in a situation where no effective competition exists; this is because it means setting prices with no reference to the market situation. So although it is the ideal pricing method, few companies are in a position to use it

• by ignoring market conditions, the firm may be missing out on the further profit opportunities offered by *price discrimination.*

**cost inflation** occurs when rising production costs force firms to increase their prices to protect their profit margins. In particular, *trade unions* are accused of making wage demands greater than productivity increases, causing employers to raise the prices of their goods, hence causing *inflation*. The usual response to this is that trade unions are only protecting their members' living standards, and if prices rise in the rest of the economy, it is unfair to expect workers to suffer a reduction in their standard of living.

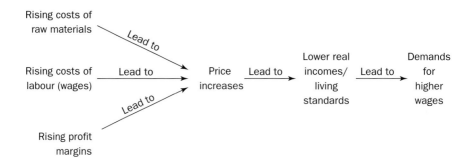

*Causes of cost-push inflation*

**Council of Ministers:** the *European Union*'s main decision-making body. Its membership comprises one government Minister from each of the member states. The Minister chosen will depend on the issue under discussion. If the meeting is focusing on the European economy, the *Chancellor of the Exchequer* is likely to be the UK's representative.

**council tax** is a tax raised on the value of houses by local authorities. If it is assumed that larger houses are owned by people who are better off, it is broadly related to ability to pay. People on benefits are generally exempt. Council tax funds a part of local expenditure, the rest coming from central government.

**counter-cyclical policy** is when a government takes steps to iron out fluctuations in economic activity (see *business cycle*, also *contractionary policy* and *expansionary policy*). When the economy is booming, the government will try to stop it 'overheating' by reducing its own spending on goods and services. In times of *recession* it will follow the opposite course. To a certain extent this is automatic; in a recession there is more unemployment, so government spending has to rise to pay for more unemployment benefit. The automatic elements are known as *'automatic stabilisers'*.

The tricky part is deciding when to apply policy measures which are not automatic. Getting the timing wrong will make the situation worse. If the *Chancellor* believed the economy was coming out of recession he might reduce government spending on, say, roads. If, however, the recovery did not happen as expected, the reduction of incomes in the road building industry would make the recession worse.

**counter-inflation policy:** if *inflation* is accelerating, the *Bank of England* may adopt contractionary *monetary policies*, by raising interest rates. This will have the effect of reducing *aggregate demand* and pressure on resources.

**countervailing duty:** an import duty which compensates for the effect of a subsidy on another country's exports.

**craft union:** an organisation set up to represent the interests of highly skilled workers, most of whom would have served *apprenticeships*. (See *trade union*.)

**creative accounting** is the name given to legal but questionable accounting practices that massage the figures (and therefore ratios) on published company accounts. The two focal points for creative accounting are the stated profit for the trading period and the balance sheet ratios relating to financial health. During the 1990s, the *Accounting Standards Board* brought in new measures to minimise the scope for presenting legal but misleading accounts.

Among the main creative accounting techniques are:

- brand accounting, meaning to obtain a valuation for brand names a company owns, and then place them on its *balance sheet*; this boosts *shareholders' funds* and therefore cuts the firm's apparent *gearing* level

- *capitalisation* of interest, by which the interest costs of financing a property development are recorded as an addition to the value of the property asset, instead of as a business cost; so instead of the interest cost being a deduction from the *profit and loss account*, it is recorded as an addition to the firm's balance sheet

- *acquisition accounting*

- *off-balance-sheet financing*

- *window-dressing*.

**creativity** is the spark that can provide an innovative solution or decision. It may be a quality that certain individuals possess naturally, but it will only become evident within an organisation that nurtures it. Some *top-down managements* lay down company policies for dealing with virtually every eventuality. This removes the flexibility of operation that is the essential background for creative solutions to problems. A firm wishing to foster creativity might:

- encourage *group discussions* among the workforce based on *brainstorming*

- accept that all ideas are worth considering

- encourage open, *direct communication*

- accept that mistakes are to be learnt from, not condemned.

**credit** exists as soon as someone has acquired goods or services without paying for them at once or by paying for them with someone else's money. A credit sale means that the organisation acquires the *current asset* of *debtors* rather than *cash*. A sale is recorded in either case.

**credit controller:** an employee in an accounts department who monitors the *debtors* of the organisation to ensure that agreed limits are not exceeded and that the cash inflows are received promptly.

**credit creation:** the process by which *banks* expand their lending by a multiple of any new deposits they receive. Not all their customers will want to withdraw their deposits at any one time. This allows the banks to keep just a percentage of their assets in the form of liquid reserves, and to use the rest to make loans. As borrowers spend the money, it is deposited once more in the bank, allowing a further expansion of credit.

**credit factoring:** see *factoring*

**credit insurance** involves paying a fee (premium) in return for the guarantee that if a customer fails to pay for a credit purchase, the insurer will pay. It is therefore a guarantee against *bad debts*. A common way of obtaining credit insurance is as part of a *factoring* service. Export credit sales can be insured through the *Export Credit Guarantee Department (ECGD)*.

**creditor days** is a measurement of the average number of days a company takes to pay its suppliers.

FORMULA: $$\frac{\text{trade creditors}}{\text{average daily sales (at cost)}}$$

**Worked example: calculating creditor days**

**Question**: the JBM Company's cost of sales last year was £1 460 000 and trade creditors amounted to £200 000. Calculate their creditor days.

**Answer**:

**Step 1** Calculate average daily sales: $\dfrac{£1\ 460\ 000}{365\ \text{days}} = £4000$

**Step 2** Apply formula: $\dfrac{\text{trade creditors}}{\text{average daily sales}} = \dfrac{£200\ 000}{£4000} = 50$

The average credit period from suppliers was 50 days.

This information is useful because:

- firms considering supplying the company can build the payment delay into their *cash-flow forecast*

- existing suppliers can check whether they are being treated fairly (if, for example, a supplier was being paid 30 days later than the average, it could justifiably complain)

- bankers and suppliers can check on the financial health of the business; a slide towards later and later payment might indicate cash-flow problems.

**creditors** are those to whom the organisation owes money, perhaps through having purchased goods or services on *credit* so that payment is still outstanding. Creditors appear under *current liabilities* in the *balance sheet*.

**creditors meeting:** a meeting arranged to confirm the appointment of a *receiver* to a company that has just gone into *liquidation*. The creditors would also have the opportunity to ask the proposed receiver questions about the likelihood of any payments of the cash they are owed.

**credit rating:** a judgement made by bankers about the financial health of a business and therefore how safe it would be to provide them with goods on *credit*. The credit rating will be based upon the strength of the firm's *balance sheet* and on its recent financial history. The best-known credit rating service is the American company Moody's. Any firm with Moody's top rating (triple AAA) is in a position to borrow at the best possible terms.

**credit terms:** the time allowed by a supplier before the customer must pay for the good or service received. This is usually 30, 60 or 90 days from the time the invoice has been presented, though customers may try to take longer to pay than this. Business credit is usually interest-free.

**criminal law** applies to those committing a criminal offence such as fraud. Such offenders should be pursued by the police and prosecuted. This contrasts with the civil law which only results in lawbreakers being sued if an individual or organisation takes them to court.

**crisis management:** the response of an organisation to a severe, probably unexpected threat to its well-being or even survival. Many firms devise *contingency plans* to cope with predictable crises (such as a fire at a key supplier's factory), but the actual crisis will rarely go according to plan. Therefore a named, top executive is likely to be put in charge. It is quite possible that this person will manage the crisis in a far more authoritarian manner than usual, due to the need for quick decision-making.

**cross-price elasticity** measures the responsiveness of demand for one good to a change in the price of another. So, if the price of apples falls, the demand for pears is likely to fall as consumers switch to purchasing apples. It is measured by applying the following formula:

FORMULA: $\dfrac{\text{percentage change in quantity demanded of good X}}{\text{percentage change in price of good Y}}$

The closer the competition between goods X and Y, the higher will be their cross-price elasticity.

**cross-section data** allows comparisons across different groups. For example, a cross-section of a number of countries could be compared by examining investment and growth rates in a single year. This compares with *time series* data, which might, for example, examine trends over a period of years in a single country.

**cross subsidy:** if there is an unprofitable activity taking place within an organisation, the losses can be offset by a profitable activity elsewhere in the same organisation. This is called a cross subsidy. When publishers bring out unsuccessful books the losses will be covered by the enormous profits made from bestsellers.

**culture:** the culture of an organisation is the (perhaps unwritten) code that affects the attitudes, decision-making and management style of its staff. Examples of different business cultures include:

● goal-orientated, bonus-seeking, youthful culture based on success at any price

● hierarchical culture based on respect for seniority, tight official communication channels and the avoidance of mistakes

● lively, growth-orientated culture based upon commitment to the product and the company.

The culture will affect *resistance to change* within the business and therefore the ability of a new boss to impose his or her style or decisions upon subordinates.

**cumulative data** is generated by adding up consecutive numbers within a series. For instance a firm with sales of 100 units per month in the period January – March has cumulative sales of:

January 100
February 200
March   300

It follows that if April's cumulative figure is 380, monthly sales have fallen to 80 units. Alternative terms for cumulative data include accumulated data and year to date.

**currency:** the notes and coins which are used as a medium of exchange in the country concerned.

**currency crisis:** if dealers on the *foreign exchange market* expect the value of a *currency* to fall, they may start selling large quantities of it. This may make it impossible for the *central bank* to buy enough of the currency to keep up its value, because its *foreign exchange reserves* are limited. This would be termed a currency crisis.

**currency swaps** are ways in which firms avoid the problems of international currencies which fluctuate in value. A swap takes place when a currency is simultaneously bought and sold. This may be done by purchasing a currency on the spot market, and at the same time selling it on the forward market. This is a way of *hedging*.

**current account:** see *balance of payments*

**current asset:** anything owned by the organisation which is likely to be turned into *cash* before the next balance sheet date, usually within one year. Typical current assets are *stock*, *debtors* and *cash*. The balance of current assets over *current liabilities* is called *working capital* and, in essence, finances the organisation's day-to-day running.

**current cost accounting (CCA)** is the attempt to allow for *inflation* in company accounts by basing asset values and profit figures on the replacement cost of assets instead of their *historic cost*. In inflationary times this would make *balance sheet* asset valuations higher, but profit figures lower. Disputes among accountants over the validity of this exercise have hindered the widespread acceptance of current cost accounting methods.

**current liability:** anything owed by the organisation which is likely to be paid in cash before the next *balance sheet* date, usually within one year. Typical current liabilities are *creditors*, *overdrafts*, *dividends*, and unpaid tax.

**current ratio:** see liquidity ratio

**curriculum vitae (CV):** the 'story of life', i.e. the itemisation of a job applicant's qualifications, experience and interests. It should provide sufficient detail to enable a recruiter to build a picture of the applicant's suitability, to provide references that can be taken up, and to give starting points for discussion at interview.

**customer service:** that part of the business activity which involves direct contact with the customer, either during the sale process, during after-sales service or during the complaints procedure.

**customs duties:** the taxes levied on imports as they are brought into the country, also known as *tariffs*.

**customs union:** a group of countries which agrees to trade freely within its borders and imposes a *common external tariff* on imports from outside the area. The European Union is a customs union. This may lead to *trade creation* and *trade diversion*. Overall it will usually promote the growth of trade and specialisation, thus allowing member countries to become better off.

**CV:** see *curriculum vitae*

**cyclical unemployment** is the consequence of an economic downturn within the *trade cycle*. Such unemployment can be expected to last for approximately as long as the *recession* itself, typically 12 – 24 months. It is sometimes lagged to the trade cycle perhaps by as much as a year. As demand falls, employers may postpone making people redundant as long as possible. Similarly, during the upturn, employers will wait to be sure that the increased demand is permanent before recruiting more staff. A government that wishes to prevent or relieve cyclical unemployment could:

- take *counter-cyclical* economic measures, reducing taxation and increasing spending
- encourage wage flexibility so that company wage bills fall automatically during recessions, without requiring redundancies. (See *profit-related pay*.)

Sometimes, governments are not willing to use counter-cyclical measures because of the perceived risk of increased aggregate demand causing excess demand and accelerating inflation. In the past, this meant that cyclical unemployment could persist for a number of years, e.g. 1990–92.

**cyclical variation:** in *time series analysis*, this is the variation which can be attributed to the economic or *trade cycle*. For example the increase in demand for *consumer durables* after a period of *recession* may be cyclical rather than indicate a change in the underlying trend.

**data:** facts of any kind, whether in number or verbal form. Although this is the correct explanation, business people are inclined to use the term to mean numerate information only.

**database:** a collection of information, usually stored on a computer. Examples of databases used in business include lists of customers and suppliers. Such information can be quickly and easily accessed, added to and interrogated, so that, for instance, it might be possible to ask the database for the names of all customers living in the North-East of England.

**Data Protection Act** came into force in 1984 to protect individuals who have information on them held on computers. Organisations which hold such information have to register with the Data Protection Registrar, and have to agree to levels of accuracy and security. The Act gives people the right to see their personal file, for example one held by a bank on a customer's creditworthiness. The 1998 Data Protection Act updated the legislation and gave employees the right to see their personnel files.

**dawn raid:** an unannounced, rapid raid intended to succeed through surprise. The term is used for *stock market* share raids, when a firm making a *take-over* buys up as many shares as possible before the bid announcement is made. This enables it to buy some shares cheaply, and to establish a base shareholding upon which to build. A dawn raid can also be used to describe the unexpected arrival of tax or *Office of Fair Trading* officials to inspect a company's books.

**day release** is *off-the-job training* for employees who are given paid time off work each week to complete a college-based course that will lead to extra qualifications. It can be an important way of making people more versatile. As employers' needs change, people's skills can be updated to fit the new requirements.

**DCF:** see *discounted cash flow*

**dear money:** if interest rates are high, borrowing will be costly and the money borrowed may be said to be dear.

**debenture:** a fixed interest, long-term security with underlying *collateral*, usually land. So a £100 000, 10 per cent debenture dated 31st December 2010 would pay £10 000 a year before tax to the registered holders until 2010. If the company defaults, the collateral can be sold to repay the lender, much like a building society *mortgage*. Debentures are an alternative to shares as a means of raising long-term *capital*. They do not dilute control but create the risks associated with raising the *gearing* level. From the investor's viewpoint, debentures are low-risk, but will not generate the capital gains which can be obtained when *equity* prices rise.

**debit:** a debit item in the system of *double-entry bookkeeping* means an increase in an *asset* or an expense, or a reduction in a *liability* or a revenue account.

**debt factoring:** see *factoring*

**debtor days:** the average length of time customers take to pay for goods bought on *credit*. The higher the debtor days figure, the longer the credit period taken by customers. This forces the supplier to tie up more of its *capital* in *debtors*, leaving less for other parts of the firm such as *fixed assets* (e.g. up-to-date machinery) and *stock*.

$$\text{FORMULA:} \quad \frac{\text{debtors}}{\text{sales} \div 365} = \text{debtor days}$$

There is no rule of thumb for evaluating the debtor days figure, though research shows that medium-sized manufacturers have to wait 80 days for payment, while shopkeepers tend to have a much lower figure (since most customers pay by cash, cheque or credit card).

**debtors** are the people who owe you money. On a *balance sheet*, they represent the total value of sales to customers for which money has not yet been received. The way an organisation manages its debtors is often a key to its *liquidity*. Successful credit control ensures that *credit* is not extended to potentially *bad debtors* and that late-payers are chased.

**debtors turnover** is an accounting ratio which measures the speed with which debtors pay up.

$$\text{FORMULA:} \quad \frac{\text{annual sales}}{\text{debtors}}$$

$$\text{EXAMPLE:} \quad \frac{\text{sales}}{\text{debtors}} \quad \frac{\pounds 1\,200\,000}{\pounds 200\,000} = 6 \text{ times}$$

A value of 6 implies that debtors pay up on average every two months. Caution is needed as sales may not be even through the year and some debtors may take much longer to pay and indeed some may be *bad debts*. The figure given could be end-of-year debtors or might be an average for the year. An alternative ratio to debtors turnover is *debtor days*.

**Debt Problem:** during the 1970s, many developing country governments borrowed large sums from banks in the developed countries. When interest rates rose in the early 1980s, the borrower countries became unable to service the debt (i.e. pay the interest). The amounts of foreign currency they could generate by exporting were insufficient to cover their commitments, even after they had cut back their imports substantially. In time they were also unable to repay their debts. This became known as the Debt Problem. Many countries have had to negotiate *debt rescheduling* with the help of the *IMF*. Some banks have written off part of the debt. Those most seriously affected include many countries in Africa south of the Sahara, as well as Mexico, Brazil and some other Latin American countries. The problem continues and is particularly acute for the poorest countries. Governments have been urged to clear these debts as soon as possible through the international organisations but so far it seems unlikely that the problem will be completely solved. Two bodies, Drop the Debt, a lobbying group, and the *Jubilee Debt Campaign*, a long-term strategy group, are continuing the process.

**debt ratio:** the amount of a country's debt in relation to the level of its exports.

**debt rescheduling** may occur when a firm with heavy borrowing finds that it cannot meet the repayments. The lenders could apply to the courts for the firm to be put into *liquidation*, or they may choose instead to reschedule the debts. This would mean extending the term of the loans and thereby postponing the repayment dates. It might also include an interest holiday, i.e. a period when the borrower does not have to pay interest on the loans. Lenders might offer these facilities because they expect to get a higher proportion of their *capital* back than if the firm was liquidated.

On the international level, debt rescheduling means lengthening the periods over which governments can repay their debts, in order to reduce the *Debt Problem*.

**debt servicing:** the payment of interest on loans.

**decentralisation** means devolving power from the head office to the local branches or divisions. This includes passing authority for decision-making 'down the line', thereby accepting less uniformity in how things are done. Traditionally, firms such as Sainsbury's and Marks and Spencer have been highly centralised.

Pros:
- decentralisation can *empower* local managers, encouraging them to be more innovative and motivated
- it reduces the volume of day-to-day communication between head office and the branches, therefore giving senior managers the time to consider long-term strategy.

Cons:
- reduction in uniformity may unsettle customers who expect every Sainsbury's to look the same, or every McDonald's hamburger to contain just one slice of gherkin
- head office is in a position to measure the success of every aspect of the product and sales mix, therefore its instructions may prove more profitable than local managers' intuition.

**decentralised wage bargaining** occurs when negotiations are between individual employers and their employees, rather than between an *employers' association* and a *trade union*, operating at a national level.

**decile:** the total accounted for by one tenth of a population. For example, if all the households in Britain were ranked in order of wealth, the lowest decile would be the 10 per cent of the population with the least wealth. To measure the distribution of wealth within society, the proportion of national wealth owned by the lowest decile could be compared with the highest decile.

**decision-making model:** see *scientific decision-making*

**declining industry:** an industry experiencing falling demand, reduced or stagnant output and falling employment. This will be associated with *structural change*.

**decreasing cost industry:** an industry in which expansion leads to a fall in average costs of production. This would occur if there were *economies of scale* to be reaped as output rose. The situation is sometimes described as *increasing returns to scale*.

**deficit:** when income falls short of expenditure. The opposite is a surplus. The terms are used generally instead of profit and loss for *non-profit-making organisations* such as charities, or in economics when describing balances such as the government's finances or the country's *balance of payments*.

**deficit spending** occurs if a government spends more than it receives in *tax revenue*. It will then have to borrow to make up the difference.

**deflation** is downward pressure on the level of economic activity, usually in an attempt to reduce *inflation*. In other words it is a period of falling demand and prices. It is usually accompanied by reduced output and rising unemployment. Deflationary policies or *contractionary policies* are those which are designed to reduce demand by the use of *fiscal* or *monetary policies*.

**deflationary gap:** a situation in which the level of expenditure is less than the capacity of the economy to produce. It will be characterised by a significant amount of *unemployment* and idle capital equipment. It may be eliminated by *injections* into the circular flow of money, i.e. by increasing investment, government expenditure or exports, or by reducing *withdrawals* (saving, taxation or imports).

**deindustrialisation** means the long-term tendency of the manufacturing sector's share of total output to decline. Writers using the term are usually looking for thoroughgoing changes in society and government policy in order to halt the trend. The main causes of deindustrialisation are said to be:

- *short-termism*
- competition from imports
- the social class divide (*them and us*)
- poor education and vocational training.

All *mature economies* (i.e. those which have had a substantial manufacturing sector for a long time) experience a tendency for resources to shift out of manufacturing and into the *service sector*. This is most marked in the USA and the UK.

**delayering** is the removal of one or more *layers of hierarchy* from the management structure of an organisation.

Pros:
- leads to a wider *span of control*
- gives greater responsibilities and workload for each staff member
- reduces the number of *intermediaries* between the bottom and the top
- reduces overhead costs.

Cons:
- staff may become overstretched (causing stress)
- may just be a euphemism for making people redundant.

**delegation** means passing authority down the hierarchy (see *decentralisation* and *empowerment*). It can only work successfully on the basis of mutual trust. The boss must trust the subordinate to complete the tasks efficiently, while the subordinate must be sure that the boss is not just passing on dull or impossible tasks. The other key element in delegation is control. Can the boss bear to relinquish control over a task? If not, the delegation is phoney.

**demand** is the desire to own a good or a service. Demand which can be translated into purchases is known as *effective demand*. When everyone's effective demand in a country is added together it is known as *aggregate demand*. An individual's demand may be influenced by incomes, tastes, or changes in the prices of other goods, be they *substitutes* or *complementary goods*.

**demand curve:** a graphical presentation of the likely level of demand for a product at a range of different prices, i.e. the relationship between price and demand. As one might expect, the curve indicates that as prices rise, demand falls (as customers switch to cheaper alternatives). This is known as a *movement* along the demand curve. A shift in the demand curve will occur if tastes or incomes change or if there is a change in the price of a related good, either a *substitute* or a complement.

*Demand curve*

**demand deficiency unemployment:** occurs when people are unemployed because the level of *aggregate demand* is well below that required to purchase *full-capacity output*. This is unemployment which could be reduced if the level of expenditure in the economy were to be increased. This might be achieved by means of *expansionary policies*. Unemployment of this kind may also be described as *cyclical unemployment* because it is likely to increase during the recession phase of the *business cycle*. Sharp increases in unemployment occurred in 1980–81 and in 1990–92 when the UK economy experienced falling demand for many products.

**demand inflation** is the process by which prices rise because there is excess demand in the economy. It is the same as when people go to an auction. If there are insufficient goods available to satisfy them, the prices of the goods which are there will be bid up. This excess demand occurs when aggregate demand is growing fast and almost all the real resources in the economy are fully employed. Shortages will appear, typically of skilled labour, and this will make it easy for people to negotiate pay rises. This in turn raises firms' costs, and they will be quick to raise their prices to cover the increase. As the economy approaches its full-capacity output, it becomes impossible to increase output to meet the growing demand, and any further increase in aggregate demand will quickly push up prices. Inflation will then tend to accelerate. This situation can be shown diagrammatically using aggregate supply and demand curves (see page 73).

**demand management** refers to government policies which aim to control the level of *aggregate demand* in such a way that there is neither excessive inflation nor high unemployment. *Fiscal* and *monetary policies* can be used in such a way as to control demand and prevent it either from growing faster than the capacity of the economy to produce, or from slowing to well below that level. Demand management policies have been associated with the work of *J M Keynes*, and are sometimes called *Keynesian policies*. They were highly fashionable in the 1960s and 70s; unfortunately they proved less easy to operate than many politicians suggested, mainly because they found it difficult to predict exactly how much of a change in demand would be needed to secure their objectives. Although demand management is seldom referred to by politicians nowadays, it is still used all the time. Interest rates (monetary policy) are adjusted in order to influence both investment and consumer spending. Fiscal policy is used less often in this way.

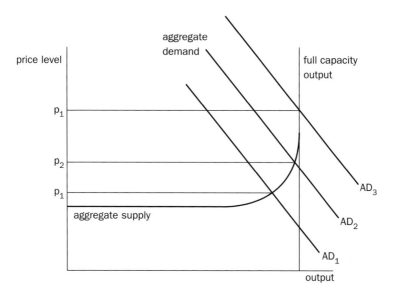

**demand schedule** gives the quantities sold of a product at a set of different prices. It gives the data from which a demand curve may be drawn.

**demarcation** is the dividing line between one job function and another. For example, it used to be common for maintenance workers in factories to be split into mechanics and electricians. Demarcation arrangements were sometimes termed *restrictive practices*, if they caused output to be lower than it could have been. Nowadays, employers favour *multi-skilling*, which does away with demarcation lines and therefore prevents *demarcation disputes*.

**demarcation disputes** are *industrial disputes* about an attempt to change existing *demarcation* lines. They occur because of the possible threat to employment if two jobs are combined into one.

**demerger** occurs when a firm is split into two or more parts, either by selling off parts, or by floating them separately on the *Stock Exchange*. Demergers occur because:

- firms involved in *take-overs* often find that their new purchases offer fewer *economies of scale* than expected, so they prefer to focus on their original business

- take-overs are often financed by heavy borrowings, so in times of economic downturn firms may try to sell off non-core business to cut their debts or interest payments.

Demergers are sometimes referred to as *divestment*. The objective may be to *stick to the knitting*.

**Deming W E (1900–1995):** an American engineer whose post-1945 work on product quality at the Hawthorne lighting plan led him to be invited to help the Japanese rebuild their industries after the Second World War. His emphasis on achieving quality through *statistical process control* was well learned and appreciated by the Japanese. They regard him as one of the founders of *total quality management* and have named their premier quality award after him.

**democratic leadership** means running a business or a department on the basis of decisions agreed among the majority. This might be done formally through a voting system, but it is much more likely to be an informal arrangement in which the leader delegates a great deal, discusses issues, acts upon advice and explains the reasons for decisions. The main difference between democratic and *paternalistic leadership* lies in the degree of *delegation* and the willingness to go along with the decisions of the majority.

**demographic profile:** a statistical breakdown of the people who buy a particular product or brand, e.g. what percentage of consumers are aged 16–25? What percentage are male? The main categories analysed within a demographic profile are the customers' age, gender, social class, income level, and region. Main uses of profile information are:

- for setting quotas for research surveys
- for segmenting a market
- for deciding in which media to advertise (VOGUE or THE SUN?).

**demographic projections:** estimates of likely population changes. These can have an impact on market size for some products.

**denationalisation** means returning to the *private sector* a business that was previously operated by the *public sector*. (See *privatisation*.)

**Department for International Development (DfID):** the government department which handles UK relations with developing countries.

**Department of Trade and Industry (DTI)** is responsible for carrying out the government's policies on the industrial base of the nation. It is involved with a wide range of activities including *regional policy*, *competition policy* and overseas trade.

**dependent population:** all those people who are either in education or too young or too old to take paid employment, or who are unable to work because of disabilities. The proportion of the population in this position varies from one country to another.

**dependent variable:** a variable which is determined by changes elsewhere in the system, and therefore depends on another variable. For example, we usually view the level of tax revenue as depending on the level of income, for a given set of tax rates. Income is thus the independent variable and tax revenue is the dependent variable.

**depletable resources** are things which are fixed in quantity and, once consumed, cannot be replaced. The term is used particularly in relation to energy: gas and oil are fossil fuels and once used, cannot be replaced, although it is possible to search for new sources. Similarly, tropical hardwoods are depletable in the sense that they cannot be replaced at the rate at which they are currently being used.

**depreciation** means the fall in value of *fixed assets* due to wear and tear over time. Businesses allocate the *historic cost* of the asset, less any forecast residual value, to its estimated useful life. The annual depreciation expense, which does not involve a movement of cash, is a notional charge to the *profit and loss account*. Each year the profit is reduced by the annual depreciation and the *net book value* of the asset is correspondingly reduced. The net book value of the asset is therefore equal to historic cost minus accumulated depreciation to date. The estimated life of the asset and its residual value are forecasts, and if the asset is ultimately sold for more than its net book value, a surplus on disposal arises.

The term depreciation may also refer to an exchange rate, the value of which is falling on the foreign exchange markets. (See *exchange rate depreciation*.)

**depression:** a prolonged period of negative growth, or growth that is well below the long-term average. Whereas a *recession* occurs regularly as the bottom phase of a country's *trade cycle*, a full-scale depression is much rarer. Where recession ends and depression begins is a matter for debate, and it may be that it is only time which turns a recession into a depression. In other words a recession becomes a depression if it continues for a long time. Few would argue that the depression of the 1930s was not one such period.

**depth interview:** a one-to-one interview in which the interviewer has no pre-set questionnaire, but tries to obtain information and ideas through informal discussion. It is a form of *qualitative research* in which a psychologist will be trying to discover the reasons behind people's attitudes or purchasing decisions.

**deregulation** is the removal of government rules, regulations and laws from the workings of business. This might include scrapping *wages councils*, or ending *monopoly* rights to supply services such as letter delivery or bus services. Bank deregulation has been important in promoting *competition* within the banking sector.

Pros:
- less regulation means fewer regulators need be employed by the government or local councils (perhaps cutting public spending and therefore cutting tax levels)
- less regulation should encourage more competition.

Cons:
- many rules affecting business were to stop exploitation; is this acceptable nowadays?
- competition does not necessarily provide what society wants; it may only provide what is profitable (such as buses in the daytime but not at night).

**derived demand:** employers' demand for labour is said to be derived demand, because they do not want labour for its own sake but for what it may be able to produce. The demand is thus derived from the demand for the final product.

**derivatives** involve a contract, the value of which is based on the value of another asset, or on an index which measures changes in values. Derivatives are used as a way of reducing risks. They may be based on interest rates, currencies, equities or commodities. They include *futures* and *options*. Futures involve an agreement to buy an amount of a commodity, or a financial asset, on a date in the future, at an agreed price. They are a way of protecting the buyer from the uncertain nature of commodity prices. If you know that you will need a certain quantity of iron ore in three months time, it may make sense to buy futures at an agreed price now, thus reducing the risk. *Financial futures* are another important derivative.

**design mix** is how the firm combines three key design elements in order to fit the market gap that has been identified. The three are:
- aesthetic appeal (appeal to the senses)
- function (how well the product works and lasts)
- economic manufacture.

**deskilling** occurs when a new machine or process changes a job that was once a source of craft pride into a repetitive or mundane task such as feeding or minding a machine.

**desk research** means finding out information from already published sources, perhaps from trade magazines, from government statistics or from on-line computer *databases*. It is also known as secondary research.

**desktop publishing (DTP)** is the use of computer software to organise material including text, pictures, shading and different font sizes on to a page or pages. The result can be seen on a VDU and then be downloaded to a printer. As word-processing packages have become more sophisticated the distinction between them and desktop publishing software has diminished.

**destocking** is the deliberate attempt to reduce a firm's stockholding by cutting orders of materials or by cutting production levels. This is usually undertaken by organisations at the beginning of a *recession*, when orders begin to fall. Businesses can cut stocks of raw materials quickly by reordering less from suppliers. This represents a cut in the suppliers' levels of *demand* which reinforces the recession. Stocks are usually financed by *overdraft* borrowing from banks on which interest is paid, so there is a strong incentive to destock when interest rates rise.

**destroyer pricing:** another term for *predatory pricing*

**devaluation:** is the deliberate decision by a government to reduce the value of its currency in relation to foreign currencies. This boosts the international competitiveness of the country's products. It also makes it more expensive for consumers to buy foreign goods, therefore making home-produced goods more attractive. Devaluation boosts the competitiveness of exports, thereby improving the balance of payments. Devaluation is a term which usually implies central bank involvement in deciding the appropriate exchange rate.

Pros:
- devaluation makes a country's exports more competitive
- it makes imports more expensive and less price competitive
- it should therefore improve the country's balance of payments.

Cons:
- devaluation may represent an 'easy option' for firms, so that they don't have to control their costs
- dearer imports may cause business costs to rise, creating inflationary pressure.

**developing country:** a country with a developing manufacturing base, but which has a national income that is not yet big enough to provide sufficient saving to sustain the investment required for more growth. Many developing countries have been dependent on *primary sector* products for their growth in the past, but as prices for such products are notoriously unreliable, growth has often been intermittent. Developing countries usually receive foreign *aid*, but the amount may vary. Some have encountered the *Debt Problem*. Others have gone on to become *newly industrialised economies*, when rapid growth of manufacturing and exports have had a major impact.

**development area:** a geographical region designated by government to receive special help due to its depressed economic circumstances. The British government may offer selective regional assistance to encourage a business to locate within a development area. Increasingly the *European Union* has played a major role in offering grants to such areas to encourage regeneration. (See *assisted areas*.)

**devolving power** means delegating it to a person or organisation at a lower level within a hierarchy. (See *delegation*.)

**dictatorial leadership:** the use of power by giving out orders, rather than consulting or delegating. It implies what *McGregor* termed a *Theory X* attitude on the part of the leader, i.e. the assumption that employees have little ability or desire to contribute fruitfully to the decision-making process. The dictatorial leader is also likely to threaten or penalise those who fail to succeed in the task they have been set. (See *authoritarian*, *paternalistic* and *democratic leadership*.)

**differentials** are the proportionate differences in pay between one grade of worker and another. They are likely to reflect different levels of skill or responsibility. When differentials are narrowed, workers on the higher rate of pay may feel that their skills and status are being downgraded.

**differentiated products** are usually substitutes for one another, but are nevertheless subtly different. Though they may perform the same function, their design features distinguish them from each other. They contrast with *homogeneous products*; with these it is impossible for the buyer to distinguish one supplier's product from another's. Differentiated products are a feature of *imperfect competition*. By differentiating their product a particular firm may be able to exert some degree of control over the market. Some firms may use *branding* or qualitative differences which make their product distinctive. (See also *product differentiation*.)

**dilution of control** occurs when an existing shareholder is unwilling to increase his or her investment in a company that is looking for extra *share capital*. For example, if a share-holder's 1 000 shares represent 10 per cent of a firm's 10 000 issued shares, the stake will be diluted to a 5 per cent holding if the firm doubles its share issue to 20 000. This issue becomes much more important if the shareholders are the family owners of the business, and the family's holding is just above 50 per cent. Then a *rights issue* might cause the family to lose control of its business.

**dilution of earnings** occurs when a firm's decision to increase its *share capital* leads to a fall in *earnings per share*. This will occur if profits (earnings) rise by a lower proportion than the increase in share capital. There are two main circumstances in which earnings dilution may arise:

- when a *rights issue* takes place
- when a firm buys up another company; if the latter proves to be less profitable than the original firm, earnings dilution is likely.

**diminishing returns** occur when, as a producer adds more of one factor of production to a fixed quantity of other factors of production, the output increases but less than proportionately. For example, if ten people have ten spades and are digging a trench, the addition of one extra person digging and allowing each person to take a break will allow the team to dig a longer trench in a given time. But if more people are added to the team, each extra one will add less and less to the distance dug, because the rest of the team will gain little benefit from further breaks.

**direct communication** means communication that is not through *intermediaries*. It is an alternative to the conventional system of communicating through official, formal channels. Professor *Herzberg* considered this a vital element in *job enrichment*, as it supported the requirement for direct *feedback*.

**direct controls:** a general term to describe the government's power to influence business and the economy through direct intervention, such as legislation or administrative action. For example, in the past direct controls were sometimes imposed by the *Bank of England* on the *commercial banks* in order to limit their lending. Such controls are more likely to be imposed by an *interventionist* government, or at a time of grave economic crisis.

**direct cost:** any cost which can be allocated precisely to a *cost centre* and which varies in direct proportion to activity or output. Common examples of direct costs are materials and piece-rate labour.

**direct labour:** the staff directly involved in the production process, who therefore represent a *direct cost*.

**direct marketing** is marketing activity that is aimed directly at the customer, such as direct mail, door-to-door selling, or door-to-door leaflets.

**director:** a senior manager proposed by the *chief executive* and elected by shareholders to represent them on the main decision-making committee, the board of directors. Directors may either be executive or non-executive. Executive directors are employees of the company, usually with the responsibility for running a large division or department. *Non-executive directors* are not company employees; they are experienced senior managers from other firms, appointed to give independent advice. It has always been hoped that non-executive directors would be sharp critics of the internal management, taking special care to look after the interests of the company's shareholders. Experience has not always borne this out, however, as too many have been friends or business associates of the chief executive.

**Director General of Fair Trading:** working from the *Office of Fair Trading*, the DGFT supervises the investigation of *cartels* and other anti-competitive practices with powers greatly strengthened by the 1998 *Competition Act*.

**directors' report:** a statutory element in a *public limited company*'s annual report which informs shareholders of: future developments, the firm's health and safety policy, any political or charitable donations, directors' shareholdings and *share options*, plus any changes in board personnel.

**direct response** (marketing) is activity designed to get the customer to contact the advertiser directly, such as by filling in a form for a holiday brochure or telephoning to buy a CD advertised on television. The great advantage of this form of advertising is that the company can measure the cost-effectiveness of each medium used, and therefore build up a picture of the best ways to spend its advertising budget.

**Worked example: measuring direct responses to a campaign advertising for members to join a Book Club**

| Publication | Type of space | Cost per advert | Number of new members | Cost per new member |
|---|---|---|---|---|
| TV Times | Colour page | £28 000 | 1 240 | £22.58* |
| Sunday | Colour page | £32 000 | 1 575 | £20.32 |
| Observer | Colour page | £14 000 | 564 | £25.71 |

* Cost per member = cost / members, e.g. £28 000 / 1 240 = £22.58

In this example SUNDAY is the most cost-effective advertising medium, as it has the lowest cost per member.

**direct taxation** is paid from an individual's, or an organisation's, income as opposed to *indirect taxes* which are paid on goods and services purchased (for instance *VAT*). Direct taxes include *income tax*, *corporation tax*, and *council tax*. They also include taxes on wealth, principally *inheritance tax*. Direct taxes are usually *proportional* or *progressive*. They also include *national insurance charges*.

**dirty float** is the term used to describe a *floating exchange rate* which operates only within certain bands. In other words the *central bank* will intervene to prevent the exchange rate exceeding those limits. If the intervention is designed merely to iron out day-to-day fluctuations and instability, it may be known as a *managed float*.

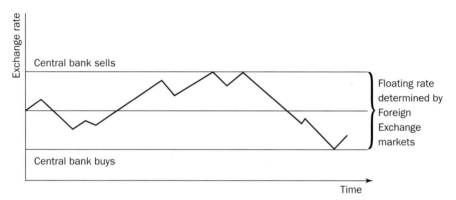

**Disability Discrimination Act 1995:** this forbids employees with disabilities being treated less favourably than others, and requires employers to make reasonable adjustments to provide working conditions and an environment to help overcome the practical difficulties of disability.

**disaster planning** became a common form of *contingency planning* during the 1980s, after a series of sudden shocks hit firms in Britain, such as the Zeebrugge ferry disaster and the Perrier Water contamination scandal. It involves visualising possible types of disaster that might hit the firm, then deciding:

● which team of senior managers would be best suited to tackling the crisis

● where they would meet

● what resources they would require (telecommunications etc.).

**disciplinary procedure** is the formal process by which employees can be taken to task for failure to meet their employment contract. If the employee does not change his or her attitude or behaviour, it will lead to verbal then written threats of dismissal. The disciplinary stages are:

1 verbal warning

2 written warning

3 final written warning

4 dismissal (if a further offence is committed within 12 months of a final written warning).

**disclosure of information** is the process of releasing factual data to enable outsiders to make a judgement or decision. For many years British *trade unions* have complained that they cannot trust the stance of managers in industrial negotiations because of their failure to disclose key facts. Company secrecy over industrial accident rates, pollution emissions and recycling levels also makes it hard for environmental campaigners to pressurise firms into accepting their *social responsibilities*. This is why many *pressure groups* feel that the law should force firms to disclose more information in their *annual report and accounts*.

**discount houses** were financial intermediaries which specialised in lending on a very short-term basis. The last ones left in business ceased to operate as such in 1998. Their functions were taken over by the relevant departments within the banks. This occurred as a result of the change in the *Bank of England*'s rules. Previously it lent directly only to the discount houses. Now it lends directly to all recognised banks.

**discounted cash flow (DCF):** an *investment appraisal* technique based on *cash flow forecasts* and the *opportunity cost* of money. A project requires a capital outlay which should generate positive cash inflows over future years. These estimated future cash inflows are each multiplied by a discount factor between zero and one, since money at some future date is worth less to the firm than the same sum in hand today. The longer the wait for a future sum, the lower its *present value*. When discounted, these future cash flows can be totalled; from this the capital outlay can be deducted to give the *net present value (NPV)* for the project. If this is positive the project is economically viable. (See *net present value* for a worked example.)

**discount rate:** this term is sometimes used to describe the rate at which the *Bank of England* lends to *banks* which are temporarily short of funds with which to meet their obligations. If the Bank of England wishes interest rates to rise generally, it can raise the discount rate. (See also *bank rate*.)

**discouraged workers:** people who have been unemployed for sometime, despite making an effort to find work, sometimes give up the search for a job. Effectively, they drop out of the labour market in the sense that they are no longer making themselves available for work.

**discretionary income:** the income left to a household after deduction of income tax, national insurance and contracted outgoings such as mortgage payments, plus the amount needed to pay for basic needs such as food and clothing.

**discretionary policy** refers to deliberate changes in tax rates or government expenditure which will affect the level of *aggregate demand*. In contrast, some changes in the level of taxation and spending are referred to as *automatic stabilisers*, because they will increase or reduce aggregate demand automatically as incomes and unemployment change over the course of the business cycle.

**discrimination:** the practice of preferring an applicant for a job because of the person's race, gender or religion. Although discrimination is illegal there is a good deal of evidence of its continuation. Preferred groups generally are able to earn higher rates of pay and may have lower unemployment rates.

**discriminatory pricing:** see *price discrimination*

**diseconomies of scale:** factors causing higher costs per unit when the scale of output is greater, i.e. causes of inefficiency in large organisations. The main factors are:

1 Communication costs: in small firms, internal communication is mainly oral, which is cheap and highly effective since *feedback* is inbuilt. Large firms have many *layers of hierarchy* so messages may be distorted as they pass through *intermediaries*.

Consequently much communication is done through memos, reports or written requests. These require the time and therefore pay of typists, filing clerks and messengers. Worse still, written messages are less effective and less motivating than conversation, so they involve more costs through inefficiency.

2   Coordination costs: in small firms, decisions are usually made by the proprietor, perhaps after consulting staff. One person taking the decisions ensures *coordination* of the firm's strategy and actions. Large firms require *delegation*, as one person cannot make hundreds of major decisions competently. Yet *empowering* managers to make their own decisions can result in different departments heading in different directions. So regular meetings are required to ensure coordination. This is why research shows that managers spend over half their time communicating. That time represents a considerable extra *overhead* cost for the firm to bear.

**disequilibrium** occurs when there is excess supply or excess demand, either in a particular market or in the economy as a whole. For example if there are large stocks of unsold butter, we can say that the market is in disequilibrium. The likely explanation will be that the price is too high for *market clearing* to take place. The diagram on the next page shows how a high price may cause excess demand. On the macroeconomic level, high levels of *aggregate demand*, in excess of the economy's capacity to supply goods and services, would indicate disequilibrium. The likely outcome would be accelerating inflation and the government might want to use fiscal and monetary policies to reduce the level of demand.

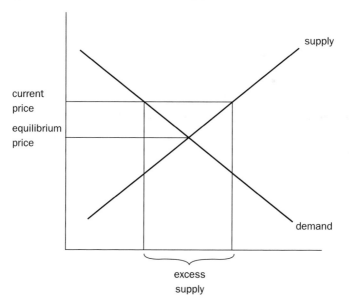

**disguised unemployment** occurs when people who would like to work do not register, usually because they are not entitled to unemployment benefit, and therefore have no incentive to do so. There can be some overlap with *discouraged workers*.

**dismissal:** being dismissed ('sacked') from a job due to incompetence or breaches of discipline. Note that this is different from *redundancy*.

**dispersion** is a measurement of the extent to which numerate data is concentrated or scattered. This is vital for marketing decision-making, such as whether to concentrate advertising effort solely upon 15–20-year-olds. Dispersion is also a key factor in *market research*, as the ideal research finding would have a low rate of dispersion (i.e. most respondents agreeing with each other).

**disposable income** is that part of your income that is available to spend as you wish. In other words your gross income of £200 per week has tax, *National Insurance*, pensions etc. deducted from it so that you may only have £150 to spend as you wish. That is your disposable income. Benefits such as income support and family credits will increase disposable income, enabling people to spend more than they can earn.

**disputes procedure:** the formal process by which a dispute between management and *trade union* will be progressed. For example, it may be laid down by written agreement that a pay dispute will be put to an *ACAS*-appointed *arbitrator* before any *industrial action* is taken.

**dissaving:** in the macroeconomic model of the circular flow of money, dissaving occurs when consumption exceeds income and is financed by drawing on past savings.

**distance learning** is the teaching of academic subjects by post (or *electronic mail*). Managers may develop their skills by specialist courses in accountancy or personnel management, or may pursue general courses such as an MBA (*Master of Business Administration*). Distance learning avoids the need to give up work while studying, and cuts out the travelling time involved in part-time academic study.

**distinctive competence** is a competitive advantage that distinguishes one firm from another. It is the skill or asset upon which future strength can be built. For example the French company Bic have developed exceptional know-how in the manufacture of disposable plastic products; that is their distinctive competence. (See *asset-led marketing*.)

**distribution:** the entire process of getting products to where customers can buy them. This sounds easy, but actually requires considerable persuasion. Shop shelf space is limited, so if a retailer is to stock your product they must destock another. Furthermore, having obtained shop distribution, manufacturers have to battle constantly to keep it. (See *distribution targets*.)

**distribution channels:** the stages of ownership that take place as a product moves from the manufacturer to the consumer (see *wholesaling*).

**Main channels of distribution**

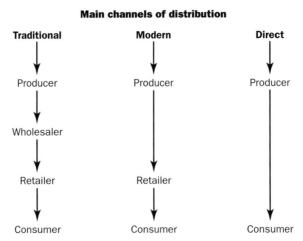

**distribution of income** is the spread of income earned by different groups of people within an economy. The intention of taxation and social security benefits is usually to redistribute income from the richer towards the poorer members of society. Since 1980, the gap between the rich and the poor has tended to widen. A relatively unequal distribution of income may increase incentives to work but may also increase tensions between employers and employees. Developing countries sometimes have a much more unequal distribution of income than developed countries.

**distribution of wealth** refers to the ownership of assets and how it is spread amongst different groups of people. Wealth can consist of bank balances, shares, property, businesses and anything else which provides a continuing income or can be sold. Wealth is a stock, in contrast to income, which is a flow. Income is paid continuously whereas wealth is held over a long period. A relatively equal distribution of wealth would imply that most people had some and few had either none or a great deal. The distribution of wealth may be affected by inheritance taxes, and by changes in property prices or ownership.

**distribution targets** are set to motivate the *salesforce* to obtain distribution in as high a percentage of target outlets as seems feasible. This might be achieved by:

* offering high *profit margins* to retailers
* heavy advertising in trade magazines
* giving sales staff big incentives to work and sell hard.

**diversification** is the spreading of business risks by reducing dependence on one product or market. It is an important business objective, be it for a small ice-cream producer wanting security from cool summers, or for *multinational* firms wanting to move into new growth markets. The opposite of diversification is *focus*.

Pros: • improves prospects for long-term company survival
       • can enable a firm to regain a growth path in a saturated market
       • provides new outlets for a firm's skills and resources.

Cons: • many diversifications have disappointed due to *diseconomies of scale* or failure to understand fully the new market-place (the customer, competition, etc.)
       • the firm's core business may be weakened as resources are redirected towards new opportunities; the American writer Peter Lynch has called this phenomenon: 'diworsification'.

**divestment** means selling off parts of the business that no longer fit the long-term strategy. This might be because they are no longer profitable, or because the firm wants to focus its management on the *core activities*, i.e. *stick to the knitting*.

**dividend cover** is the number of times the dividend declared could have been paid out of the *net profit* available after tax and interest. A figure of around three is usually felt to be desirable. Much below it and the firm is paying out such high dividends as to leave too little for reinvestment. Above it and the shareholders could reasonably question whether the firm's dividend pay-outs are too mean.

**dividend per share (DPS)** is the total dividend declared by the *directors* divided by the number of shares issued.

$$\text{FORMULA:} \quad \frac{\text{total dividends}}{\text{shares issued}} = \text{dividends per share}$$

**83**

**dividend policy:** the proportion of profits after tax a company's directors decide to pay out to shareholders in the form of annual dividends. The higher the payout, the less there is to reinvest to make the business bigger or more efficient. Higher retained profits should enable the firm to pay higher dividends in future. So the more profit that is retained today, the greater prospects of benefits tomorrow. Shareholders would have to agree to such a policy. They can vote on it at the AGM; if they disagreed with the policy they could sell their shares.

**dividends** are a share in the profits of a company distributed to its shareholders according to the rights which the shares give them. Dividends must be paid (after interest charges) on *preference shares* before *ordinary shares*. Preference share dividends are fixed but ordinary share dividends are declared annually by the directors and voted on at the *annual general meeting*.

**dividend yield** is the annual *dividend per share* expressed as a percentage of the market price of the share. The dividend is a matter of record but the market price may fluctuate constantly. If the share is being upgraded by the *stock market*, its price will rise and therefore the yield will fall. Dividend yield is an important consideration for share buyers who need an annual income from their savings to boost their regular earnings (for example, pensioners). Investors can compare a share's dividend yield directly with building society rates, to help decide where to place their savings.

$$\text{FORMULA:} \quad \frac{\text{dividend per share}}{\text{market share price}} \times 100 = \text{dividend yield}$$

**division:** a major operational part of a business. It is likely to have its own *chief executive* or *chairman* and may have a separate location from the head office. It will function as a business within a business.

**division of labour** means breaking a job down into small, repetitive fragments, each of which can be done at speed by workers with little formal training. This enables firms to hire labour cheaply and plentifully, but may lead to serious problems of low *motivation* and even *alienation* of the workforce. Professor Herzberg maintained that unless workers have a complete unit of work they cannot be motivated. Nevertheless, the degree of specialisation implied by division of labour can enable an individual to become expert at his or her job and can increase productivity. It can also make it much easier to mechanise certain parts of the production process, opening up the possibility of further productivity gains.

**divorce of ownership and control** is a phrase conveying concern that although the shareholders own public companies, managements run them. This might lead to conflicting loyalties with managements pursuing objectives that help their own careers or job satisfaction, rather than looking after shareholders' best interests. Many past *diversification* moves and *take-over bids* seem to have offered little real benefit to shareholders.

**dog:** a term used by the Boston Consulting Group to describe a product with low *market share* within a market with low growth. The Group recommend that dogs be considered for discontinuation, in order to concentrate time and resources on more profitable brands. Dogs form one part of the *Boston Matrix*.

**dollar ($):** the currency of the United States of America. Because of the importance of the US economy in terms of world trade, many goods are traded internationally in dollars. For example, oil produced in the North Sea by the UK will be sold to another country at a price given in US dollars. The euro may well become a similarly important world currency in the future.

**double-entry bookkeeping** is a system of accounting whereby one event is recorded in two accounts, as a *debit* in one and as a *credit* in another. This recognises that all financial transactions have a dual nature. For example, if you go to buy a chocolate bar, not one but two things occur. You hand over 30p (cash minus 30p) and receive a piece of (very temporary) stock (stocks plus 30p). The use of double-entry ensures that *assets* always equal *liabilities* and therefore *balance sheets* always balance (unless a mistake has been made).

**Dow Jones Index** is the name for the New York's Stock Exchange daily market index. Dating back to 1928, the index takes the average price of thirty major stocks which together account for 25 per cent of its *market capitalisation*.

**down-market:** a product or advertisement aimed at working-class or low-income households; the opposite of *up-market*.

**downside** is the possible or actual consequence of a decision turning out badly. If the downside is relatively small compared with the potential benefits of a decision, the *risk:reward ratio* is said to be favourable.

**downsizing:** reducing the size of a business to meet a new, lower demand level; the term downsizing is often used as a euphemism for a round of redundancies. Due to the negative connotations of the term **down**sizing, some firms now use a further euphemism – **right**sizing.

**downtime** is when machinery is needed but not being used. This may be because of a breakdown, lack of spare parts, or when resetting the machine for a different product specification to be manufactured. Downtime might be measured in minutes or as a proportion of the day's working hours. It represents a waste of resources and adds to *fixed costs per unit* by restricting the volume of *output* from a given *production line*.

**downward communication** is the passage of information down the *chain of command*, from senior to junior staff.

**DPS:** see *dividend per share*

**drawings** represent the salary taken out of an *unlimited liability* firm by its proprietors. What is left on the *profit and loss account* after drawings is the firm's retained earnings.

**Drucker, Peter:** a highly influential management writer and consultant who popularised the concept of management by objectives. His ideas were firmly rooted in the case histories of major corporations such as IBM and General Motors, making his writings far more business-specific than motivation theorists such as *Maslow*.

**DTI:** see *Department of Trade and Industry*

**dumping** describes the selling of a good in another country at a price which is less than its cost of production. A country may dump for a number of reasons:

- to earn foreign exchange: this was a common practice amongst countries formerly under communist control. Items such as cameras were sold at less than their cost of production in order to earn western currency
- to get rid of excess production: in the early 1990s the USA fined European steel manufacturers for such dumping

- to destroy the foreign industry in order to create a monopoly so that prices can be adjusted back to high levels in the future.

**duopoly** is where there are only two producers in the market. This may result in what appears to be a highly competitive market, usually based on *non-price competition*, such as *advertising*. However, there may also be a certain amount of *collusion*, either explicit or implicit, in order to guarantee high profits for both firms, and to keep out other potential competitors. This is sometimes referred to as *tacit agreement*. Because there are only two producers, the actions of one are clear to the other, and so each business decision will be based on how it is expected that the competitor will react to the decision, as well as how consumers will respond.

**durable:** see *consumer durable*

### Do you need revision help and advice?

Go to pages 325–341 for a range of revision appendices that include plenty of exam advice and tips.

**earnings:** when applied to a company, means *profit* after tax. When applied to employees, earnings refer to total pay, i.e. wages or salaries and any overtime or bonus payments.

**earnings per share (EPS):** a ratio showing the after-tax *profit* available for distribution to shareholders. The company directors recommend and the shareholders vote on how much of that profit will be paid as dividends and how much will be *ploughed back* into the company.

FORMULA: $\dfrac{\text{profit after tax}}{\text{number of shares}}$

**Worked example: if DG Ltd makes a profit after tax of £40 000, what is the EPS if the issued share capital is £200 000 of £0.25 share?**

DG has $\dfrac{£200\,000}{£0.25}$ = 800 000 shares issued

EPS = $\dfrac{£40\,000}{800\,000}$ = £0.05 i.e. **5p per share**

**EC:** see *European Community*

**ECB:** see *European Central Bank*

**ECGD:** see *Export Credit Guarantee Department*

**e-commerce** means electronic commerce and has two components.

- Consumers may shop on-line rather than in shopping centres. This may have the potential to cut prices in some instances. Or it may simply increase convenience.

- Firms may buy from other firms on line. This is known as the B2B market, business to business. This seems likely to be a highly significant development.

The growth of e-commerce has been slower than was predicted in 1999–2000. However, there have been some huge on-line successes, such as Easyjet, which built its business by making more than 90 per cent of its ticket sales on the Internet.

**econometrics** means, literally, the measurement of economic relationships. It involves generating hypotheses from economic models and testing them against the data, to determine what statistical support there is for the existence of particular relationships.

**economic and monetary union (EMU):** the operation of a common monetary policy within Europe, including a single currency run by a *European Central Bank*. Eleven *European Union* countries are members, including all the major economies other than Britain. The operation of the single currency (the *euro*) is the responsibility of the European Central Bank. The euro was introduced in 1999 and since July 1 2002 it has been the only legal currency throughout the *euro-zone*.

This has a number of far-reaching implications.

- Firms in the euro-zone will find it very easy to trade with one another. There will be none of the uncertainties arising from having different exchange rates.

- Prices across the euro-zone should become much more transparent. It will be easy for buyers to see who is charging the least and buy from them. This may increase competition and lead to lower prices for consumers.

- With a single *monetary policy* for all member countries, it may be difficult to determine an appropriate interest rate unless all economies have similar levels of aggregate demand. There may be times when individual countries find the interest rate either too high or too low. *Economic convergence* is thus important for member countries.

**economic convergence** is the situation when countries adopt similar economic policies and so have similar rates of *inflation* and *public-sector deficits*. It is an important pre-requisite for *monetary union*. Without it, some countries would, within a monetary union, become increasingly uncompetitive and therefore economically depressed relative to other member countries.

The convergence criteria for membership of the EMU are:

- the inflation rate must not exceed that of the three best-performing countries by more than 1.5 per cent

- interest rates on government bonds must not be more than 2 per cent above those in the same three countries

- the government deficit must be no more than 3 per cent of GDP

- the total government debt must be no more than 60 per cent of GDP

- the exchange rate must have been reasonably stable for the past two years.

These conditions would not be a problem for the UK, should the government seek membership in the future.

**economic development** is the process by which a country may experience economic growth and a *reallocation of resources* away from primary production and towards manufacturing. The term is usually used to describe what is happening in relatively poor countries which are usually referred to as *less developed countries*. Rapid economic development is usually associated with high levels of investment, and improvements in education and training opportunities, and sometimes with a policy of allowing relatively *free trade* and an increasingly *open economy*.

**economic efficiency** implies that output is being produced at the lowest possible cost in terms of resources, and in the types and quantities which most closely reflect patterns of consumer demand. Minimising costs in turn implies that there is *technical efficiency* (sometimes known as productive efficiency). This means that the production process uses the best available technology and is organised so as to eliminate wasted resources. When the structure of production reflects consumers' wants there is *allocative efficiency*, arising from *consumer sovereignty*. Another frequently used way of describing economic efficiency is to say that no one can be made better off without making someone else worse off. This is sometimes referred to as Pareto efficiency.

**economic expectations** refer to people's anticipation of the way the economy is likely to develop in the future. Such expectations can have a profound effect. For instance, firms will not invest in new *plant* and machinery if they believe they will not get an adequate return, even if the rate of interest is low. Consumers will not spend money in the shops, whatever the level of prices, if they believe that the economy is in *recession* and that their jobs are at risk.

**economic forecasting** is the process by which economists use *economic models* to predict future trends in the main economic variables. The accuracy of forecasts depends on the extent to which the assumptions on which they are based actually correspond to reality. Forecasting is made difficult by the fact that shocks may occur which are quite unexpected and have far-reaching effects which are by their nature unpredictable. The oil price rise of 1973–4 and the reunification of Germany in 1989 are examples of shocks which had a major effect on a number of countries.

**economic goods** are all those items which have a cost in terms of *real resources* and are therefore scarce in nature. A price must be paid in order to obtain them. The opposite of an economic good is a *free good* and it is actually difficult to identify examples of these. Sometimes blackberries are said to be a free good.

**economic growth** describes the way the real income of an economy increases over time. A nation's growth is usually measured in terms of *gross domestic product (GDP)*. The reasons for growth are complex, although it can be explained in terms of increasingly efficient uses of the *factors of production* to provide more and more goods and services. Important elements in the growth process include *investment*, education and training, and *technological change*. Investment increases the amount of capital per person employed and increases productivity. Education and training enhances *human capital*, again making people more productive. Technological change leads to the availability of bigger and better machines, and also helps to create better ways of managing people. These three factors in combination have a big impact on growth rates.

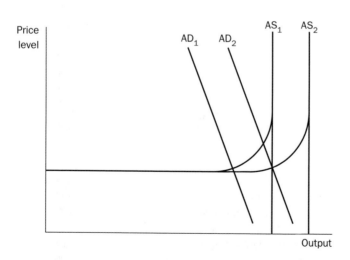

Rising capacity in the economy, as aggregate supply increases, means that output can grow without inflation accelerating

GDP figures must be interpreted with caution. A developing country may have strong growth in GDP, and also a high birth rate. This means that per capita growth is less than the growth of GDP. It is also important to note that increases in GDP do not necessarily yield increases in *welfare*, because some aspects of growth bring disadvantages such as increased noise, pollution or congestion.

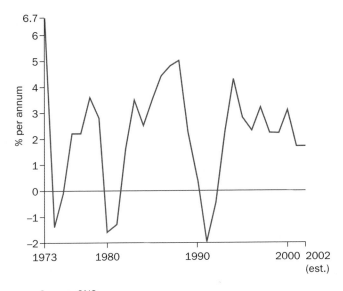

Source: ONS

*Economic growth rates fluctuate over the course of the trade cycle*

**economic indicators** are the monthly statistics that provide information on the country's economic performance. *Leading indicators* give a prediction of future events, *coincident indicators* show the state of the economy today, and *lagging indicators* show the health of the economy in the recent past. All are subject to considerable error, so it is unwise to draw any conclusions from one month's data.

**economic man** is a term based on the assumption that human behaviour is determined by rational economic motives such as the desire for financial gain and fear of financial pain. It underpinned the writings of Adam *Smith* in the eighteenth century and F W *Taylor* in the early twentieth century. It is also at the heart of what *McGregor* called a *Theory X* attitude on the part of managers.

**economic models** are constructed of relationships between different variables which enable economists to examine the connections between changes. A model may use only those variables which are most important within the situation being studied, and thus can reduce the level of complication which must be considered. In this way they may enable us to gain important insights into the way the economy works. A model may be constructed in terms of a number of simultaneous equations, or the relationships may be represented graphically or verbally. Models can be judged by their effectiveness in predicting what will happen under particular circumstances. They will not give accurate predictions if they are based on unrealistic assumptions. A model may be very simple, as in the basic supply and demand diagram, or very complex, as for example in the Treasury model of the whole economy which has over 500 equations and variables.

**economic planning:** the creation by a government of a plan for a period of years which gives a series of targets for output, investment, training and other means by which its objectives may be met. In the UK this approach to economic policy was used in the 1960s. In France it has been in continuous use for many years.

**economic profit** is the difference between total revenue from the sale of the product, and the opportunity costs of all the resources used in production. It is a reward for the taking of unquantifiable risks by the entrepreneur. Profit in excess of the full opportunity cost of the resources encourages entrepreneurs to divert more resources to production because it shows that there is a high level of demand for the product. (This is the *profit signalling mechanism.*)

**economic rent** is the amount which someone can earn which is in excess of their *transfer earnings*, i.e. what they could earn elsewhere. It is a demand-determined reward to labour and will be earned when labour is to some degree in inelastic supply. For example, doctors are in perfectly inelastic supply because the number of places available to study medicine is determined by the government and the profession. To the extent that the demand for doctors exceeds the supply, they will be able to negotiate higher salaries than most could earn as research scientists or in other occupations.

**economic sanctions** prohibit or discourage trade in certain items with a particular country, usually with a political motive. Sanctions against South Africa were partly responsible for the government of the country eventually abandoning its policy of racial discrimination.

**Economic Trends:** a monthly publication from the Office for National Statistics that lists and charts the latest government statistics on the economy. It is a usual source of *secondary data* for project or assignment work.

**economies of scale** are the factors that cause average costs to be lower in large-scale operations than in small-scale ones. In other words, doubling the *output* results in a less than double increase in costs; the cost of producing each unit falls because factor inputs can be used more efficiently. Economies of scale fall into a number of categories, divided into internal and external economies. The following are internal:

- specialisation, i.e. with a large workforce it is possible to divide up the work process and then recruit people whose skills exactly match the job requirements; staff can then be trained and become highly effective at carrying out their limited task

- technical economies, such as the use of automated equipment where it is more cost-effective than labour; this is only feasible when the *fixed costs* of the machine can be spread thinly over many units of output

- purchasing economies with the benefits of bulk buying, i.e. obtaining supplies of materials and components at lower unit costs, thereby cutting variable costs

- financial economies stemming from the lower cost of *capital* charged to large firms by the providers of finance. Banks charge lower rates of interest and equity investors are more willing to accept low *dividend yields* from bigger firms. This is because large firms are usually more diversified and less vulnerable to *liquidation* than small firms

- marketing economies which occur because some kinds of advertising, for example on TV, cost the same irrespective of how much is produced. Thus with a higher level of output, the advertising cost is spread across a larger quantity.

External economies are the advantages of scale that benefit the whole industry, and not just individual firms. So if an industry is concentrated in one geographical area it is likely that a pool of labour will be attracted and trained, perhaps by a local college, which will have specialised skills useful to the whole industry and from which each firm will benefit. Similarly, a large grouping of firms will attract a network of suppliers, whose own scale of operation should yield economies such as lower component costs. Further, the growth of the industry will make it possible to fund research which may benefit a number of producers.

**Economist Intelligence Unit (EIU):** a sister company to the ECONOMIST magazine that provides carefully researched *secondary data* on particular countries or markets. Its monthly publication RETAIL BUSINESS is a valuable source of sales and distribution information about UK consumer markets and products.

**ECU:** see *European Currency Unit*

**EEC:** see *European Union*

**effective demand** is the desire to buy backed by the ability to pay. Text books often suggest that the price of a *commodity* is determined by *supply* and *demand*. In such cases the author really means effective demand.

**effective exchange rate:** the exchange rate as measured by the exchange rate index, which values the currency as a weighted average of the currencies of the nation's major trading partners. The weights are proportional to the amount of trade involved.

**efficiency** means using resources effectively. It can be calculated in many different ways; the most common measurements are:

- labour efficiency: productivity (output per worker)
- production efficiency: *wastage* (percentage of scrap within the process)
- financial efficiency: *asset turnover* (the amount of sales generated from the firm's assets).

Efficiency is an important economic concept and has a range of more qualitative aspects; see also *allocative efficiency*, *economic efficiency* and *technical efficiency*.

**EFTA:** see *European Free Trade Association*

**EGM:** see *extraordinary general meeting*

**EIU:** see *Economist Intelligence Unit*

**elasticities** measure responsiveness to change. *Price elasticity of demand* measures the responsiveness of quantity demanded to a change in price. Other important elasticities include *income elasticity of demand*, *cross-elasticity of demand*, *supply elasticity* and *advertising elasticity*.

**electronic mail (e-mail)** involves sending messages from one computer to another, either internally or to those outside the firm. This is instantaneous communication that is especially useful for posting detailed data such as daily sales broken down by product line.

**e-mail:** see *electronic mail*

**embargo:** an order forbidding trade with a particular country, perhaps imposed by the United Nations against a country that has broken international laws or conventions.

**emerging markets:** countries which in recent years have increased manufacturing output very rapidly, while also adopting a more market oriented pattern of production. They include China, Hong Kong, India and a number of other Asian countries; Eastern European countries such as Poland and Hungary, and some Latin American countries such as Mexico and Brazil.

**emissions trading programmes** provide for companies in certain parts of the USA to trade the right to allow a certain quantity of polluting gases to escape into the atmosphere. This ensures that those companies which create air pollution actually pay for the right to do so. Companies which do not do so will have to control emissions of polluting gases. The price of the right to pollute creates an incentive to pollute less.

**empire building** is when a manager makes decisions with the objective of increasing his or her own department or sphere of influence.

**empirical testing** is the use of data to test economic theories, or the predictions of *economic models*.

**employee appraisal:** see *performance appraisal*

**employee involvement:** the extent to which employees are made a part of the decision-making process. At one end of the spectrum, managers might have a suggestion box, into which employees may put their ideas for improving production methods. At the other end of the spectrum, employees may have opportunities to participate directly in the management process, through consultation and representation on the Board of Directors. In between there may be various methods of communication which ensure that employees are regularly consulted, or there may be quality circles which create opportunities for discussion of production strategies.

**employers' association:** an organisation representing the views and interests of the companies within a sector or industry. It is financed by members' subscriptions and is expected to provide value for money by:

- its success as a *pressure group*, for example in influencing the taxes the government imposes or cuts on products
- its research success, either by compiling sales figures from all the firms within an industry, or by initiating studies that can help the members cope with foreign competition. Part of the motivation towards this research may be *public relations*
- providing a negotiating team that can agree minimum pay and conditions throughout the industry with employees' trade union representatives.

**Employment Act 1980:** the first of five Employment Acts passed by Mrs Thatcher's Conservative governments. Its main features were:

- repeal of the existing procedures for trade union recognition, thereby enabling firms to refuse to negotiate with unions
- *picketing* restricted to 'own place of work'
- lawful *secondary action* limited to direct supplier or customer
- first move against the *closed shop*, making closed shops allowable only if 80 per cent of the workforce vote in favour
- reductions in employment and compensation rights for employees of small firms.

**Employment Act 1982** provided further tightening of the 1980 rules. The main measures were:

- further restrictions on lawful *industrial action* by redefining a 'lawful dispute'
- removal of trade union immunity from authorising unlawful industrial action (making unions liable for damages of up to £250 000)
- dismissal of strikers made easier
- *closed shop* union membership agreements made harder to enforce.

**Employment Act 1988** tightened up the controls on union operations by:

- insisting that all voting members of national union committees must be elected by postal *ballot* of the entire membership
- protecting union members from being disciplined by unions for ignoring strike calls or *picketing*, even after a ballot in favour of industrial action
- laying down the specific wording to be used on voting papers in *industrial action* ballots.

**Employment Act 1989** was designed, according to the Secretary of State for Employment, to 'remove outdated, unnecessary barriers to women's employment and relieve young people and their employers of a mass of bureaucratic restraints'. Opponents argued that the 'barriers' were far from outdated. The Act's main provisions were:

- removing all restrictions on the hours of work of young people, including the prohibition of night work
- removal of discriminatory legislation against women, such as the former ban on women working underground in mines
- dissolving the Training Commission and the Industrial Training Boards.

**Employment Act 1990:** last of a series of Acts passed by Conservative governments during the 1980s designed to 'free up the labour market', i.e. to reduce the influence of government and especially *trade unions*. Its main provisions were:

- to make it unlawful for an employer to refuse to employ a non-union worker; that meant the end of the *closed shop*
- to make unlawful any remaining forms of *secondary action*
- to make trade unions liable for virtually any *industrial action* taken by their members
- to allow employers to dismiss any individual for taking part in an *unofficial strike* without the individual having the right to complain of *unfair dismissal* to an industrial tribunal.

**employment agency:** a *private sector* business that acts as a job centre, charging employers a fee if they decide to recruit one of the candidates sent along by the agency for interview.

**employment contract:** a legal document that sets out the terms and conditions governing an individual's job. It details the employee's responsibilities, working hours, rate of pay and holiday entitlement. By signing it, an employee agrees to abide by its terms. If, therefore, the employee joins in with strike action he or she can be dismissed for having broken the contract.

**employment protection:** the laws which protect the position of the employee at work. *The Employment Relations Act 1999* provides significant examples. There is some concern that there is a trade-off between protecting the employee and encouraging employers to create more jobs. Employment protection is stronger in some EU countries than in the UK and this may help to explain why these countries have higher unemployment rates.

**Employment Relations Act 1999:** this 'New Labour' legislation increased employee rights in relation to union membership and claims for unfair dismissal. Among its key measures were:

- reducing the employment qualifying period for those claiming unfair dismissal from two years to one year
- increasing from £12,000 to £50,000 the maximum courts can force firms to pay to a worker dismissed unfairly
- a statutory procedure for employees to obtain union recognition, where there is clear support among the workforce; if 50 per cent or more of the workforce are in a union, recognition cannot be refused by the employer
- rights to three months' leave for mothers and fathers when a baby is born.

**employment tribunal:** an informal courtroom where legal disputes between employee and employer can be settled. In recent years they have heard over 80,000 cases per year (and rising). The main areas of dispute covered by tribunals are:

- *unfair dismissal*
- workplace discrimination on grounds of sex, race or disability
- the *national minimum wage*
- working time.

**employment zones:** small areas of the country identified as needing extra government help in getting the longterm unemployed back to work. The target launch date for the first 15 zones was April 2000.

**empowerment** is providing the means by which subordinates can exercise power over their working lives. Whereas *delegation* might provide the power for a subordinate to carry out a specific task, empowerment is more all-embracing. It implies a degree of self-regulation; the freedom to decide what to do and how to do it.

**EMS:** see *European Monetary System*

**EMU:** see *economic and monetary union*

**end product:** the product the consumer buys, as opposed to any intermediate products used to make up the end product.

**Enron:** the US energy business that grew to be the world's biggest by 2000 but then collapsed in financial scandal in 2001. It has become a byword for the risks of investing in shares, and the problems of *corporate governance* in times of booming stock markets.

**enterprise allowance:** a regular payment from the government to those starting up a business, to help supplement their personal income during the first year of trading.

**enterprise culture:** a social climate which applauds the profit motive in general and starting a small business in particular. The term was widely used in the 1980s and formed a key element in *Thatcherism*.

**enterprise policies** are all those measures which are designed to help encourage businesses to set up and expand.

**enterprise zone:** a town or small area hit by severe unemployment that is given government *grants* or tax advantages to encourage greater business investment. When first set up in 1981, the zones were expected to act as a magnet, attracting inward investment that would spread prosperity throughout the surrounding area. Despite generous incentives such as 10 years free of local rates and 100 per cent tax allowances, enterprise zones proved a disappointment. Much of the 'extra' investment was diverted from sites just outside the zones, providing little additional employment. In 1989, when there were 27 zones established, the government announced that no more would be created.

**entrepreneur:** an individual with a flair for business opportunities and risk trading. The term is often used to describe a person with the entrepreneurial spirit to set up a new business. The entrepreneur takes the decision to produce, using *factors of production* to create a product and carrying the risks associated with bringing the product to the market place. Sometimes the entrepreneur is described as the fourth factor of production.

**entry** refers to the process by which a firm may set up in business and become part of the industry. Easy entry implies that the industry will be at least fairly competitive because profits will attract additional producers who will compete with each other. *Exit* is the reverse process. Entry and exit are an important part of the process of *structural change*.

**environmental accounts** are those sections of annual reports which attempt to evaluate the impact of business activity on the environment.

**environmental audit:** an independent check on the pollution emission levels, wastage levels and recycling practices of a firm. If measured annually and published, such an audit could encourage companies to invest in improved environmental practices. Unless forced to do so by legislation, however, it is hard to see why poorly performing companies should carry out this exercise.

**environmental economics** is the study of environmental problems and lays particular emphasis on evaluating the costs and benefits of different kinds of solutions to the problems posed by pollution, congestion and the general destruction of resources. Most environmental problems are associated with some kind of *market failure* and *externalities* which enable producers to avoid paying the full resource costs of production.

**environmental policy:** a written statement of a firm's approach to dealing with the environmental disturbance or hazards it may face or create. A paper towel manufacturer, for example, might adopt a policy that covers:

- planting a new tree for every one its suppliers cut down
- including an average of at least 30 per cent recycled paper in its products
- getting at least 20 per cent below the minimum pollution emission standards ruling within the *European Union.*

**Environmental Protection Act 1990:** this legislation introduced controls on water, land, air and noise pollution. It was designed to give added protection to employees and the public.

**EPS:** see *earnings per share*

**equality** means that people experience no large differentials in income within a society. It has seldom been the case that total equality has been achieved in any society, but some countries have for long periods had a much greater degree of equality than others. Sweden has been most notable in this respect while the USA has tended to have very little equality in its *income distribution*, though rather more equality of opportunity through its education system. (See also *equity/efficiency tradeoff*.)

**equal opportunities:** a situation where employees and potential recruits have equal chances of being employed or promoted, whatever their sex, race, colour, religion or disability. The pursuit of this goal has been frustrated by personal and organisational discrimination. For example, in Northern Ireland it can be very difficult for Catholics to gain employment in predominantly Protestant organisations. In the whole of Britain, job applications by blacks are very much less likely to succeed than those of whites. A political consensus in the 1970s enabled the *Equal Opportunities Commission* and the Commission for Racial Equality to be set up. The former seeks to promote sex equality, the latter to overcome discrimination on grounds of race.

Many large firms employ an equal opportunities officer whose job is to monitor procedures, attitudes and outcomes regarding discrimination within the business. The officer will check that:

- *job descriptions*, advertisements and application forms have no inherent bias
- the shortlisting of candidates is carried out on objective criteria (such as educational achievement)
- the interviews are conducted fairly
- the statistics of those appointed (or promoted) suggest that minority groups have been given equal opportunities
- the proportion of disabled employees meets the government target of 3 per cent (this only applies to firms with over 20 employees).

Although the above systems could work effectively to provide equal opportunities, the evidence shows that many firms give this issue a low priority. Success will require either tougher laws or a change in social attitudes. (See *Sex Discrimination Act*, *Race Relations Act*, *Equal Pay Act*.)

**Equal Opportunities Commission:** an organisation set up by the *Sex Discrimination Act 1975* to promote the ideas and practices required to eliminate sex discrimination in education, advertising and employment.

**Equal Pay Act 1970:** a statute requiring employers to provide equal pay and conditions to those doing the same jobs, or work of equivalent difficulty. This had some effect in narrowing the pay gap between men and women, though it took the European Union's Equal Pay Directive 1975, to establish fully that equal pay should be given for work of equal value. This regulation enabled shop workers to claim successfully that cash till operation is as valuable and demanding a job as working in the (male-dominated) warehouse. Despite some successes, however, women's pay remains significantly below that of men.

**equation of exchange:** connects the *quantity of money* (M), the *velocity of circulation* (V), the price level (P) and the number of transactions (T).

FORMULA:    $MV = PT$

Sometimes known as the Fisher equation, this is an identity rather than a relationship: it is true by definition. PT is the total value of all output, which is equivalent to national income. MV is the amount of money needed to pay for it, since the velocity of circulation is simply the number of times each unit of currency circulates within a given time period. It can however be used to predict the rate of *inflation* under certain circumstances. If the velocity of circulation is constant, and the number of transactions grows only slowly, then it follows that inflation will be directly related to the quantity of money in circulation.

Some economists have taken the view that velocity is constant and that the equation of exchange illustrates simply a fundamental and direct link between money and inflation. But the data on velocity in recent years rather suggests that it is not constant, at least in the short to medium term. The reality is certainly more complicated than the equation of exchange suggests.

**equilibrium** is the notion of a market where quantity demanded and quantity supplied are equal to each other. In a product market this will produce an equilibrium price; in the labour market, an equilibrium wage; and in the market for *capital*, an equilibrium rate of interest. There will be neither *excess supply*, nor *excess demand*. The market is said to have cleared.

Some markets do clear, but in others prices tend to be in a constant state of change, with equilibrium, if it is ever reached, little more than a fleeting accident. The primary importance of the concept of equilibrium is as a tool of analysis, rather than an exact description of the real world. It allows us to identify the problems in markets which plainly do not clear, such as the housing market when many potential sellers are unable to find buyers at the price they would like to get. Price theory predicts that the houses will sell if prices fall to the equilibrium level, a prediction which sellers who must sell frequently discover to be accurate, even if the exact level of the equilibrium price is not at first obvious.

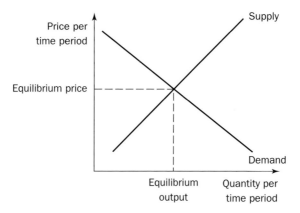

*Equilibrium in the market for goods*

In macroeconomics, equilibrium is a situation in which aggregate demand is exactly equal to the level of planned output. Thus buyers wish to buy all that firms intend to produce. There is no change in the level of stocks. If aggregate demand is greater than or less than output, stocks will fall or rise to accommodate the difference.

**equity:** a term associated with the notion of fairness. (See also *equity/efficiency tradeoff*.)

**equity capital** is the name given to shares; equity being the word for equal. Therefore equity capital means *share capital*. In the UK, equity shareholders have one vote per share and each share has an equal right to distributed profits. Some books, however, treat equity as if it means all *shareholders' funds*, i.e. share capital plus *reserves*.

**equity/efficiency tradeoff:** for governments, there may be a choice between *equity*, i.e. creating a relatively equal distribution of income, and *efficiency*, which may require some incentives. Incentives to work and take risks imply that some people receive rewards in the form of earnings or profits which make them much better off then most other people. Yet without incentives, economic growth may be slow and therefore fail to deliver the improvement in standards of living which people expect.

This area is very controversial. It is fairly clear that the limited incentives which exist in a centrally planned economy do not encourage people to improve productivity in the way that they usually will in a market economy. However, in the context of a market economy, it is not clear that measures to reduce inequality, such as progressive taxes and spending on social services, actually reduce economic growth and the quest for efficiency. Scandinavian countries have on the whole a fair degree of equality and acceptable or better growth rates.

**ethical code:** a document setting out the way a company believes its employees should respond to situations that challenge their integrity or social responsibility. The focus of the code will depend on the business concerned. Banks may concentrate on honesty, and chemical firms on pollution control. It has proved difficult to produce meaningful, comprehensive codes; NatWest Bank, for example, took two years to produce its ten-page document. The typical code might include sections on:

- personal integrity – in dealings with suppliers and in handling the firm's resources
- corporate integrity, such as forbidding *collusion* with competitors and forbidding *predatory pricing*
- environmental responsibility – highlighting a duty to minimise pollution emissions and maximise recycling
- social responsibility – to provide products of genuine value that are promoted with honesty and dignity.

Critics of ethical codes believe them to be *public relations* exercises rather than genuine attempts to change behaviour. What is not in doubt is that the proof of their effectiveness can only be measured by how firms actually behave, not by what they write or say.

**ethical investment** is the use of finance for capital investment in projects which avoid certain kinds of unethical activity. It applies mainly to investment funds such as unit trusts. Businesses which might be excluded from funding might be those producing defence equipment or tobacco products, or those which have a weak record on pollution control. Others might be excluded because they deal with governments which have a poor record for respecting human rights.

**ethical pricing** is an attempt by some organisations to pay higher prices to poor producers in *developing countries* in order to give them a fairer return for their labour. Café Direct is perhaps the best known example.

**ethical responsibility:** see *business responsibility* and *corporate responsibility*

**ethics** are the moral principles that should underpin decision-making. A decision made on ethics might reject the most profitable solution in favour of one of greater benefit to society as well as the firm. Typical ethical dilemmas in business include:

- should an advertising agency accept a cigarette manufacturer as a client?
- should a firm in a take-over battle hire a private detective to investigate the private lives of the rival executives?

- should a producer of chemicals sell to an overseas buyer it suspects will be using the goods to produce chemical weapons?

If public opinion and media pressure force firms to take the publicity impact of their decisions into account, this may change the decisions made. This would not mean, however, that the firm was becoming more ethically-minded. An ethical decision means doing what is morally right, it is not a matter of scientific calculation of costs and benefits.

**EU:** see *European Union*

**EU enlargement:** there is a queue of countries looking to join the EU. It is planned that Poland, the Czech Republic, Hungary, the Slovak Republic, Slovenia, Latvia, Lithuania, Estonia, Cyprus and Malta will join in 2004. Bulgaria and Romania may join in 2007. Turkey wants to be given a date too. However, there are still some doubts about the government's record on human rights, despite recent improvements.

Meanwhile the existing members are negotiating hard in order to make suitable changes to the decision-making process. The necessary changes may well have a considerable effect on the way the EU works.

Applicants have to be able to adopt the economic policies of the EU, must have effective competition policies and must be capable of protecting the rights of minority peoples; this means that negotiations can be very protracted.

**euro:** the name given to the single European currency introduced on January 1 1999. The currencies of the countries adopting the euro were fixed permanently to each other on that date. Euro notes and coins were introduced on January 1 2002 and by June 30 2002, individual currencies were no longer legal tender. The three *European Union* countries outside the so-called *euro-zone* are Britain, Denmark and Sweden.

Up to the time of writing, the euro has been persistently weak, falling against the US dollar and the pound. The *European Central Bank* which sets interest rates in the euro-zone has had some difficulty in establishing its credibility.

**eurocurrency:** bank balances held in currencies which are not the normal local one. For example, dollar balances held in a London bank are termed eurocurrency deposits, as are pounds held in a Frankfurt bank.

**European Bank for Reconstruction and Development** was set up to provide development finance for the transitional economies of Eastern Europe in 1990.

**European Central Bank (ECB):** the central bank established to control the workings and monetary policy within the single currency (*euro*) area. Founded in June 1998, the Bank is based in Frankfurt, Germany but controlled by the 12 member countries of the single currency. The Bank's primary objective is to keep inflation below 2.2 per cent per annum in Europe. Its main tasks are:

- to set interest rates throughout the euro area
- to determine monetary policy
- to provide a monthly report on the euro-zone economy.

There have been some doubts about the policies of the ECB. It is impossible to meet the needs of all member economies with a one-size-fits-all interest rate. The jury is out as to how it will work in the long run, as individual economies become fully integrated.

**European Commission** is the civil service of the *European Union*, but with one important difference from the UK's civil service in that the Commission actually proposes legislation. The Commission is headed by the President and 19 other Commissioners (two each from the five big states and one from each of the smaller ones). Proposals for any new EU regulations and directives pass from the Commission to the *European Parliament* for debate and possible modification before going to the *Council of Ministers* for approval or rejection. Concerns about corruption led all 20 Commissioners to resign in 1999.

**European Community** the name for the *European Union* until November 1993.

**European Court of Justice** is the supreme court of the European Union's legal system. The court makes judgements on European law and Treaties when they are in dispute. The Court has the power to fine firms and to challenge national legislation. It is the ultimate legal authority within the EU.

**European Currency Unit (ECU):** was a stable means of exchange between the foreign currencies of Europe derived from a weighted average of the value of those currencies. The ECU provided the basis for the *euro*.

**European Development Fund:** a fund created by the EU to provide finance for investment in *less developed countries*.

**European Economic Area:** the agreement signed in 1991 between the members of the *European Union* and the *European Free Trade Association*. It allows for free trade to take place between EU countries and Norway, Iceland and Liechtenstein.

**European Free Trade Area (EFTA):** set up as a *free trade* rival to the *European Union*, this economic area has reduced in importance as key members have left to join the EU. As at February 2000, it consisted of just four members: Iceland, Liechtenstein, Norway and Switzerland.

**European Monetary System (EMS):** the attempt at harmonising the financial arrangements of the member states of the *European Union* in the late 1980s. It was the first phase of the movement that led to European monetary union in January 1999. A key element of the EMS was tightening the bands of the *Exchange Rate Mechanism* (ERM), to lock European currencies closer together. This proved successful, even though Britain and Italy both suffered currency collapses in 1992 which forced them to withdraw from the ERM.

**European Parliament:** the elected chamber of the *European Union*. The members sit each month alternately in Strasbourg, France, or in Brussels, Belgium. They debate and amend proposals put forward by the *European Commission* (the European civil service) before they are passed to the *Council of Ministers* for approval or rejection. The Parliament is very restricted in its powers and can only modify or delay decisions proposed by the Commission. As the only directly elected European institution, the Parliament feels it ought to be given more powers, and indeed it is slowly having greater influence. Members of the European Parliament were first directly elected in 1979.

**European Regional Development Fund** was set up by the *European Union* in recognition of the fact that increased trade would cause adjustment problems in some regions. Southern Italy, parts of North East France and Merseyside are examples of areas which have been chronically depressed and have qualified for development assistance from the fund.

**European Social Fund** was set up by the *European Union* to improve employment opportunities for people in parts of the EU which have suffered from structural unemployment. It provides funds for training schemes and job creation.

**European Union (EU):** formerly the European Community (EC) and before that the European Economic Community (EEC), currently consists of the following members: France, Germany, the Netherlands, Belgium, Luxembourg, Italy (the first six members), the UK, Denmark, Ireland (joined 1973), Greece (joined 1981), Portugal, Spain (joined 1986) and Austria, Finland and Sweden, (joined 1995). The EU was established under the Treaty of Rome in 1957 with the objective of removing all trade barriers between member states. The background to this was the desire to form a political and economic union which would prevent the possibility of another war in Europe.

In the autumn of 1991, agreement was reached with the EFTA countries to form closer links within what is called the *European Economic Area (EEA)*. This builds on the Single European Act which came into force in 1987, and the abolition of all trade and other restrictions which was effective under the Act from January 1 1993 to form the *Single European Market*. The *Maastricht* treaty, which came into force November 1 1993, laid the foundations for even greater unity. It was seen as a move towards a federal Europe (although the UK had the word 'federal' removed from the Treaty, and secured opt-out clauses on *European Monetary Union* and the *social chapter*). Under the Treaty, the EC was renamed the European Union from 1.11.93.

The institutions of the EU are shown in the diagram below:

Pros: • it offers a huge potential market of over 375 million people. Its size offers the possibilities of *economies of scale*. The combined strength of the EU creates a potentially powerful trade bloc
 • by creating competition it reduces costs and increases efficiency as well as encouraging innovation
 • investment is encouraged, especially inward investment from non-EU countries like Japan who are seeking to produce within the EU's boundaries
 • it offers the possibility of income and wealth redistribution within Europe and offers greater career choices for EU citizens.

Cons: • the budget has not always been wisely spent. In particular the *Common Agricultural Policy* has distorted spending in favour of agriculture, has led to over-production in certain areas and has fostered corruption.

- the bureaucracy of some elements of European law making, particularly apparently odd notions from the *European Commission* has made some people think that law making should be delegated to member states. This is the idea of *subsidiarity*
- countries outside the EU bloc, especially those in the Third World see the Community as another conspiracy by the rich western economies to keep them poor (by trade advantages for EU members over non-members)
- individual members still tend to put national interests before those of the wider community. Although laws have often been passed, they have not always been applied with equal force.

*EU enlargement* in 2004 will bring in 10 new members.

**euro-zone:** a journalistic phrase for the 12 countries linked by their single currency, the *euro*. The zone represents nearly 80 per cent of the population of the *European Union*.

**exceptional item:** an entry in the *profit and loss account* which arises from ordinary trading, but is so large or unusual as to risk distorting the company's trading account. Therefore it is listed separately as an exceptional item. An example would be unusually large *bad debt* charges.

**excess capacity:** for the individual business this means having more storage or production potential than is likely to be used in the foreseeable future. Therefore the *capacity utilisation* will be low and the *fixed costs per unit* of output will be relatively high. Firms faced with excess capacity might rationalise by closing down one production site or renting out spare space to another firm. For the economy, excess capacity means that resources are being under-utilised. There is likely to be unemployment, and many firms may contract or close down because of low levels of *aggregate demand*.

**excess demand** describes the situation where *demand* exceeds *supply*, as in the diagram below. This shows *disequilibrium* in the market, which fails to clear. Excess demand can be seen when there are large numbers of people wishing to buy an item which has just become fashionable and shops have difficulty in obtaining adequate stocks. This situation will not last long as either prices will rise or supplies will increase.

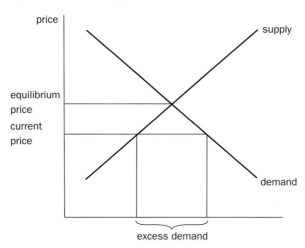

*Excess demand*

Excess demand may also occur on the macroeconomic level. If the level of *aggregate demand* is growing fast, it may outstrip the capacity of the economy to increase output.

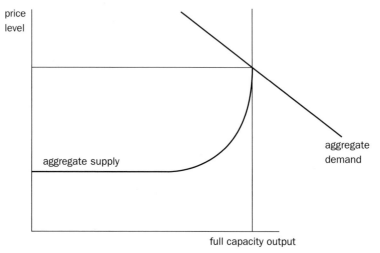

full capacity output

*Excess aggregate demand*

Shortages of goods and services, and skilled labour, may appear and both of these will mean that it is easy to raise prices and negotiate wage increases. In this way *inflation* will accelerate. Excess demand may occur at the recovery stage of the trade cycle before firms have restocked following a *recession*, and also at the peak of the cycle as all the slack in the economy has been taken up so that increasing production is very difficult.

**excess supply** occurs when the quantity supplied is greater than the quantity demanded. On the microeconomic level, it means that the price is higher than its equilibrium level, and gives producers an incentive to supply more of the product. At the same time the high price discourages buyers and the result is seen in stocks of unsold goods.

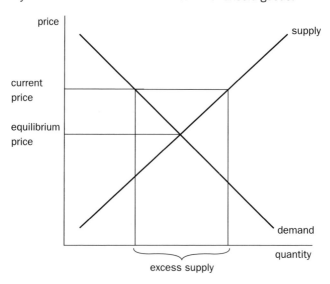

On the macroeconomic level, excess supply would imply that firms were producing more than consumers want to buy, there would be stocks of unsold goods and in time firms would adjust production downwards. This could happen at the onset of a recession when there would be falling *aggregate demand*.

**exchange** is the process by which people trade with each other, offering goods and services they have produced for goods and services they need or want. Exchange is crucial to economic life, making it possible for people to specialise in the type of production in which they have an advantage.

**exchange controls** are limits set by law on the dealings in gold and foreign currency which a country's citizens can make. In effect, it prevents a country's *exchange rate* from settling at a market-determined price, because it is a way of fixing the market. Exchange controls were abandoned by the UK in 1979, and by all the member states of the *EU* in 1993. They are still widely used in Eastern Europe.

Pros:
- can counter a *balance of payments* deficit by limiting the value of imports to the value of export earnings
- allows the internal price level to be established by the workings of the internal economy rather than external factors such as the exchange rate.

Cons:
- discourages international trade
- may encourage other countries to follow suit.

**Exchange Equalisation Account:** the account in which the Bank of England keeps the foreign exchange reserves. These may be used to influence the value of the currency as and when the need arises.

**exchange rate:** the price of one country's currency expressed in terms of another. In the press, the pound sterling may be valued in terms of the euro, the US dollar, or a 'basket of currencies' (an average of a number of major currencies). Anyone going on holiday abroad will know that there is a rate for all other currencies against the pound. The exchange rate between different countries is kept in line through *arbitrage* operations.

The exchange rate influences the prices of imports and exports, and the ease with which producers in different countries can compete with each other.

**exchange rate depreciation:** occurs if market forces cause the exchange rate to fall, so that exports become cheaper and imports dearer in terms of the domestic currency. This may happen because the demand for exports has fallen over a period of time, or because capital inflows have diminished. Either way, demand for the currency will fall and with it the equilibrium exchange rate, as shown in the first diagram.

The same outcome will occur if there has been an increase in demand for imports or a capital outflow. There will be an increase in the supply of the currency (see the second diagram) by people who want to buy foreign currency on the foreign exchange markets, leading to a fall in the exchange rate.

Appreciation leads to the reverse situation in which the exchange rate rises, imports become cheaper and exports become dearer.

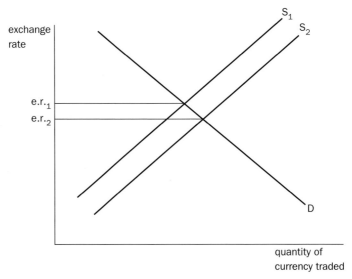

*Exchange rate depreciation*

**Exchange Rate Mechanism (ERM):** the way currencies were brought into line under the *European Monetary System (EMS)*. Countries belonging to the ERM agreed to keep their exchange rates within a range of values known as currency bands. If market forces pushed a currency down to the limit, the central bank used its reserves to buy the currency, thus defending its value. (See fixed exchange rates.)

The ERM was set up in 1979 and included most of the EU countries, except the UK which entered in 1990 and left again in 1992 when it became apparent that the pound was set at a *parity* too high to be sustainable. The ERM was superseded by *European Monetary Union* in January 1999.

**exchange rate policy:** a government may allow its exchange rate to float freely, or in consultation with its trading partners may seek to fix the rate, or it may seek to manage the exchange rate so that fluctuations are reduced. Since 1972, most currencies have floated most of the time, with central banks intervening to eliminate day-to-day fluctuations. The drawback to a floating exchange rate is that it may be unstable. EMU will remove this instability within the euro-zone, but the euro will fluctuate against all other floating currencies.

**exchange rate target:** governments may choose to maintain a target for the exchange rate, as a means of controlling inflation. Then, in the event that prices rise, domestic producers become less competitive, and demand for their products will fall on both export and domestic markets. This will discourage them from raising prices and reduce aggregate demand generally, reducing inflationary pressures. The UK government adopted this policy in the late 1980s.

**excise duty** is a tax levied by HM Customs and Excise on a number of goods, the best known being alcohol, tobacco and petrol. They raise revenue and may discourage consumption. In the case of some products this can lead to distortions. In the case of beer, for example, the duty is raised on its alcoholic content. This might encourage a brewer to weaken the beer and so reduce the excise duty paid whilst keeping the retail price the same, thereby increasing profits.

**exit:** the way in which businesses may leave the market, or close down altogether, if the product in question has begun to make losses, or just become less profitable than alternative uses of the resources. Easy exit is very important in ensuring efficiency, because without it the *allocation of resources* cannot adjust to changes in the pattern of consumer demand. Exit can be difficult in *state-owned enterprises* and may be affected by employment protection legislation.

**expansionary policies** may be used by governments which wish to reduce unemployment and achieve higher rates of growth. *Fiscal policies*, e.g. tax cuts and increases in expenditure, and a *monetary policy* of reduced interest rates will all tend to increase aggregate demand and encourage firms to take on more labour and expand output. Care must be taken not to overdo expansionary policies, lest growth leads to pressure on resources and accelerating *inflation*. Expansionary policies will not help in the long run if unemployment is structural in nature.

**expectancy theory:** the view that *motivation* depends on employees' *expectations* as to the outcome of their efforts. If people know what they want from an outcome and believe they can achieve it, they will be highly motivated towards it. This theory is mainly associated with *Vroom* and contrasts with *Maslow* and *Herzberg*'s emphasis on people's needs.

**expectations** are what people believe will happen in the future. Economists and business leaders place great importance on expectations because they assume that they influence people's behaviour. If, for example, people believe that house prices will rise sharply, they may rush to buy before the price rise occurs. The extra *demand* will pull prices up, making it a self-fulfilling prophesy.

Expectations may be very important in a macroeconomic context. Investment plans are often based on expectations about future demand. Again, optimistic expectations may provide business with a self-fulfilling prophecy. Inflationary expectations will tend to make people want to negotiate pay increases to cover whatever they expect inflation to be. So control of inflation requires that inflation expectations be reduced.

**expected value** is the average value of the possible outcomes resulting from a decision, weighted by the probabilities of achieving them. Used in decision tree analysis, it is the monetary value that would be expected on average from a decision if it was repeated many times.

**expenditure reducing policies** entail reducing the level of aggregate demand using *fiscal and monetary policies*. The term is used in relation to policies to deal with a *trade deficit*.

**expenditure switching policies** reduce expenditure on foreign produced goods and services and increase it on domestic products. They include *import controls* and *exchange rate depreciation*.

**expenditure taxes** tax spending rather than income. They include *VAT* and the *excise taxes*, but the term may also refer to a system by which people are assessed according to their expenditure rather than their income. This would give people an incentive to save more.

**expense:** a payment for something of immediate benefit to the business. It causes a debit on the accounts and is charged to the current *profit and loss account*. Maintenance costs and wages are expenses; these are also known as *revenue expenditure*.

**exploitation** means taking advantage of a situation or resource for one's own gain. The term implies that the gain will be at the expense of others. Exploitation could be used to describe the employment of labour at very low wages, or the profitable extraction of a scarce mineral from a Third World country.

**Export Credit Guarantee Department (ECGD)** is a government department offering a service of guaranteeing that if foreign importers of UK-produced goods fail to pay, then it will step in and pay instead. It is a way of insuring UK exporters against *bad debts* overseas. By offering such a service, exports are encouraged. As with any insurance policy, fees are charged, and critics of the British government have pointed out that ECGD charges much higher premiums to British exporters than the governments of France, Germany and Japan do to their own companies. In this way, the competitiveness of British exports is hindered. In 1991, the ECGD's short-term export credit insurance business was privatised. Nevertheless, in 1999 the ECGD still insured over £3 billion-worth of exports.

**export-led growth** occurs when there is rapid growth of exports which then has a *multiplier* effect on the rest of the economy. In the past Japan and South Korea have both experienced this type of rapid growth leading to improvements in the standard of living there. An *under-valued exchange rate* may be helpful in achieving this.

**export marketing:** devising a strategy for developing and sustaining profitable sales overseas. Although largely the same as UK marketing, selling overseas has certain points of difference:

- gaining *distribution* is likely to be harder and far more expensive, so most firms use local *agents* who already know and have access to the local distribution channels

- the exporter must decide whether to keep the product the same in all markets (benefiting from *economies of scale*), or to tailor make it for differing local tastes; the latter should generate higher sales, but the former will keep unit costs down and therefore might be more profitable

- brand names may have different meanings in different languages and should therefore be researched (the German soft drink Pschitt was tested in the UK but failed).

**exports:** goods and services sold for foreign currency. Goods are visible exports while services such as tourism or insurance are invisible exports.

**extension strategy:** a medium- to long-term plan for lengthening the life cycle of a product or brand. It is likely to be implemented during the maturity or early decline stages within the life cycle. Extension strategies can be divided into two categories: defensive and offensive.

Defensive: a plan designed to postpone the obsolescence of a product by a year or two, perhaps to keep sales going until a replacement can be launched. Examples include car manufacturers' 'special editions', which usually offer different paintwork, slightly different equipment and a bouncy name.

Offensive: a plan to revitalise or reposition a product to give it a wholly new, long-term market. Horlicks becoming Instant Horlicks achieved this, as it shifted a bedtime drink to an anytime drink. Even more noteworthy was Johnson and Johnson's repositioning of its Baby Powder and Baby Oil to appeal to women instead of just the babycare market.

Types of extension strategy include:

- redesigning or reformulating the product ('New improved!')
- adding an extra feature ('Now with . . . !')
- repositioning its price and image (usually downmarket)
- changing the packaging and advertising imagery to appeal to a new or additional market sector.

Note that sales promotions or extra advertising spending alone would not be regarded as extension strategies. They are ways of boosting sales that could work equally well at any stage of the life cycle.

**external balance:** a situation in which exports and imports are roughly the same in value.

**external benefits:** see *externalities*

**external constraint:** a factor outside the control of the enterprise that restricts it from meeting its objectives. Main types of external constraint include:

- changing consumer tastes
- competitors' actions
- economic circumstances (especially the level of interest rates, the value of the pound, consumer and business confidence, and the level of *aggregate demand*)
- legal constraints
- social attitudes and *pressure group* activity.

**external costs** are negative consequences of an activity that are paid for by people or organisations other than the originator of those costs. For example, the sulphur emissions from power stations cause acid rain that damages forests; the cost of this is borne by the owners of the forests, not the electricity companies. As external costs do not affect the *profit and loss account* of the firm causing the costs, it has no direct incentive to minimise the pollution. This is why government intervention is required to force the polluter to pay (or stop). There are serious external costs associated with night flights into Heathrow Airport. Local residents have been offered major restrictions on night flights as a way of softening their opposition to the building of Terminal 5. (See *cost-benefit analysis*.)

**external economies of scale:** see *economies of scale*

**external environment:** the circumstances within which firms operate that are outside their control. (See *external constraints*.)

**external financing** means obtaining capital resources from outside the firm's resources or accounts. This can only be done in one of three ways: debt, *share capital*, or *grants*.

Debt can be obtained for day-to-day (short-term) transactions or for longer-term *capital* needs. Among the ways of borrowing for the short term are: bank *overdraft*, *trade credit* and credit *factoring*. For the longer term are bank loans, commercial mortgages and *debentures*.

Share capital can be obtained via a *rights issue*, the issue of *preference shares*, or by a *flotation* of the company's shares on the *Stock Exchange*.

Grants could come from the *European Union*, the government's *regional policy* or from a local enterprise board. It should be remembered, however, that grants provide only a tiny fraction of the capital needs of business.

**external growth** comes from outside the firm, such as by acquiring or merging with another firm. This is the easiest way to grow rapidly, but results in a huge number of managerial problems based on the difficulty of integrating a new business, management and *culture*. *Internal growth* is a far safer way of expanding, though it may be too slow to allow the firm to capitalise on exciting short-term prospects.

**externalities** are those costs or benefits which occur as a result of the main operation of the business but which are not part of the firm's *profit and loss account*. Examples include *pollution* and congestion, costs that are the result of production but which are borne by the community, not the business. There are moves for some *external costs* to be passed back to organisations, such as by legislation that forces firms to pay for any smoke emissions from their factories. Where it is possible to 'make the polluters pay', firms have an incentive to minimise their costs by minimising the pollution.

External benefits can arise through the effect on local service and supply industries of new firms opening up in an area, or from the spill-over effect of new technology, such as in defence or related industries. An example of external benefit from the development of space exploration was Teflon which was used to produce non-stick saucepans.

An attempt to account fully for external as well as internal costs and benefits is made thorough *cost-benefit analysis*.

**extraordinary general meeting (EGM):** a shareholders' meeting called in addition to the normal *AGM*. This might be to gain approval for a *rights issue* or for a vote of confidence in the *chairman*.

**extraordinary items** derive from events or transactions that fall outside the ordinary activities of the company and which are therefore not expected to recur frequently or regularly. The most common example is the cost of closing a business division or factory. Extraordinary items used to be excluded from the main section of the *profit and loss account* because of their potentially distorting, one-off nature. Now, under the modern Financial Reporting Standards extraordinary items are included.

**extrapolation:** in forecasting the near future it can be assumed the recent past will be a good guide. This is known as extrapolating from the past to the future. When *trend* values have been established, they can be plotted on a graph and extrapolation by eye or by mathematical means can be undertaken. See diagram on following page.

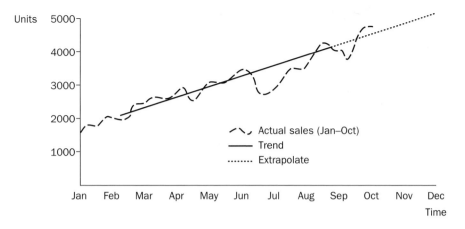

*Extrapolation of a sales trend*

**extrinsic motivation** is a drive to succeed that comes from outside the job itself. It might be stimulated by the promise of financial reward or promotion. Professor *Herzberg* characterises such a process as 'movement' rather than *motivation*, which he believes to be less desirable.

**Do you need help with the synoptic element of your Economics and Business course?**

Go to page 335 for tips and advice.

**face-to-face interview:** an interview conducted in person, so that the interviewer and the respondent are face to face. This contrasts with a telephone survey or a *self-completion questionnaire*.

Pros:
- the interviewer can assess the *body language* of the respondent when the questions are being answered
- face-to-face interviews gain higher *response rates* than self-completion questionnaires; this reduces the chance of a biased sample.

Cons:
- respondents are less likely to make critical comments face to face
- face-to-face interviewing is time-consuming and expensive.

**factor:** an organisation that provides a *factoring* service. Most are subsidiaries of banks.

**factoring** is a banking service which provides up to 80 per cent of the value of invoiced sales as a cash advance, and then organises the collection of the debt. Many organisations which sell mainly on *credit* carry high values of *debtors* in their *current assets*. This ties up cash that could be used more effectively elsewhere in the business. An alternative is to sell these debts to a specialist debt collector called a factor.

**factor markets** include the markets for labour and capital. Capital markets provide a source of *finance* for businesses and individuals. The price of capital is the *interest rate*. Labour markets are made up of the people who would like to be employed and the employers who want to hire people. The price of labour is the going wage or salary.

**factors of production** include land, *labour*, *capital* and *enterpreneurship*. Enterprise is not considered to be a special factor of production by some economists because they regard an *entrepreneur* as someone who, whilst having special skills, is nonetheless just a part of labour. Others argue that without entrepreneurship the other factors would not be combined in order to produce profit, and hence increase living standards. The factors are rewarded as follows:

- land receives rent
- labour receives wages
- capital receives interest
- entrepreneurship receives profit.

**factory farming** is the use of *production line* techniques to ensure maximum *output* from farm livestock with the minimum of inputs. This usually means that the animals live in isolation in very confined spaces, and are fattened up with the aid of hormones. It is a good example of where *profit maximisation* could be thought to conflict with *ethics*.

**factory gate prices** are the prices charged by producers for output sold to wholesalers. They provide a helpful *leading indicator* of possible future consumer price changes.

**factory inspectors** are employed by the *Health and Safety Executive* to check that firms are complying with relevant UK and EU legislation, such as the *Health and Safety at Work Act 1974*.

**Fair Trading Act 1973** set up the *Office of Fair Trading (OFT)*, the government agency responsible for providing ministers with advice on legislation and action with regard to *monopolies*, *mergers* and *restrictive practices*.

**Family Expenditure Survey:** carried out by the *Office for National Statistics*, this provides the information needed to construct the *Retail Price Index*, which measures the rate of inflation.

**fax (facsimile machine):** a way of transmitting photocopies via telephone lines, thereby enabling detailed, legally valid written information to be communicated instantly.

**Fayol, Henri** (1841–1925) was a French management pioneer who focused on the problems of organisational structure within large firms at the turn of the century. Whereas his American contemporary, F W *Taylor*, concentrated on the efficiency of shop-floor labour, Fayol looked at senior management. He was largely responsible for introducing the concepts of *chain of command*, the *organisational chart*, and *span of control*.

**Federal Reserve Bank** (known as the 'Fed') is the *central bank* of the United States. It consists of the Federal Reserve Board and twelve regional reserve banks which control the banking system within each region. The American banking system includes a large number of quite small banks and calls for a rather different system of control from that of other countries.

**feedback** is response to a piece of communication. Without it the communicator cannot know whether the communication has been received effectively. This could not only cause operational problems (such as stocks not being reordered), but may also undermine *motivation*. This is because communicators have a psychological need for response to their efforts. For instance, if homework goes unmarked students will soon lose the impetus to produce more, and any that is done will be of poor quality.

**fertility rate:** the number of births per thousand women between the ages of fifteen and forty-five. It provides a useful way of predicting population changes.

**fieldwork** is the process of carrying out field research, e.g. a *market research* survey.

**finance:** a term covering sources of funds which may be borrowed to pay for investment or consumption.

**financial accounting** is largely concerned with reporting and the production of the financial accounts according to the requirements of the *Companies Acts* so that users of accounts have an accurate view of the firm's financial position.

**financial assets** include, cash, bank and building society balances, bills, bonds, shares and pension entitlements.

**financial economies:** see *economies of scale*

**financial futures:** agreements to buy financial assets such as bonds at some date in the future.

**financial intermediaries** include *merchant* and *retail banks*, *building societies*, *pension funds* and *insurance companies* and some other financial institutions.

**Financial Reporting Standards (FRS):** an accounting standard issued under the authority of the *Accounting Standards Board*. The first standard was issued in 1991 and aimed to improve the reporting on *cash flow* in published company accounts.

**Financial Services Act 1986** set up a system of self-regulation in the City which was intended to ensure that only those considered 'fit and proper' would be able to operate within the financial markets. It was supposed to ensure that the fees and charges made by the financial services businesses would become more explicit. In fact, major providers of financial services such as the life insurance industry managed to keep their charges hidden.

**Financial Services Authority:** the organisation which supervises the operations of the financial system. It was set up in 1997 to create a new, overarching system which super-vises banks as well as other financial intermediaries, such as insurance companies. It works in close collaboration with the *Treasury* and the *Bank of England*. Supervision is important; properly carried out it can, for instance, prevent banks from making imprudent loans and financial advisers from misleading the public.

**financial year:** the national financial year runs from 6 April to 5 April and so income tax changes apply accordingly. Each individual person or company may make up its accounts annually to any date. The essence of a financial year is simply to create a consistent reporting period.

**fine tuning:** the notion that governments can adjust fiscal and monetary policy to create just the right amount of aggregate demand, keeping unemployment and inflation low and encouraging growth. The idea was fashionable in the 1960s and 70s. The results of attempts to fine-tune the economy were disappointing because it proved very difficult to decide the exact amount of change needed, and governments tended to overshoot or act too late, partly because of weaknesses in current data and uncertainty about future events.

**finite resources** are resources which are fixed in supply and cannot be renewed. They are also referred to as *non-renewable* or *depletable resources*. Oil is one example, along with many other mineral products. Others include tropical timber and fish stocks which are not being exploited in a sustainable way.

**firm:** a collection of *factors of production* brought together by an *entrepreneur* for the purpose of producing goods or services. The term is often used when theory is being employed to analyse a particular situation, in contrast to the term business, which is used in a more practical context.

**firm-specific skills** are those skills which are acquired on the job and relate to that partic-ular employer. A business will try hard not to make redundant a person with firm-specific skills because a replacement will have to be trained all over again. Their wages may be viewed as a *fixed cost* for this reason.

**fiscal policy** is government policy towards its raising of revenue and its level of (public) spending. The task of setting fiscal policy is undertaken by the *Chancellor of the Exchequer*. It is arrived at in the following order:

1 establish government economic objectives
2 decide on the correct balance between government revenue and government spending (known as the fiscal or budgetary balance)

3    make the individual decisions that are compatible with **1** and **2** and maximise political advantage. They may include increasing the tax on petrol or increasing government spending on particular things such as the National Health Service.

In the *circular flow of national income*, taxes represent a withdrawal that is balanced by government expenditure on such items as pensions, unemployment benefit and so on. If the government takes in more than it spends, i.e. runs a *surplus*, consumer spending power is reduced and *aggregate demand* falls, thus slowing down the economy. This would be a *contractionary policy*. If it spends more than it takes in, a *deficit*, then it increases demand and therefore increases economic activity.

Government spending injected into the economy has a *multiplier* effect as it moves through the economy. For instance, if an unemployed person gets a job helping to build a new road, some of his or her wages will be spent on things which previously could not be afforded, such as new clothes. This creates demand in the clothing industry, so more people are employed to make clothes, which creates more income and so on. If the clothes are made abroad, however, it is the overseas economy and workforce that benefits. Similarly, if the government cuts spending, there will be a downward multiplier effect.

Revenue can be raised either through direct taxation, e.g. *income* and *corporation tax* or through indirect taxation, e.g. *VAT*. Governments can alter the mix of the two for policy reasons, such as reducing direct taxation, which some believe has an important impact upon people's incentives to work. Indirect taxes can also be used to discourage consumption of certain products, e.g. tobacco and petrol. These are microeconomic policies.

The timing of government intervention in the macroeconomy is crucial, yet extremely difficult to judge.

Fiscal policy must be used in conjunction with *monetary policy*, and there is a good deal of uncertainty about exactly what the outcome of any given change will be. Some economists believe that government spending has a 'crowding out' effect, meaning that any boost to the economy from the *public sector* is at the cost of the *private sector*. There is no hard evidence that this is the case.

**Fisher Equation:** see *equation of exchange*

**fixed assets:** items of a monetary value which have a long-term function and can be used repeatedly. These determine the scale of the firm's operations. Examples are land, buildings, equipment and machinery. Fixed assets are not only useful in the running of the firm, but can also provide *collateral* for securing additional *loan capital*.

**fixed capital formation:** see *gross domestic fixed capital formation*

**fixed costs** are the expenses that do not alter in relation to changes in demand or output (in the short term). They have to be paid whether the business trades or not. Examples are rent, *depreciation* and interest charges. Part of the wage and salary bill may be fixed when the people concerned are not directly involved in the production process.

**fixed costs per unit** also known as *average fixed costs*, are total *fixed costs* divided by the units of output produced. While total fixed costs cannot be changed by definition in the short run, fixed costs per unit continually fall as output or activity is increased up to the *capacity* level.

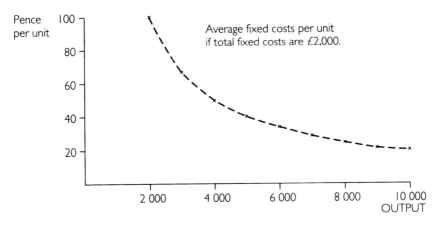

*Fixed costs per unit*

**fixed exchange rates** are currency rates which are not permitted to respond to changes in the demand for currencies. In practice, some movement may be allowed, but the rate is controlled by *central bank* intervention. If the pound came under selling pressure, the market reaction would be a fall in the exchange rate. Under a fixed system the central bank, in this case the *Bank of England* would step in to buy pounds with reserves of foreign currency. In other words it would make up for the shortfall in demand.

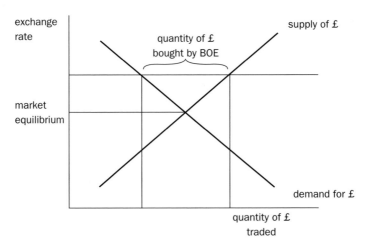

*Fixed exchange rate*

If the exchange rate reflects market forces over the long term, there may be no difficulty in keeping it fixed. If the exchange rate is overvalued, large reserves will be needed in order to defend the rate. Speculators, hoping that the rate will fall may then be able to make large sums by selling currency at the fixed rate, and later, after a devaluation or depreciation, buying it back at the new lower rate.

The existence of large amounts of money which can be moved into different currencies very easily can lead to very large capital movements and a rather unstable exchange rate, if holders of the currency do not have confidence in the ability of the government to maintain the fixed rate. The pound sterling has floated against most other currencies since 1972 but arguments in favour of fixed rates are still heard.

**fixed factors of production** are the resource inputs to a production process, the quantity of which cannot be altered in the short run. In other words the quantity of the factor employed does not change with the level of output. For example, *capital* equipment is a fixed factor because it takes time to arrange to have more or less of it. *Labour* will be a fixed factor if there are difficulties about increasing or decreasing the quantity of it as output changes, as in the case of managers.

**fixed overheads:** see *overheads*

**fixed rate loan:** a loan on which the interest rate payable is determined at the outset and does not vary with the market rate of interest.

Pros:   •   enables interest costs to be budgeted accurately
        •   the firm is protected from the potentially serious impact on *overheads* of sharp rises in interest rates.

Cons:   •   fixed rate loans are inflexible, as they are taken out for specific time periods (such as five years)
        •   timing must be right; it is easy to become tied to a high fixed interest payment just before market rates fall.

**flat organisation (or hierarchy):** a management structure based on a wide *span of control*, therefore requiring relatively few *layers of hierarchy*. This results in:

•   good *vertical communication* as there are few management layers between the bottom and top of the company

•   the need to delegate a high proportion of the tasks and decisions

•   higher motivation potential, given the greater responsibility delegated to junior managers and staff.

**flexibility** in business usually means the ability and willingness to change methods of working. This relies on a workforce that is capable of *multi-skilling* and is not too resistant to *change*. A flexible worker would be capable of doing many different jobs, perhaps when filling in for an absentee.

**flexible exchange rate:** see *floating exchange rate*. The way in which lost competitiveness can be regained through depreciation of a floating exchange rate has been mentioned by many people who oppose UK entry to EMU. Competitiveness is most commonly lost through an inflation rate which is higher than those of other countries. If the UK joins EMU and then experiences accelerating inflation, it will lose competitiveness within the euro-zone.

**flexible labour markets** occur where employers are able to take on new employees on a full-time or a part-time basis, temporarily or permanently, at wage rates which are not set by union agreements or government controls, and are able to make employees redundant without great expense. It is generally thought that there is less unemployment in a flexible labour market. The US labour market is believed to be more flexible than the UK labour market. Within the EU, the UK and the Netherlands are thought to have much more flexible labour markets than most other member countries. (See also *flexible working*.)

**flexible specialisation:** a manufacturing theory stating that because modern markets are broken down into small niches, yet customer tastes are always changing, the successful firm must be able to produce specialised products flexibly. This requires machinery that can quickly be reprogrammed, instead of conveyor-belt-driven plants designed to mass-produce a single item. Flexible specialisation implies a move back to *batch production* and places a premium upon a multi-skilled, adaptable workforce.

**flexible working**: the acceptance by staff and management that rigid *demarcation* lines lead to inefficiency, and therefore that *labour flexibility* is preferable for long-term success. The same term is also used to describe a staffing pattern that is not dependent upon full-time, permanent jobs. In this context flexible working means a willingness to work on a temporary or part-time basis.

**flexitime:** an *employment contract* that allows staff to complete their agreed hours of work at times that suit the employee. This can give a greater sense of control to workers who have repetitive jobs, and helps parents with small children.

**floating exchange rate** applies to a currency which responds to supply and demand on the foreign exchange markets without *central bank* intervention. Changes in demand and supply are brought about by changes in imports and exports or by capital movements, or by *speculation*. A floating exchange rate will undergo an *exchange rate depreciation* if demand for the currency falls or if supply rises, and an *appreciation* if demand for the currency rises or supply falls. (See also *exchange rate*.) A floating exchange rate may be managed by the central bank so as to reduce day-to-day fluctuations.

Pros: 
- requires no foreign currency reserves
- the exchange rate adapts to changes in trade patterns
- reflects market forces.

Cons:
- firms cannot predict future rates, adding to the uncertainties involved in business decision-making, which might restrict trade
- leaves the international competitiveness of a country's goods to a market that is often affected by speculative money flows; these may have little to do with the underlying state of the economy and its *balance of payments.*

**flotation:** the term given to the launch of a company on to the *stock market* by the offer of its shares to the public.

**flow production** is the manufacture of an item in a continually moving process. Each stage is linked with the next by a conveyor belt or in liquid form, so that the production time is minimised and production efficiency is maximised. The diagram on the next page shows a continuous system in which sub-components are being fed into the main production line just as streams flow into a river.

In order to operate effectively, a flow system needs high-capacity utilisation, as the highly mechanised line is likely to be expensive to purchase, install and maintain. Therefore high demand levels are needed to spread the *fixed costs* over many units of output.

**fob** means free on board, a way of valuing exports at the point at which they are loaded for transport abroad. It is of no significance for the student but appears in balance of payments data.

*Continuous flow production*

**focus** upon the core of the business represents the opposite corporate strategy to *diversification*. Focus might be achieved by selling off fringe activities or by the decision to stop developing new products outside the core market.

**focus groups:** an American term for *group discussions*, i.e. small-scale, in-depth research into the reasons behind consumers' habits and attitudes.

**Food Act 1984:** *consumer protection* legislation that has been incorporated into and strengthened within the *Food Safety Act 1990*.

**Food Safety Act 1990** is a wide-ranging law which strengthens and updates *consumer protection* in the food sector. This brought food sources, and by implication farmers and growers, specifically under food safety legislation for the first time. It made it an offence to sell food which is not of the 'nature or substance or quality' demanded by the purchaser. Other key features include:

- premises selling food must register with the local authority
- those handling food must receive appropriate training
- enforcement officers can issue an improvement notice or, in extreme cases, an emergency prohibition notice
- the harmonisation of UK laws and standards with those of Europe.

**footloose** companies are those with no firm commitment to any specific location. They are able to locate in a wide range of places because their costs do not vary much between one place and another. Traditional industries are often tied to a location for historical reasons, such as past raw material or energy availability. Recently developed industries such as electronics are likely to be footloose.

**Footsie (FT–SE 100):** a widely quoted index denoting shifts in the average share price level among 100 of the largest public companies in the UK. The market prices are plotted regularly through each working day and their *weighted average* is the basis of the index. A rise in the index indicates greater confidence in the financial community about UK economic prospects generally so the Footsie is considered an important *leading indicator*. The term stands for the Financial Times–Stock Exchange 100, though it is usually referred to as Footsie.

**Fordism:** the application of Henry Ford's faith in *mass production* run by autocratic management. This implies high *division of labour* and little workplace democracy, but with the consolation of high wages.

**forecasting:** estimating future outcomes such as next year's sales figures. Although forecasts can only be guesses of the future, the aim is to base the guesswork on the best possible information. There are three main sources for this:

- projecting an established trend forward (*extrapolation*)
- *market research* into consumers' buying intentions
- consulting experts with proven ability at anticipating trends.

Macroeconomic forecasting involves the use of sophisticated models with many equations which are used to represent the relationships between different variables in the economy as a whole.

**foreign aid** may be offered to *developing countries* with a *low per capita* income in order to help them invest. It may also be available to countries with serious famine problems. It may be bilateral, from one government to another. Or it may be multilateral, given through an international organisation, often the *World Bank* or the *European Development Fund*. There have been strenuous efforts over the years to persuade the developed countries to give more foreign aid, almost always unsuccessful. A target of the 1960s and 70s, that 1 per cent of GDP should be given by each developed country, never came near to being reached and since then aid has tended to diminish rather than to grow.

Not all aid has been well used; some has been spent on prestige projects and military objectives which have not benefited poor people. There has been some evidence of corruption in the disbursement of aid, and its usefulness has been further compromised by the tying of aid payments to a commitment to buy goods from the donor country. In some cases aid has been tied to the purchase of military goods.

**foreign direct investment (FDI)** refers to investment by companies with their head office in another country, which are setting up factories or distribution outlets. In other words, it implies that the investment is in actual productive capacity which will generate output, rather than in financial assets such as shares or bonds. Many governments have been keen to encourage FDI. Within the UK, Wales has been particularly successful in attracting foreign investors.

**foreign exchange** may mean foreign currency, the *medium of exchange* of another country. Or the term may be used differently, to mean the process of exchanging the currency of one country for that of another.

**foreign exchange market (FOREX)** is the market where dealers buy and sell currencies either 'spot', i.e. for immediate exchange, or 'forward', i.e. at a rate agreed today for some future time, such as in three months' time. Currencies are bought and sold depending on the demands of international trade but also for reasons of speculation. The major world trading markets are in London, New York and Tokyo.

**foreign exchange profits/losses:** those profits and losses which result from buying and selling a currency in the expectation that its value will rise or fall in the future. For instance, foreign exchange dealers may decide that the pound is overvalued. They therefore sell pounds and buy other currencies. If the pound then falls in value they make a profit.

**foreign exchange reserves** are the stocks of foreign currency held by the *central bank*, and available if the exchange rate needs to be maintained at its existing level at a time when market forces are tending to push it downwards, i.e. bring about a *depreciation*. The level of the reserves becomes important if there is either a *fixed exchange rate* or a *managed float*.

**formal communication** takes place within the official channels, i.e. the lines of communication approved by senior management. An example would be marketing manager talking to the marketing director: his or her immediate boss. Within that channel any form of communication is regarded as formal. Beware of muddling formal communication with written and informal with oral. (See also *informal* and *direct communication*.)

**formal economy:** that part of the economy which is recorded in official statistics. So it includes all legally organised business and all government activity, but excludes the use of resources which are not paid for such as voluntary and domestic work, and work done for cash which is not declared for tax purposes. Some of the latter will be legal but some will not.

**Fortress Europe** describes the possibility that a Europe with a single market might build an import protection wall around itself, keeping out American and Japanese imports.

**forward markets** are the markets in which it is possible to buy a certain quantity of goods or foreign currency at a price agreed today, for delivery at a specific future date. This can act as insurance against unforeseen problems that may damage the profitability of an export order, such as a sudden jump in oil prices due to war breaking out in the Middle East. Contracts made in the forward market are known as *futures*.

**franchise:** a business based upon the name, *logos* and trading method of an existing, successful business. To obtain a franchise requires the payment of an initial fee and the signing of a contract that places tight restrictions upon the *franchisee*, including:

- limitation on the area of operation
- design of premises to be exactly as laid down by the *franchisor*
- all supplies to be purchased from the franchisor
- an annual payment to the franchisor based upon a percentage of the franchisee's turnover.

Despite these costs and constraints, business start-ups based upon franchising have a far lower failure rate than independent firms. This is due to the following advantages of franchising:

- the niche, trading strategy and methods have been tried and tested elsewhere, reducing many of the risks associated with business start-ups
- the name and *logos* may have wide customer recognition and loyalty, ensuring high *demand* from day one
- part of the annual payment goes into an advertising fund that finances much larger *advertising campaigns* than could be afforded by an independent; television advertising has played a major part in the success of franchise businesses such as McDonald's and Pizza Hut.

Despite these considerable advantages, potential franchisees should never forget that running any business is very demanding and involves significant risk. Franchising has attracted some would-be *entrepreneurs* who lack the experience or the personality to lead a company.

**franchisee:** a person or company who has bought the local rights to use the name, *logos* and training method of another company (the *franchisor*).

**franchisor:** the holder of the *franchise* who will sell the local rights to suitable *franchisees*. From the franchisor's point of view, this can be a far better way to expand the company than via the traditional route of opening up more managed branches or outlets.

Pros:
- prevents the cash drain or heavy borrowings required to develop a business quickly enough to take advantage of a market opportunity; with franchising, growth is paid for by the franchisees

- franchisees have the direct financial incentive to be far more motivated than salaried managers

- a firm with many franchise outlets needs less middle management than one with managed outlets, thereby reducing the overhead costs and improving *vertical communications.*

**free enterprise:** circumstances in which firms are allowed to start up and operate free from government involvement or regulation. The term tends to be used with reference to small or medium-sized firms and implies a fiercely competitive market. This might prove inaccurate as unregulated markets can become dominated by *monopolies* or *cartels*.

**free entry** refers to the situation in which *entry* is very easy for firms which seek to break into a new market. Where the market has a large number of small businesses, e.g. hair-dressers, antique shops, accountants and so on, entry is usually fairly free. Manufacturing industries in which large potential *economies of scale* create *barriers to entry* illustrate the reverse situation. Free entry is used as a theoretical concept which helps to define *perfect competition*. Easy entry will always make for a more competitive market.

**free goods** are goods which have no price and no *property rights* associated with them, and require no *factors of production* for their enjoyment. It is rather hard to find satisfactory examples because, increasingly, it has become apparent that the traditional examples such as fresh air and sunshine are not free at all. Hence the saying, there is no such thing as a free lunch.

**freehold:** the right to own a piece of land and/or property for evermore. Freeholds can become substantial, long-term *assets* with a strong impact on the *balance sheet*. They can provide the security (*collateral*) that banks want before lending money, or be the basis of raising cash via a *sale-and-leaseback* contract.

**freelance:** a self-employed person who expects to earn a living by providing a service to different clients at irregular intervals. As they are not employed on a permanent basis, free-lancers need to work especially hard at keeping their clients satisfied.

**free market:** a market in which there is no government interference. The concept of a free market underlies the *laissez faire* principle, *capitalism* and the *market system*. In practice, a market with literally no government intervention would be totally chaotic, as there would be no legal system to ensure fair play. The term is used to describe markets where the government does not actually control decision-making.

**free rider problem:** where there is a *public good*, no one can be excluded from benefiting from it and so no one has an incentive to pay for its installation or upkeep. Streetlighting is a standard example; because of the free rider problem no individual will pay for it. All will wait for someone else to provide it, knowing that they will have the use of it without paying. This is why public goods must be provided by governments which have the legal right to tax people to pay for them.

**free trade** exists when trade between countries is not restricted in any way by *tariffs*, *quotas*, or other barriers. It is based on the theory of *comparative advantage*, which argues that every country will be better off if it specialises in producing goods at which it is comparatively more efficient. The *World Trade Organisation* (previously *GATT*) accepts the notion that more trade benefits everyone, and through successive 'rounds' of negotiations has sought to reduce trade barriers around the world.

**frequency distribution:** where events occur many times, the values they have on each occasion can be recorded to see the frequency with which each value occurs. Examples might be daily sales of a chocolate bar, or the precise length of a bolt to be used in car production. Distributions can be presented as *histograms* or as line graphs.

**frictional unemployment** occurs in the time delay between losing one job and finding another. By its nature it is temporary, as opposed to *structural unemployment* which is more fundamental and therefore longer term. Improved information flows are one way of reducing frictional unemployment. However, taking time to find the right job is often efficient from both the employer's and the employee's point of view.

**Friedman, Milton** (b. 1912) is an American economist who is most closely associated with the ideas of the monetarists. In 1976, he was awarded the Nobel Prize for economics. He retired in 1979 from the University of Chicago, where he had been Professor Economics since 1948. His work at that University, and the work of others who went there, gave rise to the idea of a '*Chicago School*' of economists. Their view of governments' responsibility for poor economic growth due to *interventionist policies* and overtaxing made them recommend a *laissez faire* approach. This view contrasted with the so-called 'Cambridge School', who supported *Keynesian* ideas including intervention through *fiscal policies*.

**fringe benefits:** any benefit received by employees in addition to their wages or salary. Common fringe benefits are a company pension scheme, a company car, discounts when buying the firm's products and the provision of sports facilities. All add to the cost of employing labour, but are expected to pay for themselves by their contribution to staff loyalty and therefore the reduction of *labour turnover*.

**full capacity output** is the highest level of output which can be achieved in the economy as a whole, given the type of resources available and their existing location. *Aggregate demand* for goods and services in excess of this level of output will lead to accelerating inflation. However there may at this level of output still be some *structural unemployment*. This will occur if the unemployed people do not have the skills which are required by employers, or if they are located in areas other than the ones in which employers are recruiting. In other words if they are *occupationally immobile* or *geographically immobile*, they may be unable to contribute to production.

**full costing** is an attempt to allocate all costs incurred in an organisation to *cost centres*. The intention is to ensure that all costs are covered and the possibility of losses by underpricing is avoided. *Direct costs* can be relatively easily allocated to an activity or a product. Some direct *overheads* may be easy to allocate but most are indirect overheads and cannot be allocated easily. An example of full costing would be allocating 35 per cent of the overhead cost of rent to the machine shop if the machine shop has 35 per cent of the factory space. A widely used alternative method is *contribution costing*.

**full cost pricing:** another term for *cost-plus pricing*.

**full employment** is the level of employment which provides jobs for all those who wish to work apart from those *frictionally unemployed*. It implies that the capital stock of the country is fully utilised. What level of unemployment in the UK now represents full employment is a matter of some debate. *Structural change*, which includes an increasing rate of technological advance, has created a high level of unemployment which does not go away even when the economy is booming. During the period 1999–2002, unemployment was lower than it had been for 20 years. This level may be the closest to full employment that the economy can get at the present time.

**full line forcing** is a *restrictive* (trade) *practice* whereby a retailer wanting to buy one brand or product from a supplier is told that unless they stock the full product range they can have nothing. As in-store space is limited, if the retailer accepts this manufacturer's full range it may not be worthwhile to stock any rival products. This is a way in which producers can attempt to achieve monopoly distribution in retail outlets (especially smaller ones). The manufacturers of ice-cream and of batteries have been accused of full line forcing in the past. Retailers wanting to fight against it could make a complaint to the *Office of Fair Trading*, but they would be worried that a powerful manufacturing firm might stop supplying them with the key brands demanded by customers.

**function:** in economics this means a relationship between two variables, one of which depends on the other. The dependent variable is said to be a function of the independent variable. For example, consumption is said to be a function of income.

Function also refers to an individual's job role, defined broadly within headings such as marketing, production, personnel or finance. Therefore a business structured by function is organised into departments such as the above. This contrasts with businesses structured by product or by *matrix*.

**functional organisation** is based on a hierarchy in which each department operates separately under the leadership of those at the top of the pyramid.

*Coordination* stems from the top, but may be hard to achieve at the lower management layers due to the separation of job functions into the different departments. This form of structure can be contrasted with the more flexible *matrix* organisation.

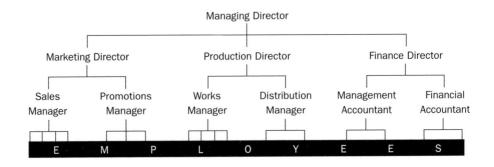

**futures trading** is when *commodities* or financial assets are bought or sold at some time in the future at an agreed price. In London such trading in financial assets occurs on the floor of LIFFE (*London International Financial Futures Exchange*). Commodities such as wheat, oil, wool, and many other products can also be bought or sold 'forward' on the commodity exchanges. This can be purely speculative, but it can also be vital for a business to protect itself against possible exchange rate or commodity price fluctuations (see *hedging*). (See also *derivatives* and *options*.)

**What other subjects are you studying?**

A–Zs cover 18 different subjects. See the inside back cover for a list of all the titles in the series and how to order.

**G7:** see *Group of Seven*

**gains from trade:** the benefits arising from trade which result in increased output from a given quantity of real resources. The theory of *comparative advantage* shows that trade allows countries to specialise in the goods and services which they produce most efficiently. By increasing efficiency, gains are made overall.

**Galbraith J K** (b. 1908): a Canadian-born economist who popularised the works of J M *Keynes* and contributed to an understanding of the workings of large corporations and of the motives of firms and politicians. His writings were sceptical of *free enterprise*, as in his criticisms of the idea that the free market satisfies people's needs. In his book THE AFFLUENT SOCIETY (4th ed., Deutsch, 1985) he spoke out strongly against the persuasive power of advertising:

> As a society becomes increasingly affluent, wants are increasingly created by the process by which they are satisfied.

Galbraith's account of THE GREAT CRASH 1929 (3rd ed., Penguin, 1988) is one of the most readable insights into that dramatic event.

**galloping inflation:** see *hyperinflation*

**game theory** applies when the bodies which are competing in the market-place exhibit interdependent behaviour. This means that for each one, the actions of the other will have an impact on the decisions taken. For example, if one business decides to cut prices, its competitor may follow suit. Game theory can be applied in a range of situations, whether the businesses are competing or colluding with each other, and whether there are gainers and losers or all may gain together.

**gap (in the market):** an identifiable market opportunity that has not yet been exploited. The term might be used in relation to:

- market segments, such as an age group that has not been catered for
- products, such as a flavour of fruit juice that has not yet been marketed
- distribution, such as a new, *impulse purchase* product that is not yet being distributed to garages, cinemas and other non-standard outlets.

**Gates, Bill:** famous for being the world's richest man, Bill Gates is co-founder of the Microsoft Corporation and has led its rise from a 1980s business start-up to a trillion-dollar business.

**GATT:** see *General Agreement on Tariffs and Trade*

**GDFCF:** see *gross domestic fixed capital formation*

**GDP:** see *gross domestic product*

**gearing** measures the proportion of *capital employed* that is provided by long-term lenders. The gearing ratio is:

FORMULA: $\dfrac{\text{long-term liabilities}}{\text{capital employed}} \times 100$

If loans represent more than 50 per cent of capital employed, the company is said to be highly geared. Such a company has to pay interest on its borrowing before it can pay *dividends* to shareholders or reinvest profits in new equipment. Therefore the higher the gearing, the higher the risk. The gearing ratio measures financial risk by use of *balance sheet* figures; the interest cover ratio measures this risk by means of *profit and loss account* figures.

**General Agreement on Tariffs and Trade (GATT)** was established after the Second World War to encourage the growth of international trade by removing or reducing *tariff* and non-tariff barriers. Agreements were reached after what were known as 'rounds' of negotiations, which often lasted many years. The latest was the Uruguay round which was started in 1986, and was concluded after very protracted negotiations over agricultural subsidies at the end of 1994. It has had an impact on trade in many products, including services.

The Uruguay Round led to GATT being transformed into the *World Trade Organisation* early in 1995. This is a larger and perhaps more powerful institution; developing countries are more involved in it than they were in GATT.

GATT was instrumental in making the world trading environment very much freer than it was before World War II. Not all its members always adhered to the general principles which it laid down, for example the *Common Agricultural Policy* of the EU is contrary to GATT principles. Nevertheless, as a forum for negotiation it led to very large reductions in tariffs which in turn led to large increases in trade in manufactures. This increase in trade has been a major factor in worldwide economic growth.

**general equilibrium** refers to the type of economic analysis which examines the consequences of changes in all of the markets which they might affect. In this way it takes account of the interrelationships between different markets. So whereas partial equilibrium analysis would consider the impact of a change in demand for restaurant meals on their price and quantity sold, general equilibrium analysis would go on to include consideration of the effect on demand for chefs, and other labour market consequences, the impact on other producers in food processing and leisure activities and so on.

**general union:** an organisation founded to represent the collective interests of employees from within any industry and with no special skills. General unions tend to attract unskilled or semi-skilled workers.

**generic brands** are those that are so totally associated with the product that customers treat the brand name as if it was a product category. Examples include Hoover (vacuum cleaner) and Bacardi (white rum). This could be said to be the ultimate marketing achievement.

**genetically modified (GM) foods:** these products of the biotechnology industry burst onto the consciousness of the consumer when the US firm Monsanto ran an advertising campaign in 1998 to persuade public opinion of their worth. The campaign backfired, leaving a widespread consumer image of GM foods as 'Frankenstein foods', of doubtful origin and with doubtful consequences for consumer and environmental welfare.

**geographical immobility** occurs when people who have been made redundant are unable to move to areas in which jobs are available and thus remain unemployed. It is made worse when there is a lack of housing for rent at reasonable prices in the areas where jobs exist. Also differences in house prices, such that areas with high unemployment have low prices, make it hard for people without jobs to move to areas with jobs.

**gilt-edged security** is a type of *government security*. It is used by governments to borrow the sums needed to cover their *budget deficits*. Originally such stock certificates were literally edged with gold leaf, hence the name. This is no longer true, but it is the case that a gilt is a totally safe form of investment because no government would refuse to pay up when the gilt matures. Gilts are also referred to as *bonds*.

**Gini coefficient:** a measurement of inequality in the *distribution of income*. (See also *Lorenz curve*.)

**glass ceiling:** the invisible barrier of discrimination that prevents women or non-whites from getting promoted to the top of organisations. In many businesses and professions, women form the majority of the workforce, yet hold a tiny minority of the senior posts. *Equal opportunities* legislation was supposed to break through the ceiling, but discriminatory attitudes have proved very hard to overcome.

**global brands** are branded products that have been marketed successfully worldwide. Examples include Coca-Cola, McDonald's and Bacardi. Although there may be a degree of tailoring to local tastes (such as more salads at McDonald's located in hotter countries) the key to global brands is standardisation. In other words, a Big Mac should taste the same in Tokyo as in Manchester. As so many global brands are American in origin, some critics worry that different national traditions are being swept aside in a shift towards the American way of life.

**globalisation** of the international economy refers to the process by which there is both an increasing world market in goods and services and increasing integration in world capital markets. This means that governments need to consult with their trading partners in order to co-ordinate their macroeconomic policies and to avoid de-stabilising capital movements. Otherwise the success of their policies is likely to be compromised.

Globalisation has been associated with the rapid growth in world trade and has encouraged economic growth. It has improved standards of living for many people. It may also have increased the power of the multinationals. Some of the growth in trade has evolved as a result of efforts to make trade easier through the trade negotiations of the *World Trade Organisation*.

**GM foods:** see *genetically modified foods*

**GNP:** see *gross national product*

**goals** are targets that act as a focus for decision-making and effort, and as a yardstick against which success or failure can be measured. The word goals is used interchangeably with *objectives*.

**going rate:** the prevailing percentage wage rise being received by employees during a *pay round*. Its level is likely to be determined by the rate of price inflation and the degree of demand for labour. If the going rate is 5 per cent, workers will see that level of pay rise as the least they can expect.

**goods** are tangible products, in contrast to services. Goods are physical objects.

**goodwill** arises when a business is sold for more than the *balance sheet* values of its *assets*. A purchaser is prepared to pay more than this for the business as a going concern because it may have an established name and reputation as well as a favourable location. Goodwill is then shown in the purchaser's balance sheet as an *intangible asset*. Goodwill is a technical accounting term which should not be confused with the everyday use of the word.

**go-slow:** a form of *industrial action* in which employees keep working, but at the minimum pace allowable under their terms of employment. This will lose them any bonuses, but will ensure that they receive their basic pay. If conducted at a time of year of high *demand*, a go-slow could be successful in applying considerable pressure upon an employer.

**government economic objectives** are the goals laid down by the political party in government. It was long thought that all governments pursued a mix of objectives including: steady *economic growth*, low *inflation*, low unemployment and a modest *balance of payments* surplus. There have been periods, however, when the pursuit of low inflation has been the primary economic objective. This has come into conflict with other aspects of policy, such as low unemployment.

**government failure** occurs when governments act to deal with *market failure*, but in the process create further distortions in the market. Very broadly, government failure may be said to occur when government intervention makes the situation worse rather than better. For example, national insurance charges raise revenue which can be used to pay benefits, but they also make it more expensive for employers to take on more labour. They thus tend to discourage job creation and raise unemployment.

**government securities** are sold by governments as a form of borrowing from households or firms. It is a way of making up for a shortfall in money raised through taxation, i.e. a *budget deficit*. The most common forms are *Treasury bills* and *gilt-edged securities*, otherwise known as *bonds*.

**government spending:** see *public expenditure*

**grant:** a government or charitable subsidy of a business investment or activity.

**grapevine:** the network of informal communication contained within every organisation. It will spread rumours that may undermine the public statements of senior management, but only if those statements are incorrect or incomplete. In firms with an *authoritarian leadership style*, the grapevine may be condemned for spreading gossip, whereas a *democratic leader* might see it as a useful supplement to other lines of communication.

**Great Depression:** the term used to describe the period following the Wall Street Crash of 1929. In the years afterwards, unemployment hit 20 per cent in Britain and 33 per cent in America and Germany. The most important lessons that can be learnt from it are:

• the impact of the economy on political life (in Germany, mass unemployment helped bring Adolf Hitler to power)

• the dangers of allowing the banking system to collapse

• that positive government action to bring about recovery can be successful.

**greenfield site:** a site for a new factory that has no history of the manufacture of the product in question. Despite the implication of the countryside, the same term would be used for an urban site. Among the firms that have succeeded on greenfield sites are Nissan UK and Toyota UK; a well-known failure was De Lorean motors in Northern Ireland.

Pros:   ●   the site can be chosen on modern not historic criteria
        ●   traditional restrictive labour practices will not hinder productivity.

Cons:   ●   no pool of local labour with the right skills or temperament
        ●   local infrastructure not geared towards the product.

**greenhouse effect:** the theory that global warming is taking place as a consequence of a build up of carbon dioxide preventing heat from the sun leaving the earth's atmosphere. Carbon dioxide is thought to be increasing due to deforestation, industrial pollution and excessive use of petrol-driven cars. Worldwide concern about the greenhouse effect put many industrial companies under pressure to reduce air pollution emissions from *pressure groups* such as Friends of the Earth.

**green pound:** an artificial exchange rate used for calculating payments to farmers out of the *Common Agricultural Policy*. If the green pound is devalued, food prices in British shops are likely to rise.

**grey market:** an unofficial market where buyers and sellers can trade legally (as opposed to the black market where trade is illegal). A grey market can develop when public interest in a new share issue is so high that people want to buy shares before the day official dealings start. More importantly, it is the grey market in goods that limits the effectiveness of price discrimination. When Fisher-Price was selling its 'Activity Centres' at a markedly higher price in Britain than in Germany, Tesco stores started buying grey market supplies from Germany and undercutting the prices charged by their competitors. Fisher-Price was furious and tried to stop this unofficial distribution channel, but had no legal power to do so.

**grievance procedure:** the method by which an employee can raise a serious complaint about his or her treatment at work. This is usually set out in the staff handbook. A common intention is that the grievance should be settled as near to the point of origin as possible.

**gross domestic fixed capital formation (GDFCF)** is the sum total of all investment in *infrastructure*, buildings, plant, machinery, and vehicles in one year. It is an important indicator because it is strongly related to the future growth of productive capacity. It includes *replacement investment*, but the higher it is, the more likely it is that it will lead to increases in productivity. It tends to be rather volatile because it is closely related to expectations and therefore to the phases of the *business cycle*.

**gross domestic product (GDP)** is the sum total of the value of a country's output over the course of a year. It differs from *gross national product* because it does not include net income from abroad. It may be calculated from expenditure, in which case it is likely to be expressed in market prices. These include expenditure taxes. It can also be calculated from income or the value of output. It is most commonly expressed at factor cost, i.e. the costs of all the inputs, which reflects the real resource costs of production.

**gross investment:** the total of all investment in buildings, plant, machinery and vehicles and *infrastructure*, including both *replacement investment* and new productive capacity. (See also *net investment*.)

**gross margin** is the percentage of *sales revenue* which is *gross profit*.

FORMULA:   $\dfrac{\text{gross profit}}{\text{sales revenue}} \times 100$

**gross national product (GNP)** is calculated by adding the value of all the production of a country (*gross domestic product*) plus the net income from abroad. Net income from abroad is the income earned on overseas investments less the income earned by foreigners investing in the domestic economy. In most countries, the growth in real GNP per head of population is the main measure of improvement in the standard of living.

**GNP deflator:** an index of prices which allows GNP to be expressed in constant rather than current prices. This means that changes in the *real* value of GNP can be compared over time. For example it might be expressed in 1995 prices. The same process can be applied to GDP, investment, consumption, government expenditure and so on.

**gross profit** is *sales revenue* minus *cost of sales* in the accounting period under review. Gross profit has not yet had *overheads*, interest and *depreciation* deducted from it and must not, therefore, be confused with *trading profit*. For a more detailed account, see *cost of sales*.

**group bonus scheme:** a performance incentive scheme based on the total *output* (or sales) of a group of workers. There are many different ways of organising such a bonus, but usually it will be based on the amount by which a target level has been exceeded. Compared with bonuses based on an individual's performance, group schemes have advantages and disadvantages:

Pros:
- encourages teamwork and thereby may improve morale
- more suitable when an individual's performance is dependent on others within the group.

Cons:
- less direct an incentive, which may reduce its effectiveness
- pressure to achieve what the group expects may result in poor production quality.

**group discussion:** a form of *qualitative research* in which a psychologist stimulates discussion among six to eight consumers chosen to represent the *target market*. The aim is partly to probe for the motives behind people's purchasing decisions (consumer psychology) and partly to use the group as a sounding board for new ideas. Usually a qualitative research programme will consist of between four and eight groups.

**Group of Seven (G7)** is the collective name given to the seven richest nations in the world: Japan, the USA, Germany, France, Canada, Italy and the UK. Because of their economic power they carry considerable political muscle, and consequently their meetings are reported widely.

When Russia is invited to participate it is known as the G8. Were China also to be invited it would become G9.

**growth:** see *economic growth*

**guesstimate:** an estimate based largely on guesswork or intuition. Although firms want to make decisions on the basis if sound data (such as *market research* findings), there may be occasions when there is no time to collect it. For example, if Galaxy announced a two-month promotion offering 20 per cent extra free, Cadbury's would have to decide immediately what effect this might have upon their chocolate sales, and decide whether to match Galaxy's offer. A sales guesstimate would be needed. *Scientific decisions* take time.

**hands-on management:** when senior executives get actively involved in the day-to-day problems of and decisions within the business. This might weaken the motivating power of *delegation*, but only if the senior manager insists on taking decisions that should be taken further down the hierarchy. Given Elton *Mayo*'s work on the *Hawthorne effect*, it is likely that active management involvement should aid motivation, though *Herzberg* would warn against over-supervision. If hands-on management is based on mistrust of the subordinates, and is effectively a form of snooping, the result could only be conflict.

**Handy, Professor Charles:** the author of many business books, notably *Understanding Organisations* and I*nside Organizations* (1990, BBC Books). Formerly an executive with BP Oil, Charles Handy has become a leading theorist about the future of organisations. He forecast the recent rise in contracted out and flexible work and the decline in the numbers employed securely as core workers. (See *shamrock organisation*.)

**hard currency** includes a number of currencies which are easily convertible and widely accepted in payment everywhere. The US dollar, the mark, the pound and the yen are examples. Indian rupees and Chinese renminbi would usually be less acceptable.

**harmonisation** (of conditions of service) represents the move to *single status*, in which manual and white-collar workers have the same terms within their *employment contracts*. This does not mean that all are paid the same amount, but ensures that all are treated the same. In the recent past it was common for factory workers to be separated from management by different eating facilities, hours of work, types of payment, and with only managers getting company pensions.

**harmonisation** (in the European Union) means making all members countries' businesses subject to the same legal framework, i.e. harmonising laws and regulations. In this way the EU tries to create a 'level playing field' so that all firms compete on equal terms within the *single market*.

**Hawthorne effect:** the beneficial impact on staff workrate and moral of an active, personal interest being shown by management. The term derives from *Mayo*'s researches into workplace behaviour at a factory at Hawthorne, USA between 1927 and 1932.

Mayo was a follower of F W *Taylor*'s methods and was attempting to measure the impact on productivity of improving the lighting conditions within the factory. He followed Taylor's scientific principles by testing the changes against a control, a section of the factory with unchanged lighting. Although productivity rose where the lighting was improved, Mayo was surprised to find a similar benefit where no physical changes had taken place.

This led him to conduct a series of further experiments which cast serious doubts on Taylor's assumptions about the absolute importance of money in motivation. The phrase 'the Hawthorne effect' remains in use worldwide as an example of the importance of *human relations* in business.

**headhunter:** a recruitment consultant who hunts actively for the right person for a job, instead of waiting for responses to an advertisement. The main benefit of this approach is that the headhunter may contact someone who is ideal for the job, but is not currently looking for work (and would therefore not notice an advertisement). Headhunting is expensive as it is labour-intensive, but it is a common way of recruiting senior managers and professionals.

**headline inflation** is inflation as measured by the *retail price index*. This includes some prices changes which may be strictly temporary in their impact on the economy, such as mortgage interest payments. This is excluded from *RPIX*. Another measure of inflation, *RPIY*, excludes changes in *indirect taxes*, again in order to measure *underlying inflation*.

**headline unemployment** is the total number of registered unemployed, not seasonally adjusted. It will obviously exclude *disguised unemployment*.

**Health and Safety at Work Act 1974** imposes on employers the duty 'to ensure, so far as is reasonably practicable, the health, safety and welfare at work' of all staff. 'Reasonably practicable' means that it is accepted that the risks of hazard can be weighed against the cost of prevention. The main provisions of the Act are:

- firms must provide all necessary safety equipment and clothing free of charge
- employers must provide a safe working environment
- all firms with five or more employees must have a written safety policy on display
- union-appointed safety representatives have the right to investigate and inspect the workplace and the causes of any accidents.

The Act also set up the Health and Safety Commission to decide on safety policy and the *Health and Safety Executive* to oversee the work of the *factory inspectors*. A major criticism of the Act, and especially of government cutbacks since 1974, is that there are too few inspectors to have a meaningful deterrent effect.

**Health and Safety Executive:** a government-financed organisation set up to oversee the implementation of the 1974 *Health and Safety at Work Act*. It employs *factory inspectors* to investigate possible breaches of the Act and to give advice on improving safety practices.

**heavy industry:** a rather loose term denoting the producers of large, heavy products usually from large-scale factories. Examples include the production of steel, lorries, cars and bulk chemicals.

**hedging** (foreign currency) is a way of covering exchange rate fluctuations so that losses and risks are minimised. Commodities or currencies can be bought now for delivery on a date in the future. *Future trading* helps firms to conduct international business without having to guess what the exchange rate or the commodity prices will be in six months' time.

**Hempel report:** a 1997 report into corporate governance, produced by a committee led by Sir Ronnie Hempel, then chairman of ICI. A follow-up to the Cadbury and Greenbury reports, it disappointed many by arguing against radical change. Hempel was content that company directors should continue to see themselves as responsible to shareholders rather than stakeholders. He argued that corporate governance should be regarded more as a matter of principles than hard and fast rules. Issues such as excessive directors' pay and perks were treated by the committee as of little importance. Critics suggested the rather tame findings were predictable given that half the committee members came from big corporations.

**Herzberg, F** (1923–2000): an American psychologist whose research in the 1950s led him to develop the *two-factor theory* of job satisfaction. Although many have criticised him for drawing conclusions about workers as a whole from a sample drawn solely from accountants and engineers, Herzberg's theory has proved very robust. Many firms have put his methods into practice, often with considerable success. Part of the reason for the interest shown by business leaders was because Herzberg offered a practical approach to improving motivation through *job enrichment*. This, he stressed, should not be confused with *job rotation*.

Herzberg's stress on redesigning workplaces and work systems to provide more fulfilling jobs was a major move away from the ideas of Ford and *Taylor*. Despite this, Herzberg could be criticised for making too little of the role of groups and teams at work. His focus on the job made him lose sight of the motivational power of team spirit.

**hierarchy:** the layers of management in an organisation, which may be many or few. Each level of the hierarchy will have authority over the one beneath. If there are many levels, the hierarchy is said to be tall. If there are only two or three, it is described as flat. In recent years there has been a trend towards flatter heirarchies, which sometimes combines with a move towards *decentralisation* of decision-making. Flat structures are also associated with a larger *span of control*.

**hierarchy of needs:** Abraham *Maslow*'s theory that all humans have the same type of need which can be classified into a single hierarchy.

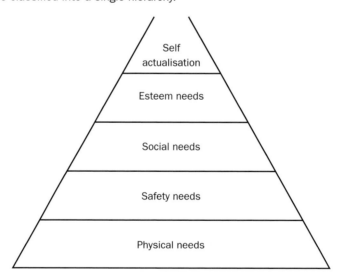

*Hierarchy of needs*

They span from the lower order, physical needs through social needs towards the higher order, psychological needs. Maslow believed that each need has to be fulfilled totally before the next becomes important. By the time all needs have been catered for, the individual will be motivated by self-actualisation, in other words psychological growth and development. Yet if the threat of *redundancy* occurs, the individual's focus will return to the basic needs, such as security.

Maslow's five categories of need:

**1** Physical, the requirement to eat and sleep (and therefore earn an income)

**2** Safety, the need for security

**3** Social, the desire for friendship, love and a sense of belonging

**4** Esteem, to gave respect from others and, more importantly, self-respect

**5** Self-actualisation, to fulfil one's potential through actions and achievements

Note that Maslow did not believe that this could be satisfied fully; in other words, people will always strive to develop further and achieve more. Hence the funnel at the top of the pyramid diagram on page 134.

**hierarchy of objectives:** a diagram to show the logical order in which a firm should determine its *objectives*. First the *aims* must be agreed, then the medium to long-term objectives, and finally the *strategies* for achieving the objectives. Although these elements can be determined in advance at board level, changing daily circumstances may force short-term, tactical objectives to be set that might not be fully in harmony with the overall aims. (See *corporate objectives*.)

**higher order needs:** see *hierarchy of needs*

**Highland Park plant:** the huge factory in Detroit (USA) at which Ford achieved the break-through to moving, conveyor belt assembly of cars in 1913. This heralded the start of the *mass production* era and therefore the beginning of the end for many craft manufacturing skills. Just prior to the switch to the mass production system, it had taken 750 minutes to assemble each car. By the spring of 1914 it took only 93 minutes an 88 per cent reduction.

**hire purchase:** a system of obtaining *credit* for the purchase of an *asset* whereby the purchaser puts down a proportion of the price as a deposit and pays the balance in equal instalments over an agreed repayment period. The purchaser becomes owner when the last instalment is paid. The hire purchaser pays a fixed monthly sum that is likely to amount to a far higher total than for outright purchase. In the short term, however, the firm may be pleased to obtain a vital asset without a large outflow of cash.

**histogram:** a diagrammatic way of representing a *frequency distribution* in which the area of the block is proportional to the value of the variable measured. A histogram differs from a *bar chart* because the width of the bars can vary as well as the height.

**historic cost** is the original purchase price paid for an *asset*. The principle of valuing assets as their historic cost lies at the heart of standard accounting. *Balance sheets* value *fixed assets*, for example, at historic cost (minus *depreciation*).

**hoarding** occurs when people or organisations keep money which is not earning interest or being used in a productive way. Savings kept under the mattress is a traditional example. Excessive current account balances would be another.

**holding company** is one which holds a majority of the shares of other companies and thus controls them without direct involvement in their running. The degree of influence can vary depending on the management style of the holding company. It can operate as little more than an industrial bank, with the head office staff simply deciding on the most profitable uses of the company's funds.

**homeworking:** earning an income from work undertaken at home. Traditionally, homework-ers have completed labour-intensive, very low-paid jobs such as hand-sewing or packing.

A B C D E F G **H** I J K L M N O P Q R S T U V W X Y Z

Modern technology offers the possibility that more professional employees could work from home, armed with communication links such as *electronic mail*, *fax* and telephone.

**homogeneous products** are identical. It is impossible to know whether an amount of the product came from one firm or another. A homogeneous product is an important feature of the model of *perfect competition*. The more homogeneous products are, the stronger the competition is likely to be in the market-place. Examples include many agricultural products, e.g. wheat, and many mineral products, e.g. iron ore.

Many businesses spend a great deal of time and money trying to persuade consumers that their products are different from others; theirs are *differentiated products*, the opposite of homogeneous.

**horizontal communications** represent the passage of information between people on the same hierarchical level within an organisation, e.g. between section heads.

**horizontal integration** occurs where a firm takes over or merges with another firm at the same stage of production. The production process starts with raw materials being processed, then moves through manufacture and assembly to be sold to wholesalers and then retailers. Horizontal integration can occur at any of these stages. The merger of two breweries would be an example of horizontal integration, and would have the following advantages and disadvantages:

Pros:    • increases market power over the next or the previous link in the process
         • enables greater *economies of scale* to occur

Cons:    • may restrict customer choice
         • unequal market influence may increase costs overall by the exercise of monopoly power, and may thus attract the attention of the *Competition Commission.*

**horizontal promotion:** the Japanese idea that as those at the top of an organisation need to have a thorough grounding in every aspect of the business, to be invited to transfer to a different department represents an effective promotion. Improved status, salary and career prospects go hand-in-hand with a new challenge, even though the individual has not moved up to a higher rung on the hierarchical ladder.

Horizontal promotion is a key element in overcoming the main weakness of a flat hierarchy (one with a wide *span of control* and few *layers of hierarchy*). Namely that few layers of hierarchy mean few opportunities for vertical promotion. This could be seen as a demotivator for ambitious employees. Therefore seeing a sideways move as promotion is important psychologically.

**host country:** one which receives foreign investment from a *multinational company*. This provides advantages and disadvantages to the host:

Pros:    • provides income and employment
         • helps the *balance of payments* initially by providing a demand for the host country's currency, and then by providing exports of finished goods
         • may provide new training and skills to the workforce
         • may encourage the growth of other domestic industries, and industrialisation in general agriculture may be shift from self-sufficiency to growing cash crops, leading to higher standards of living, at least in the short run.

Cons:
- once income and wage levels have been raised, the multinational may move on to the next source of cheap labour and/or raw materials
- the multinational may not adhere to the highest standards of safety and responsibility that it would be required to follow in other, more developed countries
- the profits will go to the shareholders, who will not usually be residents of the host country, leading to an invisible outflow on the balance of payments.

**hostile take-over bid:** this is where a *predator* company wishes to acquire a target company and its actions are unwelcome. The predator offers a price for the shares of the target and, as soon as it has acquired a majority, it has management control. It can vote in its own directors at a general meeting. According to the take-over rules, the predator has a time limit to persuade shareholders to accept the offer and during this period the two companies may publish their campaigns. By contrast, some companies agree terms and carry out an agreed *merger*.

**hot money:** speculative flows on foreign exchange markets. It is possible to hold large cash balances in order to gamble on changes in *exchange rates*. For example, during the Asian financial crisis, large quantities of yen and other Asian currencies were sold. As exchange rates fell, more and more holders of the currencies lost confidence and they in turn sold. Later, when the exchange rates had stabilised at a lower level, they bought the currencies again. Money which moves from one capital market to another in search of the best rate of return is termed hot money.

**household:** the basic economic decision-taking unit. Economists tend to talk about households rather than individuals because their consumption patterns have more in common than, say, those of a teenager living at home and a single person living alone.

**human capital** is the degree of skill and training embodied in labour as a *factor of production*. As in financial capital, its value can be increased by investment, in this case in education. The education might be paid for by the state or privately, but it explains in part why a graduate might reasonably expect to earn more than someone with no qualifications. Although that is not always the case for individuals – pop stars with no qualifications earn more than almost every graduate – it is true in general.

**human development index:** a measure of the quality of life constructed by the United Nations Development Programme. It takes into account not just income but also a range of other criteria such as literacy and life-expectancy. Canada and the Scandinavian countries usually rank among the highest.

**human relations** is the aspect of management that Elton *Mayo*'s work highlighted. The *Human Relations School* promoted the benefits to morale and productivity of a *paternalistic* style of management in which the worker was to be seen more as a member of the family than as a mere *factor of production*. Among the policy outcomes were:

- a move to more social facilities surrounding work (sports teams, social clubs etc.)
- the appointment of personnel or welfare officers whose function was to look after the well-being of the labour force
- a move to greater communication and *consultation* between the management and the factory floor.

**Human Relations School:** those managers and writers who supported *Mayo*'s views on the importance of *human relations* in the workplace. (See *Hawthorne effect*.)

**human resource management (HRM):** the responsibility of using and developing the organisation's personnel in the most productive way. This appears to be little more than restating the role of the personnel department, but HRM has some distinctive features:

- its spur has been the success of the Japanese at managing people, even though their firms rarely have personnel departments; so HRM represents a rethink by personnel professionals
- it places greater emphasis on development through training and career planning
- it has the potential to persuade all managers that the development of their human resources (subordinates) is their job, not the personnel department's.

**Human Rights Act 1998:** from October 2 2000, all courts and tribunals have been required to act in accordance with the European Convention on Human Rights.

**hunch:** the intuition that can lead a decision-maker to go against the obvious or statistically proven route. This may prove a stroke of genius or a source of great embarrassment. In support of hunches is the statement by John Sculley, Chief Executive of Apple Computers:

> No great marketing decisions have ever been made on quantitative data.

(D Rowan, THE INTUITIVE MANAGER, Little, Brown & Company, 1989).

**hygiene factors:** elements of working life that have the potential to cause dissatisfaction, such as salary, working conditions, status and over-supervision. (See *Herzberg*.)

**hyperinflation** is used to describe a situation where the value of money decreases so fast that it loses some, or all of its functions. Consequently, people resort to *barter* or to the use of some other commodity which has intrinsic value or to the use of a foreign currency. The exact level of inflation which turns into hyperinflation is not precise since it will be determined by psychological factors. The best-known example of hyperinflation occurred in Germany in the 1920s, but in more recent times many South American countries have suffered from it. Russia has also experienced its horrors. Hyperinflation can result in the breakdown of societies because it leads to a major redistribution of wealth in favour of those with debts, and against savers who are holding assets denominated in money terms, such as bank balances and building society accounts. It also strongly favours those who can negotiate higher pay, while penalising people on fixed incomes.

**hypothesis:** a theoretical connection between two variables, which can be tested against the facts. For example, we might suspect that the purchase of yachts is related to income. By examining the increase in real incomes which occurs when the economy is growing, and comparing this with the trend in yacht sales, we might find that the hypothesis was supported by the evidence.

**IBA:** see *Independent Broadcasting Authority*

**IBRD:** see *International Bank for Reconstruction and Development*, commonly known as the World Bank

**idle time** is the amount of time a work station is not operational. A work station can be a machine waiting to be used in a production process or a booking clerk in a railway station. The concept is most often met in simulation exercises.

Causes:
- machinery breakdowns, perhaps due to old age or poor maintenance
- the time taken to reset machines when a different batch is to be produced.

Effects:
- a high rate of idle time reduces labour productivity and therefore adds to wage costs per unit
- if the workforce is being paid *piece rate* or a productivity bonus, idle time hits wages packets and therefore lowers morale.

**IIP:** see *Investors in People*

**IMF:** see *International Monetary Fund*

**immobilities** occur when people are unable to take up a job which is available because they are living in another area (*geographical immobility*), or because they do not have the right skills for the job (*occupational immobility*). Immobilities are a form of *market imperfection*.

**imperfect competition** occurs when there are a number of competing firms, but the market lacks some or all of the features of *perfect competition*. Broadly there are three types of imperfect competition: *duopoly*, *oligopoly* and *monopolistic competition*. In a duopoly there are just two firms competing. Oligopoly describes a situation where there are several firms in the market. In both cases, the market will be characterised by interdependence: the competing forms will base their decisions on what the others are doing, or might do in the future. There is likely to be much *non-price competition*. Under monopolistic competition there are many competitors, each selling a differentiated product.

**imperfect information** is a market imperfection as a result of which competition is impaired by lack of easily available information. The consumer who does not know where to find a product at the cheapest price will pay more, and this protects the producer from the competition which might exist if information were fuller.

**imperfections** occur in an *imperfect market*, and include *immobilities*, *imperfect information*, government intervention, barriers to entry, small numbers of buyers or sellers and any other source of distortions which may interfere with the operation of competitive market forces. (See also *imperfect market*.)

**imperfect market** occurs when there are imperfections, i.e. distortions in the market such that competition is not as forceful as it might be. An imperfect market departs in one or more ways from the conditions of *perfect competition*. It will generally not achieve *technical and allocative efficiency*. For example, firms which have a degree of monopoly within their markets may not be forced to seek the most efficient methods of producing and as a result, prices may be higher than they need be.

**import:** the purchase of a product or service from overseas.

**import controls** are *tariffs* or *quotas* designed to limit the number of overseas goods entering the domestic market. In extreme cases, some goods are prevented from entering at all, which is called an *embargo*. Tariffs are a tax on imports. Quotas and other forms of import controls are collectively called *non-tariff barriers*, which discriminate against imported goods in a more subtle way. One example of such a non-tariff barrier would be requiring excessive paperwork for imports, resulting in delays at the frontier. Import controls are generally being reduced over the years by WTO negotiations.

**import penetration** a measurement of the share of the home market taken by importers. 25 per cent penetration means, therefore, that imports account for a quarter of sales within a market.

**import duty:** a *tariff* levied on an imported item at the point of entry to the country.

**import substitution:** some developing countries have sought to industrialise by reducing imports and developing domestic industries which would replace them. Although this has been occasionally successful, in general the protected domestic industries have never become efficient enough to compete on world markets. So the countries which concentrated on producing the goods in which they had a comparative advantage and exporting them performed better. Brazil was an exponent of import substitution for many years but has largely abandoned it in recent times.

**impulse purchase:** an unplanned decision to buy a product or brand. Certain types of product are especially prone to impulse purchase, such as confectionery and snacks. This makes it worthwhile for retailers to display the items prominently (such as by the checkout) as impulse purchase products generate extra takings. If a manufacturer knows that its products are mainly bought on impulse it is likely to:

• increase spending on packaging design and display materials at the point of sale

• offer high retail profit margins in order to maximise distribution and give the shops a strong incentive to display the product in an eye-catching position

**incentives:** financial or equivalent rewards (such as free holidays) to stimulate action from staff or customers. On a wider level, the term may be used to refer to groups of people who, for example, lack the incentive to work because they are in the *poverty trap*. Incentives can be vital in ensuring that the allocation of resources reflects the pattern of consumer demand. People may need an incentive to move from one kind of production to another.

**incidence of taxation** analyses the extent to which a specific expenditure tax falls upon the consumer or the producer. Depending on the price elasticity of demand for the produce, the producer may or may not be able to pass the tax on to the consumer by raising the price.

A tax will shift the supply curve upwards by the exact amount of the tax. The more inelastic the demand is, the easier it will be for the seller to pass the tax on to the consumer in the form of a higher price (P₁ in the diagram). If demand is elastic, then consumers will simply buy less of the product as the price rises, and the producer will have to absorb at least a part of the tax (Ep minus f₂ in the second diagram). Taxes on items with elastic demand will reduce the quantity bought and have little effect on the price, while taxes on items with inelastic demand will discourage consumption relatively little but lead to an increase in price close to the amount of the tax.

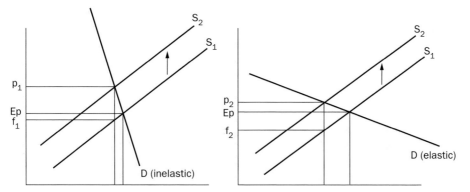

Ep is the market equilibrium price
p₁ and p₂ are the prices to the consumer after tax
f₁ and f₂ are the prices received by the producer after tax has been paid

*Incidence of taxation*

**income** is a flow of money which acts as a reward for the services of a *factor of production*. Wages and salaries are a reward to labour, and are described as earned income. Unearned income includes rent, interest and profit: rent is a reward for the owner of land or property. *Profit* gives a return on capital invested and also the efforts of *entrepreneurs*. Interest is return on a capital sum which is loaned to someone else.

**income and expenditure account:** the equivalent of a *profit and loss account* that records the year's trading for a non-profit-making organisation such as a charity or club.

**income distribution:** see *distribution of income*

**income effect:** when there is a change in a price, that change will have an income and a substitution effect. The substitution effect shows how quantity consumed changes in response to the change in that price compared to all other prices. Thus if foreign holidays become more expensive, the substitution effect will lead to more holidays being taken closer to home. The income effect shows the effect on consumption of the change in real income which occurs when a price changes. The rise in the price of foreign holidays causes a fall in real income because it reduces purchasing power. This will mean a tendency for consumption of everything, not just foreign holidays, to fall. Items with very low prices will have a very small income effect.

**income elasticity** measures the way in which *demand* changes when consumers' *real incomes* change.

FORMULA: $\dfrac{\text{percentage change in demand}}{\text{percentage change in real incomes}} = \text{income elasticity}$

## incomes policy

There are two main elements in a product's income elasticity. The first is whether it is a positive or negative figure. For example, if the demand for sausages fell by 2 per cent in a year when real incomes were boosted by 5 per cent, the income elasticity of sausages would be 2% ÷ 5% = −0.4. That the figure might be negative is because in years of prosperity, consumers buy more expensive, luxurious foods. Most goods, however, have positive income elasticity, meaning that people buy more of them when they are better off. The term 'normal goods' is given to these products, whereas those with negative income elasticity are known as 'inferior goods'.

The second key element is the degree of elasticity. As with price elasticity, a value of more than one indicates an elastic demand, while less than one means inelastic demand. Luxury items will tend to be highly income elastic, in other words quite a small drop in the living standards of consumers can lead to a substantial fall in demand for expensive sports cars, perfumes or whiskies.

Income elasticities can change significantly over the life cycle of a product. The motorbike, for instance, was a great success in the UK as incomes rose to the point where people could afford one as opposed to a bicycle. As incomes rose further, a small car became affordable and the demand for motorbikes fell, making it an inferior good at this point. Then, as incomes rose to the point where the motorbike became a recreational vehicle, income elasticity became positive once more.

Businesses selling goods and services with low income elasticity will be less vulnerable during a recession than those selling goods and services with high income elasticities. Producers of biscuits might hardly notice a recession while producers of yachts may go out of business due to lack of demand.

**Worked example: Market research reveals that following an increase in disposable income of 10 per cent, the demand for aftershave rises by 22 per cent. What is the income elasticity of demand for aftershave?**

Formula: Income elasticity of demand $= \dfrac{\text{percentage change in demand}}{\text{percentage change in income}}$

so in this example: $\dfrac{22\%}{10\%} = \mathbf{+2.2}$

**incomes policy** was used during the 1960s and 1970s as a way of controlling inflation. Usually, it meant that pay increases were limited to a certain percentage. Such policies were never very successful because they prevented wages from adjusting fully to market forces.

**income tax** is paid as a proportion of an individual's gross pay after certain allowances have been deducted. It is levied in a series of steps designed to ensure that no one can become worse off by moving into a higher tax band. The Chancellor of the Exchequer changes the tax rates every year. The following example assumes income tax bands at the 2002 level.

| Income between | Tax rate (%) |
| --- | --- |
| 0–£4615 | 0 |
| £4616–£6536 | 10 |
| £6537–£35 025 | 22 (basic rate) |
| £35 026 upwards | 40 (higher rate) |

**Worked example:**

| | Toby earns £15 000 per year | | Jill earns £50 000 per year | |
|---|---|---|---|---|
| | Tax % | Tax due | Tax % | Tax due |
| 0–£4615 | 0 | 0 | 0 | 0 |
| £4616–£6536 | 10 | £192 | 10 | £192 |
| £6537–£35 025 | 22 | £1862 | 22 | £6267 |
| £35 026 upwards | 40 | 0 | 40 | £5990 |
| Total tax | | £2054 | | £12 449 |
| As % of income | | 13.7% | | 24.9% |

Although all taxes are undesirable from the view point of those who must pay them, income tax has particular strengths and weaknesses compared with other ways of raising government revenue. Many people approve of its progressive nature; that is, it takes an increasing share of income from higher income earners (thereby reducing the burden on the less well off). Many of the better off feel that this is unfair however. In the above example, Jill is earning three times more than Toby, yet paying six times the tax bill. A further argument against income tax is that it acts as a disincentive to work hard or seek promotion (because the government takes 22 or 40 per cent of every extra pound earned). Research has never been able to prove this theory, however.

**incorporation:** the process of becoming a corporate body, that is establishing a business as a separate legal entity. Before incorporation the owners of the business are liable personally for all of its debt. Becoming incorporated requires these steps:

● preparing a *memorandum of association*

● preparing *articles of association*

● sending these to the *Registrar of Companies* and applying for a certificate of incorporation.

**increasing returns to scale** occur if output can be increased using a proportionally smaller quantity of inputs. It will tend to be associated with economies of scale.

**indebtedness** is the extent to which a business or a government owes money to banks or international organisations.

**independent variable:** where there is a relationship between two variables, one may be determined by something else and thus be termed independent. In the relationship between income and consumption, consumption is seen as depending on income, while income, the independent variable, is determined by a whole range of other things such as the level of investment, the level of government spending and the level of exports. It is therefore treated as being independent.

**indexing:** see *index-linked*

**index-linked** means linking a value specifically to the changes in the *retail prices index* (RPI) (the standard measure of *inflation* in the UK). Thus pensions or some forms of savings may be indexed or index-linked so that their real value is preserved.

**index numbers** are a convenient way of showing change in a set of data over time, called *time-series analysis*. Let us say a company had 28,000 employees in 2000, 33,600 in 2001 and 39,200 in 2002. If we make 2000 the base year and let the value for 2000 be equal to 100, then the other values are set relative to this. Therefore, in 2001 the index would be 120 ($33{,}600/28{,}000 \times 100$) and in 2002 it would be 140. The index series tells us quickly that in 2001 employment rose by 20 per cent compared with 2000 and in 2002 by 40 per cent compared with 2000. As the table shows, the benefit of indexing is that it makes trends understandable at a glance.

|  | Staff total | Staff index (2000 = 100) |
|---|---|---|
| 2000 | 28 000 | 100 |
| 2001 | 33 600 | 120 |
| 2002 | 39 200 | 140 |

**indicators** help to show what is happening in the economy. Leading indicators foreshadow changes to come: an increase in machine tool production indicated that an increase in output is likely.

**indicative planning** is a process whereby the government produces a plan for the whole economy which may help individual businesses and organisations to make their own plans in order to fit in with it. Indicative planning was widely practiced during the 1960s and is now rather out of fashion.

**indifference curve:** a line graph showing a set of combinations of two products, each of which is equally acceptable to the consumer. As part of revealed preference theory, indifference curves can be used to analyse the effect of price changes.

**indirect cost:** a cost not directly attributable to a product line or a *cost centre*. It is probably, but not necessarily, a *fixed cost*. An example might be general maintenance charges in a factory.

**indirect labour:** those employees such as office and cleaning staff who are not involved directly in the process of production or customer service.

**indirect taxation** is tax paid on goods and services, as opposed to *direct taxation* which is paid on income and profits. Examples of indirect taxation include *VAT* and *excise duty*. Indirect taxes are usually regressive, that is to say they take a higher proportion of a poor person's income than a rich person's. In 1979, the UK shifted the burden of taxation away from direct taxation to indirect, on the grounds that direct taxes are a disincentive to working harder or longer.

**individual bargaining** occurs when a firm negotiates with each employee in turn over salary levels and terms of employment. This takes place either when there is no *trade union* to undertake *collective bargaining*, or when individuals believe they can do better than the generally negotiated terms.

**individual savings accounts:** (ISAs) a type of tax-free savings scheme designed to encourage more people to save. ISAs can include cash savings, shares and life assurance policies. The interest received is not taxed.

**indivisibility** is the machine utilisation problem that some equipment may be built to a large scale and not be divisible into smaller units. If all a firm needs is 600 units a week, but the smallest machine produces 1 500, it will have to accept operating permanently at only 40 per cent of capacity. This will push up *fixed costs per unit* and put a small producer at a considerable cost disadvantage.

**induced expenditure** is spending, the level of which is determined by the level of income. Consumption, saving and tax revenue are all induced, within the framework of the basic Keynesian model of the macroeconomy.

**induction** is an introductory training programme designed to familiarise new recruits with the layout, health and safety, and security systems within the firm. The new employees might also be introduced to key personnel.

In economic theory induction is a process by which relationships may be inferred from specific observations. The process may start with an examination of the data and from this a hypothesis may be worked out.

**industrial action:** measures taken by the workforce that will halt or slow output, in order to put pressure on management during an *industrial dispute*. Types of industrial action include: *strike*, work-to-rule, and *go-slow*.

**industrial advertising:** promoting products to industrial customers such as the owners of heavy lorry fleets, or the buyers of components such as gearboxes. As the target markets tend to be small, *direct mail* is often used, though so too are advertisements in trade or industrial magazines such as THE ENGINEER.

**industrial democracy** means the attempt to provide a workforce with channels through which the decision-making powers of the organisation can be influenced. *Trade unions* tend to be sceptical of the motive behind management initiatives in this area, suspecting that either the intention is to undermine the role of the union, or that the channels provided will only give a facade of democracy. Nevertheless, when used in the right spirit, the following forms of industrial democracy can be very successful:

● *worker director*, i.e. a board director elected to the board from and by the factory floor

● *works council*, a regular meeting point between management and unions

● *workers' cooperative*, i.e. the firm's workers owning a majority of the shares, thereby giving them a great interest in its success or failure

**industrial dispute:** a disagreement between management and the *trade union* representatives of the workforce that is serious enough for *industrial action* to be considered. The dispute might be resolved by successful *conciliation* or *arbitration*. Otherwise the union will consider balloting its members on whether to take industrial action.

**industrial espionage** means using the semi-legal or even illegal techniques of spies to gain information about a competitor or customer. Although this sounds far-fetched, there have been several past cases where major firms have used private detectives in this way. What this demonstrates is the enormous importance placed on information. Just as in a war, finding out the enemy's battle plans is invaluable, so in a *take-over* battle, businesses have gone to extraordinary lengths to find out their rival's next move.

**industrial inertia** is used to describe the situation when a firm or an industry stays in its original location after the reasons for its being there in the first place have disappeared. Reasons for industrial inertia include:

● the costs of upheaval may be too great to justify a move

● there may be external *economies of scale* which justify it in staying where it is, such as local colleges which specialise in training the precise skills needed in the industry

- there may be marketing advantages which derive from a traditional location, such as Sheffield steel or Scotch whisky

(See also *industrial location*.)

**industrialisation** is the process by which a country may move from dependence on primary production to having a developed manufacturing sector. Many developing countries are in the process of this transition at the present time: for example, Mexico, India, Indonesia and many others.

**industrial location:** the decision taken on the geographical placing of firms and industries. The location of *heavy industry* was often based on the notion of '*bulk increasing*' or '*bulk decreasing*' goods. This meant that if the industrial process gained weight it would be located as near to the consumer as possible, whereas if it lost weight in the process it would be placed as near to the raw material source as possible. The soft drinks industry gains weight by adding water and so, for instance, Coca-Cola was originally sold to retailers in the form of a syrup to which soda was added at the point of sale. Even when Coke was sold in bottles, the syrup was sent to local bottling plants so that the relatively heavy product did not need to be transported very far. On the other hand, the steel industry is a considerable weight loser, and so it is located as close to its main raw materials – coal, iron ore and limestone – as possible. Today the bulk increasing/bulk reducing theory applies less because transport costs are a smaller proportion of total costs than they were. Communication links are better and the growth of the service sector has inevitably spread locations towards the consumer.

In recent years, it has been argued that profit-maximising behaviour is not always followed by some managers who locate in an area which is pleasant enough to suit their employees or themselves. Often, firms start up in a location close to the proprietor's home. This site may be clung to for many years after it has ceased to be economic to stay there (see *industrial inertia*). Also governments have affected some location decisions by offering *grants* and other incentives (see *regional policy*). This has affected the decisions of *multinationals* who are able to locate in whichever country minimises their costs.

**industrial policy:** the government's strategy for boosting economic growth by improving industrial competitiveness. This might mean making fiscal, monetary and foreign currency decisions on the basis of business needs, including:

- increasing government spending on transport and communication infrastructure
- keeping interest rates relatively low
- keeping the pound at a competitive level on the foreign exchange markets.

**industrial relations:** the atmosphere prevailing between a management and its workforce representatives, the *trade unions*. Anything that damages the relationship between the two sides might destroy the element of trust that is the key to good industrial relations.

**industrial union:** an organisation founded to look after the collective interests of all types of employee within a specific industry, e.g. the National Union of Mineworkers (NUM). Whereas most unions represent workers with a particular type of skill from many different industries (e.g. electricians), an industrial union would have clerical, skilled and unskilled members, all working in the same industry.

**inelastic demand** is where for a given percentage change in price there is a proportionately lower change in quantity demanded. It is the situation of a product that has low price sensitivity because consumers need it or think they need it. Examples of goods with inelastic demand are necessities like fuel and heavily branded items such as Levi's. If the price of Levi's rises by 10 per cent then demand might only fall by 5 per cent. In this case, the numerical value of its price elasticity would be: $-5\% \div 10\% = -0.5$. Any good having inelastic demand would have a lower number at the top (the numerator) than at the bottom (the denominator), and therefore the final value will always be less than one, but greater than zero. (Because quantity demanded almost always goes down when the price rises, the minus sign is often ignored.)

**inequality:** a situation in which there are large differences in incomes and wealth within a society. Most developed countries in Europe have a lower level of inequality than do most developing countries or the USA. Inequality has tended to increase everywhere in recent years. Inequality can be reduced by *progressive taxes* and *social security* benefits. (See also *equity*.)

**infant industries** are those just starting which are seen as needing protection from overseas competition. The argument is based on the notion that the industry will only be competitive once it has achieved *economies of scale* and therefore it needs protection until that has been achieved. This is particularly relevant to developing countries which may find it difficult to develop any industries in the face of international competition. However there are drawbacks to using import controls to protect domestic industries. There may be considerable difficulty in deciding when the industry no longer needs protection; in the meantime consumers will be paying more for the product than they would for imports. The costs to consumers may be very high.

**inferior good:** a product for which demand rises when real incomes fall. This happens because the item is bought as a cheap substitute for a product thought more desirable. Examples include supermarket *own-label* brands, to which people turn when trying to economise. Inferior goods come into their own during *recessions*, when falling standards of living force consumers to switch to more economical products. A manufacturer that produces a range of products, half of which are inferior goods, would be in an excellent position to cope with the *business cycle*.

**inflation** is a sustained rise in the average prices of goods within an economy. It is also useful to understand it as a fall in the purchasing power of money. If inflation reaches very high levels it is known as *hyperinflation*.

The causes of inflation are complex. Until the twentieth century, inflation was very infrequent and the price level was as likely to fall as to rise. Until the late 1960s, inflation remained at a relatively low level in most developed countries. Then it became much more volatile.

The precipitating cause of accelerating inflation is *excess demand* in the economy as a whole. This occurs when aggregate demand is growing faster than the capacity of the economy to supply. At first there will be evidence of skill shortages, and it will become clear that sellers can raise prices and still sell the goods. Firms will raise wages to attract the scarce skills they need to increase output. Trade unions will find it easier to negotiate pay rises.

Once inflation is accelerating it will tend to continue because of people's *expectations*. All employees will try to protect their real earnings by negotiating an increase equal to what they expect inflation to be. (See *inflationary expectations* and *inflationary spiral*.)

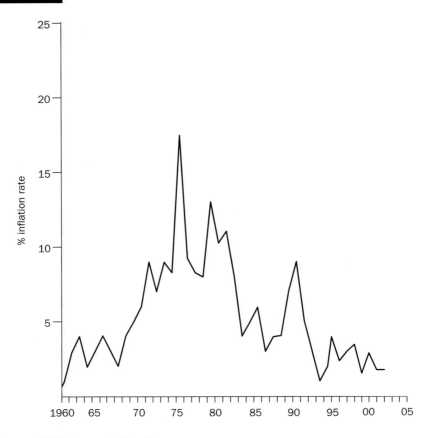

*Source: ONS, Economic Trends*

The monetarist view of inflation holds that it is caused by excessive increases in the money supply. As bank lending increases, borrowers are able to increase spending, leading to the excess demand already described.

Inflation has numerous consequences:

- for firms and households which have borrowed substantially, inflation reduces the real value of the sum outstanding, making it easier to repay the loan at the end of its life. For example, if a firm borrowed £4m. 10 years ago, and inflation since then had doubled the price level, the loan would be much easier to repay from the firm's doubled level of income. During the 1970s and 1980s, home owners typically made large capital gains as the value of their homes rose while the scale of their debt fell

- inflation increases uncertainty. While a stable rate of inflation may appear predictable, in practice, the higher the rate of inflation, the more volatile it has proved to be. This makes planning difficult for firms and individuals.

- consumers become increasingly sensitive to prices. This may benefit small producers, as theirs are usually the more *price-elastic* products. The producers of major brands suffer as the regularity of price increases in the shops causes *brand-loyal* customers to look at prices instead of just picking their favourite from the shelf. They may switch towards the more competitively priced items, thereby reducing the *value added* by brand names. The owners of the brands must either cut their price premiums, or greatly increase their advertising expenditure in order to restore their value added

- employees become far more concerned about their wage levels, for unless they can obtain a pay rise at least as high as the level of inflation, their *real income* will fall. Therefore *industrial relations* can worsen sharply in inflationary times, with workers pushing their union representatives to be far more forceful about pay increases.

*Contractionary policies* may be used to control inflation. Strict control of the growth of the money supply reduces aggregate demand, and pressures in the labour market. In time, people's expectations of inflation will fall and they will accept lower pay increases. However this process in the early 1980s and 1990s proved to be slow, and to entail a considerable rise in unemployment. *Incomes policies* were favoured in the 1960s and 70s.

Inflation is currently subdued and some have even suggested that it may be dead. It is too soon to be sure about this. There may still be inflationary pressures ready to build up in the economy if skill shortages become persistent. *Exchange rate* changes or commodity price rises could have an impact. The *Monetary Policy Committee* of the Bank of England comments on this regularly.

**inflation accounting** is the attempt to eliminate the distorting effects of price rises from the underlying financial position of a firm. The most common method is *current cost accounting*, which values *assets* and *profits* on the basis of current replacement cost instead of *historic cost*. The complexities of this procedure have prevented it from being adopted widely by the accounting profession.

**inflationary expectations** are the views of the general public as to what will happen to the rate of *inflation* in the future. Usually, people anticipate that a period of rising inflation will continue into the future. For example, if the rate of inflation has risen from 4 per cent a year ago to 7 per cent today, people are likely to expect inflation to be 10 per cent by the same time next year. Therefore they might negotiate a pay rise of 10 per cent now in anticipation of that future level. By so doing, they add to costs and help to bring about that new level, so that their prophesy becomes self-fulfilling. (See *inflationary spiral*.)

**inflationary gap** occurs when *aggregate demand* is greater that *aggregate supply* and the economy is already producing its *full capacity output*.

**inflationary spiral** is the way in which price rises in one sector of the economy cause price increases in another, so that they spiral ever upwards. If prices rise, say because the money supply has been growing and there is too much *credit*, so that the *demand* for goods and services exceeds *supply*, prices rise and people will react by negotiating pay increases. One person's pay increase becomes another's price increase and so the spiral continues. Governments attempt to break the spiral by depressing demand within the economy or by imposing wage controls, such as the *public sector* pay increase limit of 1.5 per cent in 1993–4. The latter action inevitably causes a lowering of living standards, at least in some sections of the community, for while wages are held in check, prices for a time continue to rise, and so *real incomes* fall. (See *inflationary expectations*.)

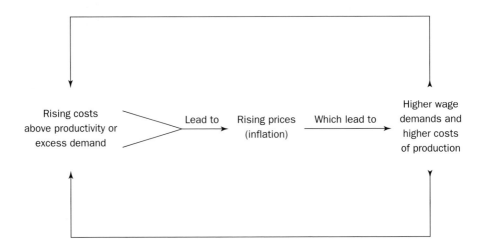

*Inflationary spiral*

**informal communication** means passing information outside the official channels. In a firm run on authoritarian lines this might be regarded as a serious breach of company discipline, especially if the message contained embarrassing information (such as details of a dangerous leak at a chemical plant). In a democratically run organisation, however, the management should not be attempting to keep secrets from the workforce, so informal communication should be accepted, even encouraged. After all, direct communication is often the quickest and most effective method, so why rely on the layers of hierarchy within the official channels?

There is, however, a danger of confusing informal with oral communication. This would be wrong because you can communicate written messages to the 'wrong' person just as easily as oral ones.

**informal economy:** that part of economic activity which is not recorded in official statistics. This includes all kinds of voluntary and domestic work, and work done for cash payments which are not declared for tax purposes. Some of this is legal but much of it consists of tax evasion or leads to fraudulent benefit claims. The amount of income which is not declared is difficult to determine and estimates vary within the range 5% to 10% of *Gross Domestic Product*. The value of voluntary work is impossible to quantify.

**informal group:** a group of employees who influence each other's behaviour and attitudes, either for or against the company's best interests. It was a key discovery of Elton *Mayo* that such groups were common, especially in organisations with weak *human relations*. He found that such groups often had unofficial leaders who wielded more effective power than the department head, especially in the setting of *group norms* regarding the work rate considered acceptable.

**informal leader:** the unofficial head of an *informal group*.

**information technology (IT)** includes the use of three electronic technologies: computing, telecommunications and microelectronics, and the way they gather, store, process and distribute information. The use of IT within an organisation tends to reflect the prevailing management style. Supermarket chains tend to concentrate on its potential for collecting vast quantities of data at shop-floor level and then transmitting it for head office analysis. So those at the top of the management hierarchy are pulling information up and then passing decisions back down to local branches. A leadership with a more democratic approach would use computer networks to allow information to flow more freely throughout the staff. This would provide an empowered workforce with the information needed for sound decision-making.

**informative advertising:** paid-for communication that provides messages based on facts rather than images. An extreme example is 'Car Boot Sale, Saturday 2.00, Town Hall'. Less clear-cut are the newspaper advertisements for electrical goods shops that scream persuasively about their sale bargains, but also provide information about prices and product specifications. The key issue about informative advertising is that it is unarguably in the public interest to be provided with useful facts. Information about prices and product ranges offered by different shops helps competition by encouraging people to shop around. When advertising is under attack from critics of its persuasive powers, the defence is often to point to the benefits of the information it provides.

**infrastructure** is the name given to the road, rail and air links, sewage and telephone systems and other basic utilities which provide a network that benefits business and the community. One of the main advantages which industrialised countries have over less developed ones is the existence of an efficient infrastructure. Building up such a system is very expensive, requiring a great deal of *capital* to be set aside, capital which poorer countries find difficult to afford. Successive British governments have been criticised for allowing our transport infrastructure to fall behind that of our main European competitors.

**inheritance tax** is currently levied on estates of more than £250,000 at a rate of 40 per cent. It thus works to create a more equal distribution of inherited wealth. (2002 figures)

**Initial Public Offering (IPO):** when shares are offered for sale to the general public for the first time. This phrase emerged in 1999 and 2000, during the wave of flotations of young, often loss-making companies. IPOs often involve the sale of fewer than 25 per cent of the shares; power therefore remains with the founders.

**injections** are items adding to the *circular flow of national income* and consist of government expenditure, exports and investment spending. They are 'matched' by *withdrawals* from the circular flow: taxes, imports and savings. When injections increase, there will be an increase in *aggregate demand*, which will have a *multiplier* effect on the economy.

**innovation** means bringing a new idea into being within the market-place (product innovation) or workplace (process innovation).

Product innovation is of major competitive significance because consumers tend to fall into patterns of purchasing behaviour that change little over time. Therefore the *market shares* of the rival products may be quite static. Product innovation can change that, to the considerable advantage of the innovator. The sources of the innovation may be based on new technology, new design or a wholly new *invention*. In recent years, James Dyson has been among Britain's leading innovators, with his cyclone floor cleaner a huge worldwide success.

Process innovation is also of great significance as it can lead to major cost advantages over competitors. When the British firm Pilkington PLC invented a new way of making glass more cheaply and to a far higher quality standard (the float glass process), it provided not only a direct competitive advantage, but also earned considerable sums in licensing fees from overseas manufacturers.

Product innovation can often play a major part in improving standards of living. The telephone is not a new product, but today's instrument is very much cheaper and more efficient than its predecessors. Process innovation is of crucial importance in leading to the growth of productivity, and ultimately to long-term *economic growth*.

**inorganic growth** occurs when a business takes over or merges with another company, thus becoming immediately bigger.

**inputs** are the elements which go into producing a good or service such as the workforce, raw materials, components and capital.

**in-service training:** courses run to broaden, update or enhance the job knowledge of those at work.

**insider dealing or trading:** profiting personally from the use of information gained from the privilege of working within an organisation. For example, if a manager knew that his or her firm was about to make a *take-over bid* of £1.40 for a firm whose shares are currently £1, a guaranteed overnight profit of 40 per cent is there for the taking. Some say this is a victimless crime, because no one loses money directly. In fact, the manager has taken advantage of the shareholder who unwittingly sold at too low a price (£1). Insider dealing is illegal, but it has proved very hard to convict those caught doing it.

**insolvency** occurs when a firm's external *liabilities* are greater than its *assets*. In practice, this is likely to be revealed through the inability to meet financial obligations, e.g. the inability to raise the necessary cash through ordinary operations, asset sales or borrowing so as to make payments as they fall due. A business which continues to trade when insolvent is operating illegally.

**Insolvency Act 1986:** the legislation that sets out the possible ways of dealing with an insolvent company. The options include:

- a voluntary agreement between the company and its creditors to restart the business
- putting the company into *administration* to try to reorganise the company in the best interests of shareholders and creditors
- *winding up* the company if there appears no way of saving it; this might be conducted by the administrator or by the appointment of a *receiver.*

**Institute of Directors (IOD):** an employers' *pressure group* that has a stronger representation among small and service businesses than its main rival, the *Confederation of British Industry*. The IOD lobbies the government to try to obtain the economic and legal conditions that most benefit its members.

**Institute of Management (IM):** the professional association of managers that acts as a *pressure group* and as a disseminator of good practice. In 1992 the organisation changed its name from the British Institute of Management.

**institutional investors** are those who manage the portfolios of the *pension funds*, *insurance companies* and *unit trust* groups which, between them, own a majority of the shares listed on the *Stock Exchange*. The influence of these financial institutions has given rise to a heated and important debate. Critics say that because the portfolio managers' performance is measured every year, they focus too much on the short-term share price performance of the firms they have invested in. This, in turn, makes them put too much pressure on companies to produce high short-term profits and *dividend* pay-outs. Few doubt that *short-termism* is a major competitive weakness of British industry; institutional investors may be one of its causes.

**insurance** is the principle by which risks are shared between all those who wish to protect themselves from unforseen eventualities. To insure against a risk, a premium is paid. The insurance company then pays compensation if the risky event happens. The premiums paid provide the necessary funds for compensation, together with an amount which covers the insurance companies' administrative costs.

**insurance companies** provide different types of *insurance* cover. Their accumulated premiums are invested in a range of assets. This makes them very important as *institutional investors* on the stock exchange.

**intangible assets:** *assets* are intangible when they do not have a physical existence, i.e. cannot be 'touched'. Whereas *plant* and equipment are tangible, *goodwill* (the value of brand names) is intangible. This is the most common example as it frequently arises when business assets are sold. Other intangibles include *patents, trademarks* and *copyrights*.

**integration** is a term used in two ways. It may refer to the bringing together of two or more companies, either by *take-over* or *merger*. (See *vertical integration*, *horizontal integration* and *conglomerate mergers*.)

Alternatively it may refer to the way in which the economies of different nation states become interdependent. For example, the EU is a powerful force for integration within Europe.

**intellectual property** derives from the invention or ownership of *patents*, *trade marks*, *logos* or any other *copyright* material. If it can be given a monetary value it can be listed on a firm's *balance sheet* as an *intangible asset*. Intellectual property may give its owner some degree of monopoly power. Often, intellectual property rights can only be protected by legal action.

**Inter-American Development Bank:** provides development finance to Latin American and Caribbean countries. It provides funds at both commercial and concessional rates of interest.

**inter-bank market** is the mechanism by which banks lend to each other on a very short-term basis to cover temporary deficits in their payments to each other.

**interdependence** is a term used in two ways. It refers to the way in which the economies of nation states have become increasingly reliant on one another in recent years, through the growth of trade and capital movements. It is also used to describe the way businesses in an oligopoly will each take decisions in the light of the behaviour, or the expected reactions, of the other firms in the industry.

**interest** is the return on capital which has been lent. The terms of a loan will usually specify a fixed percentage rate, or they may provide for the rate to rise and fall with interest rates generally.

**interest rates** represent the cost of borrowing money or, to put it the other way, the return for lending funds or for parting with *liquidity*. Interest rates also measure *opportunity cost* in that individuals give up the interest on their money by spending it on consumer goods rather than saving and receiving interest. Firms considering an investment project do so on the basis of whether the return from the project will exceed the interest paid if they borrow. If they use their own funds they forgo interest: this is the opportunity cost of the investment. Returns should exceed the interest lost.

Interest rates can also be a key weapon of economic policy. If the Bank of England pushes interest rates up, consumer and business spending is likely to fall. High interest rates can also be used to support the exchange rate by attracting flows of short-term currency into the country. The Bank of England, in common with many other central banks, does not have any easy way of controlling the supply of money, i.e. the amount banks are prepared to lend. But through its control of interest rates, it can influence the demand for money, that is, the amount businesses and individuals want to borrow.

**inter-firm comparison** is evaluation of a firm's financial performance by comparing it with one or more firms in the same industry and of a similar size. It is a commonly used method for interpreting financial ratios. For example, it is hard to know how to judge in isolation the knowledge that a firm has a *debtor days* figure of 68. If told that its closest rival's figure is 50, however, it would be clear that there are questions that need to be answered.

Useful though inter-firm comparison can be, however, it has significant limitations:

- different firms are likely to have different accounting methods (one may depreciate assets over three years, another over five years), indeed, some may be *window-dressing* their accounts; in either case the value of the comparison would be undetermined

- there is no legal requirement that firms break down their accounts into their separate operating units; a shareholder wanting to compare Cadbury's ratios with those of Mars might not be aware that the Mars accounts comprise not only confectionery but also Pedigree Petfoods (Chum, Whiskas, etc.); this would render the comparison meaningless.

**interim accounts** are those produced (and sometimes published) halfway through the financial year.

**intermediaries:** people within the official *communication channels*, through which messages must be passed in order to reach the intended receiver. As the diagram on the next page shows, if employee A wants to communicate with manager J, the message has to go via intermediaries C, F and H. This will slow the message down and may lead to it becoming distorted. Even worse, C, F or H may either forget to send it on, or decide it is not worth passing on. Therefore the greater the number of intermediaries, the less effective the communication system. This is a fundamental problem for large firms and can represent a major *diseconomy of scale*.

**intermediate goods** are purchased by producers and include such products as materials and components (for short-term usage) or machinery and equipment for the long term.

**intermediate technology** can be used in situations where high technology methods of production are not appropriate. For example, in developing countries where wages are low it is often not cost-effective to use capital-intensive approaches. In addition, such an approach may worsen poverty by creating job losses. Intermediate technology uses imaginative ways of making people more productive but does not require expensive imported equipment. A wheelbarrow may be an improvement, for moving soil, on the traditional Indian method of a basket carried on the head. It does not reduce employment in the way that a JCB might.

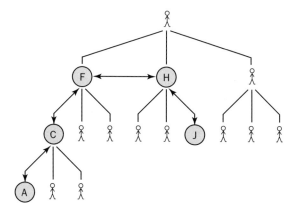

*Intermediaries*

**intermediate goods** are purchased by producers and include such products as materials and components (for short-term usage) or machinery and equipment for the long term.

**intermediate technology** can be used in situations where high technology methods of production are not appropriate. For example, in developing countries where wages are low it is often not cost-effective to use capital-intensive approaches. In addition, such an approach may worsen poverty by creating job losses. Intermediate technology uses imaginative ways of making people more productive but does not require expensive imported equipment. A wheelbarrow may be an improvement, for moving soil, on the traditional Indian method of a basket carried on the head. It does not reduce employment in the way that a JCB might.

**internal constraint:** a factor within the company's control that is restricting it from achieving its objectives. The main internal constraints are:

- finance: has the firm the *cash flow*, the borrowing capacity or the profitability to finance its plans?

- marketing: does the firm have the marketing assets required, be it a brand name with a suitable image, or the distribution strength needed for success?

- people: have the staff the skills and experience to achieve what is required? If not, can retraining make up the ground?

- production: does the firm have the spare capacity to produce the volumes required?

(See also *external constraint*.)

**internal costs** are those expenditures that affect a firm's own accounts, such as wages and materials. This ignores the costs that the firm's actions may generate, but that may be incurred by other people or organisations.

**internal economies of scale:** see *economies of scale*

**internal financing:** the generation of cash from within the company's resources/accounts. This can be obtained from:

- *retained profits* (plus *depreciation*)

- *working capital* (by cutting stocks or *debtors*)

- the sale of *fixed assets* or under-performing divisions (for example, Grand Metropolitan financed the purchase of Burger King by selling off its hotels division).

**internal growth** arises from within a company, through increasing sales of existing products and/or the launch of new ones. This is likely to be a slower, steadier process than the alternative of buying up other firms (*external growth*). Even internal growth can be risky, however, if it is financed by debt. The ideal is expansion based upon reinvested profit.

**internal markets** can be created in large organisations such as the National Health Service in order to foster a spirit of competition and thereby encourage greater efficiency. The process requires that instead of just handing work over to the department that has always undertaken it, the job be given to whichever department can offer the lowest 'price'. In this way, less efficient departments will lose work and may therefore be forced to lose staff.

**internal rate of return (IRR)** is the discount rate which, when applied to a set of cash flows, makes their *net present value* equal to zero. The IRR can then be compared with the current market rate of interest, which represents the cost of capital. If the IRR is higher, the project is attractive. Alternatively, the company may set its own minimum discount rate as a criterion to test whether projects are viable and compare the IRR with that. The diagram below shows a project with an internal rate of return of 14 per cent. This beats the prevailing rate of interest (9 per cent) but does not meet the firm's own requirement of a 16 per cent minimum. Therefore the project would not be proceeded with (unless other, qualitative factors take precedence).

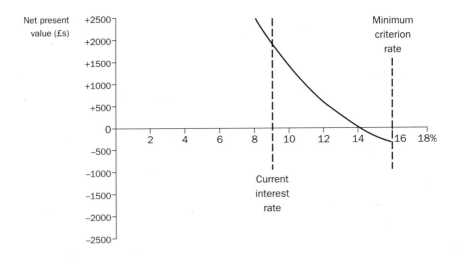

**International Bank for Reconstruction and Development** is the proper name of what is usually known as the World Bank. It was set up in 1947 along with the *International Monetary Fund*. Initially it was designed to provide finance for the post-war reconstruction of Europe and Japan. Quite quickly its primary focus shifted to the developing countries. It borrows funds on western capital markets, and lends them to *developing countries* for projects of many kinds including *infrastructure*, agriculture, industry, education and health. It charges commercial interest rates, but lends for purposes and in countries which banks might usually find too risky. Loans are often conditional on the adoption of particular policies, which may be unpopular. However this does mean that governments can shift the blame for necessary but unpalatable policies onto the World Bank.

Some of the World Bank's projects have been controversial. Although now anxious to promote environmentally sound policies, it has not always been so. Through its 'soft loan' arm, the *International Development Agency*, it lends to the poorest countries at concessional rates of interest. It also undertakes extensive research and advises developing country governments on economic policy.

**international competitiveness** measures the ability of firms to sell abroad and to compete with imports. It is determined by a number of factors, including price, quality, delivery and *after-sales service*. Such competitiveness will often be affected by the level of foreign *exchange rate*, though successful exporting countries can succeed despite high and rising exchange rates. This shows that the price of goods is often not the main determinant of competitiveness. Germany and Japan, for instance, have thrived through well-designed, high-quality products such as BMWs and Sony televisions that consumers are willing to pay a price premium for .

**International Development Agency (IDA)** is part of the International Bank for Reconstruction and Development (World Bank), undertaking lending on concessional terms. Interest rates may be lower on these loans, and they may be waived altogether for a period of time. These loans are available only to the poorest developing countries, and some of the projects supported are not strictly commercial, although they may have an important role in the development process.

**International Labour Organisation (ILO):** a member organisation of the United Nations, the ILO exists to help improve working conditions throughout the world. It maintains relationships with trade unions as well as governments, and seeks to promote social justice in the workplace.

**International Monetary Fund (IMF)** was set up at the Bretton Woods conference in 1944 and was designed to co-ordinate the international monetary system. Until 1972, it oversaw the system of fixed exchange rates which was in operation. Its objectives were to ensure the stability of the system and provide adequate finance to support the growth of world trade. Stability can itself promote trade, because it reduces uncertainty and makes forward planning easier and less risky.

Member countries contribute funds in proportion to the size of their economies. If they have problems with a persistent balance of trade deficit, they may negotiate a loan from the IMF. This will help to finance the deficit in the short term and allow time for economic policies to produce a long-term solution. Usually the IMF sends a team of inspectors to the borrower country; they advise on the conditions upon which the loan is provided. These conditions are likely to include cuts in *public expenditure* and control of monetary growth. The availability of loans helps to ensure that exchange rate changes are not excessively destabilising.

Since 1972, most exchange rates have floated. The IMF has continued to act as co-ordinator of the international monetary system, ensuring that the growth of liquidity was sufficient to finance world trade. Its role as a source of loans has increasingly been confined to developing countries. It continues to provide surveillance of all member economies, acting as a source of information and advice. It has had an important role in organising the developed countries' response to the *Debt Problem*.

During the *Asian financial crisis*, the IMF had a strong role in helping with funds and policy advice. However, its advice was widely criticised. In particular, the advice given to Indonesia to cut government spending and accept much higher import prices led to widespread political unrest which was anything but stabilising in its impact.

**International Standards Organisation (ISO) 9000/9002** is a worldwide quality certification procedure of exact equivalence to *BS 5750*.

**international trade** consists of *exports* and *imports*, both visible and invisible, between countries. Through the development of *comparative advantage*, international trade brings about an improvement in people's living standards. In the long run, there is a very clear link between international trade and *economic growth* (see bar chart below). Being able to buy a cheap imported substitute for a dearer domestic product can increase many people's purchasing power, giving them higher real incomes. However in the short run, some people may lose out as growing international competition forces the less competitive firms out of business and makes their employees redundant. This can lead to *protectionism*, a movement to reduce trade through *import controls*.

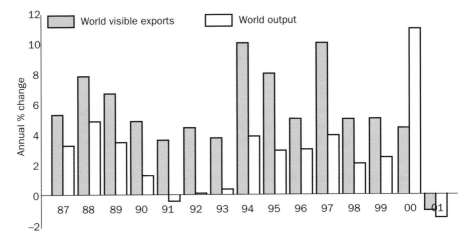

*International trade and output. Source: WTO, Annual Reports*

**inter-union disputes** are disagreements between two or more of the *trade unions* representing the workforce at a particular company. This might lead to internal bitterness or even *industrial action*, with the managers no more than onlookers.

**intervention** (in foreign currency markets) is when a *central bank* steps in to buy or sell a currency in order to stabilise its exchange rate. (See also *fixed exchange rate*.)

**interventionist:** an individual who believes that government intervention can help to make markets more efficient, and protect individuals from socially irresponsible business behaviour. Such a person is also likely to promote an active economic policy by government, as opposed to a *laissez-faire* approach.

**interventionist policies** are those pursued by governments that believe it is their duty to exert a strong influence over the running of a country's economy. Such intervention might include 'rescue packages' to help out large firms which have got into financial trouble and laws to provide stronger protection to consumers or workers. Many interventionist policies were derived from *Keynesian* beliefs that the state could help to iron out the extremes of the *business cycle*. They were much in evidence in the UK from the early 1940s until 1979, when Mrs Thatcher's Conservative Government came to power. The new Prime Minister believed that government should stand back from the detailed working of the economy because markets are the most efficient way to allocate resources. Government's role, she argued, is simply to provide an efficient background against which markets can work. The theory on which this is based is called *supply side* economics.

Among the most-favoured policies of interventionists are:

**Economic policy**
- active support for new or manufacturing firms
- *regional policy*
- *counter-cyclical* action
- faith in using *fiscal policies*

**Policy towards business**
- tougher laws and higher fines for polluting and dangerous workplaces
- *wages councils* and industrial training boards
- controls on boardroom pay levels.

**interviewing** is the process of obtaining information through questioning conducted face to face or over the telephone. There are two main business circumstances in which interviewing is used: as part of a job selection process and as part of a *market research* study. In either case, the interview can use *closed questions* to obtain specific (and quantifiable) information, or *open questions* that allow attitudes and ideas to emerge.

**intra-firm comparison** evaluates performance within the firm, often by using financial ratios. There are two methods of conducting this comparison: over time and between departments.

Comparisons over time give managers, shareholders and creditors an impression of the firm's progress. If a firm's *acid test ratio* this year is 0.6, it would be very reassuring to hear that last year it was 0.5 and the previous year 0.4. For internal users of the accounts, comparisons over time give important messages about trends in the firm's performance in relation to its objectives. External users, however, may be handicapped if the firm has changed its accounting practices or indulged in *window-dressing*.

Comparisons between departments are an essential piece of management analysis. Only if the firm knows that department A is obtaining a 30 per cent return on capital, while B generates only 12 per cent, can it decide how best to allocate its *capital expenditure* for coming years.

**intranet:** links between computers within a company to provide the same facilities to browse information and send e-mails that exist worldwide on the *Internet*. The advantage of an internal Internet (intranet) is that information confidential to the company can be published internally without outsiders having access. Glaxo, for example, uses an intranet to keep its research scientists up to date with discoveries made throughout the business.

**intrinsic motivation** means a drive to succeed that is from within the person. It occurs when individuals are doing a task they find satisfying, challenging or significant in the achievement of a meaningful goal. These are the drives that Professor *Herzberg* called the motivators, and can be contrasted with causes of *extrinsic motivation* such as pay and fringe benefits.

**invention** the creation of a new product or process. If it represents a scientific or technical first, an invention can be *patented* to ensure that any user of the idea must pay royalties to the inventor. Britain has an impressive record at invention (including penicillin and the hovercraft), but a far poorer record at achieving the crucial next stage: *innovation*, i.e. bringing new ideas to the market-place.

**inventory** another term for *stock*

**inverse relationship:** when two *variables* are related, such that they move in opposite directions, they are said to be inversely related. For example, quantity demanded is usually inversely related to price. As the price rises, consumers will be discouraged from buying the product.

**investment** means doing without consumption today in order to use *capital* to generate future returns. To an economist, investment means the purchase of capital equipment such as *plant* and machinery. On the *stock market*, investment means buying shares. In accounting terminology, investment might be in *fixed assets* or *working capital*. On the macroeconomic level, investment is important because it increases productive capacity and promotes *economic growth*. Investment spending is an injection into the circular flow of money and will have an upward *multiplier* effect on income.

**investment appraisal:** the set of techniques for determining whether a capital investment project should be undertaken or not, or for ranking investment projects in order of desirability. The techniques include methods using *discounted cash flows* such as *net present value* and *internal rate of return*, as well as *average rate of return* and *payback*. The advantage of using appraisal methods is that they avoid reliance on *hunch* or intuition alone. Nevertheless, it should be remembered that all four quantitative techniques are based on a forecast of the *cash flows* from an investment, which is not only subject to many variables but also to *bias* on the part of the forecaster.

**Investors in People (IIP)** is a government standard for employee consultation and training that establishes a procedure for 'relating training to your business plan'. In order to achieve the standard, assessors will ask:

- have goals been set for the business?
- have these been explained to the workers?
- have workers the right skills to meet those targets?

**invisible export:** the sale of a service to an overseas customer. As well as services such as banking, airline travel and insurance, visits by foreign tourists are counted as invisible exports, since they bring income in from overseas.

**invisible hand:** Adam *Smith's* famous term for the way the free market successfully and efficiently brings together willing sellers and willing buyers (through the *price mechanism*). If the product loses popularity, the lack of *demand* will force the price down, so that producers begin to make losses. In time they will cut production, and fewer resources will be devoted to the product which has become less popular. The reverse happens when demand increases. Profits will be made and will attract resources into the industry. In this way the profit-signalling mechanism in the market-place will invisibly secure an allocation of resources which balances supply and *demand*. Adam Smith believed that people acting entirely out of self-interest unwittingly serve the community as a whole through the operation of this 'invisible hand'.

**invisible import:** the purchase of a service from an overseas supplier.

**invisible trade** consists of imports and exports of services. They include financial services such as banking and insurance, as well as tourism and shipping. Invisibles account for approximately a quarter of world trade. Traditionally, the UK has enjoyed a surplus of invisibles, which has helped to pay for the long-standing deficit on *visible trade*.

**invoice:** another word for a bill. Where goods are sold for cash, an invoice may be given as proof of purchase and title. In the case of a credit sale the invoice should state the terms, e.g. payment within 30 days.

**inward investment** is the *capital* attracted to a region or a country from beyond its boundaries. An example of such investment is a Japanese car manufacturer opening an assembly plant in the UK. There has been a big increase in inward investment, which is one element in the process of *globalisation*.

**IPO:** see *Initial Public Offering*

**IRR:** see *internal rate of return*

**ISA:** see *Individual Savings Accounts*

**ISO 9000:** see *International Standards Organisation*

**issued share capital:** the amount of a firm's authorised share capital that has actually been issued (sold) to investors. The *memorandum of association* states the authorised share capital of a company, but not all the shares need be issued at once. Thus, under *shareholders' funds* in the *balance sheet*, both the authorised and issued share capital may be listed. Shareholders can see whether further shares can be issued which would raise further funds but also dilute the ownership.

**IT:** see *information technology*

**Do you know we also have A–Zs for:**

- **Accounting**
- **English Literature**
- **Mathematics**
- **Psychology?**

Ask for them in your local bookshop or see the inside back cover for ordering details.

**Japanese way:** a term summarising the Japanese approach to management. Although there is a danger in over-simplifying (because Toyota and Nissan are as different from each other as Ford is from Rover), the Japanese way comprises three main elements:

- a strategic focus on the long term, in which the goal of a strong market position is more important than short-term profit
- a highly educated, highly trained workforce that is given a key role in improving production methods and quality; the *kaizen* (continuous improvement) group and the *quality circle* are ways of achieving this
- *lean production*, eliminating wastage of materials and time; hence *just in time (JIT)* production and *stock control* and the reduction in product development time that enables Toyota to get a new product idea to the market-place in half the time taken in the West.

**Japanisation:** the process by which Western firms have attempted to follow the *Japanese way*.

**jargon:** the terms used among specialists that form a language which may mean little to outsiders. This may, indeed, be the motive behind its use. Individual businesses may have their own jargons.

**J-curve:** the short-term response of the *current account* of the balance of payments to a sharp fall in the exchange rate. *Depreciation* makes imports dearer and exports cheaper. Other things being equal, exports will rise and imports will fall. However, this takes time and during the process of adjustment, as buyers react gradually to price changes, imports will cost more and exports bring in little more than they did before. So the current account may actually worsen before it gets better.

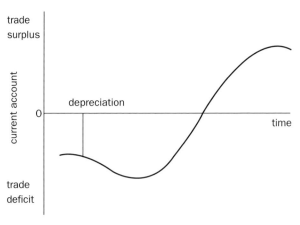

**JIT:** see *just in time*

**job analysis:** an investigation into the demands of a job to identify the tasks and skills required for high performance (to draw up a *job description*). These can then be related to the abilities demanded from the employee in order to draw up a *job specification*.

**job description:** a detailed statement of the nature of the job, identifying the precise tasks and responsibilities involved. It is likely to form part of the individual's *employment contract*.

**job design:** deciding how the tasks required within a production process should be subdivided or grouped into specific job functions. The key decisions are between:

- high *division of labour* and a complete unit of work
- close supervision and self-checking.

The role of job design is crucial in *job enrichment* and in *motivation* generally.

**job enlargement:** increasing the number of tasks and possibly responsibilities involved in a job. Examples of job enlargement are *job rotation* and *job enrichment*.

**job enrichment:** the attempt to motivate by giving employees the opportunity to use their abilities. This definition is closely based upon Professor *Herzberg's* work, as job enrichment was the main policy recommendation that stemmed from his theories. Herzberg suggested that an enriched job should ideally contain:

- a range of tasks and challenges at different ability levels, some of which should be beyond the employee's experience to date
- a complete unit of work, in other words a meaningful task rather than a repetitive fragment
- direct *feedback*, by which the employee could know immediately how well he or she was performing.

**job evaluation:** comparing the demands of different jobs in order to establish a systematic structure of gradings and pay scales. This will involve identifying the skills, experience and responsibility involved in each job. Given the psychological significance of *status* in the workplace, a job evaluation exercise may cause great disquiet. Those that receive lower gradings than expected may become demotivated.

**job flexibility:** see *flexible working*

**job production** means producing a one-off item that has been tailor-made to suit a special customer. Although most of this type of production is undertaken by small firms (because there are no *economies of scale*), shipbuilding may operate on the same job basis. Also very common among smaller firms is a combination between batch and job methods. A baker might bake a dozen celebration fruit cakes. Some are then tailor-made into wedding cakes while others are decorated for birthday cakes.

**job rotation:** widening the activities of a worker by switching him or her around a number of work tasks. For example, a shop worker might spend two hours on the checkout, two filling shelves and another two in the warehouse. This is intended to relieve the tedium of the work, but has the useful side-effect of ensuring that if one person is absent, others can cover the job without difficulty.

**job satisfaction:** the degree to which an employee feels positively towards his or her present job function. Many writers have pointed out that the term is not only hard to define but also to measure. Indeed several believe it to be virtually irrelevant to managers, as it has not been possible to prove that higher job satisfaction results in higher job performance. Despite these reservations, the huge research effort and the management time spent considering the problems and opportunities involved suggests that job satisfaction is of great importance. Most clearly, job dissatisfaction can lead to *absenteeism*, high *labour turnover* and poor *industrial relations*. (See *Herzberg* and *job enrichment*.)

**job security:** the extent to which a job is, or seems to be, guaranteed for the foreseeable future. Although lack of job security would prevent a worker's *lower order needs* from being satisfied, it is possible that the implied threat would stimulate greater effort.

**jobseekers' allowance:** the benefit paid to someone who is unemployed for the first six months.

**job sharing:** when employees agree to divide the working week on a job in two, so that they each do half of the one job. This can be very useful for parents with young children, and may provide the employer with the bonus of having two, fresher minds on the one task.

**job specification:** a statement or listing of the characteristics required to do a job successfully. So whereas the *job description* describes the job, the job specification specifies the person. Drawing up a 'job spec' is one of the first stages in the recruitment process. It provides a yardstick against which the job applicants can be measured. Typical elements in a job specification include: educational qualifications, experience, impact on others, and special aptitudes (such as speed of thought).

**joint consultation:** regular meetings between management and *trade unions* to discuss important issues other than *collective bargaining*. A joint consultation committee is a communication forum in which the management's long-term strategy might be outlined, with requests for comments from the shop-floor.

**joint demand** occurs when two items are consumed together, i.e. are complements. Examples might be shoes and shoe laces or CDs and CD players. An increase in sales of one may lead to an increase in sales of the other.

**joint-stock company:** the traditional term for describing a limited company, i.e. a separate legal entity financed and owned by individual shareholders. Joint-stock companies may be *private limited companies* (Ltd) *public limited companies* (PLC).

**joint supply** occurs when the production of one good also entails the production of another. This often happens in the chemical industry where one chemical may be produced as a by-product of another. Meat and leather provide another example. A fall in the market price of one may affect the quantity supplied of the other.

**joint venture:** when two or more firms set up a business division that will be operated jointly. This method avoids the need for a complete *merger*, with all the managerial problems that can entail. The potential problem with a joint venture is that the common interests that brought the firms together may shift, leaving the possibility of a messy divorce. Joint ventures have proved to be a useful way for developed country businesses to invest in *developing countries* with which they are not familiar (e.g. China and India).

**Jubilee Debt campaign:** the movement to persuade developed country governments to find ways of reducing the debt owed by the poorest and least developed countries. The original objective was to clear all the debts of the world's 22 poorest countries before the end of 2000. In the event, the debt was reduced from $2.9 billion to $2.1 billion. (See also *Debt Problem*.)

**junk bond:** a fixed interest loan offering higher annual *dividends* than most bonds, but with far less security. The issuing of junk bonds was a major factor in the huge credit boom in America in the 1980s. It resulted in American firms becoming very highly geared, thereby turning the early 1990s *recession* into the longest for 60 years.

**just in time (JIT)** a manufacturing system which is designed to minimise the costs of holding *stocks* of raw materials, components, work-in-progress and finished goods by very carefully planned scheduling and flow of resources through the production process. It requires a very efficient ordering system and delivery reliability. It is usually implemented in conjunction with a shift from *mass* to *cell* production.

JIT also has enormous implications for managing the workforce. High stock levels act as a cushion against workforce indiscipline, be it absenteeism or strike action. Without them it is essential that managers encourage cooperation instead of confrontation. Factory workers need to be treated as valued members of a complete team - trusted, trained and consulted.

As a result, JIT can lead firms to rethink their approach to factory work. The traditional approach of splitting work into repetitive fragments results in an uncooperative workforce. So firms organise the workforce into teams, working together on large units of work instead of working in isolation on the same boring task.

From its origins in Japan, the JIT approach has spread widely throughout the West. In Britain, Rolls Royce has divided its car plant into 16 zones, each acting as a business within a business, responsible for purchasing, cost, quality and delivery. Rolls Royce's new approach has halved the break-even level from 2 800 cars per year to 1 400.

**Do you need revision help and advice?**

Go to pages 325–341 for a range of revision appendices that include plenty of exam advice and tips.

**k:** a common abbreviation of thousands (of pounds).

**kaizen:** a Japanese term meaning continuous improvement. The importance of this element in the *Japanese way* has often been overlooked. When General Motors realised how far their efficiency had slipped behind the Japanese car firms, they invested billions of dollars in brand-new, highly automated production lines. Yet in the period it took to design, install and test the plant, the Japanese firms had moved the productivity goalposts by their continuous improvement policy. Furthermore, the Japanese improvements cost relatively little, as they were just shop-floor ideas on how to complete tasks more efficiently. Most were generated by kaizen groups that met regularly to discuss problems and solutions.

The diagram below shows the kaizen effect on productivity growth as compared with the traditional Western approach of large, technology-based leaps forward. Note that whereas the Western version would probably entail large-scale *redundancies*, steady productivity improvements are more likely to be accommodated by rising demand or output or by *natural wastage*.

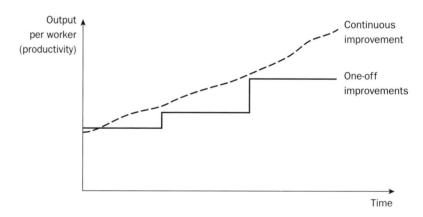

*Kaizen: continuous improvement*

**kanban:** the Japanese system of order cards that pull component supplies through a factory. This is the practical basis of the *just in time* production system. It often operates on the simple basis of two component bins. When one is empty, it is wheeled to the component production section with its kanban order card. That triggers production of the component that must be completed just in time before the other bin runs out of supplies. This approach minimises the amount of semi-completed stock within the factory, focusing minds on the need to avoid production hiccups that could quickly bring the factory to a halt.

**keiretsu:** a Japanese term for a group of companies that have interlocking minority share-holdings in each other. This encourages them to consult closely on long-term planning. Well-known keiretsu include Mitsui and Mitsubishi.

**Keynes J M** (1883–1946): unarguably the most important British economist of the twentieth century. His most important works included THE ECONOMIC CONSEQUENCES OF THE PEACE (first published 1919; latest edition Macmillan 1989), and THE GENERAL THEORY OF EMPLOYMENT, INTEREST AND MONEY (first published 1936; latest edition Macmillan 1973). Keynes combined in remarkable measure a capacity to develop economic theory with a strong grasp of the practicalities of running the economy. He was a major influence on Britain's successful handling of its wartime economy 1939–1945, and his ideas were adopted worldwide in the long period of economic growth between 1945 and 1970. (See *Keynesian*.) He was instrumental in the creation of the International Monetary Fund just before his death. His approach to economic policy has had a lasting impact and is still visible from time to time in the policy pronouncements of politicians. His work on unemployment in the 1930s reflected a profound concern for the welfare of the unemployed. At the same time he was a strong advocate of prudent management of the monetary system.

**Keynesian:** a person whose economic ideas can be traced to those of J M *Keynes*. At the risk of over-simplification, these include:

- scepticism that the economy tends to stabilise at full employment; Keynes believed that government action might be needed to push an economy out of *recession* (such as extra public expenditure)
- conviction about the desirability of *counter-cyclical policies* by government
- the belief that allowing people to suffer (through unemployment, for example) while waiting for the free market to bring the economy into balance is morally and socially unacceptable

Whereas the *classical economists* believed that unemployment would lead to falling wage rates, which would in turn increase the quantity of labour demanded by employers, and gradually eliminate unemployment, Keynes showed that a fall in money wages might reduce consumption and so cause the economy to settle at an equilibrium level of output well below that of full employment. Hence the need for increased injections to raise *aggregate demand*. Increased government expenditure could be financed by borrowing until such time as the economy recovered.

For a time, Keynesians were at odds with the group of economists known as monetarists, who saw government expenditure as a source of inflationary pressures, and emphasised the importance of controlling the growth of the money stock in order to prevent *inflation* from accelerating. During the early 1990s, the debate came to hinge upon the impact of rising aggregate demand on the labour market. Keeping large numbers of people unemployed can help to reduce inflationary pressures, but it also has serious implications for the welfare of the unemployed themselves.

**kitemark:** the symbol that shows that a consumer product has met the standards laid down by the *British Standards Institute (BSI)*.

**Kondratieff cycle:** the theory that in addition to the normal five to ten year *trade cycle*, there exists a 50-year cycle of economic upturn and downturn. The theory was put forward by the Russian economist Kondratieff in the early twentieth century. It was dismissed by

**167**

many economists until the *Great Depressions* of the 1880s and 1930s were duly followed (50 years later) by the frequent and severe *recessions* of the period from 1975–1992. The most widely accepted explanation for the Kondratieff cycle is that the introduction of a new technology causes disruption, but once established it forms the basis for many new products and jobs. In the 1930s the car was displacing rail, while in the 1980s the microchip was replacing mechanical technology.

**Kyoto Agreement:** the agreement made at the Climate Conference in 1997, by which 38 developed countries set targets for the reduction of greenhouse gases. The US, the EU and Japan, the three biggest polluters, committed themselves to cut emissions from 1990 levels by 7, 8 and 6 per cent respectively by 2012. The US pulled out in 2001, after the election of George W. Bush. Japan has also backed out.

**Do you need help with the synoptic element of your Economics and Business course?**

Go to page 335 for tips and advice.

**labour:** the factor of production which involves people, working to produce goods and services. Labour involves both doing and thinking. Labour is often referred to as if it were a single type of resource. In practice there are many different categories of labour, depending on their respective capabilities, which are referred to as *human capital*. This can be increased through education and training.

**labour, demand for:** the demand for labour reflects the demand for the product and is thus a *derived demand*. There will be a demand schedule for labour just as there is a demand schedule for the product, and the numbers employed will depend partly on the going wage rate. At any given wage, more labour will be demanded if the price of the product rises, or if more can be sold.

If labour productivity rises, there are a number of possible outcomes. Costs will fall, so prices may be cut, sales may rise and more labour will be demanded. Alternatively, the increased productivity may make it possible to pay higher wages, but in that case costs will not fall.

The demand for labour is thus closely related to the product market, and changes in the pattern of demand work their way through the labour market into the overall allocation of resources. There is also a close relationship between the demand for labour and the price of capital. If wages rise relative to the price of labour saving capital equipment, employers will tend to substitute capital for labour and the demand for labour will fall.

**labour flexibility:** the ease with which a firm can change the jobs carried out by its staff. This is an important element in a firm's ability to cope with change within its market-place. The main factors determining labour flexibility are:

- workforce attitudes, including any *resistance to change*
- traditional labour practices, which may be restrictive and entrenched, such as rigid job *demarcation*
- the general skills of the labour force (have workers been encouraged to take general training courses or do they only know their specialist function?)
- the strength and attitude of the local *trade union.*

Labour flexibility will tend to increase when the threat of unemployment is serious. However increased flexibility can make it possible to pay higher wages if productivity rises.

**labour intensive:** a work process in which labour costs represent a high proportion of total costs. Such a situation is most likely to exist in the service sector, in a small firm, or in a firm operating on a *job* or *batch production* system. This contrasts with firms that are *capital-intensive*.

**labour market** is the supply of labour (i.e. all those offering themselves for work) and the demand for labour (i.e. employers in both the *private* and *public sectors*), which together determine wage rates. Talking of a single market for this *factor of production* is rather misleading because it is made up of a vast number of smaller markets which have quite different characteristics: road repairers, brain surgeons and pop stars for instance. However in many instances these smaller markets are interlinked.

**labour mobility** is the extent to which labour moves around in search of jobs, called *geographical mobility*, or the extent to which labour moves between jobs, which is known as *occupational mobility*. It is an indicator of a dynamic economy if such mobility is high. Geographical mobility depends on such things as available housing, costs of moving, communications and the importance of family ties, whilst occupational mobility depends on training facilities and a willingness to learn. (See also *immobility of labour*.)

**labour turnover:** a measurement of the rate at which employees are leaving an organisation.

$$\text{FORMULA:} \quad \frac{\text{numbers of leavers per year}}{\text{average number of staff}} \times 100$$

High labour turnover may be caused by:

- pay levels falling below comparable rates locally
- low morale, perhaps due to ineffective or *authoritarian leadership*
- an economic upturn creating many other job opportunities.

The main effects of high labour turnover are:

- heavy overheads due to the costs of recruiting and training replacement staff frequently
- productivity reductions as new staff acclimatise
- the difficulties of building teamwork with an ever-changing team.

**lagging indicator** is a term used to describe a signal which lags behind the true state of economic activity. Unemployment figures often lag behind in this way because, as the economy moves out of *recession*, firms experience an increase in their order books and respond by increasing output, initially by working overtime rather than by taking on more staff. Only when firms are convinced that the recovery is well under way will they employ more people. Therefore, unemployment tends to fall some time after the economy has begun to grow.

**lags** may occur whenever a change in one variable has an impact on another, but after a lapse of time. It is usual for decision takers to take time to adjust to new circumstances. A change in prices will usually lead to a change in the quantity demanded but only after existing contracts have been completed.

**laissez-faire** is a political and economic philosophy rooted in the work of Adam *Smith* which believes that governments should avoid interfering in the running of business or any other part of the economy. A laissez-faire economist places faith in the ability of the free market to maximise business efficiency and consumer satisfaction. *Interventionists* note that the theory of laissez-faire was devised in the eighteenth century when small firms did compete freely. Today, many markets are dominated by a few large firms, so the theory of laissez-faire is less persuasive. However since the early 1980s there has been a swing back towards less interventionist policies, associated with Thatcherism in the UK and with the transition to market economies in Eastern Europe and Russia.

**laissez-faire leadership** occurs where the leader has minimal input, leaving the running of the business to the staff. *Delegation* would lack focus and coordination, making it hard for employees to feel a sense of common purpose. This style can stem from a leader's inability to provide the framework necessary for a successful democratic approach. Or it may be a conscious and brave policy decision to give staff the maximum scope for showing their capabilities. Some people will love the freedom provided, and produce highly creative work. Others will hate their unstructured job with its low input from the leader. (Also see *democratic*, *authoritarian* and *paternalistic leadership*.)

**landfill waste tax:** a tax imposed per ton of waste dumped in landfill sites. Started in October 1996, this tax was intended to make the polluter pay. This should provide an incentive for companies to minimise the waste they dump and maximise their efforts at recycling. The rate of tax rose from £7 to £10 per tonne in 1999 and the government announced the rate would rise £1 per year between 2000 and 2004.

**lateral communication:** another term for *horizontal communication*.

**lateral thinking:** the ability when faced with an apparently unsolvable problem to think creatively and either find a radical solution or realise the situation can be sidestepped altogether. This kind of creative thinking can pay especially handsome dividends in product development and in marketing, where originality can lead to exciting *innovations*.

**launch:** the programme of *stockpiling*, *distribution*, *advertising* and publicity required to thrust a new product before its *target market*. The launch may be national or regional depending upon the firm's confidence in the product, its available production capacity, and any known regional taste differences. Once sufficient stocks of the product are ready, the launch is likely to consist of three phases:

1 *Trade advertising* plus aggressive *salesforce* activity to get wholesalers and retailers to stock the product.

2 A large-scale *merchandising* campaign to achieve high visibility at the point of sale, e.g. display stands near the shop checkouts.

3 A consumer advertising campaign, perhaps of TV commercials plus posters.

**layers of hierarchy** means the number of ranks within the organisational structure, i.e. the number of different supervisory and management layers between the shop-floor and the chief executive.

**LDC:** see *less developed countries*

**leadership style:** the manner and approach of the head of an organisation or department towards the staff. The leader's manner affects the personal relationships involved. Will the leader inspire loyalty, affection, respect, trust? The style includes the use of *delegation* and *consultation*, plus the degree to which he or she gets involved personally in the daily problems of the business. Both aspects will be handled differently by each and every leader, but there are four categories of leadership style that are used widely for purposes of analysis: *democratic*, *paternalistic*, *authoritarian* (or dictatorial) and *laissez-faire*.

**leading indicator** is a term used to describe a signal which predates or predicts the true state of economic activity, such as the level of orders for machine tools. The *stock market* often leads in this way. For example, growing confidence that signs of a recovery are under way is often translated into rising share prices, as investors predict improving profits in the next year to eighteen months. The opposite also holds, with sharp falls in share prices indicating a falling off of activity in advance of the reality. Such leading indicators can be predictors of what is likely to happen to the 'real economy'.

**lead time:** the length of time a firm needs between receiving an order and delivering the finished product or service. Efforts by management at reducing lead times could result in considerable benefits in terms of customer satisfaction and faster turnover. Nevertheless, many customers would rather have a 100 per cent reliable delivery date than an apparently faster, but actually less reliable service.

**leakages** are savings, taxation and imports, which leak out of the circular flow of money and reduce aggregate demand. (See *withdrawals*.)

**lean production:** a term used to describe the range of waste-saving measures inspired by Japanese manufacturing firms. These include *just-in-time*, shorter product development times and *flexible specialisation*. To the authors of THE MACHINE THAT CHANGED THE WORLD (Womack, Jones & Roos, Macmillan, 1990), lean production has replaced mass production as the world's most efficient system. Its efficiency stems from the focus upon minimising the waste of any resource that does not add value to the product or service. Time spent re-checking and re-working the output of others is time wasted, therefore focus on getting the work right first time. Whereas time spent discussing how to improve the product or process can add value to the product, therefore improvement (*kaizen*) groups are encouraged. (See also the *Japanese way*.)

**Learning and Skills Councils:** the bodies responsible for ensuring that local training opportunities meet local needs. They are composed of representatives of local businesses and work in collaboration with Colleges of Further Education to set up appropriate courses.

**learning curve:** the process of gaining experience and knowledge that depends on learning from your mistakes. New employees and firms new to a market both go through the same learning process. The successful ones will be those that move up the learning curve as rapidly as possible, probably through a combination of good research and a willingness to experiment.

**learning organisation:** an enterprise that makes *continuous improvement* a central theme of its management approach. Therefore it is always willing to listen to new ideas and make the necessary changes – however radical.

For this to be successful there needs to be an open style of management, excellent internal communications and a sense of common purpose amongst managers and staff alike.

**lease:** a way of acquiring property for a restricted period of time; after the lease runs out, ownership returns to the freeholder. As it has value for the years of its life, a lease is recorded as a *fixed asset* on a firm's *balance sheet*.

**leasing:** a method of acquiring non-property *assets* without the need for the initial cash outlays implied by purchasing. This can also be done by renting or hiring equipment, though leasing is cheaper per month because the firm must contract to lease the assets for a period of two or more years. Leasing avoids the damage to *cash flow* caused by purchasing and releases *capital* for other, perhaps more profitable uses. But in order to provide the leasing company with a profit, it is inevitable that in the long run most leasing arrangements will prove more expensive than outright purchase.

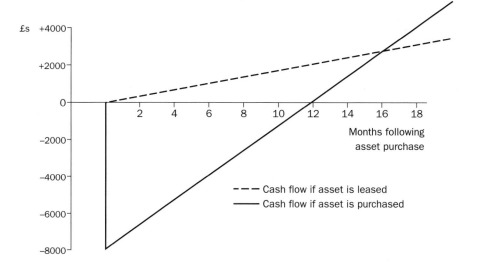

*Leasing compared with purchasing an asset*

**least developed countries:** the forty-one countries identified by the UN in 1990 as having the lowest per capita incomes. Many African countries are included. Together they account for 8 per cent of the world's population but only 0.7 per cent of world GDP.

**legislation:** laws passed by Acts of Parliament.

**lender of last resort:** an important function of the Bank of England, which guarantees to lend to banks which find themselves temporarily unable to meet their customers' requests for withdrawals. This does not mean that the Bank will bail out any bank at any time; a bank which has been mismanaged or involved in fraud may still fail or be sold, as in the case of Barings in early 1995. But it does mean that the Bank will try to ensure the stability of the banking system as a whole.

**less developed countries:** a general term which covers all those countries which have relatively low levels of GNP, poorly developed infrastructure and a large part of their resources engaged in agricultural production. The World Bank defines as low income countries those which in 2000 had per capita GNP of less than US$755 a year. These are sometimes described as the least developed countries. Middle income countries are defined as those with between $756 and $9,265 per capita income in 2000. Malaysia and Mexico belong to the latter group, a number of which might be described as being well on the way to being developed countries.

**level playing-field:** a phrase that sums up the need within a *market economy* for all firms to be competing on the same terms. If one national government is subsidising its steel producers, for example, they will have an unfair advantage over those from a country like the UK, which offers no State-aid to steel. The *single European market* is an attempt to provide a level playing-field in relation to laws and regulations governing traded goods within the EU. If product and factory regulations could be made the same throughout the union, the trading field would have been levelled out.

**leverage:** the American term for *gearing* (i.e. the level of borrowing).

**liability:** a debt that may have to be paid within 12 months (current liability), after 12 months (long-term liability), or at no specified time (*shareholders' funds*). For an understanding of *balance sheets*, it is useful to remember that liabilities are sources of finance. They are the means by which the *assets* have been acquired. For example, an *overdraft* (current liability) is a source of short-term finance for the firm.

**liberalisation** is a term used to describe the freeing up of international trade from barriers such as *tariffs* and *quotas*. The *General Agreement on Tariffs and Trade (GATT)* was established to negotiate reduced barriers under a succession of so-called 'rounds'. The *World Trade Organisation* has now taken over from the GATT.

**licensing:** when the holder of a *patent* or *copyright* allows other firms to use their creation in return for a *royalty*. The royalty might be an agreed percentage of the value of the sales made by the licensee, or a fee per unit sold. The holders of the Star Wars name and *logo* might, for example, charge licensees £1 per Star Wars T-shirt and 10p per Star Wars pencil. Licensing can be a way of preserving intellectual property rights.

**LIFFE:** see *London International Financial Futures Exchange*

**light industry:** manufacturers of all items other than the large-scale output of *heavy industry*. Typical examples include food manufacture and printing.

**limited company:** a firm that enjoys *limited liability*. In other words the owners (shareholders) are only risking the amount they have invested in the company rather than their personal wealth.

**limited liability** is the idea that the owners (shareholders) are financially only responsible for the amount they have invested in the company rather than their personal wealth. Thus if a firm becomes insolvent, the maximum *creditors* can receive is the shareholders' original investment. In order to protect and inform creditors, the word 'Ltd' (standing for Limited) or 'PLC' (standing for Public Limited Company) appear after the company's name. The importance of limiting the amount of a shareholder's liability is that it encourages people to invest with relatively little risk.

**limit pricing** involves selecting a price that is below the profit-maximising price. A company may choose to do this if it seems likely to discourage new entrants to the industry. This may help to preserve its competitive position. High profits could attract new entrants which would compete strongly. It is likely that this is an element in the pricing strategies of many firms producing consumer durables.

**line extension:** adding a new flavour or model type to a product line. For example, once Walls had launched 'Magnum' successfully, 'White Magnum' soon followed.

Pros:
- a line extension can offer more variety to regular customers, encouraging higher levels of *repeat purchase*
- it can also be used to segment a market, as, for example, a plain chocolate choc-ice will appeal more to adults than to children
- most importantly, a line extension can protect a successful product from competition; once the success of 'Magnum' had become clear, competitors would look for ways of getting into this market sector; the easiest way would be to offer a 'Magnum' imitation (*me-too*) with a point of differentiation; if Walls had not offered 'Magnum White', a rival would have done so.

Cons: • line extensions can cannibalise your existing products, in other words much of the demand for 'Magnum White' may have come from buyers of 'Magnum'. By spreading sales among more products, each one's chance of gaining high retail distribution is reduced.

**line management:** managers who have been delegated specific authority over people, decisions and results within the management hierarchy. Line personnel are distinguished from staff because the latter hold no direct responsibilities for meeting *company objectives*. The term 'line manager' comes from the line of command (also known as *chain of command*) that forms a vertical line of delegated authority within the organisational structure.

**liquid assets** are the *assets* that are closest to cash, namely bank deposits (cash) and *debtors*. In the case of banks, liquid assets include *bills* and short-term loans.

**liquidation** means turning *assets* into *cash*. The term is usually used in the context of a firm ceasing to trade in its current form, probably due to *insolvency*. The closure may be the result of a *creditor* taking the firm to court to seek compulsory liquidation due to non-payment of debts. In this case a *receiver* will be appointed to attempt to raise the cash to satisfy the creditors. If the firm has sufficient assets, or a fundamentally strong trading position, it may well be that the receiver is able to find a buyer for the firm or to keep it going. More common is *voluntary liquidation*, in which the firm's directors decide that they wish to stop the firm continuing to trade as at present. This might be because an elderly proprietor wants to retire and can find no buyer for the firm. The main alternatives to liquidation are *administration* and financial *restructuring*.

**liquidity:** the ability of a firm to meet its short-term debts. As bills can only be paid with *cash*, liquidity can also be understood as the availability of cash or near-cash resources. Liquidity can be estimated from a firm's published accounts using the *acid test ratio*.

**liquidity crisis:** a loss of confidence in a firm's ability to meet its short-term debts. This may encourage bankers or *creditors* to demand payment before others get at the firm's money. Inability to meet those payments might lead to *liquidation*.

**listed company:** a firm that has its shares listed on the main London *Stock Exchange*. In order for this to be possible, the firm must be a *public limited company* (PLC). See below for how to obtain a *listing*.

**listing** refers to those public *joint-stock companies (PLCs)* which appear on the *Stock Exchange* list. Among the advantages and disadvantages of a full listing are:

Pros: • gives access to a large potential source of *capital*
      • shareholders receive some protection from fraud because of the stringent requirements of the Stock Exchange Council
      • raises the profile of the company, giving it publicity and therefore (perhaps) greater credibility.

Cons: • the *flotation* process is time-consuming and expensive, requiring a lengthy *prospectus* prepared by a *merchant bank*
      • it makes the company more vulnerable to *take-over bids*; this may lead to *short-termism* in managerial decision-making
      • a great deal of information about the firm has to be made public. It is possible to be quoted on the *Alternative Investment Market (AIM)* which has less stringent requirements, and which is often a 'halfway house' between being a private company and a PLC

**Lloyds** insurance market is one of the world's main centres for obtaining insurance cover on anything from a car to an oil rig. Lloyd's members underwrite risks from throughout the world, earning Britain considerable sums of foreign currency; making insurance one of Britain's main *invisible exports*.

**loan capital:** medium- to long-term finance, either from banks or from *debenture* holders. Loan capital plus *shareholders' funds* represent a firm's *capital employed*. When raising extra loan capital, a firm should consider its *gearing* level, i.e. the extent to which it is reliant on borrowed money. If loans represent more than 50 per cent of capital employed, the firm is considered over-geared.

**Loan Guarantee Scheme (LGS):** a government-backed loan insurance scheme which guarantees bankers that up to 80 per cent of the money they lend to a business will be guaranteed by the *Treasury*. This was introduced in 1980 as a way of encouraging banks to lend to small and medium-sized companies thought too risky to justify a conventional loan. In return for its financial risks, the government charges a fee of around 2.5 per cent of the annual value of the loan. The precise terms of the LGS are often changed in the annual *Budget*, but would easily be available from the *Department of Trade and Industry* or from any high-street bank.

**lobbying:** putting your viewpoint across directly to a person in a position of power and influence. The term comes from the central lobby of the Houses of Parliament, which is where protesters go to put their case to their Members of Parliament. Although intended as an aid to the democratic process, lobbying has become tainted by the number of MPs who are paid to represent special interests such as the tobacco industry. (See *pressure groups*.)

**local area network:** the linking of personal computers within a network operating system, usually within the same company.

**local content:** the proportion of the value of output that is produced within the country where the product is assembled. This is an important issue within the *European Union*, because products imported directly from the Far East are subject to restrictions and taxes, whereas *free trade* exists for products made within the EU. Yet that opens the possibility that a Japanese firm might set up in Britain, import all components from Japan, and simply bolt them together in this country. Other EU countries are keen to ensure that a product with such a low local content is treated as if it is a direct import from Japan.

**local government** is responsible in the UK for most school education, social services, local roads, planning, and a range of other services. Changes in local government, and the trend towards unitary authorities (single authorities responsible for all locally provided services), may affect the way these services are organised.

**localised industry:** where one area has a particular advantage for an industry, that industry will tend to develop there rather than in other locations. In the past the existence of coal often created an industrial area involving steel making and engineering. *Industrial inertia* may mean that these industries have continued to be located in the same place. Other possible local advantages include a supply of appropriately skilled labour with a tradition in the industry concerned.

**local multiplier:** when spending in one particular area increases, then a local multiplier effect will be observed. Extra spending will generate employment: if a new bridge is being built, people will be employed to do the building. These people will then spend some of their earnings locally, thus creating further demand and increased employment in the immediate area.

**location of industry:** see *industrial location*

**lock-out:** when an employer decides to bring an *industrial dispute* to a head by preventing the workforce from getting in to work. This might happen if a *trade union* has organised a successful work-to-rule or series of disruptive, one-day strikes. Management might fear that the workers will be able to continue *industrial action* indefinitely.

**logistics** is the process of ensuring the right supplies and products are in the right place at the right time, at a competitive cost. The main functions covered are:

- materials ordering and handling
- *stock control*
- *distribution* and delivery

**logo:** a visual symbol of an organisation or brand. It might be the design of the brand name (such as the Coca-Cola signature) or pure creation, such as the 'golden arches' yellow M that symbolises McDonald's.

**Lomé Conventions** of the EU allow many of the ex-colonies of EU states to have preferential access to EU markets. Four separate conventions, the most recent in 1990, have provided a forum for the negotiation of these arrangements with *ACP* states. They compensate to some extent for the loss of the trading arrangements which these countries lost through the development of the EU. They are not especially generous, given that the countries concerned are mostly very poor. India is among those not included in these trading arrangements.

**London International Financial Futures Exchange:** LIFFE (pronounced 'life') was the financial market where companies could obtain forward currency or hedge their future currency commitments. In 1990 LIFFE was merged with the Traded Options Market to form the *London Derivatives Exchange*.

Liffe is now known as Euronext.Liffe. The exchange was taken over by Euronext, the owner of similar exchanges in Amsterdam, Brussels and Paris.

**long-run:** the period of time in which all factors of production can be varied. For example, it is possible to invest in new capital equipment and build new factories. Similarly, some businesses may enter or exit from the market-place, so changing the size of the industry.

**long-term liabilities:** debts (*creditors*) falling due after more than one year. These include medium- and long-term loans, *debentures* and (possibly) *provisions* for tax payments or other long-term debts.

**long-term unemployed** are people who have been unemployed for more than a year.

**Lorenz curve:** a graphical representation showing inequality. In the diagram, the Lorenz curve will run along the 45° line if, for example, the range of percentages of the population are the same as the share of total income which they receive. The more unequal the distribution of income, the more the Lorenz curve will be bowed out below the 45° line. For example at point A, 20 per cent of the population have 10 per cent of the total income. So the closer the curve is to the 45° time, the greater is the degree of equality and vice-versa. Lorenz curves can be used to compare other frequency distributions which are not equal, such as the number of firms and cumulative market shares. The Gini coefficient is the area between the Lorenz curve and the 45° line, and gives a measure of inequality.

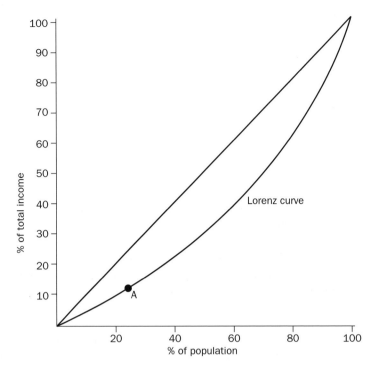

*Lorenz curve*

**loss leader:** a product sold at or below cost in the hope of generating other, profitable sales. The method is most commonly used in retailing, where a shop may advertise a loss leader heavily, enticing in customers who will probably buy other, full-priced items as well. The same term can also be used to describe a manufacturer who prices a lead item cheaply, knowing that usage of the item requires further, full-priced purchases. For example, publishers of sticker collections may charge only 50p for a large, glossy album, but 30p per pack for the cheap stickers that go inside.

**lower order needs:** see *hierarchy of needs*

**lower turning point** is the lowest point in the *trade cycle*, where the economy moves out of *recession* or *depression*. During the downswing of a recession, economists and politicians attempt to forecast when the lower turning point is to be reached. In fact it is often only six to nine months afterwards that it becomes clear when it happened.

**Ltd:** see *limited liability*

### What other subjects are you studying?

A–Zs cover 18 different subjects. See the inside back cover for a list of all the titles in the series and how to order.

**Maastricht** is the name of a city in the Netherlands where the Treaty on European Union was signed by all the member states of the *EU* in December 1991. The Treaty planned the introduction of the single currency in 1999 and formulated a number of areas for combined policy action including industrial and social policy, health and education, common foreign policy and defence. The Maastricht Treaty attempted to push the pace of European unity forward. The Treaty came into force on November 1 1993. For a time, the UK opted out of the social chapter but complied fully from 1997. It has still not joined *EMU*.

**McGregor D** (1906–1964)**:** an American psychologist whose book THE HUMAN SIDE OF ENTERPRISE (first pub. 1960; Penguin, 1987) popularised his view that managers can be grouped into two types: *Theory X* and *Theory Y*. McGregor had researched into the attitudes of managers towards their employees. He found that the majority of managers assumed that their workers were work-shy and motivated primarily by money; he termed this type of manager Theory X. The alternative, minority, view was that workers look to gain satisfaction from employment and therefore evidence of low achievement levels should make managers question whether they were providing the right work environment. In other words, the Theory Y manager's first assumption should be that the blame for poor workforce performance lies with management rather than the workers themselves.

The Theory X Manager assumes:

- workers are motivated by money
- unless supervised closely, workers will under-perform
- that workers will only respect a tough, decisive boss
- that workers have no wish or ability to help make decisions.

The Theory Y Manager assumes:

- workers seek job satisfaction no less than managers
- that, if trusted, workers will behave responsibly
- that low performance is due to dull work or poor management
- staff have a desire and the right to contribute to decisions.

McGregor's use of the easily memorable X and Y has made his work widely used in management training. This is despite the fact that it is largely derived from other theories. Theory X is derived from the work of F W *Taylor* and from Adam *Smith*'s notion of 'economic man'. Theory Y stems clearly from *Mayo*'s human relations approach and *Maslow*'s work on human needs. Nevertheless, just the introduction to THE HUMAN SIDE OF ENTERPRISE will give the reader a clear understanding that McGregor's writing has much more to contribute than just the memorable X and Y.

**machine tools:** the capital equipment needed to make the machines used in manufacturing. In other words, not the robot welder on the car *production line*, but the machinery to make robot welders.

**macroeconomic:** a term indicating the study of the whole economy (macro means 'large'). The main elements within the macroeconomy are firms, consumers, the government and other countries. The way they depend on each other is shown by the *circular flow of national income*. Macroeconomics is concerned with aggregate demand and aggregate supply, and with total consumption, investment and expenditure. Thus the *sales revenue* of an individual firm is a part of the microeconomy; by adding up the sales revenue of all firms (their aggregate income) the size of the macroeconomy can be measured. The study of the macroeconomy leads on to consideration of macroeconomic policy. As there are large areas of macroeconomics which are still poorly understood, policy prescriptions are usually controversial.

**macroeconomic policy** aims to bring about desirable outcomes by influencing the economy as a whole. The objective might be to raise the rate of economic growth, or to make the economy more stable, by making adjustments in the level of *aggregate demand*. This could be done by making changes in:

- *fiscal policy*, using tax changes or government expenditure changes. Reducing taxes and increasing expenditure will increase aggregate demand and tend to stimulate the economy. Provided there are some unemployed resources output will increase.

- *monetary policy*, using interest rate changes to influence levels of spending on investment and consumer goods, will also affect aggregate demand and activity in the economy as a whole.

- *exchange rate* policy may also be used because a falling exchange rate may stimulate demand for exports and discourage imports. Alternatively, a rising exchange rate may make imports cheaper and tend to reduce inflationary pressures.

In all macroeconomic policy decisions, it is important to consider how close the economy is to *full capacity output*. *Expansionary policies* used when the economy is close to full capacity output and there are *supply constraints* will encourage inflation to accelerate. Equally, if unemployment is largely structural in nature, expansionary policies will not help. They may defeat the objectives which the government is aiming for. In these circumstances *supply-side policies* may provide a more appropriate strategy. See also *demand management*.

**mainframe computers** are the largest computers in the series beginning with *microcomputers* and going through *minicomputers*. Their size enables many functions to be processed simultaneously with large reserves of memory. They are mainly used by large corporations, research organisations and where defence or space applications are needed.

**maintenance factors:** another term for *hygiene factors*.

**make-or-buy decision:** the management choice between buying in components or making them in-house.

**managed exchange rate:** a *floating exchange rate* may still be managed to ensure that day-to-day fluctuations are kept to a minimum. The central bank buys when the exchange rate is falling, and sells when it is rising, so as to keep the exchange rate from deviating too far from its current market level. (See also *fixed exchange rate*.)

**management accounting:** the production and use of accounting information for internal managerial purposes of analysis, planning, review and control rather than for historical financial record. The diagram below sets out the main types of information considered part of the management accountant's function. In all cases it will be treated as highly confidential, in contrast with the completed company accounts that are published after the *financial year* has been completed.

Management accounting

| Budgetary control | Cost or profit centres | Investment appraisal | Break-even analysis |
|---|---|---|---|
| Cash-flow forecasts | Overhead allocation | Pay-back, ARR NPV and IRR | Contribution costing |

**management buy-in:** when managers from outside a company buy up the shares in order to take control. The managers do it because they (and their financial backers) believe that they can run the firm more efficiently than the current management. As with a *management buy-out*, a buy-in is likely to be financed largely by borrowed money, causing *gearing* to be uncomfortably high.

Note that a buy-in differs from a buy-out because the latter is when managers buy their **own** firm from the shareholders, whereas a buy-in is when **outside** managers buy in to a firm.

**management buy-out (MBO):** when the managers of a business buy out the shareholders, thereby buying ownership and control of the firm. It is hoped that this will give the management the incentive it needs to maximise the productiveness of the organisation. Many MBOs involve buying a single business unit from a large parent company. This gives the added benefit of separating the firm from its potentially *bureaucratic* (and therefore high overhead) parent.

However, some MBOs have been financed in a risky manner, with high debt levels. If the business is successful, the managers stand to make millions as the value of their shareholding soars. Failure, however, may lose not only the managers' investment but also the workforce's livelihood. So whereas the managers are taking a risk which may pay them handsomely, the workforce stands to gain nothing, but may lose everything.

**management by objectives:** a method of coordinating and motivating a workforce by dividing the company's overall goal into specific targets for each division, department, manager and possibly employee. Peter Drucker, in his book THE PRACTICE OF MANAGEMENT (Heinemann, 1955) put forward the view that management by objectives is the only effective way of delegating authority in a large firm. He urged that targets should be agreed after discussion, not imposed from above. A *Theory Y* management would be expected to take the former approach; *Theory X* managers would take the latter.

**management by walking about (MBWA):** an extension of *human relations* theory suggesting that managers can best express their interest in and focus on shop-floor activity by regular, informal visits. By inviting complaints or ideas, senior managers can cut through the *layers of hierarchy* that hinder *vertical communication*. As with many developments in motivation theory, this idea originated in America but was adopted most enthusiastically in Japan.

**management consultant:** an individual or firm which specialises in giving independent advice to companies. The advice may relate to internal management issues such as *delayering* or *restructuring*, or on divisional issues such as obtaining better production technology or tackling a marketing problem. Management consultants are expected to have greater breadth of experience than the company's own management, since they are likely to have tackled the same problems before at a different firm. No less important is that the consultant has no *vested interest* in ensuring that one department triumphs over another in a reorganisation.

**management succession:** the issue of who will take over the key positions in the company when the current directors retire. This can be a very important issue for family businesses, should there be no obvious successor. It can also worry the shareholders in a large *public limited company* that has been dominated by one or two people. Such worries might lead to a flagging share price that would leave the firm vulnerable to a *take-over bid*.

**management trainee:** an employee selected to participate in a training programme designed to equip the individual for a management post. This is likely to be a process lasting between six and 24 months, including:

- a personal development programme designed to encourage self-confidence, assertiveness and time management
- an academic programme based on finance, marketing, motivation theory and the law
- a work experience programme in which trainees will spend some weeks or months in several different departments in order to gain a full understanding of the workings of the organisation.

**managerial economies:** see *economies of scale*

**M and A:** see *mergers and acquisitions*

**manpower planning:** deciding on the type and number of staff required in the future, given the firm's sales forecasts, plans and *objectives*. Having decided how many workers are needed and what their skills should be, the *human resource* manager can plan by:

- carrying out a manpower audit, i.e. checking on the skills of all the present workforce
- identifying the known future leavers (those reaching retirement, for example), to exclude them from the calculations
- consulting, then deciding on how many existing staff could and would like to retrain for the job functions of the future
- preparing a recruitment plan stating how many new staff need to be recruited and how the firm will set about the process.

**manual worker:** an employee who works with his or her hands, usually in a factory context. Manual workers are often subdivided into three categories:

- skilled, e.g. welders and qualified electricians
- semi-skilled, e.g. van drivers and production line workers
- unskilled, e.g. cleaners and road sweepers.

**mapping** means selecting the key variables that differentiate the brands within a market and then plotting the position of each one. Usually this is done on a two-dimensional diagram as shown below. Here, ice-cream brands are plotted against the key criteria of customer age and product price. By contrast, the criteria for cider might be trendy or traditional and strong or standard (alcoholic strength). Brand mapping enables a firm to identify any gaps or niches in the market that are unfilled.

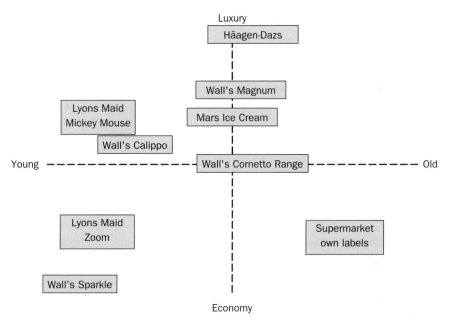

*Brand mapping for ice-cream (based on authors' estimates)*

**margin:** a commonly used shorthand way of referring to a *profit margin*, i.e. the proportionate difference between revenue and cost.

**marginal analysis:** economic theory analyses decisions taken at the margin. That is to say, people usually decide not whether to do something at all, but whether to do a little more, or a little less. They may produce, or consume, a little more or a little less. Producing a little more will bring in marginal revenue and have a marginal cost. The profit maximising producer will carry on producing up to the point where these two are equal. This is economically efficient because the price a consumer is prepared to pay for that last unit is exactly equal to the real resource cost of producing it.

**marginal cost:** the change in the total cost of a product or service which results from changing output by one unit more (or less). In the short run, only *variable costs* can be altered so marginal cost in the short run is entirely variable cost. Marginal costing is an alternative term for *contribution costing*.

**marginal cost pricing:** an item may be priced at its marginal cost, thus ensuring that the price is equal to the opportunity cost of the resources foregone in producing it. This principle has been used in the pricing of goods produced in the public sector. The drawback is that the price may fail to reflect some of the fixed costs of production and so lead to losses being made.

**marginal efficiency of capital or investment:** the extra revenue generated by one more unit of capital invested. This will need to at least equal the interest rate on borrowed funds if the investment is to be seen as worthwhile. From this can be derived the theory of the demand for investment funds, which is a part of the basic *Keynesian model* of the macro-economy.

**marginal product:** the extra output generated by the addition of one more unit of an input.

**marginal productivity theory** gives one explanation of how wages are determined. The theory is that wages will be equal to the value of the marginal product of labour. Profit maximising employers will hire people up to the point where the costs of doing so (the wage) is just equal to the value of the output added. Although this can be quite helpful in giving an understanding of the forces underlying the demand for labour, it has little practical usefulness in that it is usually rather hard to tell exactly how much output one particular person has added to the total.

**marginal propensity to consume (MPC):** the proportion of an increase in income which will be spent on consumption. It is important within the Keynesian model of the macro-economy because, along with the *marginal rate of taxation* and the *marginal propensity to import,* (i.e. the *marginal rate of leakage*) it helps to determine the size of the *multiplier*. The higher the marginal propensity to consume, the larger the multiplier will be.

**marginal propensity to import:** that proportion of an increase in income which is spent on imports.

**marginal propensity to save:** that proportion of an increase in income which is saved.

**marginal rate of leakage:** that proportion of an increase in income which leaks out of the *circular flow of money* in the form of saving, taxes and imports. The marginal propensity to consume and the marginal rate of leakage together are equal to one by definition. So a high marginal rate of leakage will be associated with a small *multiplier*.

**marginal rate of tax:** the proportion of an increase in income which is taken in tax. This may be used as a macro- or a microeconomic concept.

**marginal revenue:** the extra revenue which comes from selling one more unit of output. In a highly competitive situation this will usually be the price of the product. Where the firm has some monopoly power, it may be less than the price, because selling one more unit of output may entail reducing the price.

**marginal social benefit:** includes all the benefits which result from a change in the output of a particular product, whether they are felt by the person who bought the product, or by some third party. It thus takes in any positive *externalities*. If people spend money on extra clothes, they benefit from feeling good in them. There is an additional benefit to anyone else who appreciates their appearance. The marginal social benefit of devoting additional land to sheep farming in mountain areas includes the benefit of the meat and wool produced, and also the benefit to people who like to see the countryside farmed in the traditional way.

**marginal social cost** includes all the costs of producing one more unit of output, whether they be the costs of production incurred by the business, or the external costs, which may be born by third parties. So the marginal social cost of producing more electricity in coal-fired power stations includes the cost of the coal and other inputs, and also the cost to people in the neighbourhood of the increased atmospheric pollution. This may show up in health problems, or any other result of pollution of this kind.

**market:** a term used to describe buyers, sellers and their means of communicating and trading.

**market-based pricing:** a collective term for pricing methods that are based on market rather than cost considerations. (See *pricing methods*.)

**market capitalisation:** the value placed on a company by the *stock market*. It is the number of shares issued multiplied by their market price. It is important to realise that this is only one way of valuing a company and there are others based on asset values. A *take-over bid* is another way.

**market clearing:** the process by which price changes until the amount which sellers wish to sell is exactly equal to the amount which buyers demand. If this process does not occur, then there is said to be *market failure*.

**market economy** is an economy which allows market forces to determine the allocation of resources. Within it there are factor markets where the price of *factors of production* are determined by the supply and demand for those factors, and product markets, where the price of goods and services are determined in the same way.

Pros:
- automatic: no need for regulation
- offers freedom of choice
- efficiently allocates resources
- leads to greater economic growth.

Cons:
- means those with the most money have greatest power
- leads to inequality of income
- the price of a good may not reflect its cost to society; these costs are called *externalities*
- monopolisation within market-places can lead to inefficiency and exploitation.

The main advantage of relying on the *market mechanism* is that it is automatic and has the potential to lead to both *technical efficiency* and *allocative efficiency*. However, the existence of *market failure* in some instances means that such efficiency is not always achieved. Furthermore, market economies do tend to exploit the weakest members of society. For these reasons they are always modified or regulated in some way by governments. The extent to which this regulation takes place is a political decision: in the formally communist countries, free markets were almost completely eliminated and replaced by central planning, but this proved to be a mistake, not only because it was expensive and inefficient to operate, but also because it stifled initiative, and led to lower living standards. A compromise between a wholly planned and a market economy is called a *mixed economy*.

**market failure** occurs when the mechanisms of supply and demand fail to allocate resources in the most efficient way, because of *market imperfections*. Also the market may fail to produce goods that are wanted (e.g. *public goods*). The market may fail to clear, as in the case where large numbers of people are unemployed. Or it may clear, but in a way that has been distorted, e.g. where organisations have some degree of monopoly power. Markets also fail when *externalities* such as water and air pollution are not costed, so that firms make private profit at the cost of social welfare. In these cases it is argued that governments should intervene.

**market forces** are the forces of supply and demand in the market-place. When demand is growing, other things being equal, the price will rise. If supply is rising but demand is constant, prices will tend to be pushed downwards. Market forces lead to price changes which reflect underlying changes in demand and supply, and influence the allocation of resources so that production is in line with consumer demand and reflects the real resource cost of production.

**market imperfections** come in many forms, each of which is a departure from the conditions of *perfect competition*. The main ones are:

- few firms in the market
- differentiated products
- imperfect information
- immobile factors of production.

**marketing:** the all-embracing function that links the company with customer tastes to get the right product to the right place at the right time. Marketing decisions are made through the *marketing model*, based on the findings of *market research*, and carried out through the *marketing mix*. At all stages in the marketing process, the firm needs to work closely with the production department and *research and development*, to ensure that what is promised is delivered.

**marketing mix:** the main variables through which a firm carries out its marketing strategy, often known as the four Ps:

- product (including range of pack sizes and/or flavours or colours)
- price (long-term *pricing strategy* and *pricing method*)
- promotion (*branding*, *advertising*, *packaging* and *sales promotions*)
- place (choosing *distribution channels* and seeking shop distribution).

Textbooks tend to treat each of the elements of the mix with equal importance. Few marketing companies would agree. The most important element of the mix is the product, which needs to be designed to meet the requirements of those within the *target market*. If this process has been achieved successfully (probably through extensive *market research*) the other three elements of the mix become clear. The price must be suited to the pockets of the *target market* and to the image of the product. The promotion will be through the media that they watch or read, while the place should be the shops visited by those types of people.

The only one of these elements that is outside the company's control is place, for obtaining shop distribution is a very difficult task in crowded modern market-places. No retailers have spare shelving, so in order for your product to gain distribution, another product will probably have to be removed from the shelves. Needless to say, every manufacturer is fighting hard to keep its distribution as high as possible, so it is never easy to gain or to keep hold of high distribution levels.

**marketing model:** a framework for making marketing decision in a scientific manner. It is derived from F W *Taylor*'s method of basing decisions on scientifically gathered research evidence.

The model has five stages:

**1** Set the marketing objective based on the company's *objectives*. For example, if the corporate goal is *diversification*, the specific marketing objective may be to launch a product into a new market that can achieve minimum sales of £5 m. within 18 months.

**2** Gather data: this will require the collection of *quantitative* and *qualitative* data about the market's size, competitive structure, distribution pattern and consumer attitudes.

**3** Form hypotheses, theories about how best to achieve the objective. For example a producer of canned food might consider whether to:

● move into the frozen-food market

● move into the chilled-food market

● take the more radical route of moving into petfoods.

**4** Test the hypotheses: this may be done solely through *market research* or, more thoroughly, by *test marketing* new product ideas. After the results are evaluated, a decision can be reached on how to proceed.

**5** Control and review: making decisions is only one part of the marketing function; implementing them is no less important. The means of implementation will be via the *marketing mix*. The effectiveness of the distribution, pricing or promotion policies must be controlled, with careful conclusions drawn from the success or failure of the project.

Having completed the task, the managers must look towards new objectives. So the process begins again.

**marketing objectives** are the goals a marketing department must achieve in order to help the company achieve its overall objectives. Marketing objectives may include:

● halting a decline in market share

● making a brand's image younger

● boosting the awareness of a brand that has faded from consumers' memories.

**marketing plan:** a report detailing a firm's marketing objectives and strategy, including: costings, forecast results and contingency plans. The stages of constructing a marketing plan are as follows:

**1**  Conduct a marketing audit to ensure full knowledge of the firm's marketing assets. This could be supplemented by a *SWOT analysis* (identifying the firm's marketing strengths, weaknesses, opportunities and threats).

**2**  Set clear objectives for the coming year based on goals for three to five years ahead. These might include targets for sales, *market share*, distribution levels and brand image ratings.

**3**  Devise a strategy for achieving the objectives that operates within a defined budget and covers: new product development, new product launches and going brands.

**marketing research:** see *market research*

**marketing strategy:** a medium- to long-term plan for meeting marketing objectives. The word 'strategy' suggests a carefully thought-out, integrated plan. It should set out the balance of marketing activity between new and existing products – with carefully costed budgets. The strategy is likely to be fully researched and then implemented through the *marketing mix* – the four Ps of product, price, place and promotion. A successful marketing strategy is one that achieves the objectives without going over budget. See also *marketing plan*.

**market-led pricing:** setting a price for your product based upon what the market can bear. This contrasts with producer-led pricing methods such as cost-plus. Market-led pricing will be particularly important in markets where *product differentiation* is low and therefore *price elasticity* is high.

**market makers** are people who find buyers and sellers for *stocks and shares*. As it may not be possible to match a buyer with a seller immediately, market makers often have to take the customer's order on to their own books. Hence they are 'making a market' in the shares. Formerly they were known as stockjobbers, and were forbidden from dealing directly with the public, that function being performed by *stockbrokers*.

**market manipulation** is the idea that it is possible to influence markets to make them less than perfectly competitive. Firms attempt to manipulate markets in a number of ways, for instance by *collusion* with other producers, or by cross-subsidising one market by another in order to force out the competition. Even *advertising* could be said to represent manipulation, if it makes consumers willing to pay a premium price for a good which is not really any different from one produced by other firms.

**market mechanism** is the operation of demand and supply, which together determine price. If the market mechanism works smoothly it should allocate *factors of production* in the most efficient way to produce those goods which consumers want in the right amount and at the right time. In practice there is bound to be a degree of *market failure*, especially since there is a time lag between changes in demand and changes in supply. In particular, economic theory often assumes that the market mechanism is working under conditions of *perfect competition*. This is not usually the case. (See also *market forces*.)

**market niche:** a gap in the range of products or services offered within a market. Having identified that such a gap exists, a business must decide whether the niche is large enough to be profitable and if so, how best to fill it. (See *niche marketing*.)

**market orientation:** the extent to which a firm's strategic thinking stems from looking outwards to consumer tastes and competitive pressures. The main alternative is *production orientation*, where the firm looks inward to its own production needs and limitations. For many years, British firms were criticised for their lack of market orientation, but that changed in the 1980s. However, there is a danger that market orientation results in lost power and status for engineers and production managers, which might affect long-term technological competitiveness.

**market penetration:** a pricing strategy for a new product based on a desire to achieve high sales volume and high *market share*, perhaps with the effect of discouraging competitors from entering the market. Penetration pricing would mean setting the price relatively low, thereby accepting low *gross profit* margins with the expectation that the high *turnover* will allow *overheads* to be covered.

Pros: • very useful if the market is one in which customers build up *brand loyalty* (prices can be pushed up later)
• sensible if you have only a small technological edge, because competitors will be arriving soon.

Cons: • loses the opportunity to charge higher prices to those willing to pay them for being first or innovators
• once a low-price image has been established in the customers' mind, it is hard to shift, and may always be associated with low quality.

**market period:** the period of time in which the quantity supplied cannot be altered. For example, the quantity of a crop product such as potatoes cannot be altered until the next season. This means that supply is perfectly inelastic, i.e. the quantity is fixed. The length of the market period will vary from product to product. For some manufactured products it will barely exist.

**market positioning:** where a manufacturer positions a brand within a market-place, in terms of image, pricing and distribution. *Upmarket* or *downmarket*? Young and trendy or old and established? For specialists or for the general public? Such a decision is fundamental to the long-term marketing strategy of a product. (See *mapping*.)

**market power:** the degree to which a firm has power over its market. Any person or business may acquire market power if they are able to distinguish what they offer for sale from that which is on offer elsewhere, or if there is little competition from other sellers. Similarly, a *monopsony* develops market power when it has more influence in the market than the seller does.

A person with scarce skills which are in strong demand will have some power in the labour market because buyers of those skills are competing for the few people who have them. A business will have some market power if it has few competitors. Marketing strategies are ways of increasing market power and reducing the threat from competing products. Market power opens up the possibility of being able to determine the price at which the product sells.

A firm like Heinz, for instance, has a more than 50 per cent *market share* in several large food market segments. It therefore has power when negotiating with raw material suppliers, power over the retailers whose customers expect Heinz on the shelves, and influence over consumers through the strength of its brand names and the size of its advertising budget.

Market power leads to reduced *price elasticity*, and therefore presents an opportunity for increasing prices and *profit margins*.

**market price** is the one at which the demand for a product exactly matches its 'supply'. It is therefore also known as the 'market clearing' price. (labelled MP on the diagram).

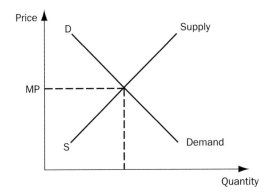

**market research:** the process of gathering *primary* and *secondary data* on the buying habits, lifestyle, usage and attitudes of actual and potential customers. The intention is to gather evidence that can enable marketing and production decisions to be made in a more scientific way than would otherwise be possible. Most large consumer goods firms would agree with Sherlock Holmes (in SCANDAL IN BOHEMIA), 'It is a capital mistake to theorise before one has data.'

Market research can be subdivided as shown in the following diagram:

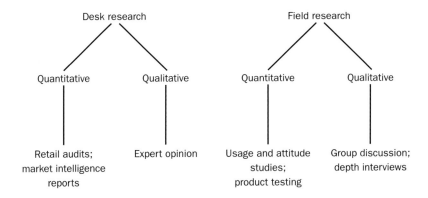

**market saturation** occurs when all those who want a product already have one. If the product is a *durable* (such as a freezer), demand will dry up until wear and tear creates a replacement market. With *consumables*, market saturation should not result in falling sales, but will inevitably prevent sales growth.

**market segmentation:** analysing a market to identify the different types of consumer. By matching the consumer categories to the types of product on offer, unfilled *market niches* may emerge. The potential profitability of filling these gaps can then be assessed. The main ways in which a market can be segmented are:

- demographically, e.g. by age, social class or sex
- psychographically (by attitudes and tastes), e.g. trendy versus staid, or home-loving versus adventurous
- geographically, by region

**market share:** the percentage of all the sales within a market that are held by one brand or company. This can be measured by volume (units sold) or by value (the revenue generated). Analysing trends in market share is important for a firm because it shows its position in relation to the market as a whole. It may not be good enough, for example, to have a 5 per cent sales increase if the market is rising at 10 per cent, as market share is being lost. The 5 per cent sales increase may boost profits this year, but if the market becomes highly price competitive as it reaches *maturity*, the firm's products may not be strong enough to survive.

**market-sharing agreement:** a *restrictive practice* in which a number of firms in an industry agree to allow each a profitable part of the total market. Generally this is illegal as it means that price competition is being suspended (forcing consumers to pay excessive prices). A market-sharing agreement is only likely if *supply* is dominated by a small number of firms (an *oligopoly*), and if it is hard for new competitors to enter the market. See also *Competition Act 1998*.

**market size:** the total sales of all the producers within a market-place, measured either by volume (units sold) or by value (the revenue generated). This information is needed to:

- assess whether the market is big enough to be worth entering
- calculate the *market share* held by your own products and brands
- identify whether the market is expanding or contracting

**market standing:** the reputation of a firm amongst its suppliers, distributors and customers. If its market standing is high, a firm can feel confident that its new products will get *distribution* and *product trial*.

**market structure** describes the competitive forces within a market. For example, in the biscuit market, one firm has 50 per cent of all sales, whereas the market for frozen food has many competitors, each with less than 20 per cent of sales.

**market testing** is an investigation by a *public-sector* business of the price that *private-sector* firms would charge to supply a service. As a consequence they might contract private companies to supply services such as accounting (and, by implication, make their own accountants redundant).

**mark-up** is the amount of *gross profit* added on to the direct cost per unit, usually expressed as a percentage.

FORMULA: $\dfrac{\text{gross profit}}{\text{cost of sales}} \times 100 = \text{profit mark-up}$

**Worked example: A shirt bought by a shop for £8 and sold for £12 has a mark-up of:**

$\dfrac{£4}{£8} \times 100 = \textbf{50\%}$

**market value** is the price determined by supply and demand. Sellers often say things like, 'My motorbike is worth £1000', but when they come to sell it the bike realises only £400, which is its true 'value'. In the harsh world of economics, goods have no intrinsic value; in other words it makes no difference how much it costs to produce them, their true value has to be related to the amount people are willing to pay for them.

**Marshall A** (1842–1924): an economist who worked mainly at Cambridge, laying the foundations of microeconomic theory. He invented the term price elasticity and developed the basics of price theory which students of economics still learn.

**Marx K** (1818–1883): the thinker and writer who did most of all to promote the ideal of social equality. He perceived capitalism as one stage in economic development, because it would eventually bring about its own destruction. It would create the conditions in which revolution brought about by workers would overthrow capitalism and replace it with the collective ownership of the means of production. Workers would be paid according to their needs rather than their market power, and in this way capitalists (owners of capital) would no longer be able to exploit their employees by paying them less than the value of what they produced.

The development of communism in Russia (from 1917) and later in Eastern Europe and China (from 1948) was based on Marx's thinking. In all cases communist revolutions created much more egalitarian societies than those which preceded them. But the system was eventually found wanting because most of the countries involved experienced rather low growth rates. This meant that they were unable to reduce poverty as effectively as many capitalist economies had done. When free elections were held in Russia and Eastern Europe in 1989, the communist party attracted relatively few votes and the economies concerned began the transition to the market system. China, Cuba, North Korea and Vietnam still have communist governments but are becoming steadily more market-oriented. Watch this space.

Marx was banished from his native Germany in 1849, for his political activities, and settled in London where he did most of his writing in the Reading Room of the British Museum. He died long before his ideas came to fruition.

**Maslow A** (1908–1970): an American psychologist whose work on human needs has had great impact upon management theorists. Best known for his work on the *hierarchy of needs*.

**mass production:** the system devised by Henry Ford that turned raw materials into finished product in a continuously moving, highly mechanised process. Mass production's great strength was its high productivity, but this relied on manufacturing vast numbers of an identical product. This was epitomised in Henry Ford's famous phrase about his Model T, 'You can have any colour you want . . . as long as it's black.' As modern markets have become increasingly segmented, mass production has given way to *lean production* or *flexible specialisation*.

**maternity and paternity regulations** set out the entitlement to leave from employment during and after pregnancy.

**matrix management:** the willingness to organise the management of a task along lines that cut across normal departmental boundaries. A new product development team might be formed from an engineer, a research chemist, a marketing manager and a designer. This means that each team member can end up with two bosses: their department boss and the project leader. This has the potential to cause problems, though the Japanese seem to use this system effectively.

Pros:
- ensures that projects are better coordinated than with four departments meeting occasionally
- if many different project teams are organised, it gives more people an opportunity to use their abilities.

Cons:
- individuals may suffer if both bosses make heavy demands on them
- there is a failure to provide the clear line of accountability present when everyone has just one boss.

**mature economies** are those which have been fully industrialised for some time, and are now experiencing a shift of resources into the service sector. The USA and the UK are examples of economies where the manufacturing sector has tended to shrink while a number of services have shown above average growth rates. Financial services, tourism, health care and a variety of personal and professional services have all been growing. (See also *deindustrialisation*.)

**maturity** is the peak sales period of a *product's life cycle*. It is likely to be a phase of fierce competition from new producers attracted to the market during the growth stage. This may cause a shake-out in which the less successful withdraw in the face of heavy losses. The survivors could then enjoy a highly profitable decline stage. Alternatively, mature products may be relaunched in *extension strategies* designed to rejuvenate and thereby postpone sales decline.

**Mayo E** (1880–1949): Elton Mayo was a follower of F W *Taylor* whose experiments led him to conclude that scientific management could not explain key aspects of people's behaviour at work. Many of his findings derived from his direction of research studies at a factory at Hawthorne, USA, from which stemmed the phrase the *Hawthorne effect*. He gave rise to what became known as the *Human Relations School* of management thinking.

**mean:** see *arithmetic average*

**means-tested benefits** are social security payments which are available only to those whose incomes are below a certain level. Examples include income support and *Working Families Tax Credit*.

**measure of central tendency:** an attempt to describe a *frequency distribution* in a single measure. These are three main measures: *mean*, *median* and *mode*.

**media advertising:** paying for advertising space or time in national, regional or local media. Media advertising aimed at consumers is known as above the line marketing.

**median:** a *measure of central tendency* which divides the distribution into two equal parts. If the items in the distribution are ranked in ascending order, the *median* is the middle item. One advantage of the median is that it is not affected by extreme values. A disadvantage is that it gives findings that are biased towards the most numerous and away from the most important.

**media planning:** the process of selecting media to advertise to your target market as cost-effectively as possible. This function is usually carried out by the media department of an advertising agency. It is a four-stage process:

## media selection

1   Gather the research data to identify your target market.

2   Decide (in discussion with the creative team) the broad media choice: television, newspapers, magazines, cinema, radio or posters.

3   Select exactly which magazines or television regions would be most cost-effective (e.g. VOGUE for reaching wealthy, fashion-conscious women).

4   Allocate the media budget as cost-efficiently as possible between the chosen media (e.g. buy more television commercials on the station that reaches your market more economically).

Stages 3 and 4 are undertaken by comparing the cost of an advertising space with the number of readers that publication has in your target market. The following table shows how this might work for a brand of cider targeted at 18–35-year-old women.

| Publication | Cost of colour page | Thousands of 18–35 women readers | Cost per thousand readers |
|---|---|---|---|
| Cosmopolitan | £24 000 | 1 650 | £14.55 |
| Woman | £32 000 | 2 950 | £10.85 |
| Hello | £18 000 | 2 422 | £7.64 |

In this example each thousand women in the target market could be reached at half the cost in HELLO magazine than in COSMOPOLITAN, so HELLO would be the best value medium.

**media selection:** see *media planning*

**mediation:** another term for *conciliation*

**medium of exchange:** a function of money, which allows people to exchange their labour or other *factors of production* for the goods and services they want to consume. Without money as a medium of exchange, we should be reduced to *bartering* and straight swaps of one item for another, which would be very inconvenient.

**memorandum of association** shows the *objectives* of the company, the amount of *authorised share capital* as well as the classes of shares and the voting rights of the shareholders. It is one of the two documents needed for a firm to become incorporated as a *limited liability* company (the other being the *articles of association*).

**mentor:** an experienced and trusted advisor to a new recruit; in effect, an appointed father-figure. This is a modern development of *human relations* theory that ensures that all recruits have a senior figure they can turn to for advice. The mentor will keep any comments or complaints confidential, and could therefore be a more effective advisor than the recruit's boss.

**merchandising:** visiting retail outlets to ensure that a company's products are displayed in as attractive and prominent a way as possible. Merchandisers might offer special display stands or shelves to retailers, hoping that they will use these, in effect, point-of-sale advertisements for the company.

**merchant bank:** a form of specialised commercial bank which performs a variety of banking functions, although rarely those directly concerned with the public. Merchant banks developed through the activities of overseas traders who dealt originally with the financing of imports and exports. They still fulfil this role, but their most important functions today are as issuing houses, and as advisers to businesses, particularly on matters concerned with mergers and take-overs. As issuing houses they advise firms on the right time for and methods of raising capital on the *Stock Exchange*. They also act as underwriters to the issue by guaranteeing to buy stock which is not immediately sold at the time of issue. In recent years, many merchant banks have become part of larger banking *conglomerates*, but some of their names live on. Employees of some merchant banks can be seen on the television offering expert advice on economic and financial events and issues.

**merger:** an agreement between the managements and shareholders of two companies of approximately equal size to bring both firms together under a common board of directors. (See *take-over*.)

**mergers and acquisitions (M and A)** is a collective term used by American-influenced City institutions to denote the general area of corporate *mergers* and *take-overs*. Many *merchant banks* have M and A departments that can charge substantial fees for advising companies on how to win or to defend against *take-over bids*.

**merit goods** are provided by the government for those who are deemed to need them. Examples include health care, education and social services.

**merit pay:** a form of bonus payment received by employees considered to have performed at a high standard during a year or half-year. To evaluate who deserves a merit pay award, *performance appraisal* is often used.

Pros: • merit pay is a reward system that can apply to all employees (whereas commission, for example, will only be received by those involved in direct selling).

Cons: • often involves tiny sums: a 5 per cent bonus may seem poor reward for outstanding work
• offers scope for mistrust and misunderstanding if some workers suspect there has been favouritism in the allocation of the bonuses.

**method study:** analysis of the method by which workers approach a task with the intention of identifying opportunities for improvement. This was F W *Taylor*'s scientific companion to *work study*. First, the consultant would decide how to subdivide the whole production process into small units of work, then method study would decide how each task should be carried out. Method study was carried out by timing each action and recording the motion and effort used. The presence of the so-called time-and-motion men was quickly to become a cause of *industrial relations* disputes.

**me-too product:** a new brand that is largely an imitation of a successful existing one. Usually me-toos struggle to get distribution in shops and are looked down on by customers. So they can only gain sales if they sell at an unprofitably large discount to the price of the original product. Occasionally, though, a firm with an exceptionally wide and powerful distribution network can make me-toos more successful than the original. Walls Cornetto was a me-too of Lyons Maid's King Cone, and Magnum a me-too of the Häagen-Dazs Stick Bar. In both cases, consumers became so familiar with the Walls product that its origin was soon forgotten.

**microcomputers** are the smallest computers in the series beginning with *mainframe computers* and going through *minicomputers*. They are generally used by small or medium-sized businesses.

**microeconomics** is the study of how individual markets work. It includes price theory, the theory of the firm, and the study of labour markets. It provides a theoretical framework for analysis of decisions made by firms and individuals concerning consumption, production and the way factors of production are to be put to use. Analysis may be of one particular market (*partial equilibrium analysis*) or it may involve the interelationships between different markets (*general equilibrium analysis*). The former would, for example, look at the way an increase in demand for bicycles might affect the price and quantity of bicycles sold, while the latter would go on to look at the impact on numbers employed in the industry and their wage rates, and the secondary effects on any other products.

**middleman:** the *agent* or wholesaler who brings together buyers and sellers. It is often assumed that middlemen serve little function, but merely add their *mark-up* to the retail prices of items. Some middlemen could be regarded as parasitic (such as arms dealers), but most are fulfilling the normal *wholesaling* function of breaking bulk.

**milking a product:** maximising the profit from a brand, usually by pushing its price up as far as possible without forcing regular purchasers to switch to another brand. This high price level is likely to discourage new users from starting to buy the product, therefore the brand's *product life cycle* will be shortened. So milking a product implies short-term profit maximisation, even at the cost of the brand's long-term prospects.

The Boston Matrix shows the situation in which a firm might milk a product. If the firm has two brands with a high *market share*, one in a growth sector and another in a declining sector, the correct strategy would be to milk the *cash cow* and use the funds to support the 'rising star'.

**milk round:** the slang term used for the annual practice of some large firms to visit many universities and recruit the best of those interviewed as management trainees.

**minimum efficient scale (MES):** the lowest level of output at which costs can be kept at their minimum. In the diagram this is the lowest output at which average total cost is minimised.

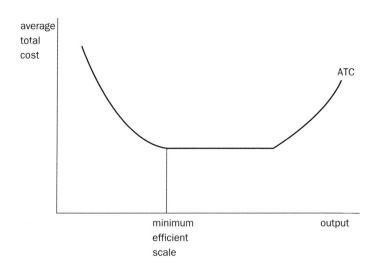

For most types of production, efficient production is possible across a range of output levels, so the average total cost has a flat-bottomed U-shape and the minimum efficient scale is on the extreme left of the bottom of the curve.

**minimum unit cost:** at a certain level of output, costs of production will be the lowest possible.

**minimum wage:** the legal minimum hourly wage rate an employer is allowed to pay an employee. The national minimum wage was introduced in April 1999. The rate for 2002 was:

| | |
|---|---|
| Up to 18 | no minimum applies |
| 18–21 | £3.20 per hour |
| over 21 | £4.20 per hour |

The Low Pay Commission is responsible for reviewing the rates regularly. The objective is to prevent employers from paying very low wages. Opponents of minimum wages hold that they reduce the demand for labour, thus creating unemployment. Effectively, they keep wage rates above the equilibrium level and lead to an excess supply of labour. The evidence suggests that this may not be the case. Employers interviewed since the introduction of the minimum wage in the UK mostly say their employment levels have not been affected.

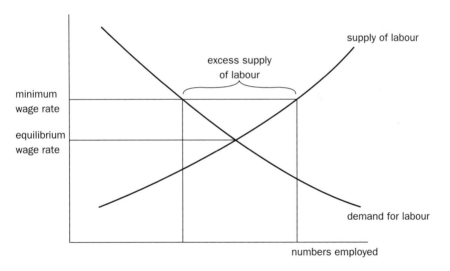

*Minimum wage rate may reduce employment*

**minority interest:** this arises where a *subsidiary* of a *holding company* is not wholly owned and a minority of the shares is owned by others. In the holding company accounts, the minority shareholdings of the subsidiaries are *long-term liabilities* and the profits due to the minority shareholders are deducted from *profit* after tax.

**Mintel:** standing for Marketing Intelligence, this is one of the leading sources of secondary marketing information. Every month Mintel analyses the *consumers*, producers, *advertising* and *distribution* within a range of markets. One month they might look at chocolate confectionery, ice-cream and washing-up liquid; the next it might be cosmetics, fruit juice and detergents. A Mintel report is likely to contain most of the *secondary data* a firm needs for its marketing planning (or a student needs for the background to a business project). As Mintel is very expensive to subscribe to, few public libraries have it.

**Mintzberg H** (b. 1939): an American writer on organisation theory who sought to explain what managers actually do. He rejected the traditional notion that managers plan, organise, coordinate and control. His research showed that most senior and middle managers spend little time thinking ahead. Their days are spent on a series of small tasks related to the problems of the moment and use mainly *oral communication*. Mintzberg recommended that managers should undergo far more training into their role and their use of time.

**mission statement:** a document detailing the aims that should provide the sense of common purpose to direct and stimulate the organisation. Their purpose is set out by Sir John Harvey-Jones in his book ALL TOGETHER NOW (Heinemann, 1994): 'Ultimately the businesses that win are those where all the people have the same aim and give freely in their commitment to it.' Advocates of mission statements believe that their focus on goals, such as high quality and customer service are far easier for employees to relate to than profit. Critics suggest that the statements are little more than public relations exercises.

Examples of mission statements include:

- James Dyson: 'Long term business success based on newly invented, innovatively designed products.'

- The Body Shop: 'Tirelessly work to narrow the gap between principle and practice, whilst making fun, passion and care part of our daily lives.'

**mixed economy:** one which combines a *market economy* with some centrally planned or State-run enterprises. A wholly market-led economy has certain disadvantages. Certain members of society, usually those who are economically the weakest, may receive very low real incomes. Also, left to themselves, businesses may fail to provide certain items which consumers do want: these are known as *public goods*. Consequently governments regulate the workings of the market through legislation, or by providing some goods and services through state enterprises. This is known as a mixed economy. In the UK, those industries run indirectly by government have included coal, steel, gas and electricity production, and services such as British Rail and the Post Office. Since 1979, there has been a move towards *privatisation*, which has extended the influence of the market and reduced the size of the public sector in most countries.

| Centrally planned economy | Mixed economy | Market economy |
|---|---|---|
| Production organised and run by the State | Some production State-run, e.g. large-scale, 'essential' services | Production market-driven |
| Labour force directed and paid by the State | State and private firms compete for factors of production and customers | Wages determined by the market |
| Prices of goods and services controlled | | Prices determined by supply and demand |

**mode:** the most frequently occurring result within a set of data. This is a *measure of central tendency*.

**model:** a representation of reality designed to provide insights into how and why an event has occurred or is expected to occur. Models may be presented in graphical form (such as a *break-even chart*), or they may be stored as a series of equations within a computer program. These equations represent the relationships between the variables which are included in the model. (See also *Treasury model*.)

**modem:** an accessory that enables one computer to be linked to others.

**modern apprenticeship:** a training programme which teaches craft skills and which is provided by the *Learning and Skills Council* in collaboration with local employers and colleges.

**monetarism** is an economic theory associated with the American economist Milton *Friedman*. The theory holds that the supply of money is at the centre of economic activity, and since the government is the only authority which can increase or decrease the supply of money, it is the government's responsibility to control the supply with care. If governments print too much money or allow too much credit, *inflation* will result, since *supply* will outstrip *demand*. Monetarists often believe also that governments should minimise their involvement in the economy and allow markets to determine the efficient allocation of resources. They tend to be rather pessimistic about the government's chances of bringing about any improvement in the allocation of resources. They see the control of inflation as a far more important objective of government policy than reducing unemployment. Their views have been contrasted with those of the Keynesians, for whom unemployment has generally been the top priority. The differences of view hinge on the question of the extent to which monetary growth should be controlled.

**monetary policy** is concerned with the *money supply*, rates of interest, exchange rates and the amount of *credit* available, in order to control the level of spending within the economy. Its importance was enhanced when Conservative UK governments made tax cuts an objective. This has meant that fiscal changes were unlikely to be made for reasons of macroeconomic control. So the main mechanism for altering the level of *aggregate demand* was monetary policy.

The Bank of England, in common with other central banks, has for some years found it difficult to control the supply of money (the amount of credit created) directly, so the thrust of monetary policy has been through control of the demand for money. This is achieved by varying interest rates. The Bank will announce a change in its *base rate*. Borrowers will economise and reduce their demand for loans as fast as they are able. The growth of bank credit will be reduced. This means that borrowers, be they investors or home buyers, bear the brunt of a tight monetary policy.

The experience of 1988–90 provides a useful example. In 1988, inflation was accelerating and the economy was clearly overheating. The Bank raised interest rates quite sharply. The increased cost of borrowing made businesses cut back their investment plans, reducing injections into the economy and producing a downward multiplier effect which ended in recession, 1990–91. At the same time, the cost of mortgages became much higher, and many people had difficulty in making their monthly payments. There was an immediate drop in consumer spending, because more of home-buyers' incomes were being spent on the interest payments. People who were not in debt were virtually unaffected by government policy, until it began to slow down the whole economy.

It is important to remember that monetary policy will always operate with a time lag. Most spending decisions take time, and the full effects of a change in interest rates may take up to two years to work its way through the economy. In May 1997 the Chancellor of the Exchequer made the Bank of England much more independent of the government. Monetary policy is now decided by the *Monetary Policy Committee* of the *Bank of England*.

**Monetary Policy Committee:** the group of Bank of England officials and independent experts which decides monetary policy. The committee meets monthly to agree any change to interest rates. If it wishes rates to change it will announce a change in *base rate*. The Governor of the Bank of England takes the chair and minutes are published two weeks later. The MPC's target for the underlying rate of inflation rate is currently 2½ per cent. If the rate diverges by more than 1 per cent from this, they will have to write to the Chancellor of the Exchequer explaining why and what should be done. The MPC itself has decided that earnings growth must be kept below 4½ per cent if inflation is to be kept low.

**monetary squeeze** describes a *monetary policy* which attempts to restrict spending in the economy by raising interest rates and thus limiting the amount of *credit*.

**monetary union:** see *economic and monetary union*

**money:** anything which is generally acceptable as a means of payment. Money is usually defined according to its functions. These are: a medium of exchange, a unit of account, a store of value and a standard of deferred payments. Keep in mind that these functions may be affected when money loses its value during a period of rapid inflation.

**money illusion** refers to the mistake people make when they confuse an increase in money values with an increase in *real* values. It is most obvious when people complain about increasing prices while overlooking the fact that they have had an increase in income. It is possible that they may think they have had an increase in real income when in fact prices have risen by the same percentage as their income.

**money income** is the measure of a person's income without taking price levels into account. So, if your money income was £10 000 this year and it rises to £20 000 next, you are twice as well off in money terms. If prices have doubled during the same period (ignoring taxes etc.), your *real income* will not have changed at all.

**money market:** where buyers and sellers of financial securities and loans come together at an agreed price, or interest rate. There is no single physical market-place, since transactions are usually conducted over the phone, through on-line computer links or through faxes. The term money market is usually taken to refer to the market for short-term loans of various kinds.

**money supply** can be measured in a number of ways, from a very narrow definition simply including notes and coins in circulation, to a much wider one which includes *credit*. The reason why broad definitions are used is because goods and services can be bought on credit as well as with cash, and so that will affect overall spending power. In the UK there are two measures of money supply. M0 is the narrow measure of money. M0 is defined as notes and coin in circulation plus banks' balances held with the Bank of England. In itself this total is of no great significance, since only a proportion of transactions are completed using notes and coin. However it has been found to be a useful indicator at times. M4 is notes and coin plus all UK residents' deposits with banks and building societies. This provides a broad measure of spending power. The money supply must be allowed to grow in line with output. The figures have to be interpreted with caution because they can be affected by a wide range of events, and there is often considerable uncertainty about their true meaning. This makes *monetary policy* difficult at times. In recent years the money supply figures have received less attention in the press than they used to.

**Monopolies and Mergers Commission:** a government-financed organisation whose function was to oversee proposed *mergers* and to check that where *monopolies* did exist, they were not against the public interest. In 1999 it was renamed the *Competition Commission*.

**monopolistic competition** occurs when there are many firms in the industry, each selling a slightly *differentiated product*. The market is characterised by easy *entry* and *exit*, so that small businesses can easily be set up and there is thus strong competition. Yet each has a small degree of *monopoly* power because the differentiated product allows consumers to choose to buy from a particular producer. Restaurants, hairdressers, estate agents, potteries and many others illustrate situations of monopolistic competition. It merges into *oligopoly* if there are relatively few producers, or a few large ones and many smaller ones. Building societies provide an example of the latter situation.

**monopoly** is in theory a single producer within a market. This represents one end of a spectrum of competition, at the other end of which is *perfect competition*.

In practice such dominant producers rarely exist, especially as the definition of the market widens. The potential danger of monopolies is that they will exploit the *consumer*, either by charging excessive prices, or by offering a poor service, or they will simply waste scarce resources by being inefficient. In some cases, monopolies exhibit all these characteristics, and hence governments exercise legal or voluntary restraints on their activities. In the UK monopolies can be investigated by the *Competition Commission*. The legal definition of a monopoly is a firm with 25 per cent or more of the market. The former nationalised utilities such as gas, electricity and water have *regulators* appointed to control them.

**monopoly legislation** covers the full range of laws which restrict the ability of firms to develop monopoly power. It is operated through the *Office of Fair Trading* and the *Competition Commission*, and also through the *EU*. As well as providing for the investigation of mergers and anti-competitive practices, the OFT deals with *restrictive practices* and restrictive trade agreements.

**monopsony** means a single buyer, as opposed to a *monopoly* which is a single seller. A single buyer is in a strong position to exploit the supplier of the good or service required. This can be done by forcing the supplier to lower the price, delay payment, or impose quality standards. It is sometimes said that large Japanese corporations act as monopsonists, pushing stock holding requirements to their suppliers and forcing each to compete very strongly for business. Large employers in areas where there is not much choice of jobs may exert monopsony power over their employees. This may enable them to hire people at lower wage rates than would otherwise be possible.

**Monthly Digest of Statistics:** the publication that provides regular government statistics on output, the *balance of payments* and many other business, economic and social topics. It is an invaluable *secondary data* source and is stocked by many public libraries. It is published by The Stationery Office.

**morale** is a measurement of the confidence and pride of a workforce. High morale should lead to good quality work and a commitment to participate in problem-solving and decision-making. For a manager, few challenges are more daunting than the attempt to transform a group with very low morale into one with far higher self-confidence and pride.

**morality** (in business): the willingness to make decisions on the basis of principle rather than profit, self-interest, or convenience. This may be easier to achieve for the proprietors of a family business than for the directors of a *public limited company*. The former run the business they own, whereas the latter are answerable to shareholders for whom *profit* may be an overriding consideration.

**Morita A** (1921–99): co-founder of the Sony Corporation, Akio Morita built up his business through innovations such as the transistor radio, the portable television and, most famously, the Walkman. The latter was Morita's conception and he pushed it through to worldwide success even though research suggested that people would have no use for it. From a British viewpoint, Morita's other contribution was to set up one of the first Japanese factories in Britain: the Sony factory in South Wales. This was successful in achieving Japanese standards of and quality, helping to prove that Japanese management methods can work with a British workforce. More inward investment from other Japanese firms followed, as did a substantial shift in attitude by British managers. (See the *Japanese way* and *Japanisation*.)

**mortgage:** a form of commercial loan, secured against a specific property asset. It may or may not be at a fixed rate of interest.

**motivation:** as defined by Professor *Herzberg*, is the will to work due to enjoyment of the work itself. He argues that it should be distinguished from 'movement'. According to the Professor, 'If you do a good job because you want to do a good job, that's motivation. If you do it because you want a house or a Jaguar, that's movement' (JUMPING FOR THE JELLYBEANS, BBC Books, 1973). Many other writers and business people use the term motivation differently, to mean anything that causes people to achieve more than they would otherwise do.

**motivational research:** see *qualitative research*

**motivators** are the aspects of a job that can (according to Professor *Herzberg*) lead to positive job satisfaction on the part of the employee. They include:

- achievement
- recognition for achievement
- meaningful, interesting work
- psychological growth and advancement at work (such as learning new skills or learning more about yourself).

**moving average:** a calculation of the trend that exists within a series of data over time. It enables erratic and seasonal factors within the data to be smoothed out so that the underlying trend can be identified (see the diagram below).

There are three steps required to calculate a moving average:

**1** Decide on an appropriate number of time periods for calculating the average; usually this will be to cover a full year, e.g. four quarters.

**2** Add up the values over the first available time period and average them, e.g. year 1 quarters 1, 2, 3 + 4 (divided by 4).

**3** Repeat the process for the next time period, e.g. year 1 quarters 2, 3 + 4 plus year 2 quarter 1 (divided by 4). Carry this process through until the last four quarters within the data series.

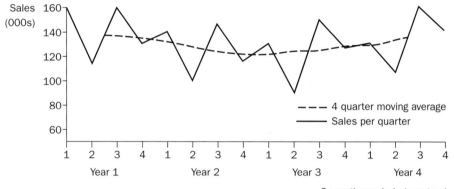

*Using a moving average to show the underlying trend*

**multilateral** negotiations or agreements are those conducted between many parties (usually countries). The negotiators might be representatives of the major *trading blocs*, such as the *European Union*. The most widely known multilateral trade agreement is GATT, the *General Agreement on Tariffs and Trade*, now superseded by the terms of the *World Trade Organisation*. A relatively recent development, the *North American Free Trade Agreement*, NAFTA, is also very important.

**multilateral trade** involves trade, which need not be reciprocal, between a number of countries. For example, if China buys office equipment from the UK, while the USA buys toys from China, and the UK buys computers from the USA, multilateral trade has taken place.

**multinational:** a firm which has its headquarters in one country, but with bases, manufacturing or assembly plants in others. Developing countries are often delighted to welcome multinational companies, but there are two sides to the argument:

Pros:
- they provide employment and income and therefore better living standards
- they may improve the level of expertise of the local workforce and suppliers
- they improve the country's *balance of payments* because imports are reduced.

Cons:
- the jobs provided may only require low-level skills
- they may export all the profits back to the 'home' country

- they may cut corners on health and safety or pollution, which they could not do in their 'home' country
- they have been known to exert excessive political muscle.

**multiple** (retailer): a store chain that has a number of shops that run on similar, head-office dominated lines. Their size provides the opportunity for tough negotiation over the unit prices of the stocks being purchased.

**multiplier:** an increase in *injections* adds to the *circular flow of income*, an amount which will be multiplied as it goes through the economy, raising incomes as it goes, although by smaller increments. For instance, if the government decides to build a new rail link it will inject say, £100 m. into the economy by paying for wages, raw materials and so on. The money will go to the workers and shareholders of the companies concerned, and they will in turn spend more on goods and services, raising wages and profits in consumer-orientated industries. Steadily, then, beneficial knock-on effects are spread through the economy. A decrease in *withdrawals* may have the same effect. Similarly, increased withdrawals or reduced injections will lead to a downward multiplier effect, with a cumulative fall in income. The size of the multiplier depends on the extent to which an increase in income leads to an increase in saving, tax revenue and imports.

**multi-skilling** means training a workforce to be able to work effectively across a wide range of tasks. This is necessary if *demarcation* barriers are to be broken down and the scope of jobs is to be enlarged. Multi-skilling has many short- and long-term benefits:

Short-term:

- staff can cover for absent colleagues
- trained staff can spot maintenance or other problems before they become serious
- faults can be corrected without the need to wait for a series of different tradesmen.

Long-term:

- staff promoted from the shop-floor will have a far wider knowledge and understanding of the process they are now managing
- changes to working practices or to products will be far easier to achieve with a multi-skilled workforce
- wider responsibilities and expertise may help to improve motivation.

**municipal services:** council-run facilities such as leisure centres, community centres, refuse collection and street cleaning. Many of these have been contracted out in recent years, opening the way for private companies to bid for the contract, often in competition with council workers.

**NAIRU:** see *nonaccelerating inflation rate of unemployment*

**national bargaining** occurs when *trade unions* negotiate with employers on behalf of members throughout the country. This has become far less common as firms have looked towards plant (local) bargaining or rejected *collective bargaining* totally, in preference for individual contracts.

**National Debt:** the sum total of all past debt accumulated by the government. It has tended over the long run to rise sharply during war time. In relation to national income, it has fallen during periods of rapid *inflation*. It is currently about 32 per cent of GDP.

**national income** is the sum of all incomes within an economy after allowing for depreciation in one year. It can be arrived at by three methods. The income approach sums all forms of income, wages, salaries, profits (whether distributed to shareholders or not), rents, and net income from abroad. The expenditure approach sums consumption, investment, government expenditure, and exports less imports. The output approach takes the total value of all output. All three methods in theory come to the same, as they each reflect a different aspect of the circular flow of money. In practice, there are discrepancies which reflect the statistical problems of gathering the data.

**national income accounts** are the full range of accounts on the macroeconomy, drawn up by the Office for National Statistics, which show all of the component parts of *national income*.

**National Insurance** is the social framework established in the UK after the Second World War whereby all employers, employees and the self-employed make contributions which provide a number of benefits. These include a safety net in the event of illness or unemployment, pensions beyond retirement age, child and maternity benefits, and various other grants. The increasing cost of state benefits, especially as the population ages into the twenty-first century, has become a matter of concern and some debate since a smaller working population will have to support an ever-growing number of dependents.

**National Insurance charges:** the payments made by employees and employers as their contributions to the funds needed to cover benefit payments.

**nationalisation** describes the transfer of firms and industries from the *private* to the *public sector*. Much of this took place during the Labour government of 1945–51. The objective was to run the industries concerned in the public interest. The nationalised industries included the railways, steelmaking, coalmining, British Airways and BP. Later shipbuilding, Rolls-Royce, and British Leyland (now Rover) joined the list. In time it became apparent that the public sector was not necessarily best placed to make the necessary business decisions; many of the nationalised industries were prone to large losses, and not just because many were declining industries. Since 1979 there has been a policy of denationalisation or *privatisation* which has returned most of them to the private sector.

**national minimum wage:** see *minimum wage*

**national product:** the value of all income earned by factors of production owned by residents. It includes income from investments overseas and excludes interest and profits earned by foreign investments within the country concerned.

**National Saving** is a form of government borrowing which encourages people to save by offering not only a reasonable interest rate free of tax, but also offering absolute security for the money itself. From the government's point of view, National Savings provide a reasonably cheap source of finance.

**National Vocational Qualification (NVQ):** a government initiative to provide young people and employees with a widely accepted, job-focused qualification at a variety of different skill levels.

**natural monopolies** exist where the scale of business operation is so large that it is only economic and practical to have one supplier of the service. For example, to have competing gas mains running side by side to every house would involve duplication, a waste of resources. It was often argued by those who believed in *nationalisation*, that many industries represent natural monopolies, including power supply, water supply and telecommunications. Admirers of *privatisation* say that this is no reason for the state to have direct control, and many of these industries have now been passed into private hands. The debate continues, however, since some public *monopolies* which have been privatised are now perceived as private monopolies instead, with little or no effective competition.

**natural rate of unemployment:** see *nonaccelerating inflation rate of unemployment*

**natural resources:** include land and supplies of basic raw materials such as oil reserves. They may also include sites with development potential, which may for example be turned into deep water ports or hydro-electric schemes.

**natural wastage:** the process of natural labour turnover as employees retire, leave to have children, or leave for other jobs, i.e. for any reasons other than *redundancy* or *dismissal*. The rate of natural wastage will differ depending on demographic factors such as the number of older workers and the proportion of young women. If the rate is relatively high (for instance 12 per cent per annum), then it is possible for the company to reduce its workforce rapidly without needing to resort to redundancies.

**negative cash flow** occurs when the *cash flow* entering the company is less than that leaving it, i.e. cash outflow is greater than cash inflow. This may be perfectly normal for a firm in its off season, but if negative cash flow persists it will drain the business of its *liquidity*.

**negative externalities:** occur when an economic activity affects third parties, i.e. people other than the producers or the consumers, in some way which reduces their quality of life. For example a polluting factory creates a negative externality for people living in the area affected by the pollution. They may encounter health problems which are a cost to the community. This cost is not borne by the producers or the consumers. The price of the product to the consumer is lower than it would be if it covered all of its *social costs*, and the producer's profits may be higher than they would be if the social cost were included in the costs of production.

**negative income tax:** a unified tax and benefits system, such that people could be taxed or receive benefits according to a single set of rules. Its attraction is that it could be used to eliminate the *poverty trap* which sometimes means that people lose money by taking a job.

**negative skew** is a *bias* within a distribution towards low values. In other words the majority of the values are below the average. For example, the diagram below shows a research finding into the frequency of school library usage by age of user. It shows that although the average age of a school library user is 15 years, the distribution is skewed towards younger, less frequent users.

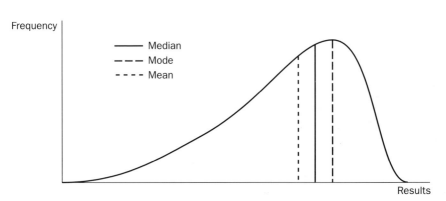

**negligence** is a legal term implying that an individual or company has failed in its duty to have regard for the interests of others. It may therefore be possible for the injured party to sue for damages.

**negotiation** is a method of joint decision-making involving bargaining between different firms or between workforce and management representatives within a firm. The objective is to arrive at mutually acceptable terms. A distinction can be made between negotiation and *consultation*, as the former term implies competitive rivalry between conflicting interests.

**neo-classical economics:** a set of economic ideas based on the work of Marshall, making heavy use of *marginal analysis*, and studying the way in which markets create an optimum allocation of resources. (See also *technical efficiency* and *allocative efficiency*.)

**neo-Keynesians:** those economists who have generally followed the teaching of J M *Keynes*, and sought to develop his ideas in the context of recent economic conditions.

**net assets** is taken by some exam boards to mean the same as assets employed, i.e. *fixed assets* plus *net current assets* (*working capital*). In published company accounts, however, *long-term liabilities* are deducted, making net assets mean the same as *net worth*. When faced with exam questions about accounting terms such as net assets, candidates can be assured that the examiners will allow any of the different versions in usage:

      Examiners' version:   fixed assets + net current assets = net assets

      Business practice:    fixed assets + net current assets − long-term liabilities
                   = net assets

**net book value** is the *historic cost* of a *fixed asset* minus its accumulated *depreciation* and is the figure which is written down in the company's *balance sheet*. It is not necessarily a measure of the *market value* of the asset, which depends ultimately on what someone is prepared to pay. Where an asset is sold for more than its net book value a surplus is recorded under *shareholders' funds*.

**net current assets:** also called *working capital*, comprise *current assets* minus *current liabilities*. It is the finance available for the day-to-day running of the business.

FORMULA:   current assets − current liabilities = net current assets

**net investment** is gross (i.e. total) investment less *replacement investment* (also known as *capital consumption*). Net investment thus represents the value of the addition to total productive capacity which has taken place over the year. It gives a good indication of the extent to which the economy is able to increase *aggregate supply* in the future.

**net national product:** another name for *national income*, being *gross national product* less *capital consumption*.

**net margin** is the percentage of *sales revenue* which is *net profit*. Unlike the gross margin, fixed *overheads* have been taken into account within this ratio. Therefore it is of far greater business significance.

FORMULA:   $\dfrac{\text{net (operating) profit}}{\text{sales revenue}} \times 100 = \text{net margin}$

**net present value (NPV)** is the value today of the estimated *cash flows* resulting from an investment. It is found by discounting the future cash flows to make allowance for the *opportunity cost* of tying up *capital* in the investment. Each year's discounted cash total is added together and taken from today's cash outlay on the project. If the resulting figure (the NPV) is positive, then the project is viable. The following worked example shows an investment where the *discounted* (future) *cash flows* are <u>not</u> enough to justify the initial outlay.

**Worked example: calculating the NPV on the purchase of an industrial robot**

| Assumptions: | • the robot costs £200 000 and should last four years |
| | • it will cost £20 000 per year to run but save £80 000 of labour costs |
| | • interest rates and therefore the discount factors are at 10 per cent |

| | Cash in | Cash out | Net cash | Discount factor | Present value |
|---|---|---|---|---|---|
| **Now** | − | 200 | (200) | 1 | (200) |
| **Year 1** | 80 | 20 | 60 | 0.91 | 54.6 |
| **Year 2** | 80 | 20 | 60 | 0.83 | 49.8 |
| **Year 3** | 80 | 20 | 60 | 0.75 | 45.0 |
| **Year 4** | 80 | 20 | 60 | 0.68 | 40.8 |
| | | | Net present value: | | (9.8) |

All figures in £000s; negative figures in brackets.

**net profit** is *gross profit* minus expenses such as the *overhead* costs. In other words it is *sales revenue* minus all the operating costs of the business. It can therefore also be termed *operating profit*.

**net realisable value** is the money an *asset* could be sold for, after allowing for any expenses involved. Stock is usually valued on a *balance sheet* at the lower of *historic cost* or net realisable value.

**networking:** the establishment of business contacts and communication links by socialising, attending professional meetings or by belonging to the right clubs. People do this in the belief that 'it's not what you know, it's who you know.'

**networking (IT):** interlinking computer hardware to enable users to have access to information, applications software and computer resources without knowing where any of them are located. As many schools and colleges are aware, computer networks sound excellent in theory, but can be a disappointment due to their unreliability.

**net worth:** the value of a firm's *assets* after all external *liabilities* have been allowed for, i.e. assets employed – *long-term liabilities*. This figure balances with *shareholders' funds*, which gives a good indication of its meaning. A firm's net worth is its net wealth, the real value of the firm according to its *balance sheet*. Therefore if the company is liquidated, by selling off all the assets and paying off all the debts the firm should arrive at a cash sum equal to its net worth. This sum would then be distributed to the shareholders.

FORMULA:    assets employed – long-term liabilities  =  net worth

**New Deal:** a second chance for adults to find work-related training or a job in a government-funded initiative. Although focused originally on 18–24-year-olds, it is now open to those over 25 and those with disabilities. It is a key part of the government's welfare to work strategy – an attempt to stop the benefit system from trapping people into a 'culture of dependency'. Critics of the programme consider it an expensive way of forcing people off benefits.

**newly industrialised country (NIC):** the term used in the past for *newly industrialised economy* (NIE).

**newly industrialised economy (NIE):** one which has moved from having a dominant *primary sector* (agriculture and mining) to a fast growing and substantial *secondary sector* (manufacturing). The best-known examples are countries around the Pacific Rim such as Singapore and Taiwan. They experience rapid growth, often through attracting *multinationals*, especially while wage rates remain far behind those of developed economies such as Japan and the United States.

**New International Economic Order:** in 1974, the *United Nations Conference on Trade and Development* began a campaign to bring about a range of improvements in the trading arrangements affecting developing countries. These included the provision of more aid, and improved access to developed country markets. The intention was to help improve growth rates in the poor countries of the world. The measures called for have not on the whole been adopted.

**new product development (NPD)** implies all the functions required to identify, develop and market new product opportunities. This requires close cooperation between *research and development*, *market research* and general marketing functions. A great deal of new product development is based on *qualitative research*, in which psychologists probe for the reasons behind consumer attitudes and actions. This is because radical new products are rarely the result of scientifically conducted research; they stem from insight into the minds of the customer.

**new technology** is used to describe the rapid changes in communications and other processes resulting from the exploitation of the silicon chip. The innovations resulting from the use of new technology can be split into three main types:

- by process, that is advancements in manufacturing technology and automation
- by product, that is new product opportunities using microelectronic technology such as the fax machine and the electronic games
- by communication links, that is *information technology.*

**niche marketing:** a corporate strategy based on identifying and filling relatively small market segments. This can enable small firms to operate profitably in markets dominated by large corporations. It can also be a strategy pursued by a large firm that prefers to have five brands selling 50 000 units in each of five niches, rather than one brand selling 250 000 in the mass market.

Pros:
- the first company to identify a niche market can often secure a solid market position as consumers see the original product as superior
- consumers are willing to pay a price premium for a more exclusive product.

Cons:
- lack of *economies of scale* may make costs too high to achieve satisfactory *profit margins*
- the firm's production system must be flexible enough to cope with relatively small quantities of several products (see *flexible specialisation*).

**NIEO:** see *New International Economic Order*

**Nikkei Index** is Japan's Stock Exchange Index, equivalent to London's Financial Times Stock Exchange (FT-SE100) index (*Footsie*).

**NIMBY:** see *not in my back yard*

**noise:** factors that can distract from the accurate reception of a piece of communication. These include: communication overload, i.e. when too many points are being communicated simultaneously to the same person; and a poor or faulty *transmission mechanism*.

**nominal value** means a face value, not a *market value* or a value based on cost. It most commonly applies in the case of financial securities or shares where the value written on the face of the certificate is not related to its market price. In other words a £1 share may currently have a market price of £3 because the firm is prospering. The term nominal value also applies when something is sold at a trivial or merely nominal price.

**nonaccelerating inflation rate of unemployment (NAIRU):** the level of *unemployment* at which *inflation* is stable. Once unemployment falls below a certain level, some skills will be in short supply and there will be a tendency for wages to be bid up and for inflation to accelerate. Higher rates of unemployment induce people to settle for moderate, or no, pay increases. So there is a *trade-off* between inflation and unemployment. But *structural unemployment*, which is long term by its nature, tends to continue even when rates of inflation are low and stable. This is the main component of NAIRU.

There is some debate about the actual level of NAIRU in the UK. It certainly rose during the 1970s and 80s. It can be reduced by training in areas of skill shortage and other measures which make it easier for people to suit themselves to the jobs available. It might fall if after the recession of the early 1990s more ways can be found to reduce disincentives such as the *poverty trap*.

There is some evidence that NAIRU is falling. During 2002, unemployment (claimant count) stood at less than 1 million, with little evidence of a tendency for inflation to accelerate. Structural unemployment may have responded to measures to make benefits less of a disincentive, and to make training more easily available.

**non-excludability:** a feature of *public goods*, the consumption of which by one person does not exclude consumption by others. The security provided by the police force is one example.

**non-executive director:** a part-time director of a company who has no day-to-day involvement or executive powers. The function of a non-executive director is to supply unbiased advice, specialist expertise and act as a control on the executives. Often a non-executive director may represent a large shareholder such as a pension fund. Following the scandal of Robert Maxwell's raid on his employees' pension fund, the *Cadbury Committee* report on *corporate governance* recommended a strengthening of the role of non-executive directors. The Committee's view was that non-executive directors are far more likely than executives to show independence from the senior management. They can therefore act as a brake on the actions of a dominant chief executive.

**non-price competition** is all forms of competitive action other than through the price mechanism. Examples include *advertising*, sales promotions, *packaging*, *branding*, *point-of-sale* activity and *sponsorship*. Non-price competition is a particular feature of market structures which fit the pattern of an *oligopoly*.

**non-profit-making organisations** may be run in a business-like way, but their objective is not the conventional one of the profit motive. Examples include charities and schools that have opted out of the local authority funding system.

**non-renewable resources:** see *finite resources*

**non-tariff barriers (NTBs)** include *quotas* and other restrictions on trade which do not involve taxing imports. Many of them are contrary to either the spirit or the letter of international regulations under the *WTO*. Quotas involve an upper limit on the level of imports. One particular type of quota is the *voluntary export restraint (VER)*. This is negotiated with the exporting country's government. Other barriers may take several forms:

- constantly changing technical regulations which make compliance difficult for importers
- forcing importers to use specified points of entry where documentation is dealt with only slowly
- regulations which favour domestic producers, e.g. packaging, and labels which conform to local language requirements.

Because barriers to trade tend to reduce the level of trade, they also reduce the real incomes of the countries which employ them, by depriving consumers of cheap substitutes for domestically produced goods. They may be popular with voters though because they are thought to protect the jobs of domestic producers.

**normal curve:** the bell-shaped curve of the *normal distribution* as shown on the next page.

**normal distribution:** a *frequency distribution* which is bell-shaped so that half of the variables lie to the left of the *mean* and half to the right. Due to the symmetry of the curve, the mean, *median* and *mode* all coincide at the same value. If data is collected on an event that occurs many times over, variations in the result will tend to form a pattern that is known as normal distribution. This means that the results will tend to be clustered around the average, and will be split equally between results above and below the average (see the diagram above). Normal distributions can be standardised so that the width of the distribution is about six *standard deviations*. The areas within each standard deviation can be very useful in statistical analysis, for example in *significance testing*.

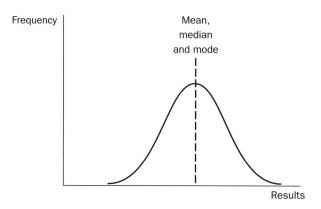

**normal goods** have demand that responds positively to changes in the *real incomes* of customers. In other words if people become better off, they buy more of this type of product. Typical examples include hairdressing, furniture, cars and eating out. All luxury goods fall into the category of normal, as do the majority of everyday items. Those that are not normal are termed *inferior goods* (for which demand rises when consumers are worse off).

**normal profit:** that level of profit which is just sufficient to keep the resources employed in production of a particular product from being used for some other purpose. Any profit in excess of that amount, termed *super-normal profit*, will tend to attract additional resources into the industry; in other words there will be *entry* into the industry by new firms. If less than normal profit is earned, some resources will leave the industry to exploit more *profitable opportunities* producing other things. Normal profit is an important feature of *perfect competition* the theory predicts that under perfectly competitive conditions, only normal profit will be earned in the long run, because the entry of new competitors will force prices back down to the level which just covers the costs of all resources used in production. (See also *profit signalling mechanism*.)

**normative:** involving a value judgement. A normative statement is one which cannot be tested against the facts. It is likely to be a matter of opinion. It contrasts with a *positive* statement which can be tested against the evidence. 'The Chancellor ought to raise taxes and increase pensions' is a normative statement, because different people will have different opinions on it, depending perhaps on their age and values.

**North American Free Trade Area (NAFTA)** consists of the US, Canada and Mexico. As a *free trade area*, it is different from the EU because it does not have a *common external tariff* against the rest of the world. Also it does not on the whole attempt to harmonise its regulations. However, it has been successful since its inception in 1993 in increasing trade between member countries. As a major trading bloc, it has potential to influence future *trade negotiations* quite strongly.

**no-strike agreement:** a contract signed as part of a firm's *negotiation* and *disputes procedure* that bars the *trade union* signatories from calling or encouraging a strike. When signed with Japanese employers, British trade unions have ensured that the disputes procedure provides for binding *arbitration* by an independent person or panel (usually appointed by *ACAS*). Often the binding element has been in the form of *pendulum arbitration*. Although no-strike agreements have been quite common with Japanese firms, by no means all Japanese companies insist on them.

**not in my back yard (NIMBY)** is applied in a number of areas of economic life. It generally applies in situations where everyone agrees that something has to be built for the good of all, but no one wants it near their own home. The most common example is motorways, which everyone agrees are extremely useful and which most people use, but which cause uproar and extreme resistance from those immediately affected by their construction. The same thing happens with potentially dirty or hazardous production processes. This is why both motorways and these factories are often located in areas where residents are poor, lack access to the media and are therefore unable to resist effectively.

**NPD:** see *new product development*

**NVQ:** see *National Vocational Qualifications*

**Do you know we also have A–Zs for:**

- **Accounting**
- **English Literature**
- **Mathematics**
- **Psychology?**

Ask for them in your local bookshop or see the inside back cover for ordering details.

**objectives** are the medium- to long-term targets that can give a sense of direction to a manager, department, whole organisation or government. If a team can be given a sense of common purpose, it becomes much easier to coordinate actions and to create a team spirit. For maximum effect objectives should be measurable and have an explicit timescale, for example to boost *market share* from 8 per cent to 10 per cent within the next three years. They must also be realistic, as an objective that seems unattainable can be demotivating. Consequently it is desirable for objectives to be agreed rather than set.

Objectives form the basis for decisions on strategy, i.e. the plan for the achievement of your goals. Therefore questions about business strategy should not be answered until the individual or company's objectives have been considered fully. (See *aims*, *corporate objectives*, and *strategy*.)

**obsolescence** occurs when a product, service or machine has been overtaken by a new idea that provides the same function in a better or more attractive way. Often obsolescence occurs as a result of *new technology*, though it may also be due to changing lifestyles, fashions or scarcity of resources. The threat of obsolescence encourages most firms to update their products regularly and to look for new products that can replace declining ones. Some firms, however, look to gain financial advantage from two specific types of obsolescence: built-in and planned.

Built-in obsolescence means designing and building failure into a machine, in order that the user needs to buy a replacement. This is a way of overcoming the effect of *market saturation* on the sales of a *durable* item. In other words if everyone who wants a lawnmower has one, sales will fall to zero. This tempts manufacturers to build the products so that they wear out after three or four years. The customer must then go and buy a new one.

Planned obsolescence is the creation of a feeling on the part of customers that they should replace items that are in fact still usable. This is largely done through restyling and adding new features to durable items such as cars. In other words, although your car may be in good physical shape, you want to get the latest model. Environmentalists would regard both built-in and planned obsolescence as equally undesirable ways of encouraging wastage of the earth's resources.

**occupational immobility** occurs when people have been trained in a skill which is no longer in demand, and have difficulty in re-training, in a skill which is in demand.

**OECD:** see *Organisation for Economic Cooperation and Development*

**off-balance-sheet financing** is 'the creative accounting trick which improves companies' balance sheets' (Roger Cowe, THE GUARDIAN). It is a device by which the business's debts can be removed from the *balance sheet*. This shrinks the firm's stated *gearing* and therefore apparent risk level. The most common method is by the creation of a *subsidiary* company which the firm controls, but does not consolidate into its accounts. This subsidiary may have obtained the loans essential for running the entire business, but these may not need to be listed on the firm's consolidated accounts. The *Accounting Standards Board* is trying to ban off-balance-sheet financing.

**Office of Fair Trading (OFT)** is the government body set up to ensure that firms are complying with the *Fair Trading Act 1973*. The OFT's director-general has four main duties:

- to consider whether *take-over bids* should be investigated by the *Competition Commission* on the grounds of being against the public interest
- to investigate suspected anti-competitive practices (such as *market-sharing agreements*)
- to investigate existing monopolies
- to consider whether to register or reject *restrictive practices* notified by firms.

The OFT was greatly strengthened by the *1998 Competition Act*, which gave it new powers of investigation, including the power to stage a dawn raid if it is likely that a firm will try to obscure important evidence. Also, it can give a firm immunity from fines if it informs on other members of a *cartel*. And it can fine firms which collude up to 10 per cent of their UK turnover for up to three years.

Recent cases show that the OFT is taking a much tougher line in the way that it implements competition policy.

**official development assistance** is the *foreign aid* given by governments to *developing countries* in the form of grants and loans.

**official finance transactions** are payments made by the Bank of England to offset inflows and outflows on the balance of payments.

**official reserves** are the *reserves* of foreign exchange held by the central bank. They may be used to defend the *exchange rate* if market forces are pushing it down. (See also *fixed exchange rate*.)

**off-the-job training** includes all forms of training apart from that at the immediate workplace. It may be conducted internally, for example in a conference room, or externally, at a college. Employees attend college during working hours either through *day release* or *block release*. The training is likely to be focused on skills, attitudes and theories that relate to work.

**OFGEM**, the Office of Gas and Electricity Markets, is the regulator for the gas and electricity industries. Both have had regulators since *privatisation* in the late 1980s. The two were combined in 2000, partly because some companies are supplying both products. Ofgem regulates the extent to which gas and electricity prices can be raised and also the value for money which customers get. It can require suppliers to restrain their activities in order to ensure that the market remains competitive. Because both industries are to some extent *natural monopolies*, regulation is needed to protect the interests of consumers.

Since 1999, neither British Gas nor the electricity suppliers have had a monopoly position; consumers can choose where to buy. Choice has brought potential savings of £60 per year on gas bills and £20–35 on electricity bills, depending on the area.

*Regulation* has at times brought OFGEM and its predecessors (Ofgas and Offer) into dispute with shareholders. To the extent that suppliers' profits may be reduced, shareholders sometimes object when prices cannot be raised.

**OFLOT:** the regulator for the National Lottery.

**OFT:** see *Office of Fair Trading*

**OFTEL** is the regulator for the privatised telephone industry, set up at the time of privatisation in 1984. It has been instrumental in opening the telecommunications market to many competing suppliers. This has created strong price competition and brought down the cost of telephone calls. In spite of this, OFTEL is currently thought to have been rather soft on BT in the past. BT moved slowly on opening up its telephone exchange facilities to other firms which wanted to develop broadband networks. OFTEL could perhaps have insisted more strongly that this had to happen. This situation may now be changing. (See also *regulatory capture*.)

**OFWAT** is the regulator for the water industry, set up at the time of privatisation in 1989. In spite of its efforts to hold down price increases, many people think that the water companies continue to act like monopolies. Water remains a true *natural monopoly* in that it is not usually possible to choose between competing suppliers and the need for a pipe network makes duplication of facilities wasteful and inefficient. In fact, prices have risen in part because of the need for extensive investment in improved water supplies. It is hard to tell how effective regulation has been in this case.

**ogive:** another term for a cumulative *frequency distribution* curve.

**oil crisis:** a situation in which supplies of oil are threatened and prices rise as it becomes more scarce. The precipitating cause could be war in the Middle East, as in 1973. *OPEC* has in the past been able to restrict production with a view to raising prices.

Because demand for oil is very inelastic, a relatively small fall in production can bring about a much larger increase in prices. Shortages are likely to disrupt economic activity because of the crucial role of oil in industry and distribution. A very short oil crisis occurred in late 2000 when protesters blockaded refineries to prevent supplies of petrol reaching the public. The oil companies were quick to raise prices but came in for much public criticism and prices soon fell again.

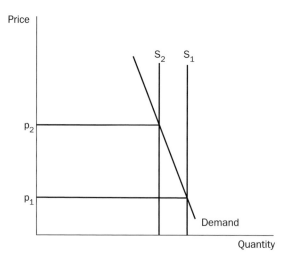

*A small fall in quantity supplied leads to a large increase in price if demand is inelastic*

**oligopoly** exists when a market is dominated by a small number of large firms (see *monopoly*). It is characterised by *differentiated products* and *barriers to entry*. It may be possible for firms to make *super-normal profits* in the long run, because the barriers to entry prevent new competitors from coming into the market. The relatively small number of competing firms is likely to include *price makers* and *price takers*. The former will tend to set prices and the latter will tend to follow.

An oligopoly can appear highly competitive, because each producer fights hard for particular *market niches* and for *market share* in general. However this competition is usually in non-price form, such as special offers and *advertising* because there is often a degree of *collusion* which keeps overall prices and therefore profits at an acceptable level. Occasionally though a *price war* may break out, in which one firm begins aggressive price cutting strategies, and others follow, each trying to undercut the other in a bid for increased market share. This is good for consumers in the short run, but may lead to the least profitable firm going out of business. Then competition is reduced and a return to tacit agreement is likely.

Analysing oligopolists' behaviour is difficult because each producer will be aware that whatever action it takes will inevitably result in a reaction from its competitors. This situation is known as one of *interdependence*. Therefore, it must attempt to take this reaction into account before undertaking anything. The UK markets for soap powder, chocolate, and ice-cream are often quoted as examples of oligopolies.

**on-balance-sheet financing** means generating extra cash using internal or external sources of finance that will show up on the firm's balance sheet. This contrasts with the deceptiveness of *off-balance-sheet financing*.

**one-off profit** is a financial surplus that has resulted from an event that is unlikely to be repeated. For example, if a firm sells a plot of land for £2m. that is on its books at £600 000, it has made a £1 400 000 one-off profit. When company accounts include one-off items, it is wise to try to extract them from the figures. Then a judgement can be made about the underlying position of the business.

**one-way communication** is the passage of a message without gaining *feedback* on whether it has been received or understood by the right person or people. It is an undesirable form of communication, as it lacks effectiveness and the potential to motivate. Examples of one-way communication include the newsletter, the lecture and the notice-board.

**on-line:** the linking of computer terminals so that information can be passed instantaneously. A common example is the electronic checkout at supermarkets that can provide on-line information to head office or even to suppliers about the numbers of each item being sold.

**on-the-job training** is instruction at the place of work on how the job should be carried out. It may be a matter of observing how an experienced employee carries out the task, or being talked through the job by a supervisor.

**OPEC:** see *Organisation of Petroleum Exporting Countries*

**open economy:** an economy in which foreign trade is important. Exports contribute significantly to aggregate demand and imports are a significant proportion of total purchases. For example, the UK economy is a more open economy than the US. Luxembourg is even more so.

# open questions

**open questions** are those that invite a wide-ranging, reflective or imaginative response. On a questionnaire, they are questions that do not have specific answers to be ticked. In an interview, they are the (harder) questions that demand more than just a factual answer. An example of an open question would be, 'Tell me a bit more about yourself.'

The term may also be used more generally to mean a question which has no right or wrong answers, but on which disagreement must be expected.

**operating profit:** the measure of profit which an organisation earns on its normal operations and excluding any *extraordinary* or *exceptional items*, which might distort a true appreciation of its usual business. Therefore, clear comparisons with previous years or with similar firms may be made.

**operating profit margin:** see *net margin*

**operational research (OR):** a set of multi-disciplinary techniques which are an aid to organising and planning operations such as production, scheduling and resource allocation. An *optimum* is usually sought, subject to a set of *constraints*. The distinctive approach is to develop a mathematical model of the system under investigation, including measurement of factors such as chance and risk. This model can then be used to predict and compare the outcomes of alternative decisions, strategies or controls. Devised at the time of the Second World War, OR techniques predated modern computers, yet are ideally suited to them.

**operations management:** the modern term for production management. It suggests a wider brief than just factory management. For example, it allows for service industries to be seen as requiring management of their operations, as has always been acknowledged in manufacturing.

**opportunity cost** measures cost in terms of the next best or highest valued alternative foregone. It may be measured in money terms or not. The cost of an evening of studying might be the missed opportunity of seeing a film. One important use of this concept is in *investment appraisal*. The cost of a project is the rate of interest paid on the funds invested. Even if an organisation used its own funds, it foregoes the interest on its money, so the real cost is the same.

The idea of opportunity cost may be applied in any situation where choices are being made. For example, consumers' decisions involve choices between items; one will be chosen, and the one foregone is the opportunity cost. Similarly labour market decisions may involve choices between work and education or between two possible jobs. And the government may find that the opportunity cost of, say, more money for the NHS is less money for roads or social services.

**optimise:** to aim for the most favourable point or circumstances. For example the optimum strategy might be one that is profitable, but not so much so as to attract *me-too products*.

**optimum** means the best possible outcome e.g. maximising *capacity utilisation* or consumer satisfaction, or minimising cost.

**option:** the right to buy or sell a commodity or a financial asset at some time in the future at a price agreed now.

**OR:** see *operational research*

**oral communication** means conveying information by the spoken word. This carries certain advantages and disadvantages compared with written communication.

Pros:
- enables feeling and emphasis to be conveyed more clearly
- has the potential to generate far more powerful *feedback* (especially if one-to-one or small-group communication)
- creates no specific costs, such as paper and filing cabinets.

Cons:
- lacks the legal status (evidence) provided by written communication
- ineffective for conveying details information such as regional sales figures
- prone to get distorted if used for a message that must pass through many *intermediaries.*

Large firms can suffer from the difficulty of communicating orally through many intermediaries. They become overly dependent on written communication, which can slow down decision-making and cause heavy *overhead* costs and *diseconomies of scale.*

**order book:** the total number of orders taken from customers, usually expressed in terms of time. Thus an order book of three months means that the factory has that amount of work on order.

**ordinary share** or equity represents part ownership in a *joint-stock company*. Ordinary shareholders receive a *dividend* on the *capital* they invest, but only after *debenture* holders, *preference* shareholders, long-term debt holders and the government (through taxes) have been paid. If the company goes into *liquidation*, ordinary shareholders are the last group of people to receive any return, after all other *creditors*. In return for these potentially high risks, ordinary shareholders enjoy the chance to benefit fully from their company's successes. Rising profits will lead to higher annual dividend payments and an increase in the *market value* of the shares they hold.

**organic growth** means expansion from within the firm, i.e. not as a result of mergers and acquisitions. It also implies that the finance for the expansion has come from internal sources rather than from shareholders or loans. As a result, organic growth is likely to be steady, even slow, but very secure.

**organisational chart:** a diagram showing the lines of authority and *layers of hierarchy* within an organisation. To be effective, the *chain of command* should be clear, with no one answerable to two people. An organisational chart should show:

- the different business functions and divisions
- who is answerable to whom
- the *span of control* in each division
- the official channels of communication.

**Organisation for Economic Cooperation and Development (OECD)** was set up in 1961 and provides a forum for discussion on economic growth and trade. It also helps to coordinate international *aid* for developing countries. Its members are mainly drawn from the developed world. Some of its most effective work has been in the collection and publication of worldwide economic and social data, standardised so that inter-country comparisons are possible.

**Organisation of Petroleum Exporting Countries (OPEC)** is the name of the *cartel* which sets output quotas in order to control crude oil prices. The members of OPEC are countries of the Middle East, South America and Africa, but not the United States, Russian or European producers. OPEC wielded great power in the 1970s when it controlled 90 per cent of the world's supply of crude oil exports. However, by forcing up the oil price the exploration of marginal fields such as the North Sea and Alaska became worthwhile, thereby reducing OPEC's influence.

**other things being equal:** see *ceteris paribus*

**output** is the finished product coming from a production process. It can be measured by volume or by value (volume times price). The level of output should not be confused with output per worker (productivity).

**outsourcing** is the process by which businesses buy services, component inputs or even finished products from independent suppliers, rather than produce them themselves. This practice increased as many businesses have found it to be cheaper to rely on other producers than try to do everything themselves. Sometimes new cheap sources of inputs can be found overseas; this has been an important element in *globalisation*.

**overcapacity** exists in a market where the maximum capacity of all the producers is significantly above current and anticipated *demand*. This threatens each producer with the possibility that demand will fall below the *break-even point*. The likely consequences of overcapacity are:

● that the weakest producers will sell out or go into *liquidation*

● that all producers will try to cut their fixed *overheads* by *rationalisation*

● that prices will fall as producers try to utilise their own capacity by boosting demand.

**overdraft:** a facility that enables a firm to borrow up to an agreed maximum for any period of time that it wishes. An overdraft is a very flexible way of raising credit in that it need not even be drawn at all and the amount borrowed may fluctuate daily. Banks may offer overdrafts without security, though for larger sums they will take security by a floating charge on all the *assets* of the business. The actual sum borrowed through an overdraft facility at the end of the financial year is recorded as a *current liability* on the *balance sheet*

**overhead allocation:** the *overheads* or *fixed costs* of an organisation are difficult to allocate to *cost centres* as they do not vary with activity in the short term. Most methods of allocation are arbitrary and run the risk of being influenced by those who want their own department to look efficient.

**overheads** are costs that are not generated directly by the production process. The term is often used interchangeably with *indirect costs* or even *fixed costs*. In fact overheads can be fixed or variable, though the overwhelming proportion are fixed. Examples of fixed overheads: salaries, rent, heating and lighting. Examples of variable overheads: *salesforce* commission, postage (for a mail-order company), advertising (for a direct marketing company).

**overheating** occurs when *aggregate demand* exceeds *aggregate supply*. The *excess demand* which results reflects the fact that *supply constraints* are preventing producers from increasing output. There will be a tendency for *inflation* to accelerate and for imports to rise as the pressure of demand increases.

**overmanning:** using more labour in the production process than is strictly necessary. It can occur when firms are run inefficiently yet survive because they have a degree of monopoly power. Or it can occur when agreements are made between unions and management not to make people redundant. This means that employees are kept on the payroll even though it would be possible to supply the existing quantity of the product without their help.

**overtime ban:** a form of *industrial action* that attempts to disrupt the employer while keeping employees' basic wages unaffected. It can only be effective if a significant proportion of work in a key section is done on overtime. This is only likely to occur in seasonal production peaks.

**overtrading** occurs when a firm expands without securing the necessary long-term finance, thereby placing too great a strain on *working capital*. Increased *demand* creates the need for more cash to finance extra raw material stocks and *work in progress*. In the absence of extra long-term funds, the firm is forced to apply pressure to *debtors* and *creditors*. If a creditor demands early payment, there is a severe danger of being forced into *liquidation*.

Overtrading is a particular problem for small firms in high growth sectors, but is also difficult for many firms when the economy moves out of *recession*. Rising demand during the recovery encourages overtrading which, in turn, can result in company failure.

**overvalued currency** is one which is trading on the foreign exchange markets at a price which makes the country's exports uncompetitive, and imports very desirable. This results in a *balance of payments* deficit. Since the deficit causes a greater supply of the foreign currency than there is demand for it, the exchange rate will eventually fall back to an equilibrium position. Market forces will create downward pressure on the currency's price. This may or may not be counteracted by central bank action to maintain the exchange rate by buying it and so supporting its value.

**own-label** (own-brand) products are branded with the retailer's own name, or with a name invented by the retailer. Such products are made by manufacturers to the recipe or specification laid down by the retailer. The products are usually made with a particular price level in mind, often around 10 per cent below the price of the *brand leader*. From the retailer's point of view, the advantages and disadvantages of own label products are:

Pros:    •    can build a brand identity for your own shop (for example Marks and Spencer) and thereby add value
        •    gives a much stronger bargaining position then when dealing with the owners of powerful brand names, therefore buy supplies more cheaply.

Cons:    •    unless your own brand has a good name, the shop's image will be cheapened
        •    requires backroom staff to check quality of own-brand produce, adding to *overheads*.

**Do you need revision help and advice?**

Go to pages 325–341 for a range of revision appendices that include plenty of exam advice and tips.

**packaging:** all the design and cost elements involved in the physical protection and presentation of a product. Packaging has been referred to as the 'silent salesman'. An eye-catching pack design that conveys the right image and information about the product can be a highly effective promotional tool. It is a key element in the *marketing mix* for any consumer good.

**P and L account:** see *profit and loss account*

**pan-European marketing** means treating Europe as a single market by selling the same products in the same way throughout Europe. This strategy is used by *multinationals* such as Levi's, Kelloggs and Ford. It reduces marketing staff costs in each country and can help ensure a consistent image (especially important for firms such as Levi's). Most commentators believe that pan-European marketing will spread rapidly as the *single European market* develops.

**paradox of thrift:** when people start to save a larger part of their incomes, the resulting leakage from the circular flow of money has a downward *multiplier* effect on aggregate demand, which eventually leads to a fall in the level of saving. This is a prediction of the basic Keynesian model of the macroeconomy, in which saving is directly related to income because a rise in the rate of saving implies a fall in consumption.

**parallel imports** are goods brought into a country by *entrepreneurs* working outside the official *distribution* network of the manufacturer. If cans of Coca-Cola were being sold for 60p per can in France and 40p in Britain, it would be profitable for a parallel importer to bring container loads of the drink in from Britain to distribute in France. Producers try any legal way they can to stop parallel imports, as they interfere with the pricing differentials that enable profits to be maximised. (See *price discrimination*.)

**Pareto analysis:** see *eighty/twenty rule*

**Pareto efficiency** or Pareto optimality, refers to a situation in which it is impossible to make anyone better off without making someone else worse off. This means that there must be an optimal *allocation of resources*, such that inputs are used in the most efficient way (*technical efficiency*) and output yields the maximum possible *utility* to consumers (*allocative efficiency*).

**parity** is a term used in the context of exchange rates. We may speak of a fixed parity, meaning a value for the exchange rate which will be kept fixed.

**participation rate:** the proportion of the population which is either in work or registered unemployed. It is thus a measure of the size of the total workforce available, and the extent to which the population is economically active.

**partnership** is a legal form of business organisation where two or more people trade together under the Partnership Act of 1890. It is usual for partnerships to have *unlimited liability*, which means each partner is liable for the debts of the other partners, including their tax liability. Because this requires a high degree of trust, partnerships are most common in the professions, such as in medicine and the law. Forming a partnership allows more *capital* to be used in the business than is the case with a *sole trader*, and some of the strain of decision-making is taken off the shoulders of individuals. It also allows partners more personal freedom, for example, they can take holidays when they like, but unlike private or public companies they retain major responsibilities for the success of the organisation, and their ability to raise finance remains somewhat limited.

**partial equilibrium analysis** examines individual markets on the assumption that events in that market can be viewed in isolation from all other markets. This is easier to do than the alternative, general equilibrium analysis, which requires the inclusion of all the knock-on effects which occur in other related markets and takes in the labour and capital markets as well as the product market.

**par value:** see *nominal value*

**passed dividend** is when a firm decides that it cannot afford to pay any dividend to shareholders this year. It is then said that the dividend has been passed.

**patent:** the right to be the sole user or producer of the *invention* of a new process or product. To register a patent the inventor must:

- provide full drawings of the invention for the *Patent Office*
- demonstrate that the ideas have original features
- promise that the ideas are his or her own.

Under the Copyright, Designs and Patents Act 1988, patent holders have the monopoly right to use, make, license or sell the invention for up to 20 years after it has been registered. Although this grants the inventor rights that can be very valuable, there is no agency for enforcing patents. Therefore the holder has to be willing to take to court those that infringe the patent. An individual inventor is very unlikely to be able to afford the legal costs, so new patents are often sold on to larger firms. A successful patent can give its owner a substantial degree of monopoly power, as happens with certain drugs, which can be sold for a high price as long as the patent lasts.

**Patent Office** is the only authority with the right to grant *patents* and *trade marks* within the UK.

**paternalistic leadership style** is reminiscent of the way fathers treat their children, i.e. deciding what is best for them. The paternalistic approach is *autocratic*, though decisions are intended to be in the best interests of the workforce. The leader is likely to explain the reasons for his or her decisions and may even have consulted staff before making them, but *delegation* is more unlikely. The paternal company treats its workforce as family, taking care of its social and leisure needs. Its emphasis is on *human relations (Mayo)* and social needs (*Maslow*).

**payback period:** a method of *investment appraisal* that estimates the length of time it will take to recoup the cash outlay on an investment. Although regarded by academics as simplistic, this is the most commonly used method of investment decision-making by businesses in Britain. Most set a *criterion level* such as two years. Projects will only be considered by senior management if they have a shorter payback period than that. If forecast cash flows are constant, the following formula applies:

$$\text{FORMULA:} \quad \frac{\text{investment outlay}}{\text{contribution per month}} = \text{payback period}$$

**Worked example: calculate the payback period from a £450 000 investment given the following forecast cash flows:**

|  | Cash in | Cash out |
|---|---|---|
| Now |  | + £450 000 |
| Year 1 | + £180 000 |  |
| Year 2 | + £180 000 |  |
| Year 3 | + £180 000 |  |
| Year 4 | + £180 000 |  |

Monthly contribution towards the investment outlay is:
$$£180\ 000 \div 12 = £15\ 000$$

$$\text{Payback} = \frac{\text{initial outlay}}{\text{contribution per month}} = \frac{£450\ 000}{£15\ 000} = \textbf{30 months}$$

Payback has several advantages and disadvantages over the other methods.

Pros:
- particularly useful for firms with difficult *cash flow* positions, as it helps them to identify how long it will take for the cash to be restored
- the further ahead a forecast looks, the less likely it is to be accurate, as uncertainty increases over time; since payback only focuses on the short term (the period until the money is recouped) it is less likely to be inaccurate.

Cons:
- the method focuses on time but ignores *profit*, making it of limited use unless supplemented by other methods such as *average rate of return*
- may encourage a *short-termism*.

**PAYE** stands for 'pay-as-you-earn' which is a system of *income tax* payment allowing employees to have their tax assessed for the year and then divided into 12 if they are paid monthly, or 52 if they are paid weekly. It avoids people receiving a large income tax bill at the end of the year, and so discourages *tax avoidance*.

**payment by results (PBR)** wage systems provide financial incentives for achieving a high or a fast rate of output. The best known methods are *piece-rate* and commission.

**payroll tax:** a tax paid by the employer which rises with the number of employees. The common example is the social security taxes which exist in most countries of the European Union. In the UK these are called employers' National Insurance contributions. They have the effect of raising the costs of employing labour. They therefore have the potential to reduce employment if the employer is likely to look for labour saving ways of producing.

**pay round:** the annual process by which employers and *trade unions* negotiate pay rises to compensate for price inflation and perhaps achieve an increase in real living standards. At times of low inflation the pay round is barely noticeable. It should not be forgotten, though, that pay expectations are affected not only by inflation but also the rises achieved by staff whose negotiations came earlier in the pay round.

**PBR:** see *payment by results*

**peak pricing** may be used where there are substantial variations in demand over the course of time. For example, rail fares are set in such a way that it costs more to travel during the rush hour. This is a way of raising revenue, and charging higher prices to those customers who put the most pressure on the capacity of the organisation to provide for them. (See also *price discrimination*.)

**peer group:** the circle of friends and workmates whose views on workplace behaviour and attitudes may be highly influential.

**pendulum arbitration:** a system of binding *arbitration* in which the independent arbitrator must decide in favour of one side of the dispute or the other. No compromise is allowable. For instance, if a *trade union* claims a 10 per cent pay rise while the management offers 4 per cent, the arbitrator must decide which is closer to the 'correct' outcome. If the arbitrator believes 6 per cent to be appropriate, the management's 4 per cent offer will be imposed on both sides.

Although it sounds extreme, pendulum arbitration encourages compromise, as both sides learn to adopt softer bargaining strategies. For example, a trade union official who expects the arbitrator to judge that 6 per cent is a fair outcome should pitch the wage claim at 6.5–7 per cent. A higher claim will increase the risk that the management side will win. Similarly, the management should push their offer towards the anticipated 6 per cent.

**penetration pricing:** the setting of a low price designed to gain sufficient market share so that customers recognise the brand within that market. This is a short-run tactic. See also *market penetration*.

**pension funds** are investment institutions that gather the pension contributions made monthly by employees and employers and invest them for long-term growth. The money is invested in well-spread portfolios of shares, property and *government securities* with the intention that the growth achieved will enable the contributors to receive generous pensions when they retire. Pension funds, together with insurance companies and *unit trust* firms are the main institutional shareholders that own the majority of shares in most of Britain's *public limited companies*. As such, they are a very important source of funds for investment.

**per capita** means 'per head', and is often used in data where an individual measure is required, such as income per capita as opposed to total income.

**percentile:** a one hundredth part of a set of observations. A person who is among the highest one per cent in terms of income earned may be said to be in the top percentile. The fiftieth percentile corresponds to the median observation, and so on.

**per employee** means the same as per capita, though it is more commonly used in a business context such as sales per employee. That would represent a ratio measuring the effective productivity of staff, especially the *salesforce*.

$$\text{FORMULA:} \quad \text{sales per employee} = \frac{\text{total sales}}{\text{number of employees}}$$

**perfect competition** exists when a market exhibits the following characteristics:

- a large number of small buyers and sellers, none of whom can influence price on their own

- a *homogeneous product*, i.e. all the rival products are identical

- *perfect knowledge*, i.e. all consumers know the prevailing price, and all producers have access to the same technology
- perfect freedom of entry into, and exit from, the market
- *perfect mobility* of factors of production
- all the firms in the market are profit maximisers
- in the long run, only *normal profit* can be earned.

These unrealistic conditions mean that perfect competition is simply a model which is useful as the starting point for analysing the behaviour of firms in the real world, but which cannot be a true representation. It does show how both short- and long-term efficiency can be achieved, however, if at least some of the conditions prevail.

*Technical efficiency* can be achieved under perfect competition because there will always be many sellers competing, and they will need to keep costs to a minimum in order to survive. *Allocative efficiency* can be achieved because *free entry* to the market means that there will always be a producer seeking to meet consumer demand at a price which reflects costs of production.

**perfect knowledge** is a condition of *perfect competition* implying that both consumers and producers are fully informed about the conditions in the market and about the best ways of producing. Consumers know all about the prices and availability of the products they may purchase, and producers are all able to use the best technology available at the time.

**perfect mobility** is a condition of *perfect competition* and means that both labour and capital can move from one use to another. People will be able to move from one occupation to another without difficulty, and also move to a different geographical area. Funds for investment will be able to move out of a less profitable use and into a more profitable activity.

**performance appraisal** is the process of judging the effectiveness of an employee's contribution over a period of time. It might be conducted every quarter, every six months or, most commonly, every year. The appraisal is carried out by a fellow employee, often the immediate superior, though it is usually based more on discussion than inspection. A performance appraisal might follow these stages:

- at the start of the year, discuss the appraisee's personal objectives, i.e. hoped-for achievements and developments
- towards the end of the period, ask the employee to complete a self-appraisal form
- use the latter as the basis for discussion of the employee's achievements, strengths, weaknesses, training needs, career intentions and future objectives.

The process is intended to provide employees with *feedback* on their performance and therefore be motivating. However it can be stressful if the appraisal is used to judge *performance-related pay* awards.

**performance indicators** are ways of measuring achievement in relation to an objective. The form of measurement is likely to be quantitative, such as sales figures, speed of response, or the quality reject rate. Schemes such as *performance appraisal* need an element of numerate data, so performance indicators are often devised as a way of making appraisal more meaningful.

**performance ratios:** the accounting ratios which help to evaluate performance, namely: *return on capital employed* (ROCE), *profit margin* and the *asset turnover* ratio. The first two measure profitability while asset turnover ratio shows how hard the capital assets are being made to work. It is important to compare like with like – different types of business have different ratios, so comparisons over time are often more meaningful that comparisons with different businesses.

**performance-related pay (PRP)** is a bonus or salary increase awarded in line with an employee's achievements over a range of criteria. For a receptionist the criteria might include helpfulness, efficiency, appearance and attendance. An employee performing well above average might get an 8 per cent pay rise while average achievers get only 3 per cent.

**peripheral** (workforce or business) means business elements or activities that do not form part of the core. As a result they are the most vulnerable to an economic downturn or a change of corporate strategy. Professor Handy has suggested that in the future, organisations will have a core of lifelong, highly rewarded and highly skilled employees supplemented by peripheral workers who are hired and fired as seasonal, cyclical or market changes dictate.

**peripheral workers** are those on the edges of an organisation's labour force. They may be employed part-time, on temporary contracts or on zero hours contracts. Unlike the salaried, core workforce, these people are used flexibly, allowing the firm to avoid fixed costs that prove a burden during periods of low demand. If the firm employs too high a proportion of peripheral workers, there is a risk that communication, teamwork and efficiency may be harmed.

**periphery:** places which lie outside the 'core' areas for particular economic or business activities. Industries tend to locate in the areas where their costs are likely to be lowest. This may be because of accessible markets, or convenient infrastructures, or some other local advantage. Centres of activity – the so-called 'core' – then generate further activity amongst supplier businesses and consumer goods production generally. Areas beyond the 'core' become known as the periphery. In the UK the core has traditionally been the South-East and West Midlands. Income levels have been lower and unemployment levels have been higher in the more peripheral areas of other regions. In the EU, Ireland and southern Italy occupy peripheral positions.

**permanent income hypothesis:** a theory of the determination of the level of *consumption*, which holds that consumption is directly related to expectation of income over the long run. This theory was set out by *Friedman*, and contrasts with the view of *Keynes*, who saw consumption as depending on current income.

**personal allowance:** the amount of an individual's income which is free of *income tax*. This amount is usually raised in line with inflation in the *Budget*, unless the Chancellor wants to increase the real level of tax revenue.

**personal computer (PC):** a computer small enough to be either desktop or laptop, yet with the computing power of the *mainframe computers* of some years ago. PCs can either be stand-alone systems or networked to other PCs and data sources. The main uses of PCs are for word processing, *spreadsheet* recording and analysis and *database* information processing.

**personal disposable income** is the income which remains to individuals to spend as they wish, after all *direct taxes* have been deducted.

**personal sector:** that part of the economy which consists of transactions made by individuals. The corporate sector involves all decisions by businesses, and these two and the financial sector together constitute the *private sector*.

**personnel department:** the section of the organisation that is responsible for the recruitment, training, welfare and discipline of staff. This has often been seen as a passive bureaucratic function, hence the modern shift towards *human resource management*.

**persuasive advertising** is communication to customers designed to appeal to the emotions. Favourable or distinctive images are used to encourage the target market to identify with the product or service being promoted. A long-running example of persuasive advertising is 'Bounty – a taste of paradise'. The power of the moving image makes television and cinema advertising the favourite media for persuasive advertising campaigns.

Some pressure groups criticise the power of persuasive advertising to press people to buy – or long to buy – products that may have little merit (such as expensive children's toys) or actually be harmful, such as fatty foods or alcohol. *Informative advertising* rarely attracts such criticism.

**PEST analysis** (political, economic, social and technological analysis): a systematic means of analysing the external factors that may present opportunities or threats to a business.

**petroleum revenue tax** is levied on the profits from production of oil within the jurisdiction of the UK government. The oil companies can offset the cost of exploration against the tax.

**Phillips Curve** is named after A W H Phillips (1914–75) who studied the data on increases in money income and levels of unemployment between 1851 and 1957, and showed that as unemployment rose, the rate of increase of wages and hence prices (*inflation*) declined. This conclusion appears obvious, since higher levels of unemployment mean that workers are in a less-powerful position to bargain for wage increases, and so the pressures on inflation are reduced. From a government policy point of view it did have important implications however, because a low-inflation policy became inconsistent with full employment, and vice versa. In the period from 1995 to 2002, unemployment fell without inflation accelerating. It is likely that there is still a trade-off between inflation and unemployment, but it may be at a lower level of unemployment than previously.

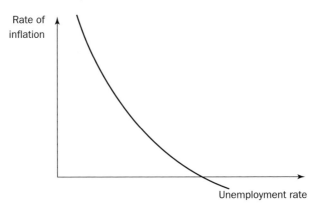

**physiological needs** are the physical needs of human beings, such as food, warmth and the avoidance of pain. They form the lowest level of *Maslow's hierarchy of needs* and are therefore often referred to as lower order needs.

**picketing** occurs when strikers stand at entrances to the venue of an *industrial dispute* in the attempt to persuade others not to cross the *picket line*, thereby breaking the strike action. Employment legislation limits the number of pickets to six. This makes illegal the use of mass picketing, which can intimidate those thinking of going in to work.

**picket line:** a group of workers on an *industrial dispute* who gather at the factory gates to attempt to dissuade people from strikebreaking. Employment legislation limits the number of pickets to six.

**pictogram:** a *histogram* or *bar chart* in which the bars are presented in pictorial form. An example would be chocolate bars stacked on top of each other, with the number of them denoting the growth in overall sales of chocolate.

**pilot study:** a preliminary stage in *market research* in which a small number of interviews are conducted to see whether the questionnaire achieves the research objectives. Any unclear questions can be rewritten before the full survey is undertaken.

**place:** the term given to *distribution*. The key marketing questions regarding place are:

- which types of outlet do we want to be distributed in? (Newsagent, supermarket or Harrods?)
- what level of distribution should we seek to achieve?
- how are we to achieve that level?

Of far lesser significance is the choice of *distribution channel* by which the goods change hands between the producer and the customer.

**planned economy:** an economy in which all the resource allocation decisions are taken by government departments. So decisions about what is to be produced, and how, and how it will be distributed all become a matter for the bureaucracy. North Korea, Cuba, China and Vietnam are still centrally planned to a degree, and many countries' governments still plan centrally some parts of economic activity.

**planned obsolescence:** see *obsolescence*

**planning permission** (or planning consent) is required from a local authority before any new construction can be started. This applies to shop signs, house extensions and change of use as much as to house, factory and office construction. It is designed to protect the environment from haphazard development.

**plant** is the *infrastructure* of a factory, especially the buildings and services (such as ventilation). It would be represented as *fixed assets* on a company *balance sheet*.

**ploughed-back profit** is another term for *retained profit*. It signifies the profit left after all deductions that is reinvested into the business to finance renewal and expansion.

**poaching** employees means attracting workers from a rival firm that have already been trained in the skills you need. This saves you the cost of the training process and means that your competitor has wasted its resources. If done widely within an economy, employers would stop (or cut down on) training new employees since it would become a pointless exercise. This would damage the skill-level and therefore competitiveness of the workforce. Poaching can be seen as an example of *market failure*.

**poison pill:** a defence to a *take-over bid* by which the company under threat signs an agreement or buys out another firm that would represent a long-term drain on the resources of the bidder. As a consequence the bidder should decide against swallowing up the poisoned pill (company), and give up their bid. An example of a poison pill is giving staff *employment contracts* with a three-year notice of termination clause. This would add greatly to the cost of taking over and reorganising the firm.

**policy:** another term for *strategy*. In other words, a plan for meeting *objectives*.

**poll:** a *quantitative research* survey, either into political or consumer opinions.

**poll tax:** a fixed amount of tax which must be paid by each person as an individual. It was tried as a means of raising revenue for local authorities in England and Wales over the period 1990–93, but was highly unpopular. This was partly because poll taxes are *regressive* i.e. they take a higher proportion of a poorer person's income and a lower proportion of a richer person's income.

**polluter pays principle** is the idea that polluting emissions should be taxed so that the businesses which create the pollution carry the full cost, i.e. both the private and the social cost, of the pollution they create.

**pollution** means contamination of some kind. It is usually referred to in the context of the environment, where pollution can take many forms: air, water, noise and many others. Increasingly, firms are being held responsible financially and otherwise for any pollution they produce. (See *environmental audits*.)

**population:** a statistical term meaning all the people within the criteria chosen for a *market research* exercise. For example, it might be all lager drinkers, in which case a sample would be drawn from the lager-drinking population.

**portfolio:** a spread of assets or interests to provide *diversification*. A share portfolio would be spread among large and small, UK and overseas companies. A brand portfolio should have *inferior* and *normal, price elastic* and *price inelastic* products. In this way, it would be extraordinary for circumstances to arise in which the firm cannot succeed.

**portfolio analysis** is the examination of all the brands held by a firm to identify their strength and potential. A useful method is the *Boston Matrix*, which analyses products in terms of their *market share* and market growth. This helps a firm allocate its resources, usually away from brands in declining markets and towards those with growth prospects.

**positional goods** are things which by their nature are fixed in supply and therefore, ultimately, accessible only to those who can afford to pay rising prices if demand increases. Examples include quiet beaches and unrestricted rural views. As population pressures and economic growth continue, demand for such things increases while supply diminishes, pushing the price up, and limiting access to the relatively few people who can buy themselves a privileged position. Another example might be a seat on the centre court at Wimbledon, or any other item the desirability of which is increased by its scarcity.

**positive skew** is *bias* within a distribution towards high values. In other words, the majority of the values are above the average. For example, the diagram on the following page shows the frequency with which people take driving tests, analysed by age.

**positive statements** can be checked against the facts in order to decide whether they are true. They contrast with *normative* statements, which involve *value judgements*, and will reflect personal opinions.

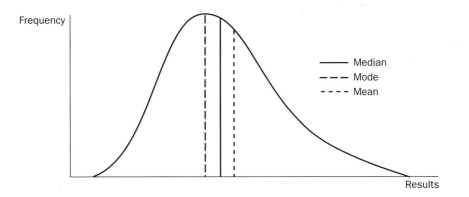

Frequency

— Median
– – Mode
- - - Mean

Results

*Positive skew*

**post-tax profit:** profit after the deduction of *corporation tax*. This is the profit that is available for distribution to shareholders. It is also known as 'earnings' which, when divided among the number of shares issued by the firm, provides the ratio *earnings per share*.

**poverty** is a situation in which people's *standard of living* is low. It may be measured in either absolute or relative terms. *Absolute poverty* means that a person's basic human needs for food, clothing and shelter are not being met, and a poor standard of health may also result. This applies to people suffering from malnutrition or without homes. Relative poverty depends on the standards being applied, and implies that within a particular society a given standard of living is unacceptably low. So people may be described as living in relative poverty if they are unable to participate in activities which are considered normal in that society, even though they have enough to eat and somewhere to live. Thus poverty may mean having basic needs satisfied but being unable to go to a football match or a short time at the pub, or pay for children's books or outings.

There is some evidence that poverty is on the increase because income distribution has widened in the past fifteen years, worldwide, under the impact of market forces.

**poverty trap:** a situation in which a person may be worse off working than living on *means-tested benefits* because the marginal rate of taxation and the rate at which benefits are lost in combination remove the incentive effects of the earnings. This results from low *tax thresholds* combined with a sharp tapering off of means-tested benefits as income rises.

**PR:** see *public relations*

**predator:** a company attempting to buy up another firm in a hostile *take-over bid*.

**predatory pricing:** setting a price low enough to drive competitors out of the market, or out of business. This anti-competitive practice is hard to prove, though the pest control firm Rentokil has been warned by the *Office of Fair Trading* to stop doing it. Their tactic had been to target small but successful local competitors; whilst keeping their national prices high (thereby remaining profitable) they cut their local prices in a predatory manner. Once the competitor had withdrawn from the market, Rentokil's prices were pushed back up. Carried out on a rolling basis around the country, this enabled the firm to keep overall prices high, yet maintain their high *market share*. Predatory pricing can be a feature of *price wars*.

**preference share:** a share paying a fixed *dividend* that offers greater security than an ordinary share. It is like a compromise between an *ordinary share* and loan capital

A B C D E F G H I J K L M N O P Q R S T U V W X Y Z

**231**

(*debenture*). If the company goes into *liquidation*, preference shareholders would be repaid in full before ordinary shareholders receive anything. This is also true of dividends, which are paid to them after loan repayments have been made, but before ordinary shareholders receive theirs. From the investors' point of view the preference share carries less risk than an ordinary share, but no right to a share of the firm's profitability.

**prepayments** are items paid for in advance, or on which a deposit has been paid. The *balance sheet* item *debtors* is really debtors plus prepayments.

**present value** is the *cash flow* for a future year discounted to become a present-day value. When all the present values are totalled and the initial outlay is deducted, the result is the *net present value* (NPV) of an investment.

**press release:** a *public relations* statement issued to the media in the hope of obtaining favourable editorial publicity. Successful press releases will offer stories that can either be treated as news items or form the humorous items and pictures that press media and television like to use.

**pressure group:** an organisation formed by people with a common interest who get together in order to further that interest. Pressure groups exist in a wide variety of forms, such as the Licensed Victuallers Association, who pressure the government in the interests of the brewing trade; Greenpeace, who fight for environmental issues; and *trade unions*, who look after the interests of their members.

**pre-tax profit:** profit before the deduction of *corporation tax*.

**preventive maintenance** means building into a production schedule the maintenance programme for equipment and machinery. In this way, mechanics can work to prevent faults rather than cure them. This is essential to ensure that a production schedule can be relied upon 100 per cent, without which a *just in time* production system cannot operate efficiently.

**price:** the money value of anything which is bought and sold in the market-place, including goods, services, assets and factors of production. In competitive markets price is determined by market forces, i.e. supply and demand. Businesses with some monopoly power may be able to decide prices within limits. In some cases prices are decided by governments, e.g. prescription prices in the UK, or all prices in a centrally planned economy.

**price competition** means the rivalry between firms which use price as a way of attracting consumers. It contrasts with *non-price competition*, which involves other ways of attracting consumers, e.g. through advertising.

**price controls** are government restrictions on the pricing freedom of firms that can be acquired through legislation. In the mid 1970s, firms could only put their prices up by more than 5 per cent if the government's Price Commission approved. This was a way of limiting *inflation* by the use of *direct controls* on the economy.

**price discrimination** means charging different prices to different people for what is essentially the same product. This is done in order to maximise revenue by charging more to those that can afford, and are willing to pay more. Price discrimination is a response to the recognition by a firm that different types of people may have different *price elasticities* of demand for a product. For example, under 16s get half-price entrance to most cinemas and football grounds because the owners know that higher prices will cut demand substantially. In this case, as in all considerations of price discrimination, it is essential that there should be the minimum of crossover between market segments. In other words, if many adults could get in for half-price, the point of the discrimination would be lost.

**price:earnings ratio (PE ratio):** a measurement of how highly a firm's shares are valued in the *stock market*. The ratio divides the stock market value of the shares by the firm's earnings (profit after tax). The higher the PE figure, the higher the company's share price in relation to its profit.

FORMULA:    $\dfrac{\text{market share price}}{\text{earnings per share}}$ = PE ratio

**Worked example: PE ratio**

$\dfrac{£1.50p}{10p}$ = **15 times**

Conclusion: the stock market rates the shares at 15 times earnings; this means it would take 15 years of this year's profit level to justify the current share price. Is this realistic? If the firm is Marks and Spencer, one could feel confident of sustained profits. It is a small computer software firm however, 15 years of profitability cannot be guaranteed. Therefore the share may be overpriced.

**price elastic:** refers to situations in which an increase or decrease in price leads to a proportionately greater decrease or increase in the quantity sold, i.e. its elasticity is greater than one. (See *price elasticity*.)

**price elasticity of demand** is a measure of the way the *demand* for a good responds to a change in its price. In order to avoid the problems with absolute numbers, it is always measured in proportionate or percentage terms, thus:

FORMULA:    $\dfrac{\text{percentage change in quantity demanded}}{\text{percentage change in price}}$

So if the price of a good rises by 10 per cent, and its demand falls by 20 per cent as a result the value of price elasticity is:

$-20\% \div 10\% = -2$

A numerical value greater than one is called *price elastic*, whilst a value of between zero and one is called *price inelastic*. In purely mathematical terms, the value of price elasticity should be negative, since an increase in price will cut demand, and a fall in price will increase demand. As this is always true the minus sign is sometimes ignored.

There is a link between price elasticity of demand and sales revenue. If demand is elastic and prices rise, the greater-than-proportionate fall in quantity sold will mean that sales revenue will fall, and vice versa. In the diagram, the box showing lost revenue is larger than the box showing gained revenue. With inelastic demand, a price increase will result in a rise in sales revenue. In the diagram on the next page, the box representing revenue gained is larger than the box representing revenue lost.

Price elasticity of demand is of considerable significance because it may affect decisions about price. Raising the price of an item which has elastic demand may not help to cover rising costs. Also price elasticity affects the impact of certain *indirect taxes*, e.g. those on petrol, alcohol and tobacco (see *tax incidence*) and of *tariffs* and *quotas* on *imports*.

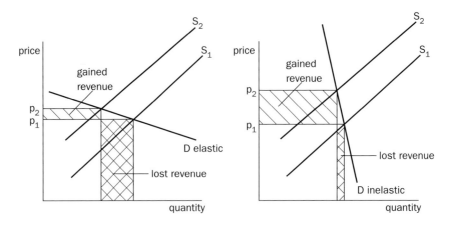

*Price elasticity of demand*

**price elasticity of supply:** see *supply elasticity*.

**price index:** a way of measuring changes in the general level of prices using *index numbers*. The *Retail Price Index* measures inflation generally. The *Wholesale Price Index* measures changes in wholesale prices and provides a useful leading indicator of inflation.

**price inelastic:** where a proportionate change in a product's price leads to a proportionately smaller change in the quantity sold, i.e. elasticity is numerically greater than zero but less than one. Such goods tend to have high *product differentiation*, meaning that consumers perceive them as having no acceptable substitutes. This may primarily be due to the effectiveness of their *branding* and *advertising*, e.g. Levi's. For the manufacturer, the advantage of a price inelastic product is that if its costs rise, it can pass them on to its customers with minimal effect on demand.

**price leader:** a brand that is in such a powerful position within its market-place that it can largely dictate the prevailing price level. The managers of rival brands know that consumers see the price leader as **the** salad cream, baked beans, coconut chocolate bar or whatever. Therefore the price set by the rivals has to be in relation to the leader. For instance, HP baked beans has to be priced at least 2–3p below Heinz, otherwise its market share will dwindle. If HP's costs rise, it may be unable to risk putting its price up until Heinz decides on a price increase. Therefore being second-best in a market with a price leader can be a dangerous position. Price leadership is a characteristic feature of oligopoly.

**price maker:** another term for *price leader*. Contrasts with *price taker*, the firm which follows the price leader.

**price mechanism** is the interaction of *demand* and *supply* which determines prices, and hence the allocation of scarce resources. Price rations the available resources among competing buyers.

**prices and incomes policy** is a way of controlling *inflation* by government restrictions on increases in prices, wages and salaries. The policy was not very successful.

**price sensitive** refers to a good whose *demand* will react very strongly to a change in its price. For instance, a small increase in price will result in a large reduction in quantity sold. Therefore price sensitive means the same as *price elastic*.

**price supports** are used where governments want to keep prices above their freemarket level. This can be done if the government is willing to buy the surplus which develops. The *Common Agricultural Policy* of the European Union provides an example of the extensive use of price supports.

**price system:** the mechanism which causes prices to rise when *demand* exceeds *supply*, and vice versa, so ensuring that prices send signals to producers about the nature of changes in consumer demand. This in turn enables the *allocation of resources* to change in response to consumers, thus preserving *consumer sovereignty*.

**price taker:** a firm with products that are insufficiently distinctive to stand out amongst the competition. As their *price elasticity* is high, these products must be priced at or below rival brands. This *competitive pricing* is the only way to ensure satisfactory sales levels.

**price theory:** the area of economics which is concerned with the determination of price, through the study of demand and supply and their interaction. The focus of price theory is on equilibrium and disequilibrium prices, and it seeks to predict the outcome of a variety of possible changes in the market-place.

**price war:** a clash between rival companies in which prices are being cut in a cycle of thrust and counter-thrust. The situation in which a price war is most likely to start is when there is oversupply, i.e. *capacity utilisation* is low. So firms attempt to keep their *overheads* covered by boosting their *market share*. If only one firm cut price to boost market share, it could benefit. When a price war breaks out, however, no company benefits, only the customer. Even that is only in the short term, however, because many price wars end when one firm withdraws from the market. In the longer term, that may enable the remaining producers to push up their prices sharply. (See also *predatory pricing*.)

**pricing methods** are the different ways in which a firm can decide on the price level to set for its products. The methods can be split into two: cost-based and market-based methods. In either case however, psychological factors can and should be taken into account. (See *pricing psychology*.)

Cost-based:
- *mark-up* pricing, as used by most small firms, means adding a standard profit proportion to the direct costs; clothes shops, for instance, tend to work on a 100 per cent mark-up, so a dress bought for £40 will be priced at £80
- *cost-plus pricing* is similar, except that a profit is added to the full cost of the good or service; in other words an allowance for *overheads* is added to the *direct costs* and then a profit percentage added to the total.

Market-based:
- *competitive pricing* means taking your price level from the prices set by others within the market-place; a new petrol station, for example, would have to charge prices in line with local competitors; too high a price would mean inadequate sales volume
- *contribution pricing* is more sophisticated, taking advantage of the fact that different prices can be charged in different circumstances for the same product (as long as all prices exceed *variable costs*)

- *profit maximising pricing* is achieved by researching to find the likely level of demand at different prices, then calculating which is the most profitable.
- *penetration pricing* is the setting of a low price, designed to gain sufficient market share so that customers recognise the brand within that market; it is a short-run tactic.

In addition to the above, firms may price tactically, in other words to achieve a short-term goal. Examples of pricing tactics include *loss leaders* and *predatory pricing*.

**pricing psychology** is of importance because consumer perceptions and images of products have a major impact on *demand*. In particular, price cutting will boost demand in the short term, but may undermine the long-term image. Consumers do not want 'cheap' Mercedes or Chanel. (See *psychological pricing*.)

**pricing strategy** is the medium- to long-term plan of the price level that a firm wishes to set for a product. For a new product there are two fundamental strategies *market penetration* (pricing low to maximise sales) or *skimming the market* (pricing high to maximise profit margins). A further possibility for an existing product is *price leadership*. This is only feasible if the product in question has the dominant image within the mass market (examples would include Hellman's Mayonnaise and Benson & Hedges King Size cigarettes). There are many other ways in which a firm might determine the price of product. (See *pricing methods*.)

**primary data:** first-hand information that is related directly to a firm's needs. *Secondary data* may be useful, but is unlikely to provide the answers to the exact questions you are interested in. For example, secondary data might provide information about total consumer spending on soft drinks. To find out about consumer attitudes to 7Up would require *primary research* to gather primary data.

**primary efficiency ratio:** another term for *return on capital*.

**primary research** is the gathering of first-hand data that is tailor-made to a firm's own products, customers or markets. This is carried out by fieldwork, whereas *secondary* (second-hand) *data* is gathered by *desk research*.

**primary sector** is that part of the economy consisting of agriculture, fishing, forestry and the extractive industries such as oil exploration and mining.

**Prince's Trust** was set up by the Prince of Wales to provide *grants* for young people wishing to start up their own businesses.

**private benefits** are the benefits which accrue to the individual buyer and seller of a product. In contrast, the *external benefits* are those which accrue to third parties.

**private costs** are the costs of production which are born by the business which produces the product. For example, private costs will include wages and salaries, interest and the costs of raw materials and components, as well as any research and development costs. They do not include *external costs*, i.e. those which are borne by third parties. These might be the costs to health and welfare of pollution which results from the production process, or of congestion.

**private enterprise** includes all economic activities which are undertaken for *profit* within the *private sector*. The owners of the business will be individuals operating as sole traders or a shareholders, or other private-sector organisations. In contrast, *public enterprise* involves the government. Private enterprise is normally subject to market forces, with decisions being made according to conditions of demand and supply.

**Private Finance Initiative (PFI):** a strategy begun in 1992 to invest in UK *infrastructure* using a mixture of private and public sector funding. The objective was to modernise the infrastructure without being committed to a big increase in government spending. It has been used to encourage private sector approaches to increasing the efficiency of building programmes in health, education and transport. Projects are run by private sector contractors, using private sector funds. The public sector body concerned undertakes to pay an annual fee for a given length of time (sometimes twenty years) which covers the costs. The most controversial such plan is to modernise the London Underground through a PFI. It is too soon to say whether the costs of PFIs are worth the benefits. See also *public private initiatives*.

**private label:** a retailer's own brand, which often carries the company name (such as Sainsbury's) but may also be an invented name (such as John Lewis' 'Jonelle' brand). For the retailer, the great advantage of a strong private label is that instead of buying supplies from a powerful branded goods manufacturer (at high prices), it can obtain supplies from whoever is willing to provide the right quality at a low price.

Accordingly, private label goods generate far higher profit margins for the retailer than branded goods. (See also *own-label*.)

**private limited company:** a small to medium-sized business that is usually run by the family that own it. Within such a firm, the family can determine its own *objectives* without the pressures towards short-term profit that are so common among *public limited companies*. At the same time, the shareholders are risking only the money they put into the company and their personal property cannot be used to pay the company's debts. However, if the business is growing, the need for additional finance may favour a shift to PLC status.

**private sector** is that part of the economy operated by firms that are owned by shareholders or private individuals. In Western economies it is the dominant sector; the remainder is called the *public sector*. Within the private sector, decisions are made on the basis of *market forces*, with businesses responding to the conditions of *supply* and *demand* so that changes in consumer demand will be reflected in decisions about what to produce.

**privatisation:** the process of returning firms or industries to the private sector after being run by the state. The policy of privatisation was vigorously pursued by Conservative governments in the 1980s and 1990s. It became a model for many other countries where it was felt that the mix between state and private sector organisations had become unbalanced. The surprise to many was that the 1997 Labour government continued to part-privatise Air Traffic Control and the London Underground.

Privatisation has a variety of meanings, from the contracting out of refuse services within a local authority, to the deregulation of bus routes. It is as much a way of thinking as a closely defined programme. However, the majority of people when they talk of privatisation tend to mean the high profile transfers of nationalised industries into public limited companies, such as British Telecom (BT), British Airports Authority (BAA) and British Airways (BA).

Among the arguments for and against privatisation are the following:

For:        As has been proved in the former communist countries, the state is not a good decider of how to distribute factors of production. The bureaucratic processes involved with decision making prevent efficiency gains which come about through the market mechanism.

Against:     Many state-run enterprises operated in areas where people have a basic right to enjoy the good or service without effective rationing by price. Examples would include water, gas, and electricity.

For:     Many state-owned companies were monopolies which exploited the public. Privatisation introduced competition into fields such as telephony, leading to the huge range of choice we have today.

Against:     Many nationalised industries were natural monopolies, meaning that there was only room for one producer in the market. The creation of privatised monopolies has allowed the water companies and others to exploit customers more than ever before.

**proactive:** a decision or action that initiates rather than responds to the initiatives of others. For example, if a *recession* occurred, the proactive company might develop a range of new, lower-priced products. The reactive firm would copy that initiative.

**probability** is the likelihood of an outcome occurring, expressed as a numerical value. Most managers would tend to refer to probabilities in percentage form ('a 50/50 chance') or as a fraction ('the chances are only 1 in 10'). Statisticians use a third method which is based on the fact that all the possible outcomes from an event must add up to 1. Therefore if the chances are 1 in 10, the statisticians describe that as a 0.1 chance.

The most important aspect of probability for business students is to recognise what is known as the gambler's fallacy. If a roulette player sees the ball land on red four times in a row, there is a tendency to think, 'Ah, well next time it's bound to be black.' In fact, every time the ball is put into play the chances of red and black are even. Therefore a firm that has launched two new product flops should not be kidding itself that, 'Our luck should turn.'

**process innovation:** improvements in the way a product is produced, arising from new technologies. This is a powerful way to cut costs and become more efficient for many businesses. It can lead to big increases in productivity.

**process theory** is an examination of the psychological processes that are involved in *motivation*. This contrasts with content theories such as those of *Maslow* and *Herzberg*. The best-known element of process theory is *Vroom*'s work on the importance of people's expectations about the chances of an action achieving a desired outcome.

**producer goods** are goods bought as inputs into the production process for consumer goods and services.

**product development**: fulfilling marketing objectives by developing new products or upgrading existing ones. This might be in order to boost sales/market share or to add value and therefore price. Successful product development relies upon excellence in research and development and in design, plus the technical ability to turn good designs into well engineered products or services. Product development can be through marginal changes (low risk, small reward) such as 'new, improved Ariel' or major innovations (high risk, high reward) such as Sony's wide-screen TV.

**product differentiation** is the extent to which consumers perceive one product as being different from its rivals. A highly differentiated product is one that people think of as so distinctive that it has no acceptable substitutes. With low differentiation, a product would be one among many, with many direct, acceptable competitors. As a result, products with weak differentiation need to charge relatively low prices in order to hold their *market share*.

There are two main sources of product differentiation:

- actual product advantages, such as better design, better manufacture and higher quality standards
- psychological factors such as *branding* and *advertising*

In contrast, *homogeneous products* are not differentiated at all. They are indistinguishable from their competitors. Similarly, commodity products are sold in large quantities and are standardised so that there is very little product differentiation.

**product innovation:** creating new products or improving existing ones. See also *innovation* and *product life cycle*.

**production** is the process of organising resources in order to meet a customer requirement. In a manufacturing context, production is the whole process from: obtaining raw materials to goods inward inspection, to production processes, to assembly and finishing, to delivery. The term 'production' can also be applied to the supply of services.

**production chain:** the entire sequence of activities required to turn raw materials into a consumer purchase. The chain will include *primary*, *secondary* and *tertiary sector* activities, with the latter involved at every stage. A highly simplified example for beer production is shown in the following diagram.

**production function:** a mathematical relationship which links the quantities of inputs to the production process, to the quantity of output.

**production line:** the arrangement of a flow production system so that parts move systematically from one stage to the next. Within such a process, *division of labour* is likely to be high and production line workers may feel threatened by the prospect of automation.

**production orientation** is a term used by many writers to indicate an old-fashioned business that ignores customer tastes and needs. The management is assumed to be inward-looking, focusing upon the convenience of producing the same old product in the same old way. This is contrasted with more thrusting, market-orientated companies that spot new trends and devise the products to meet them. Although there is truth in this, production orientation does have some important strengths:

- implies a commitment to focus on the firm's strengths rather than diversifying into unknown markets

- will often be associated with high quality, even to the point of producing an item that is stronger or better than the market thinks it needs (but that can boost long-term *corporate image*)

- may lead to longer-term planning for new capital investment than in a market-orientated firm.

**production possibility frontier:** the set of combinations of products which can be produced within an economy if all resources are being fully utilised. It is usually shown in diagrammatic form as being a curve, showing combinations of two goods which are possible. This curve will be concave to the origin, because resources vary as to the efficiency with which they can be used to produce particular items. Giving up some of one product may be possible but may not lead to much more of the other product being produced, if all the resources suited to its production have already been used.

Combinations of products outside the frontier (e.g. at point A) are impossible because they require more resources than are currently available. Combinations of products inside the frontier (e.g. at point B) entail unemployment of labour orcapital or both. If the quantity of resources available increases, e.g. as a result of investment, then the frontier may shift outwards, allowing more of both goods to be produced.

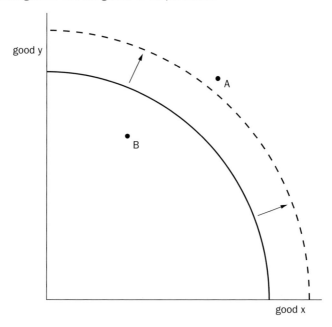

**productive capacity** refers to the ability of the economy to produce. An increase in productive capacity, which might result from an increase in investment, implies that it will be possible to increase output.

**productive efficiency:** see *technical efficiency*

**productivity** measures the efficiency with which resources are used. The most commonly used productivity measure is output per person employed. When people speak of productivity, this is usually what they mean. However, it is possible also to measure output per unit of capital employed – the productivity of capital.

Productivity can be measured within the individual firm or for the economy as a whole.

On the international level, differing levels of productivity growth (efficiency) are important in explaining variations in industrial performance and rates of economic growth. These in turn have a major impact on standards of living.

In recent years, productivity growth in the UK has improved. Productivity grows for a number of reasons including:

- increased capital investment, so that labour inputs are working with better quality or larger amounts of capital equipment

- technological change, so that production processes are more efficient

- improved management techniques, so that people work more effectively together. Examples of the possibilities would be *multi-skilling* and *teamwork*.

Rising productivity can cause unemployment, which may persist for a number of years, if demand does not rise as fast as the productivity gains. (This happened in the UK in the early 1980s). Despite this, it is difficult for an economy to grow healthily in the long run without productivity improvements. In the period 1960–1980, UK productivity grew very slowly compared to other developed countries. Recent experience has been much improved, though still not without cause for concern in some areas.

*Productivity increase, 1995–2001*

| US | Japan | France | Germany | Italy | UK |
|---|---|---|---|---|---|
| 14.4 | 7.7 | 6.1 | 6.1 | 4.2 | 9.2 |

Source: National Institute Economic Review, 2002

**productivity bonus:** a financial *incentive* to encourage a workforce to work hard. Employees receive a basic wage supplemented by a bonus related to their output level. The bonus rate can be calculated on a group or individual basis. *Herzberg* would describe such a system as a way of achieving movement, not *motivation*.

**productivity deal:** an agreement between management and union representatives that the former will provide some financial or other benefits in exchange for higher output per employee. If a 5 per cent pay rise has been granted in exchange for 5 per cent higher productivity, this would leave labour costs per unit unchanged and therefore have no harmful effects upon competitiveness or *inflation*.

**product life cycle:** the theory that all products follow a similar life course of conception, birth, growth, maturity and decline, although products pass through these stages at different speeds. The modern cigarette was born in 1873 and sales peaked in 1973 (implying a product life cycle of around 200 years), whereas the entire sales life span of Pokemon cards was three years.

Factors affecting the length of a product's life cycle:

- durability: if the item need be bought only once (such as a sandwich toaster) then *market saturation* can hit demand, as all those who want the item, have it
- fashion: if the item's sales grew because of fashion, it is likely that they will die quite quickly, for the same reason
- technological change can be very significant in turning the customer away from a product that now seems obsolete.

An important implication of the theory is that as every product will eventually decline and die, it is necessary for firms to carry out continuous new product development programmes. Ideally, new products should be financed from the *cash flows* generated by mature brands, and should be launched before maturity turns to decline. The product life cycle relates to company cash flow in the following way:

- during the development phase there is substantial negative cash flow from the money spent on research and development, *market research*, product design, and setting up a *production line*
- if birth turns to growth, more cash must be ploughed into expanding factory capacity
- once sales have stabilised, the firm can reap the cash rewards from their success
- in the decline phase, brands with a high *market share* can provide the cash for the development of replacement products (see *cash cow*).

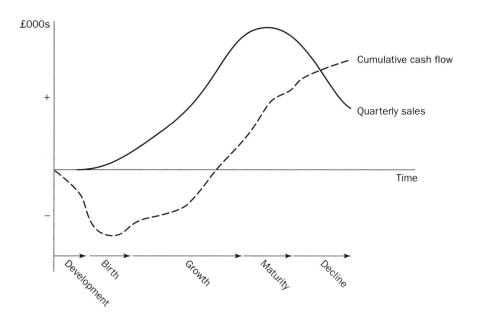

**product mapping:** see *mapping*

**product placement** occurs when a manufacturer gets a brand placed in a scene of a film or television programme. If the hero of a worldwide box-office hit insists on Bacardi and Coke several times in the film, it may be because the producers have paid for the product to be placed there. In effect this is a form of advertising.

**product portfolio** is the full range of products offered by a company. See also *portfolio*

**product positioning:** careful planning of the *product portfolio* so as to have products which appeal to as many different segments of the market as possible.

**product proliferation** is the tendency for successful market sectors to become over-crowded by a large number of new product launches. This proliferation makes it hard for shopkeepers to find shelf space for all the products available, and can lead to confusion on the part of the customer.

**product range:** the full listing of the products offered by a firm.

**product trial** is the rate at which consumers in your *target market* buy or try your brand for the first time. It forms one of the three prime objectives for a firm launching a new product:

1   distribution

2   product trial

3   repeat purchase.

Most firms set quantitative targets for each, such as to get a chocolate bar distributed in 80 per cent of sweetshops, tried by 50 per cent of chocolate buyers and repeat purchased by 12 per cent of trialists. In markets such as chocolate, product trial is heavily influenced by *packaging, promotions* and *advertising*. If the market is more fashion orientated, word of mouth is likely to be the main single influence upon the rate of trial.

**production possibility curve:** see *production possibility frontier*

**profit:** a simple definition of profit is what is left from *revenue* after costs have been deduct-ed. Profit is also a return on capital invested: it compensates the owner of the capital for the loss of the capital for any other potential use.

Economists distinguish *normal* and *super-normal profit*. The former is that amount of profit which is just sufficient to keep the resources employed in their current use. The latter is profit in excess of this amount, and indicates that buyers are prepared to pay a price above the costs of all the resources used in production. In time this will attract more resources into production and increase output in line with consumer demand. (See also *profit-sig-nalling mechanism*.)

Ways of arriving at different versions of profit are listed within the *profit and loss account* (see below).

FORMULA:   revenue − costs = profit

(See also *surplus*.)

**profitability ratios:** *gross profit* and *operating profit margin* and *return on capital invested* give different measures of profitability.

**profit and loss account:** a statement recording all a firm's *revenues* and costs within a past trading period. Although firms have a degree of leeway about how they present their 'P & L account', most adopt the format set out in the example below. To show how the cal-culations work, sample figures are included on the right-hand side.

**Worked example: profit and loss account**

|  |  | £000 |  |
|---|---|---|---|
|  | Revenue | 940 |  |
| minus | Cost of sales | 610 |  |
| equals | **Gross profit** | 330 |  |
| minus | Overheads | 180 |  |
| equals | **Trading/Operating profit** | 150 |  |
| plus | One-off items | (30) | (a £30 000 loss) |
| equals | **Pre-tax profits** | 120 |  |
| minus | Tax | 30 | (25% of pre-tax) |
| equals | **Profit after tax** | 90 |  |
| minus | Dividends | 40 |  |
| equals | **Retained profit** | 50 |  |

**profit centre:** a division or department of a company that has been given the authority to run itself as a business within a business, with its own *profit and loss account*. Before the start of the year, a senior manager will discuss with the leader of the profit centre the likely *revenues* and costs for the forthcoming year. From this a *budget* will be drawn up from which the profit statement will be derived.

Pros:
- enables power to be delegated to the local level, which should speed up decision-making
- the local profit and loss account can form the basis of financial incentives for all the workforce at the centre.

Cons:
- hard to coordinate the activity of several different 'small firms', all wishing to grow rapidly, but with the possibility that they may end up competing with each other
- the performance of a profit centre may bear no relation to the effort and skill of its management; after all, a blazing summer would make high profits in the ice-cream market an inevitability.

**profit margin:** *profit* as a proportion of *sales revenue*. It can be expressed as a total (the percentage of sales revenue which is profit), or it can be calculated on a unit basis (profit as a percentage of the selling price). The margin is different from the *mark-up* as the margin is a percentage of price while the mark-up is profit as a percentage of cost.

**Worked example: a sofa is bought by a furniture shop for £550 and sold for £625**

Profit margin

$$\frac{\text{profit}}{\text{selling price}} \quad \frac{£125}{£625} \times 100 = \textbf{20\%}$$

Mark-up

$$\frac{\text{profit}}{\text{cost}} \quad \frac{£125}{£500} \times 100 = \textbf{25\%}$$

**profit maximisation** is often taken to be the reason why firms exist and to be their primary *corporate objective*. In economic theory it is often assumed that forms always maximise profits. In practice, most firms have a hierarchy of objectives. When a firm's survival is threatened, it may profit-maximise in order to restore its financial health.

Otherwise it is likely to pursue longer-term *objectives* such as *diversification*. Another possible strategy is *satisficing* – earning enough profit to stay comfortably in business.

**profit-maximising pricing** is achieved by researching to find the likely level of *demand* at different prices, then calculating which is the most profitable. If the product has a relatively low *price elasticity*, the price set through this method is likely to be quite high. That is likely to attract new competitors who may make serious inroads into your medium-term *market share*. Therefore profit-maximising pricing may benefit the firm's short-term performance at serious cost to its longer-term future.

**profit motive:** the objective of the entrepreneur, who will seek sales revenue over and above the level of costs of production, as a reward for taking risks and organising the business. Economic analysis usually rests on an assumption that all *entrepreneurs* are motivated by profit. In fact, although it is important to make a profit to ensure longterm survival, many businesses have other motives as well.

**profit quality** refers to the likelihood of a profit source continuing into the future. If a profit has arisen from a one-off source (such as selling property at above its *book value*), its quality is said to be low. High-quality profit is *trading profit* that can be expected to be repeated in future years.

**profit-related pay:** a system of *remuneration* in which a proportion of each employee's salary varies in line with the firm's profit level. So, instead of being paid £20 000 a year, an employee might be paid £15 000 plus 0.01 per cent of the firm's trading profit. If the firm's profit last year was £60m., then the employee can expect a salary of £15 000 + (0.01% of £60m = £6 000), i.e. £21 000. Since 1987 the government has offered *income tax* incentives to encourage the adoption of profit-related pay, but take-up has proved slow.

**profit share:** a bonus paid on top of employees' salaries to ensure that a proportion of the firm's profit is shared out among staff.

Pros:
- could help to bridge any '*them and us*' divide between staff and management or shareholders
- provides staff with a personal *incentive* to keep costs down and productivity up (at John Lewis, for example, the profit share has amounted to over 20 per cent of annual salary)

Cons:
- unless it amounts to a substantial sum, the profit share may be disregarded by staff, or even seen as insultingly low
- research evidence has shown that profit sharing, on its own, has little effect on performance, partly because individuals cannot believe that their own efforts will make a significant difference to the whole firm's profit level

**profit signalling mechanism:** when demand for a product is increasing, prices will tend to rise and the product therefore becomes more profitable. This encourages entrepreneurs to expand activities in the profitable lines of production by moving resources into them. When losses are being made the reverse happens: resources will be moved out of the unprofitable lines. In this way *profits* signal the existence of unsatisfied consumer demand, and ensure that the *allocation of resources* falls into line with the pattern of consumer demand.

**pro forma:** a projected table of data. Hence a business plan for a new firm might include a pro forma *profit and loss account* for the first 12 months.

**programmed trading** is the use of computer programs that decide when to buy or sell shares or foreign currencies. The computer might be instructed, for example, to automatically sell any share that has fallen by 10 per cent or more (to prevent a client from losing everything).

**progressive tax** takes a higher proportion of an individual's income the more that individual earns. An example is *income tax*. Having a tax-free allowance, then a band of income which is taxed at 10 per cent, means that people on lower incomes are taxed less, while people on higher incomes will pay tax at the standard rate of 22 per cent or the higher rate of 40 per cent.

**promotion** has two different meanings:

- being appointed to a more senior or more desirable job (though see *horizontal promotion*)

- the promotion of a product as part of the *marketing mix* by the use of *advertising*, *branding*, *sales promotion* and *public relations*.

**property rights:** owners of assets have a right to charge people who want to make use of those assets. For example, owners of fishing rights may charge for the use of them by other people.

**proportional tax:** a tax which takes an equal proportion of income whatever the person's income level.

**proprietor** is the person who owns and runs a business, usually a *sole trader*.

**prospectus:** a document which companies have to produce when they go public, i.e. become *quoted* on the *Stock Exchange*. It gives details about the company's activities and anticipated future profits. It has to conform to the *Companies Act 1985* and be handed to the *Registrar of Companies*. Any false declarations in the prospectus carry heavy penalties because it is construed as fraud to encourage people to buy shares on the basis of incorrect information.

**protectionism** describes policies of erecting barriers to trade such as *quotas, tariffs* and *non-tariff barriers*. Because of the benefits of trade derived from the law of *comparative advantage*, protectionism is discouraged under *WTO* agreements. The most notorious period of protectionism was between the wars, during the *Great Depression*, where country after country put up barriers in the hope of maintaining its level of employment. However there has been an increase in protectionism in some product areas in recent years. *Voluntary export restraints* in the EU and USA have been placed on imports from the Far East of cars, steel and electronic goods. Despite the benefits of trade generally, people with vested interests in certain industries are sometimes able to bring pressure to bear on their MPs or Congressional representatives so that they will support protectionist measures.

**prototype:** a sample product manufactured on an experimental basis to see if the engineering and design ideas work in practice. The prototype can be tested both from an engineering and from a *market research* perspective, before the firm decides whether to start full production.

**provisions:** allowances made in accounts for likely, but not definite, future *liabilities*. An example would be if a firm has been sued for damages which it believes it will probably have to pay.

**PSBR** stood for public sector borrowing requirement, which is now generally known as *public sector net borrowing*.

**PSDR:** see *public sector debt repayment*.

**PSNCR:** see *public sector net cash requirement*.

**psychological price barrier:** the price level that changes consumer perceptions of the product's value for money. £10 000 would represent such a barrier for many car buyers, hence the large number of cars on offer for £9 950. Technically, *price elasticity* increases at the psychological price barrier. Therefore a 1 per cent price increase from £9 950 to £10 049.50 will have a far greater effect upon demand than a 1 per cent change from £9 500 to £9 595.

**psychological pricing** means setting a price based on the expectations of the consumers within your *target market*. If, for example, a perfume producer has identified a *market niche* for a special occasion fragrance for mid-teenage girls, the price may be set above the level of the competition. This will help to reinforce the image set by the perfume's *packaging* and *advertising* messages. In this way, the price level becomes an integral part of the product's *marketing mix*.

**psychometric test:** a selection test designed to reveal the personality of a candidate for recruitment or promotion. It is usually done through multiple-choice questions which may use word association to look for candidates' sense of teamwork, their honesty or their sense of commitment. Japanese employers are very keen on this, because it tests whether the individual is likely to fit in.

**public borrowing** means borrowing by the government to finance current and capital expenditure. See *public sector net borrowing*.

**public corporation:** the technical name for a nationalised industry, i.e. an enterprise that is owned by the state but offers a product for sale to *public* and *private sector* customers. It should not be confused with a *public limited company*, which is in the *private sector*.

**public enquiry:** can be held in planning permission cases that are thought to be of particular public interest. A typical example might be the building of a motorway through a site of outstanding natural beauty.

The case is usually heard by an inspector appointed by the *Department of Trade and Industry*, and will hear evidence from the proposers and the protesters. The enquiry has the power to turn the planning application down.

**public enterprise** refers to state-owned organisations which produce for the market, for example the Post Office.

**public expenditure** is spending by the government, for example on social security, defence, education and health. Public expenditure in 2002 was 40 per cent of GDP. (See *fiscal policy*.)

**public finance** refers to government expenditure and the ways in which it is financed through taxation and *public sector net borrowing*.

**public goods** are items which must be provided by society as a whole, because no one can be excluded from benefiting from them, and their consumption by one person does not prevent their consumption by someone else. Examples include street lighting and the police force.

**Public Interest Disclosure Act 1998:** legislation aimed at protecting 'whistle-blowers', in other words, those who expose wrongdoing by work colleagues/bosses. The Act is supposed to encourage socially responsible whistle-blowing of crimes or potential crimes, but few commentators expect it to be effective.

**public limited company (PLC):** a company with *limited liability* that has over £50 000 of *share capital* and a wide spread of shareholders. PLCs are the only type of company allowed to be quoted on the *Stock Exchange*. The drawbacks of being a quoted company are illustrated by Richard Branson of Virgin. He decided that having become a public company he wished to return to the status of *private limited company* again to avoid the loss of control and the share price fluctuations which accompany quotations on the Stock Exchange. (See also *divorce of ownership and control*.)

**public ownership** refers to *nationalised industries*, which produce for the market, but are owned by the government and are therefore part of the *public sector*.

**public private initiatives** are projects which aim to use private finance to invest in the development of public services. Many are related to public transport developments. A particularly controversial scheme involves the London Underground which is badly in need of expensive modernisation. See also *Private Finance Initiative*.

**public relations (PR)** is the process of obtaining favourable publicity via the editorial columns of press media, or in television or radio broadcasts. The PR expert has the contacts within the media to ensure that the client's story or side to a dispute is reported sympathetically. Public relations can be a positive process,such as organising interviews on Breakfast TV shows or setting up launch parties for new products. However, there have also been cases where PR personnel have spread negative stories about rival firms. This is legal but unethical.

The Institute of Public Relations explains that public relations involves:

● liaising with the media; writing press releases, answering press enquiries, setting up interviews

● producing and writing publications; newsletters, annual reports, leaflets and brochures

● organising events; exhibitions, conferences, product launches and opening events

● planning publicity campaigns and measuring results.

**public sector:** the organisations and activities that are owned and/or funded by national or local government. These include *public corporations* (nationalised industries), public services (such as the National Health Service) and municipal services (such as local council-run leisure centres).

**public sector net borrowing** is the amount by which *government expenditure* exceeds revenue from taxation and other income. It varies from year to year, depending on government policies at the time and on the state of the business cycle.

High levels of borrowing may necessitate *high interest rates*, in order to encourage people and organisations to buy government bonds. This can be a problem if the result is to make borrowing more expensive for businesses which want to invest. It also means that there is a link between the way government expenditures are financed and *monetary policy*. High levels of borrowing can make it difficult to pursue prudent monetary policies in order to reduce inflation.

Borrowing increases in times of *recession* as tax revenues tend to fall and expenditure on benefits increases. The reverse may happen in a boom.

**Public sector net borrowing as % of GDP**

| 1996 | 1997 | 1998 | 1999 | 2000 | 2001 | 2002 (est) |
|------|------|------|------|------|------|------------|
| +3.6 | +1.0 | −0.4 | −1.1 | −1.6 | −0.9 | 1.3 |

Source National Institute Economic Review, 2002

A negative figure implies that there is a *public sector debt repayment*. Some governments at times have difficulty in keeping borrowing under control. One of the requirements for entry to EMU is that borrowing be less than 3 per cent of GDP per year.

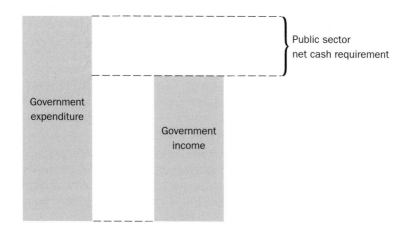

**public sector debt repayment (PSDR):** if government expenditure is less than tax revenue, then the government will be able to pay off some of its debts. This occurred from 1987 to 1990, partly because the government was receiving large payments for shares in the privatised industries. It occurred again in 1999–2001 as tax revenues rose.

**public spending:** see *public expenditure*

**public works:** expenditure by the government on infrastructure or socially useful projects, which may be of particular value in times of high unemployment.

**purchasing power:** the real value of a given sum of money in terms of what it will buy. *Inflation* causes the purchasing power of the currency to fall.

**purchasing power parity:** an approach to international comparisons of standards of living which takes into account price levels in different countries. It uses exchange rates which have been adjusted to give accurate comparisons of purchasing power.

**put option:** the right to sell shares in the future at today's price. Such a transaction would be entered into by someone who believes that the share price is about to fall. It is the way in which an investor who feels 'bearish' about the *stock market* can make money out of their pessimism.

**pyramid:** this usually refers to the company hierarchy, in other words the formal management structure, including the numbers of management layers and the *span of control*.

**pyramid selling:** is a clever (though generally illegal) way of encouraging inexperienced people to part with their cash in exchange for the right to sell a questionable product to others at high prices. Those at the top of the pyramid can benefit hugely from the commissions that those lower down pay on anything they sell. The nearer to the bottom you go, the more you encounter disillusioned people who realise that they have spent money on items that most consumers do not want.

**Do you need help with the synoptic element of your Economics and Business course?**

Go to page 335 for tips and advice.

**qualitative research** is in-depth research into the motivations behind consumer behaviour or attitudes. It is usually conducted by psychologists among small groups of people within the *target market* for the product (these are called *group discussions* or *focus groups*). The other main technique used by qualitative researchers is the *depth interview*.

The idea behind qualitative research is that when people are asked direct questions (as in a *questionnaire*) they may give answers that make them sound sensible or rational. Yet many purchasing decisions are based on emotion, not logic. Consumers pay £20 extra for the 'right' pair of jeans. Qualitative researchers aim to find out consumers' real thought processes during a relaxed discussion that has no pre-set questions. It can therefore lead wherever the psychologist feels the truth lies.

Pros:
- can reveal the motivations behind consumer decisions
- as discussion can range freely, it can discover the unexpected (whereas questionnaires can only consist of questions that were known beforehand to be significant)
- group discussion can provide ideas about how to solve a marketing problem from the most important people of all: the customers.

Cons:
- each interview or discussion is expensive, therefore few firms can afford to conduct many; this leads to possible concerns about whether the sample is representative
- the unstructured nature of the responses means that the data cannot be quantified.

**quality assurance:** the attempt to ensure that quality standards are agreed and met throughout the organisation, to ensure customer satisfaction. Among the key factors that must be considered are:

- the time, effort and technology input into product design
- the quality of supplies of materials and components
- the commitment of the workforce
- the system of quality monitoring and control
- the ability to deliver on time
- the quality of advice and *after-sales service* provided.

**quality circle:** a discussion group that meets regularly to identify quality problems, consider alternative solutions, and recommend a suitable outcome to management. The members are usually drawn from the factory floor, but may include an engineer, a quality inspector and a member of the sales team (to provide the customer angle). This method

**251**

was first devised at the Toyota Motor Company in Japan in the 1950s. Its success as a form of *consultation* and *job enrichment* led to its wider adoption in Japan and then, in the 1980s, in the West. The two principles behind the quality circle are that:

- no manager or engineer can understand production problems as fully as the shop-floor workers, therefore their knowledge is a huge untapped asset for the firm
- workers appreciate the opportunity to show their knowledge and talents in a problem-solving environment.

**quality control:** the process of checking the accuracy of work bought-in or completed. This is usually carried out by quality inspectors, though some modern factories encourage employees to check their own quality. This conforms to *Herzberg*'s view of the importance of personal responsibility and self-checking.

**quantitative research** means research using pre-set questions among a large enough *sample size* to provide statistically valid data. In practical terms that means using a *questionnaire* to poll at least 200 consumers within each segment of a market. It is a way of discovering data such as:

- a product's *consumer profile*
- the way a market can be segmented
- probable sales at a given price level
- estimated sales of a new product
- the results of a *blind product test.*

Large firms tend to use group discussions (see *qualitative research*) to help understand customer views and then write a questionnaire based upon them. Interviewers can then be employed to conduct the survey upon a representative sample of the population. The three main ways of drawing a sample are: *random, quota* and *stratified.*

**quantity theory of money:** the theory which links the quantity of money in circulation with the rate of *inflation*. The simplest version of this is given by the *equation of exchange*. This states that $MV = PT$, where M is the quantity of money, V is the *velocity of circulation*, P is the price level and T is the number of transactions. (In itself, this is in fact an identity: it is true by definition.) The theory holds that if M rises while V and T are constant, P will also rise.

This theory was important in economics in the early part of the twentieth century, but was superseded when Keynes and other economists observed that V and T might not be stable. It was replaced by a more sophisticated theory relating money and prices, developed by the proponents of *monetarism*, of whom the most notable was Milton *Friedman*. These ideas were influential during the early 1980s and became associated with Margaret Thatcher's time as prime minister. The policy prescription which resulted from monetarism was one of strict monetary control which would bring down the rate of inflation.

**quartile:** the total accounted for by one quarter of a population. For instance, a computer might rank all of a firm's 1 000 customers in order of sales value. The 250 biggest customers (the top quartile) could then have their sales totalled, which might reveal that they buy 80 per cent of the firm's *output*. The smallest 250 customers (the bottom quartile) might be worth less than 2 per cent of the firm's output. This information would help the company to make decisions on its sales and distribution strategies.

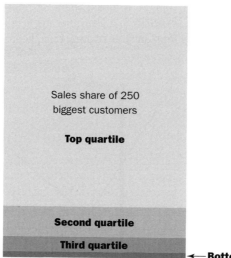

Sales share of 250
biggest customers

**Top quartile**

**Second quartile**

**Third quartile**

←—**Bottom quartile**

*Analysing data into quartiles*

**Queen's Award for Industry** is given for an outstanding contribution in particular business areas such as exporting or training.

**questionnaire:** a document containing a series of questions designed to discover the information required to meet a firm's research objectives. When writing questionnaires there are four main principles to bear in mind:

- each question should ask only one point.
- questions should not contain *bias* (e.g. 'How much do you like cider?')
- the time, cost and ability to quantify the analysis of the answers depends on whether the questions are closed or open. *Closed questions* are far more common (e.g. 'Have you bought cider within the last week?' Yes ☐ No ☐
- the questions must be asked in the right sequence, leaving personal details such as age, address and occupation until the end, and making sure that earlier questions do not bias the answers to later ones.

**quick ratio:** see *acid test ratio*

**quorum:** the minimum number of group members present at a meeting to enable decisions to be valid. For example in a committee of 12 it may be agreed that a minimum of six members must be present for a quorum to exist.

**quotas (import):** a form of *import control* that limits the sales of foreign goods to a specified quantity or *market share*. This will reduce the *supply* of the item, so if *demand* stays constant, the price is likely to rise. The more inelastic the demand for the imported product, the more the price is likely to rise. Above the level of the quota, the supply is fixed and the price is demand determined.

A common form of quota is the *voluntary export restraint (VER)*; these are often placed on imports of cars, electronic goods and steel to the EU and the USA from the Far East. Quotas are strongly discouraged by *WTO*, but are nevertheless widespread in some product areas.

This is because there has been support in recent years for protectionist policies on the grounds that they may save jobs. In reality it is likely that the loss of output caused by the restraint on trade is more serious for standards of living than the loss of jobs. (See diagram below.)

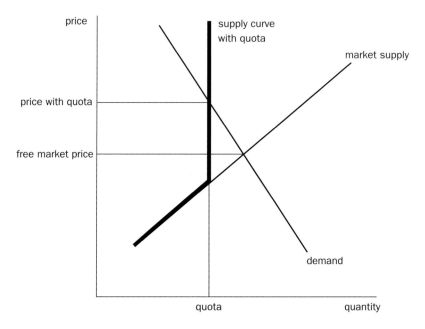

**quota sample:** the recruitment of respondents to a *market research* exercise in proportion to their known *demographic profile*. Therefore if you know that 25 per cent of your buyers are men, you would instruct interviewers to recruit one man for every three women within your sample. This is a far cheaper method of recruitment than *random sampling*.

**quoted company:** a firm that has its shares listed on the *Stock Exchange* or the *Alternative Investment Market*.

**What other subjects are you studying?**

A–Zs cover 18 different subjects. See the inside back cover for a list of all the titles in the series and how to order.

**Race Relations Acts 1968 and 1976** make it unlawful to discriminate at the workplace against any person on grounds of colour, race, ethnic or national origin. Specifically, the Acts make it unlawful to refuse employment, training or promotion on these grounds, or to select someone for *dismissal* on grounds of race. The 1976 Act set up the Commission for Racial Equality with power to investigate and issue non-discrimination notices against employers or *trade unions* found to be acting in a discriminatory manner. Individual complaints should be taken to an industrial tribunal.

**R and D:** see *research and development*

**random sample:** contacting survey respondents so that every member of the population has an equal chance of being interviewed. This sounds straightforward but is, in fact, both hard and expensive to achieve. The reason is that random must not be confused with haphazard. If all that an interviewer did was to stand outside Marks and Spencer one Tuesday afternoon and interview as many people as necessary, various distortions would occur in the sample:

- relatively few men would be interviewed
- few working women would be interviewed
- few hardworking students would be interviewed
- in other words, the sample would be mainly pensioners, parents of pre-school children and the unemployed.

In order to avoid these pitfalls, random samples are drawn from local electoral registers, and interviewees are contacted at home. The interviewer must call three times before giving up on an address. This is to overcome the problem that busy people are the least likely to be at home. The need to visit and revisit specific addresses adds considerably to fieldwork costs. So although random sampling is common in social research, businesses tend to use *quota samples*.

**rate of interest:** the amount which will have to be paid annually for the loan of funds. This will be higher for risky borrowers than it is for known, reputable borrowers. The lowest interest rates are those used by banks when they lend to each other. (See also *interest rates*.)

**rate of return:** a measure of the profit earned in relation to capital invested. Various definitions of profit may be used and comparisons of different investments may be made in order to determine which is most profitable.

**rates** are taxes paid by businesses to the local authority in their area, and are usually known as the *Uniform Business Rate*. Rates used to be payable on all properties but now individuals pay *council tax*.

**rate support grant:** the block grant from central government to local authorities. It means that not all of local spending needs to be financed by local taxes (i.e. by *council tax* and the *Uniform Business Rate*). It also allows the government to provide extra money to those areas with the greatest needs. In recent years it has been reduced somewhat.

**ratio analysis:** an examination of accounting data by relating one result to another. This facilitates more meaningful interpretation of the figures.

There are four main users of ratio analysis:

- internal managers, wanting to measure their own performance compared with previous years and with their rivals: the main ratios of interest would be those relating to perfor-mance (such as *return on capital employed* and *asset turnover*) plus those relating to profitability, such as *gross* and *net margins*

- *creditors* or potential creditors, for whom the security of their loans or credits would be the prime consideration: *liquidity* measures such as the *acid test ratio* would be of par-ticular interest

- shareholders or potential shareholders should examine key indicators such as return on capital employed, acid test and *gearing*.

- the staff (perhaps through *trade union* representatives) would be interested in the financial security of the firm (acid test and gearing ratios) and in its profitability: widening *profit margins* would make a substantial pay claim seem far more plausible

**rational expectations:** an economic theory which holds that because people learn from past experience, their reactions can be predicted, for example in relation to inflation. The theory was in important element in the body of thinking known as monetarism, which was particularly influential in the early 1980s. After that it became clear that people sometimes take some time to learn from past experience, and therefore there may be long time lags in their reactions.

**rationalisation** means reorganising to increase efficiency. The term is mainly used when cutbacks in *overhead* costs are needed in order to reduce an organisation's *break-even point*. This may be achieved by:

- closing one of a company's factories and reallocating the production to the remaining sites

- closing an administrative department and delegating its tasks to the firm's operating divisions

- *delayering* (removing a layer of management).

*Public relations* officers often use the term rationalisation as a euphemism for *redundancies*.

**rationing** means imposing a physical limitation on individuals' consumption of a good or service. For instance, in time of war it might be necessary to limit each car driver to one gallon of petrol per week. Rationing is often achieved through the *price mechanism*, in that only those who can afford a good will be able to have it.

**raw data** is unprocessed *primary data*. Usually the term refers to statistical information such as the sales figure for a product. Even after elementary processing such as collection into a time series (month 1, month 2 etc.) it is still considered raw. Among the main forms of analysis of raw data are: *indexing*, *seasonal adjustment*, *smoothing* and *weighting*.

Until it is processed it may be hard to use and interpret raw data, as shown in the following figures for sales of T-shirts.

**Worked example: T-shirt company sales**

|  | Raw sales figures | Seasonally adjusted sales index (base: Jan–Mar) |
|---|---|---|
| Jan–Mar | 1 647 920 | 100 |
| Apr–Jun | 2 486 729 | 105 |
| Jul–Sept | 3 842 166 | 107 |
| Oct–Dec | 1 946 771 | 112 |

It is only after allowing for the seasonal influences on *demand* that the underlying pattern of sales growth can be identified.

**raw materials** are *commodities* bought by a firm in a virtually unprocessed state. Examples would include sugar for making chocolate and sand for making glass.

**real** means that the item in question is being expressed in a way which removes the effects of inflation. (See *real incomes*.) For example, real earnings show the actual change in the *purchasing power* of what people are earning. In contrast, *nominal values* are expressed in money terms, without allowance for inflation.

**real incomes** are money incomes deflated by the level of prices. For instance, if you earned £100 last year and £200 this, but in the meantime prices had doubled, your real income would remain the same. To calculate real incomes, i.e. deflate to the prices of a base year, divide money income by the current price index and multiply by the index for the base year, i.e. the year of comparison.

**real interest rates** are the rates above (or below) prevailing rates of *inflation*. For instance, if inflation is 5 per cent per annum, and interest rates are 8 per cent, real rates are 3 per cent. During periods of rapid inflation, a seemingly attractive rate will often be negative in real terms. For instance, an attractive interest rate of 20 per cent will actually be minus 5 per cent, if inflation is 25 per cent per year.

**reallocation of resources:** when the pattern of consumer *demand* changes, resources are reallocated in line with the new pattern of demand, through the *price mechanism*. This process was first described by Adam *Smith*, who characterised it as the *invisible hand*. Reallocating resources is not always easy; it may entail some *structural unemployment* as some industries decline while others grow and people take time to adjust to the new composition of output.

**real resources** are all the things which can be used to create products for which there is a demand. So they include the *factors of production*, *land*, *labour* and *capital*, *human capital* and *natural resources*.

**real terms:** a figure or series of figures presented after stripping out the effects of inflation. For example, a firm may boast that its revenue has grown by 6 per cent in the past year; but if inflation is running at 7 per cent, the firm's revenue has fallen by 1 per cent in real terms.

**receiver** is appointed by *creditors* when a company has insufficient assets to cover its *liabilities*. The receiver's job is to try to sell the company to any other interested parties as a *going* concern so that those who are owed money can get it back. If he or she fails to find a buyer, then the company will be sold off in parts, and will be liquidated.

**recession** is that part of the *business cycle* which is characterised by falling levels of *demand*, very little investment, low business confidence and rising levels of unemployment. It is neither as long lasting nor as severe, however, as a *depression*. The official definition of a recession is two successive declines in quarterly *gross domestic product*.

**reciprocity** is the principle by which countries agree to grant the same trade concessions to their trading partners as they are receiving from them. When countries are negotiating trade arrangements through the WTO this principle is often important in securing agreement.

**recognition:** see *union recognition*

**recovery** is that part of the *business cycle* which is characterised at first by slowly rising levels of *demand*, some investment, patchy business confidence and falling levels of unemployment. Later in the recovery, optimism returns and investment grows faster.

**recruitment** is the process of identifying the need for a new employee, defining the job and the appropriate person for it, attracting a number of suitable candidates, then selecting the one best suited to the job.

**recycling** means dismantling and/or sorting products so that they can be collected and reused. This reduces the need for more raw materials to be mined or grown. As the cost of *raw materials* increases, technology improves, and the legal, moral and ethical implications of polluting become more critical, firms will move into recycling more of their own, and other firms' products. The decision, whether or not to recycle, usually entails careful consideration of the costs and benefits of doing so.

**redeployment** means moving people to new job functions either because their department has been closed down or because they are not good enough in their current post. It is often used as a polite way of telling staff that they are being moved sideways or even demoted.

**redundancy** occurs when a job function is no longer required. Therefore the employee holding the job becomes redundant through no fault of his or her own. If an organisation requires a large number of redundancies in order to reduce its *overheads*, it may ask for volunteers, offering financial inducements to those that accept. If insufficient numbers of the right types of employee apply to leave, compulsory redundancies may have to follow. The staff involved are legally entitled to the following minimum payments:

| Age of employee | Payment per year of service |
|---|---|
| 18–21 years | Half a week's pay |
| 22–41 years | One week's pay |
| Over 41 years | One and a half week's pay |

These terms only apply to those with over one year of continuous employment.

**refinancing** means injecting more *capital* into a business which has become short of liquidity. A refinanced business might, therefore, have received a high proportion of its extra *capital* in the form of loans.

**reflation** means stimulating aggregate demand by using *expansionary policies* in order to increase the rate of economic growth and reduce unemployment. These could be *fiscal* *policies* such as tax cuts or increases in government spending, or *monetary policies* such as reducing interest rates.

**Regional Development Agency:** a government-funded organisation with the objective of boosting the economy in its region of the country. England has eight RDAs, one for each region. Wales, Scotland and N. Ireland have had their own for some years. The English RDAs were set up in 1999 and presented their ten year strategies to the government in October of that year. The strategies included:

**East Midlands** – to aim to be in Europe's top 20 regions by 2010, as measured by national income per person; in 1999 the East Midlands was 38th.

**Yorkshire Forward** – aims to improve business birthrates and survival rates ... and to become an e-business region centred on Leeds.

The other six regions are: North West, One North East, Advantage West Midlands, South West of England, South East England and the East of England.

**regional policy** is the government's attempt to correct imbalances of income and employment by stimulating the local economy of less prosperous areas. (See *enterprise zones* and *development area*.)

Pros:
- reduces inequality of incomes and of opportunities
- reduces the hardship associated with structural decline
- reduces congestion in other regions
- by reducing unemployment it reduces the waste and cost of keeping workers on the dole.

Cons:
- there is little evidence that it works to change long-term trends
- firms often move a very short distance to take advantage of the incentives, but in so doing create no extra jobs or incomes
- to be effective it requires substantial government spending; successful firms might argue that they are subsidising less successful ones.

**regional test:** a form of test marketing in which a real experiment is undertaken within a whole marketing region. An example would be launching a new product within the North-West. This would find out whether the product can achieve a high enough *market share* to be profitable if launched nationally. A regional test is a far more expensive experiment than *market research*, but should yield far more accurate information. (See also *test market*.)

**Register of Members' Interests:** a document in which Members of Parliament specify any group with which they are associated which might influence the way they speak or vote in the House of Commons. By declaring such interests it is allowable for MPs to advance the causes of those groups.

**Registrar of Companies** maintains a record of all *joint-stock companies* in the UK, including their *memorandums of association* and for larger companies, their *annual report and accounts*. All the information held by the Registrar is available to the public at *Companies' House*.

**regressive tax** is one which takes a smaller proportion out of someone's income the more they earn. It is important to realise that a tax like VAT which is set at a fixed rate, is in fact regressive. If two people buy identical goods on which there is £10 of VAT, the £10 represents only 1 per cent of someone's income if they are earning £1 000, but 10 per cent if they are earning £100. The regressiveness of VAT is greatly reduced by the fact that it does not apply to food and housing, among other things.

**regulation** is one way in which companies are constrained by law, for instance on the maximum permitted level of pollution. Many firms complain that the existence of many consumer protection, employment and pollution regulations imposes excessive overhead costs upon business. For example, many staff are required to ensure that laws are being complied with. Furthermore, dislike of dealing with rules and regulations may put people off starting new businesses.

One of the objectives of privatisation was the removal of excessive restrictions, but it was necessary to introduce regulators such as OFTEL and OFWAT to limit the activities of British Telecom and the water companies and so avoid their exploitation of powerful market positions.

**regulator:** an independent person appointed by the government to exert control over the activities of privatised *monopoly* companies such as British Gas. (See *OFTEL*, *OFWAT*.)

**relative price:** a price may stay the same in money terms but rise or fall in relation to that of another if the price of the other good changes. For example, wage rates may stay the same while the cost of capital equipment may fall due to technological developments. Decisions about how much capital to acquire and how much labour to employ depend on their relative prices, and the relative rise in the price of labour may lead to capital being sub-stituted for labour in the production process and fewer people being employed.

**relativities** are comparisons between levels of pay in different grades, occupations or industries. They are used in pay negotiations to establish what might be an appropriate pay rise. For example a pay rise at Ford may be used to establish relativities in other car companies or in manufacturing generally.

**remuneration:** the entire package of material rewards received by an employee. These may comprise: pay, pension contributions, and *share options* plus *fringe benefits* such as a company car and private health insurance.

**renewable resources** are natural resources which can be regenerated. For example forests which are replanted after felling has taken place are renewable, and hydro-electric power is renewable because it is continuously available. In contrast, electricity from a gas or coal-fired power station is not a renewable resource because fossil fuels which have been used are not replaceable – they have been taken from the earth's crust.

**rent** is the payment made for temporary use of a property. Income from rent is the return on the capital invested in the property. *Economic rent* has a specialised meaning: it is a payment made for a factor of production which is fixed in supply, and therefore receives more than its *transfer earnings*. The economic rent reflects its scarcity in relation to the demand for it.

**reorder level:** the quantity of stock considered the minimum before more need be ordered from the supplier. To decide on the appropriate reorder level a firm must take into account the following factors:

- how long suppliers take to deliver after an order has been placed (their *lead time*)
- the level of *demand* for the product
- the level of *buffer stock* set by a firm.

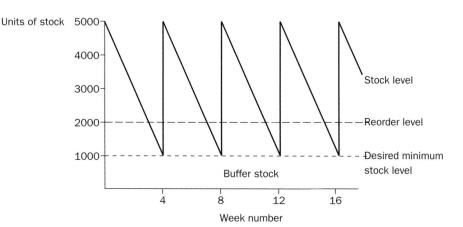

*Stock recorder level*

**repeat purchase** occurs when a first-time buyer purchases the same brand again. If this keeps happening, the process could be described as developing *brand loyalty*.

**replacement investment:** the level of investment needed to maintain the existing stock of capital equipment. This is sometimes known as *capital consumption*. *Gross investment* less replacement investment gives the level of *net investment*. This is the addition to the capital stock, which takes place each year.

**replacement rate:** the percentage of a person's income, when employed, which would be replaced by benefits if he or she is unemployed.

**repo rate:** the technical term for bank rate or base rate. It is the interest rate charged by the *Bank of England* to banks which borrow from it whenever they are short of funds. Repo is short for 'sale and repurchase', the mechanism by which the Bank lends. The banks sell bills and bonds to the Bank, at a discount equal to the repo rate, with an agreement that they will be bought back by the banks within about two weeks. It is thus a very short term loan. Because the banks need to borrow in this way on a regular basis, the repo rate underpins the structure of interest rates generally, and gives the Bank of England its controlling influence over the rates charged to borrowers.

**repossession:** when a borrower is unable to make interest and debt repayments on a loan which has been given specifically for the purchase of a home or a consumer durable the property is security for the loan and may be taken back by the lender to cover the outstanding debt.

**resale price maintenance** forced retailers to abide by the prices set by producers. This protected small independent shops from price competition, thereby ensuring that more survived to serve their local communities. Only after resale price maintenance was abolished in Britain in 1964 was there a substantial shift towards the concentration of *market share* among multiple retailers such as Sainsbury's and Tesco.

**research and development (R and D)** means scientific research and technical development. This is directed at improving the product, rather than at finding out what the consumer wants and thinks. (The latter information is the function of *market research*). The innovation which results from R and D may be either product or process innovation. The former results in a new product, the latter provides better, cheaper ways of producing a similar product. R and D is an important aspect of *innovation*.

**reserves** are a company's accumulated, retained *profit*. When they were made, these profits represented an important source of long-term finance for the business. There is no reason to assume, however, that they are still held in the form of cash. Therefore it is a mistake to suggest that a firm can 'use its reserves' to finance investment; it can only use cash.

In the macroeconomic context, the term reserves usually means reserves of foreign currencies held by the central bank. These may be used to manage the exchange rate, so that its value is kept stable.

**resistance to change** occurs as a result of: fear of the unknown; mistrust of the motives of those proposing change; and worries about loss of job security, income or status on the part of the staff concerned. Research has shown that in most organisations, middle managers are the staff most resistant to change. This is because middle managers have more to lose in any reorganisation than those below them in the hierarchy.

To reduce resistance to change, senior management needs to:

- have established in advance a sense of common purpose and of trust between the employees and management of the organisation
- explain and discuss the reasons for change in an attempt to achieve a consensus that it is essential
- if possible, guarantee staff that the changes will not result in any compulsory *redundancies* or pay cuts
- consult fully on the options available for implementing the change, ensuring that employee views have a significant impact on the eventual strategy
- set a clear timetable for the entire process of change; this prevents rumours circulating about what may happen next.

**resources:** sources of inputs needed for production processes.

**resource allocation:** see *allocation of resources*

**respondent:** an individual who responds to a *market research* exercise and is therefore part of the actual *sample*.

**response rate:** the proportion of those contacted within a *market research* survey who become *respondents*. This is an important element in determining how representative the *sample* is. A low response rate might introduce *bias*, as those who choose to respond may have different views from those that do not. This is a major disadvantage of using *self-completion* or postal questionnaires instead of *face-to-face interviews*.

**response time:** the length of time it takes for decision-takers to adapt to a change. Policy or price changes may require a review of existing strategies.

**responsibility** for decisions or results can be implied by *delegation*, but should remain with the directors, for they are ultimately responsible for the organisation's strategy and for the appointment of the staff involved. Nevertheless, there have been many occasions in business and in politics when the chief executive or government minister has refused to accept responsibility for actions taken by subordinates. In which case no one appears to be responsible for organisational errors or misdeeds. See also *social responsibility* and *business responsibility*.

**responsible marketing:** focusing the business not only on what customers want, but also on what is ethically or environmentally justifiable.

**restrictive practice:** a term used in two separate contexts. Restrictive trade practices are active interferences by producers in the free working of markets. This reduces competition and is therefore likely to lead to higher consumer prices. Among the main restrictive trade practices are *full line forcing*, *market sharing agreements* and the sharing of technological or marketing information. Practices such as the latter can be registered with the *Office of Fair Trading* and would therefore be legal. Unregistered restrictive practices can result in prosecution under the *Fair Trading Act 1973* and action by the European Commission under Article 85 of the Treaty of Rome.

Restrictive working practices are past agreements between producers and workers that limit the management's flexibility to decide who should work where and in what way. A common example is tight job *demarcation*, whereby a plumber may refuse to change a fuse because that is the job of an electrician. As the Japanese have demonstrated the benefits of workforce *flexibility*, British managements have tried to negotiate or to force through an end to job demarcation.

**restructuring** means reorganising with a view to improving efficiency. This may involve a restructuring of the management hierarchy (perhaps through the introduction of *profit centres*) or of the production capacity. Often, in fact, the word 'restructuring' is used as a euphemism or excuse for large-scale *redundancies*.

**retail audit:** a form of secondary research that measures the retail sales and *market share* of all major brands within a representative sample of shops. Individual producers may then decide to subscribe to this service on a weekly or monthly basis. Among the benefits of retail audits are:

- provides analysis of the composition and trends of sales within different types of outlet (supermarkets, chemists etc.)
- gives producers an early warning of changes in consumer purchasing patterns that will soon feed through to *demand* (via changes in wholesale stock levels)
- provides data on shop *distribution* levels.

**retail banks:** the banks which cater for the needs of individuals and small businesses. These include well-known banks such as Barclays, Lloyds and HSBC and a number of banks which used to be building societies. The remaining building societies also offer many retail banking services. In contrast, *merchant banks* deal mainly with the long-term needs of large businesses.

**retail cooperatives** are usually part of the national cooperative movement, which was established to provide consumers with goods at a fair price and with all the profits being paid back to the shoppers themselves.

**retailer:** a shop which sells goods to the general public.

**retail margins:** the percentage *profit* received by a shop on each item (or the average item) it sells. This is the retailer's *gross margin*, i.e. it does not allow for *overhead costs*.

**retail prices index (RPI)**

FORMULA: $\dfrac{\text{selling price} - \text{purchase price}}{\text{selling price}} \times 100 = \text{retail margin}$

**Worked example: if a furniture shop buys chairs from a manufacturer for £200 and sells them for £500 its profit margin is:**

$$\frac{£300}{£500} \times 100 = 60\%$$

**retail prices index (RPI):** shows changes in the price of the average person's shopping basket. The RPI is the main measurement of *inflation* in the UK and is calculated through a *weighted average* of each month's price changes.

It starts with a study of people's spending patterns, to try to assess the average household's weekly expenditure. This is in order to provide the base weights. About 16 per cent of household spending is on transport; it therefore carries a weight of 0.16 within the RPI. So if transport prices rise by 10 per cent, this adds 1.6 per cent to the overall RPI (10% × 0.16). The bigger the proportion of household incomes spent on an item, the bigger the effect of any price change upon the overall inflation figure.

**Worked example: The formula for the construction of an index number is:**

$$\text{Index} = \frac{\Sigma(\text{price relative} \times \text{weights})}{\Sigma \text{weights}},$$

where the price relative is the index of the change in the individual price. ($\Sigma$ means 'the sum of'.) If Year 1 is to be the base year and if there are just two products, a price index for them can be constructed in the following way. This gives the average increase in prices and reflects the relative importance of each item in the total budget.

| Product | Year 1 price | Year 2 price | Price relative | Weight | P.R. × weight |
|---|---|---|---|---|---|
| Potatoes | 16p | 20p | 125 | 6 | 750 |
| T-shirts | £4 | £4.40 | 110 | 4 | 440 |

$$\text{Index} = \frac{750 + 440}{10} = 119$$

A problem with the RPI is that it is weighted towards the average household's spending pattern. Yet many people who rely on the level of the RPI for annual increases in their government benefits or pensions have quite different spending patterns. For instance, pensioners spend twice the proportion of their income on heating as the average household. So if electricity and gas prices rise 10 per cent in a year when most prices have risen by 3 per cent, the RPI figure (of perhaps 4 per cent) will fail to reflect the inflation experienced by pensioners.

**retail selling price (RSP)** is the actual price of an item charged to customers in a shop. This will differ from the wholesale price to a degree that depends on the price *mark-up* decided on by the retailer. In making calculations about manufacturers' *revenues* or *profits*, it is important to remember that they will not receive the full RSP of the product.

**retained profit** is the profit left after all additions and deductions from *sales revenue*. These include trading costs, one-off profits or losses, taxation and *dividends*. Retained profit (the so-called 'bottom line') represents an important source of long-term, internal finance for the business. It adds to the *balance sheet* reserves, and therefore to *shareholders' funds*.

**retraining:** giving people who are part of the way through their working lives different or improved skills which are likely to be in demand in the future. Where people are occupationally immobile, this can enable them to take the jobs which are available.

**return on capital employed (ROCE)** is the percentage return the firm is able to generate on the long-term *capital* employed in the business. Its importance is illustrated by the fact that it is sometimes referred to as the primary efficiency ratio. A firm's ROCE enables a judgement to be made on the financial effectiveness of all its policies. If, for example, it is unable to generate a higher ROCE than the prevailing rate of interest, it could be argued that the firm should close down, sell off its *assets* and put the money in the bank. Apart from in times of *recession*, the average firm generates a return of around 20 per cent on its capital employed. Within its growth phase, however, the Body Shop generated figures closer to 100 per cent, which meant that the firm was generating enough profit to double the size of the business each year.

FORMULA: $\dfrac{\text{operating profit}}{\text{capital employed}} \times 100$ = return on capital employed

**Worked example: if a firm has an operating profit of £252 000 and capital employed of £2m., its ROC equals:**

$$\dfrac{£252\,000}{£2\,000\,000} \times 100 = \textbf{12.6\%}$$

**return on equity** is the percentage return the firm is able to make on its *shareholders' funds* (the capital owed to the holders of *ordinary shares*). This is a similar ratio to *return on capital* and can be evaluated in much the same way. The only difference is that return on equity ignores any loan capital held by the firm.

FORMULA: $\dfrac{\text{pre-tax profit}}{\text{share capital + reserves}} \times 100$ = return on equity
(shareholders' funds)

**return on investment (ROI):** an American term that is sometimes used to mean *return on capital employed* (ROCE), and sometimes to mean return on capital outlay (ARR).

**return on net assets:** operating profit for the year, expressed as a percentage of the firm's *net assets*. As net assets balance with shareholders' funds (the equity), this ratio gives exactly the same result as *return on equity*.

**returns to scale:** the relationship between the level of output and the quantity of inputs needed to produce it. If there are possible *economies of scale*, there will be *increasing returns to scale*. A given increase in output will require a proportionately smaller quantity of inputs in order to produce it.

**revaluation** is an upward valuation of the *assets* of a firm, probably as a consequence of *inflation*. The only asset that is commonly subject to revaluation is *freehold* property. In the interests of objectivity, the new valuation would be carried out by independent surveyors. However, the firm's own directors would still have influence over the new figures.

In the macroeconomic context, revaluation refers to the value of the *exchange rate* and to a move to increase the value of the currency in relation to all other currencies. This might occur if there is a *fixed exchange rate*. This is likely to happen if the country has a long-standing surplus on the current account of the *balance of payments*.

**revenue** is the total value of sales made within a trading period.

    FORMULA:   price × quantity sold

**revenue expenditure:** another term for *revenue spending.*

**revenue spending** is expenditure on all costs other than *fixed asset* purchases. It is charged in full against *sales revenue*. Examples include materials, expenses and salaries.

**reverse take-over** takes place when a smaller company takes over a larger one. This could be where the issued *share capital* of the victim is larger than that of the aggressor, in which case financing the reverse take-over involves raising more loan capital or issuing more shares. An alternative is where a *private limited company* takes over a *public limited company*. An example is the Royal Bank of Scotland's successful February 2000 takeover of Natwest, a bank twice its size.

**reward for risk:** a way of evaluating profitability through comparison with the presumed risk-free investment of resources in a bank deposit account. The reward for risk is the amount by which the percentage rate of profit exceeds the prevailing interest rate. The higher the reward, the greater the risks it is worth taking.

**Worked example: a new computer software firm is making a 10 per cent return on capital while interest rates are 7 per cent. Is this satisfactory?**

Quantitative analysis: the reward for risk is 10% − 7% = 3%; if research shows that, each year, one in ten software firms goes into liquidation, the 3% reward would not justify the 10% risk.

Qualitative analysis: if the firm has a well-diversified product range, a wide spread of customers and management of proven quality, the level of reward may outweigh the low level of risk.

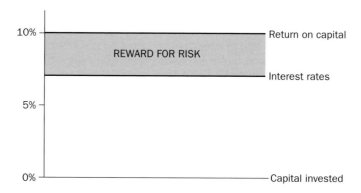

*Diagram to show how to interpret an average rate of return (ARR)*

The same method of analysis can be applied to the investment appraisal methods: *average rate of return* and (without subtracting the interest rate) *internal rate of return.*

**rework** is the extra labour and material cost involved in correcting manufacturing faults on a production line. Most modern procedures for improving quality (such as *total quality man-*

agement, *quality circles* and *zero defects*) aim to eliminate rework altogether. This would cut costs and enable customer deliveries to be speeded up.

**Ricardo, David** (1772–1823): an economist whose most enduring contribution was the Theory of Comparative Advantage. This shows how each country will have a *comparative advantage* in producing different goods and services, and if each specialises in the products in which it has the comparative advantage, it will be possible to increase total output, thus making everyone at least somewhat better off.

**rights issue:** so called because it offers existing shareholders the right to buy more shares before anyone else. It occurs when a company wishes to raise more *capital* relatively cheaply. The company will ask its existing shareholders if they wish to buy more shares at what might seem an advantageous price, i.e. lower than the price at which the shares are currently trading. However, because the rights issue has the effect of supplying more shares to the market, the share price will fall after the rights issue has taken place. For the original shareholders who do not wish to take up the rights issue their share value is protected because they are able to sell their rights to make up the difference.

**risk:** the possibility that events will not turn out exactly as expected. Risks are quantifiable, and probabilities can be assigned to them. Sometimes it is possible to insure against them, the insurers using the probability of their happening as a basis for setting the insurance premium. In contrast, uncertainty is not quantifiable.

**risk identification** is the attempt to determine and then quantify any threats to the firm's continued operations. Identifiable risks may include:

- financial risks, arising from the firm's *liquidity* position (short-term ability to meet debts), or from its *gearing* level (its dependence on debt): these risks can be quantified using *ratio analysis*

- trading risks, stemming from the price sensitivity of the firm's products, the degree of competition, and whether producers are working at full capacity or far below it: quantification could be achieved if the firm could discover its *price elasticities*, its *market shares* and the degree of *capacity utilisation*

- transactional risks, arising from reliance on large orders for materials that are subject to changes in market prices, or from reliance on foreign currency: substantial shifts in the price of materials or currencies may turn expected profits into heavy losses

- crises, such as when Perrier Water became contaminated.

**risk management** is the attempt to identify and plan for threats to the firm's stability or profitability (see *risk identification*). Managers can apply a long-term strategy of risk minimisation by addressing each of the main areas of business risk:

- financial risks: avoid low *liquidity* and high *gearing*; ensure careful *cash-flow forecasting* and control

- trading risks: avoid over-reliance on one product or market; work at strengthening the *product differentiation* of your brands

- transactional risks: hedge your forward risks if they are substantial; consider buying on the forward market (giving a guaranteed price today for your needs in three, six or twelve months' time)

- crises: prepare *contingency plans*

**risk:reward ratio** is an assessment of the risks of making an investment compared with the anticipated rewards. This ratio is rarely quantified because of the difficulty of determining precise data. A typical example of its use is by investors in West End musicals. The failure rate is known to be very high, but the rewards from investing in a successful production can be so huge as to make some people consider that the risk:reward ratio is favourable.

**rivalrous marketing:** where a small number of businesses are competing fiercely, their marketing strategies may be quite clearly targeted at each others' products. Advertising may be designed to invite unfavourable comparisons. Products may be designed so that they compete directly. This type of behaviour is very typical of an oligopoly, where a small number of large firms compete on price and on a number of non-price features.

**rivalry:** competition between firms may lead to intense rivalry as each seeks to outdo the other in the market-place. This is a likely outcome where there is an oligopoly using both price and non-price competition, intensely preoccupied with increasing market share.

**robotics** is the science of using robots in production processes to replace people, especially where such processes are monotonous or hazardous. Increasingly, however, scientists are investigating wider ranges of activities for robots involving primitive 'thought' processes.

**ROCE:** see *return on capital employed*

**ROI:** see *return on investment*

**role-play exercises:** a standard element in management training courses in which individuals adopt roles assigned to them in a problem-solving or decision-making context.

**rolling over** (of debts) is an agreement between a company and its bankers that loans due to be repaid at a certain date will instead be 'rolled over' into the future. In other words, the company is being given longer to repay the debt. This is not necessarily a charitable act by the banks as they will not only receive extra interest on the debt, but are also likely to charge a substantial arrangement fee to the company concerned.

**RONA:** see *return on net assets*

**royalty:** an agreed percentage of *sales revenue* paid to the owner of a *patent* or *copyright* for the use of the idea, process, name or work.

**RPI:** see retail price index

**RPIX and RPIY:** RPIX is the retail price index excluding mortgage interest payments, thus giving a measure of inflation which is not distorted by interest rate changes. RPIY excludes indirect taxes as well as mortgage interest.

**safety margin:** the amount by which *demand* can fall before a firm incurs losses, i.e. how close the firm is to the *break-even* level of output.

FORMULA:    demand − break-even output  =  safety margin

**safety policy:** the term for the legal requirement that firms should display a written statement of their policy towards the health and safety of the workforce. This is laid down in the *Health and Safety at Work Act 1974*.

**Sales of Goods Act 1994** lays down the contractual arrangements implied by the purchase of an item. It specifies that goods must be of 'merchantable quality', i.e. fit for the purpose for which they were purchased.

**salesforce:** the team of sales representatives employed to achieve high *distribution* in wholesale and retail outlets, or to sell direct to consumers. A national sales force represents a major *overhead* cost to firms, as representatives will be required for every region. As a result, building up an effective salesforce is a major financial strain for new, small firms. Yet without a strong salesforce, a firm may find too few outlets to achieve a *demand* level above the *break-even point*.

**sales promotion** is the use of short-term incentives to purchase, such as free offers, competitions etc. The strategy behind the use of sales promotions may be aggressive or defensive. An example of the latter would be to defend the brand against a competitive attack by a new or existing product. An aggressive promotion would be attempting to gain sales and *market share*, and would therefore be targeted at purchasers of rival brands.

The main purpose of sales promotion are:

- to create the initial surge of demand to persuade shops to stock a newly launched product
- to attract new buyers who the firm hopes will become regular customers
- to lock customers in to buying your product when under threat from a new competitor.

**sales revenue** is the value of sales made within a trading period. For ordinary calculations, it is enough to realise that:

FORMULA:    quantity sold × price  =  revenue

This does require some explanation however, in order to distinguish revenue from cash received. This is because a firm includes within revenue any sales made on credit. Therefore revenue comprises cash sales plus credit sales. This may sound a trivial matter, but because profit calculations are based on sales revenue, it follows that company accounts can present a healthy-looking profit position even though the firm is desperately short of cash.

**sales tax:** a tax on goods sold which is included in the price to the customer. Examples include VAT and excise taxes.

**sales turnover:** another term for *sales revenue*.

**sales value** means total sales measured at selling price, i.e. quantity times price. It is usually used as a way of measuring *market size*. For an individual firm, sales value is the same as *sales revenue*.

**sales volume** is the quantity of goods sold, either by an individual firm or throughout a market-place.

**sample:** a group of respondents to a *market research* exercise selected to be representative of the views of the *target market* as a whole. There are four main methods of sampling: *random*, *quota*, *stratified* and *cluster*. In consumer research, the quota sample is the one used most commonly.

**sample size:** the number of *respondents* to a research survey or to a specific question within the survey. The sample size is important as it needs to be large enough to make the data statistically valid. A sample of 20 people, for example, is so small that a different 20 could easily have quite separate views. When deciding on an appropriate sample size for a survey, a firm should bear in mind the following:

- the higher the sample size, the more expensive the research and the longer the fieldwork will take

- the lower the sample size, the greater the chance that random factors will make the results inaccurate

- if the research is to assist in a decision of great importance to the firm, it should invest the time and money into a large sample size (if it can afford to).

**sanctions** are rules made by international organisations or pressure groups which prohibit trade with countries which are behaving in ways which are considered unacceptable. The United Nations may place sanctions on a country which is considered to be behaving aggressively, as with Serbia and later Iraq. South Africa was eventually forced by sanctions to abandon overtly racist policies. It is possible to prohibit trade in particular items, e.g. arms.

**satisficing:** a term used to describe the acceptance of what is satisfactory instead of pursuing the best or maximum result. There are two main circumstances in which this applies:

1 Setting a strategy based on a satisfactory compromise between objectives. For example, if two divisional directors are each attempting to persuade the firm to pursue a different strategy, the managing director might satisfice by deciding on a mixture of both.

2 Aiming for an achievement that is less than the maximum, perhaps because the firm does not want to draw attention to its powerful *market position*. For example, instead of aiming for *profit maximisation* a firm might pursue a profit level just high enough to finance its expansion plans.

**saturation point:** the point at which demand for a product will stop increasing because everyone who wants the product now owns one. From that point onwards only replacement purchases can be expected.

**savings ratio:** that proportion of household income which is saved. The proportion can have a considerable impact on the development of an economy. Savings provide funds which can be used to invest in new *plant* and equipment, which clearly helps growth. So in the long term, the growth of an economy depends upon a high rate of saving, although in the short term a rise in the savings ratio can cut consumer spending and reduce aggregate demand.

In the past savings were thought to be at least partly determined by interest rates. That link now appears rather weak. Savings could be determined by expectations, so that the threat of rising unemployment might make saving increase. However this has proved to be a weak link too. A stronger connection can be made between the savings ratio and the rate of *inflation*. A higher rate of inflation can erode the value of money-denominated assets and therefore lead people to save more for a while in order to rebuild the real value of their assets.

In the basic *Keynesian model*, saving is directly related to the level of income. (See also *average propensity to save* and *marginal propensity to save*.) This shows that if consumers save rather than spend then *demand* may be insufficient to sustain business confidence, and growth may slow.

**scab:** a term of abuse by strikers or *pickets* to describe strikebreakers. Hence 'scab labour' means workers who cross picket lines and take the jobs of those on strike.

**scale of production**: a measure of a company's output level, usually in relation to competitors or to trends over time. So 'large-scale production' implies that the firm is one of the major producers in its market place; 'increased scale of production' may be from very small to quite small. As their scale of production increases, firms are likely to enjoy *economies of scale*. To a certain extent these will be counterbalanced by *diseconomies of scale*.

**scarcity:** the term used to describe the fact that people's wants and needs always exceed the resources available to satisfy them. In practice choices must be made and those choices determine the *allocation of resources*.

**scenario planning** is the process of anticipating possible changes in a firm's situation and then devising ways of dealing with them. For example a chocolate producer could ask itself: 'What if next summer brings a three month heat-wave? How will we cope with the collapse in demand for our products?' Having conceived the scenario, the management could consider options such as providing special display cartons suitable for retailers' chilled cabinets, or even supplying their own chocolate chillers.

**Schumacher, F** (1911–77): a writer whose book SMALL IS BEAUTIFUL (Vintage, 1993) began a serious rethink of the effectiveness of large business corporations, and of the environmental damage caused by modern business practices.

**science park:** an industrial estate placed next to a university or research centre with the intention that the businessmen and the academics can get together to discuss practical applications of new developments or theories.

**scientific decision-making** is the use of a formal procedure to ensure that decisions are arrived at in an objective manner. It attempts to eliminate *hunch* or *bias* by ensuring that decisions are based on factual, numerical evidence. The decision-making model on the following page is widely used:

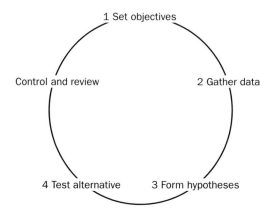

1 Set objectives

Control and review

2 Gather data

4 Test alternative

3 Form hypotheses

*Scientific decision-making model*

**scientific management** is the attempt to make business decisions on the basis of data that is researched and tested quantitatively. The principles were laid down by F W *Taylor* in his book, THE PRINCIPLES OF SCIENTIFIC MANAGEMENT (HarperCollins, 1947). He considered it to be management's duty to identify ways in which costs could be accounted for precisely, so that efficiency could be improved. Although F W Taylor is remembered mainly for his advocacy of financial incentives and high *division of labour*, his most influential legacy has been his advocacy and part-invention of such tools of scientific management as cost accounting, *work study* and *method study*. (See *scientific decision-making*.)

**scrip issue:** issuing extra, free shares to existing shareholders in proportion to their holdings; for instance one new for every one held. Although there are technical reasons for doing this, the main motive is to reduce the market share price. The problem here is that if a company is very successful and its share price shoots up to reflect this (perhaps to 380p each), sharebuyers are put off by a price that looks expensive. A one-for-one scrip issue would double the number of shares in circulation and therefore should halve the value of each share. At 190p each the shares appear to be priced more reasonably, which may make them more attractive.

**SD:** see *standard deviation*

**seasonal adjustment** is a method for identifying and eliminating regular seasonal variations from a data series in order to identify the underlying trend. This statistical procedure is especially important for data that has a direct impact on decision-making. The monthly unemployment figures might affect government economic policy, and a poor month's sales might lead a firm to halt a 'failed' advertising campaign. Yet unless seasonal influences have been taken out of the figures, the data might look gloomy when the underlying trend is quite positive.

**seasonal unemployment:** unemployment which rises and falls according to a seasonal pattern. Wintry weather can lead to unemployment of construction workers or of people employed in tourism.

**seasonal variation** is the degree to which actual figures vary from the trend within a given month or quarter. Although some text books measure the variation as a number (actual minus trend), it seems more logical to take it as a proportion (actual over trend).

**secondary action** is *industrial action* at a place other than where the dispute originated. All such forms of action were made illegal through a series of *Employment Acts* during the 1980s, culminating in the 1990 Employment Act.

**secondary data** is information collected from second-hand sources such as reference books, government statistics or market intelligence reports. Such data can provide information on *market size* and market trends for most product categories. It may be accessible publicly and therefore free, but is in any case not as expensive to gather as *primary data*. (See the entries for: *Annual Abstract of Statistics, Business Monitors, Economic Trends, Economist Intelligence Unit, employers' association, Mintel*.)

**secondary picketing** means setting up a *picket line* at a place other than where an *industrial dispute* originated. As with all other forms of *secondary action*, this is illegal.

**secondary sector:** the part of the economy concerned with the manufacture of products. *Primary sector* industry extracts materials from land or sea, while the *tertiary sector* provides business and consumer services. Although the secondary sector is Britain's most important supplier of exports, less than a quarter of the workforce is employed in manufacturing. It is a feature of developing economies that the secondary sector grows faster than primary industry. In developed economies such as Britain, however, the secondary (manufacturing) sector tends to grow less fast than service businesses.

**sector:** the economy can be divided up into sectors, each of which consists of a group of decision-takers with features in common. For example one distinction is between the *private sector*, the *public sector* and the overseas sector. The economy can also be divided up into the personal sector, the corporate sector and the government sector. The personal sector consists of all individuals, the corporate sector of all businesses.

**seedcorn capital** is the initial *share capital* that enables a new business to be born. It might be invested by family or friends, or by a *venture capital* firm. It should provide sufficient funds for an *entrepreneur* to test out a business idea fully. Many business start-ups fail, therefore providing seedcorn capital is very risky. However, the occasional great success may make sufficient profit to more than cover the losses made on the failures.

**segmentation:** see *market segmentation*

**self-actualisation** is psychological self-fulfilment, i.e. feeling enriched or developed by what one has learned or achieved. *Maslow* considered this the highest need of human beings. (See *hierarchy of needs*.)

**self-completion questionnaires** are questionnaires that respondents must fill in themselves (unlike a *face-to-face interview*). They may be sent by post or left for people to pick up and complete. This represents a much cheaper form of *market research* than the face-to-face interview, but is likely to suffer from low *response rates* (which can bias the results).

**self-employed** workers operate as their own bosses, either working *freelance* or with the permanent task of running their own businesses. Self-employment has various tax advantages over regular employment, especially in claiming expenses that can be offset against *income tax* bills. In 1999, it was estimated that 11 per cent (3.2 million) of the labour force was self-employed.

**self-regulation** occurs when an employers' organisation decides to issue codes of behaviour to encourage the firms in an industry to act more responsibly. Traditionally such organisations have been founded when pressure for regulation from the public or parliament has become too great to ignore. The employers hope that the agreement to regulate themselves will pre-empt the need for government intervention.

**sellers' market:** a market in which there are more buyers than sellers, so that the sellers can raise the price and still sell. The term applies most often in a housing boom, when prices are rising steadily.

**semi-variable costs** are costs that vary with *output*, but not in direct proportion. Therefore, in order to calculate total costs at a specific level of output, a manager would have to work out the semi-variables especially. This makes them hard to deal with, notably in break-even analysis. Examples of semi-variables include maintenance expenditure and telephone bills. In the latter case, it is clear that although a doubling of customer demand would not nec-essarily double a firm's telephone calls or bills, it is reasonable to expect that they would increase. Therefore the telephone is neither a fixed nor a variable cost. (Note that if a cost such as a telephone bill comprises a fixed rental element plus a variable usage charge, a firm would split the cost up into its fixed and variable elements.)

**separate legal entity** occurs when a firm becomes incorporated as a limited company, in which the business becomes legally separated from the owners or shareholders. After that, if the company runs into debt or is sued for negligence, it is not the owner who is liable, but the company.

**separate status** occurs when the employment terms and conditions for managers are quite different from those for the workforce. Although this is considered a very old-fashioned, *'them and us'* approach, it remains quite common. Typical examples of separate status include:

|  | Factory workers | Clerical and managerial |
| --- | --- | --- |
| Working hours: | 08.00–16.30 | 09.30–17.30 |
| Remuneration | Hourly wage or piece-rate | Monthly salary |
| Pension: | State only | Company pension scheme |
| Notice: | One week | Three months |

**service contract:** an *employment contract* covering the length of notice and compensation arrangements (in case of dismissal) for company directors or senior managers. Such contracts often specify lengthy notice periods, and therefore form the basis of high com-pensation payments.

**service sector:** see *tertiary sector*

**set aside:** the scheme by which farmers are paid not to cultivate a portion of their land. The *Common Agricultural Policy* of the EU currently has a set aside policy, as does the US gov-ernment. This is to ensure that farmers in the country concerned do not produce so much that farm prices fall and farm incomes are reduced.

**Sex Discrimination Act 1975:** a law forbidding discrimination against either sex in relation to *recruitment*, terms and conditions, and access to training or promotion. Despite the existence of this Act, the difficulty of obtaining legal proof has meant that much discrimina-tion has persisted. As with other issues of *social responsibility*, the passing of laws has not proved a substitute for ethical behaviour.

**Sex Discrimination Act 1986:** an Act enabling a common retirement date to be imposed on men and women. In 1993, the government stated its preference for a retirement age of 65.

**sexual harassment** is distress caused by unwelcome verbal or physical advances of a sexual nature. Although the term usually refers to men harassing women, it may be vice versa. Sexual harassment can be a reason to claim *constructive dismissal* from an industrial tribunal.

**shamrock organisation:** a term invented by Professor Handy to describe the modern business with three types of workforce:

- a permanent, highly valued and skilled core, assured of lifetime employment
- the contractual fringe (suppliers of services that can be contracted out, such as cleaning)
- a flexible labour force, hired and fired to cope with seasonal and cyclical changes in demand

Handy suggests that such an organisation will be slimmed down, with core staff taking on highly responsible tasks including the coordination of the fringe and flexible workforce. The shamrock organisation can be contrasted with the traditional *paternalistic* but *bureaucratic* corporation.

**share:** a certificate entitling the holder to *dividends* and *shareholders' rights* in proportion to the number of shares owned.

**share capital:** the value of the sum invested into the company by ordinary and preference shareholders. As these investors cannot get their money back from the firm, the managers know that they can rely on these funds permanently into the future. Investors can, of course, sell their holdings to other investors through the *Stock Exchange*.

**shareholders' funds** are that part of a firm's long-term finance owed by the company to its shareholders. It comprises the *share capital* invested by the shareholders plus the accumulated profits made by the firm over its years of trading (the *reserves*).

> FORMULA:    share capital + reserves = shareholders' funds

**shareholders' rights** are the legal entitlements of owners of ordinary shares. These include:

- the right to attend the *annual general meeting*
- the right to vote on new directors
- the right to take part in a *vote of confidence* in the *chairman*
- the right to receive an *annual report* into the financial state of the business.

In practice, small shareholders have rights, but usually very little power. On occasions, however, they can exert considerable influence, as when Alan Sugar, founder of Amstrad, wished to end his company's Stock Exchange *listing* and return the company to the status of a *private limited company*. Mr Sugar offered to buy Amstrad shares at a price which his shareholders considered derisory; they gathered together and turned the offer down.

**share options:** a financial incentive that offers managers the right to buy shares in the company they work for at a future date, at a price set today. For example, a director might be given an option to buy 250 000 shares at a price of 50p at any time between three and five years hence. If the share price rises to 90p, they can take up the option and sell the shares on the *stock market*. By buying at 50p and selling at 90p, a profit of 40p × 250 000 = £100 000 will have been made. Supporters of this kind of scheme believe that share options will provide key employees with the incentive to perform at their best. Critics suggest that it might lead to *short-termism* (when the options are due), and can lead to excessive financial rewards in the boardroom, when the workforce may deserve just as much credit as the directors.

**share register:** the list of all the shareholders in a company together with the size of their holding. Firms regularly check their share registers to see if a particular person or company is building up a large enough share stake to launch a *take-over bid*.

**shift in demand:** this refers to the demand curve, which shows the relationship between price and quantity demanded. The curve shifts if there is a change in market conditions such as a change in incomes, a change in the price of a substitute product or a change in tastes or fashion. (See also *demand curve*.)

**shift in supply:** this refers to the supply curve, which shows the relationship between price and quantity supplied. The curve shifts if there is a change in costs of production, which might result from a change in technology. There may also be a shift in the supply curve if some other product becomes more profitable, diverting resources towards the most profitable items. (See also *supply curve*.)

**shift work** is regular work that takes place during non-standard working hours. It may be a morning shift (e.g. 2 a.m. – 8 a.m.) or a night shift (8 p.m. – 2 a.m.). Shift work is essential in services such as the fire brigade and is often used in manufacturing, especially if there is an expensive, *flow production* process requiring high *capacity utilisation*. Some organisations recruit workers for a specific shift; others have a rotation of two weeks of days, two of evenings etc. There may be shift payments that offer a higher rate of pay to compensate for the unsociable hours worked.

**shocks** are events which have a major impact on the economy, such that many things change. Examples include the reunification of Germany in 1989, which created a major shock for Germany and a somewhat smaller one for its EU partners and the oil price rises of 1974 and 1979. A change in commodity prices will be a major shock for a country which depends on export revenue from the sale of that commodity.

**shop-floor:** the place where direct labour is carried out, either by shop assistants or by factory workers.

**short run:** a time period in which only some variables may change. For example, the short run may be the time in which inputs only of *variable factors of production* can be altered. The input of fixed factors cannot be changed. So more employees might be put to work with the same stock of equipment. In contrast, in the long run, inputs of all factors of production may be changed. The definition of the short run may change according to the context in which it is being used.

**short-termism** is a phrase describing the state of mind of managers for whom rapid results are the top priority. Examples of short-termism include:

- setting a short *payback period* as an investment criterion
- increasing prices up to their most profitable level (thereby attracting in competition)
- cutting back on spending on research and development or training.

Such an approach can be contrasted with the Japanese pursuit of long-term goals such as total quality and technological superiority. It seems likely that the main causes of British short-termism are:

- the absence of a tradition of loyalty to one company, which may make our executives too keen to make their mark quickly

- the greater number and influence of accountants in British boardrooms (compared with engineers in Germany and Japan)

- the threat of a *take-over* may encourage firms to keep short-term profit high in order to bolster up the share price: British firms are much more likely to have a majority share-holding available on the *stock market*, so this is a more important issue in Britain than in Germany or Japan.

**significance testing:** checking the statistical validity of a sample result, usually in relation to an objective of 95 per cent certainty. An example would be checking whether a 54 per cent preference for product A is statistically significant compared with the 46 per cent choice for product B. If the *sample size* is very small, this difference is of no significance since it can be explained by purely random factors.

**single currency:** the *euro* is the single currency of the 12 EU countries which have joined together in the *Economic and Monetary Union* (EMU). In 2002, national currencies went out of use and the *European Central Bank* issued notes and coins. The costs and risks associated with foreign exchange transactions were eliminated within the member countries. It is possible that euro transactions will increase in the three EU countries which are outside EMU (UK, Sweden and Denmark) even if they do not join soon. At the time of writing the UK government is still undecided about joining. The economy must of course meet the convergence criteria. Also, Chancellor Gordon Brown has outlined his five economic tests:

- will EMU create better conditions for *foreign direct investment* in the UK?

- how will the UK financial services sector be affected?

- are the eurozone and the UK *trade cycles* moving reasonably closely together?

- will EMU be flexible enough to cope with problems as they emerge?

- will joining lead to higher growth, greater stability and low unemployment?

Will these give us the answer?

**single European market:** the agreement between the EU countries that from January 1 1993, the trading differences between member countries would be eliminated so that businesses could treat the whole of the area as their home market. This was intended to be achieved by the abolition of three trading restrictions: *non-tariff barriers*, physical customs controls, and different technical standards and taxation levels. Despite much optimism about its impact, the full effects of the single market are hard to evaluate.

There is a long way to go on both technical standards and tax. In a 1999 European Commission survey, 41 per cent of companies considered different national standards and specifications a continuing barrier to the single market. Nevertheless 50 per cent felt barriers were reducing compared with 5 per cent who thought they were increasing.

**single status** occurs when a firm has eliminated all the physical and contractual barriers between grades of staff. These forms of class discrimination might include: separate

**277**

canteens, different working hours, different pay terms and conditions (management on salaries, workers on *piece-rate*), or *clocking in* for shop-floor workers only. Once a firm has removed such divisive features, it can hope to eliminate the feeling of *'them and us'* that pervades many organisations. Japanese firms go so far as to insist on the same overalls for all managers and workers, or even morning exercises. Both are to establish single status by demonstrating that all employees wear the same work clothes and participate in the same morning activity.

**single union agreement** means the recognition by a firm of just one workforce representative body for *collective bargaining* purposes. This removes the potential disruption caused by *inter-union disputes* and reduces the time spent on *negotiations*. Toshiba's agreement with the electricians' union in 1981 is believed to have been the first of its kind in Britain. Such agreements have often included *pendulum arbitration* clauses, with some adding *no-strike* agreements.

**skewed result:** a *frequency distribution* in which the number of findings is not balanced around the *mean* figure. The findings may be skewed towards values below the mean (a *negative skew*) or above the mean (a *positive skew*).

**skill shortage:** even when there is substantial unemployment, shortages may develop of people available for work and possessing the skills required. This is likely to happen if the economy has been growing and the employment of skilled people has been increasing. Employers may offer higher pay in order to attract the type of people they require. In time this may create an incentive for more people to acquire the necessary skills but this cannot happen immediately.

**skills mismatch:** a situation in which the people available for work have skills which are not required by the employers who are seeking to hire people. This will be associated with occupational immobility. It occurs because people have been made redundant from declining industries. The skills required by growing industries are different. This is a feature of *structural change*.

**skimming the market** means pricing a new product at such a high level that it is only purchased by trend-setters, enthusiasts or people who are well off. The firm may choose to hold this high price in the long term, or cut prices when competition arrives. Skimming the market is a viable option only for an innovative product. (See *market penetration* and diagram overleaf.)

Pros:
- the price tax placed on a product affects consumer perceptions of its quality and desirability; pricing high can be an important element in establishing an up-market image
- skimming can be used as a form of *price discrimination*, ensuring that trend-setters pay the high price they are willing to pay, then lowering the price to attract the mass market later on.

Cons:
- a high price may make it easy for a competitor to launch a successful, lower-priced imitation
- by failing to maximise sales at the start, the firm may not be able to hold on to a viable *market share* when competitors arrive.

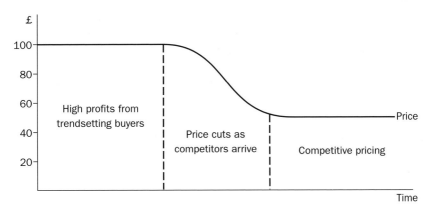

*Skimming the market*

**sleeping partner:** a contributor of finance to a business partnership who takes no active role within the firm, and therefore can arrange to hold *limited liability* status.

**slogan:** a catch-phrase used regularly by an advertiser to communicate a sales message in a highly memorable way.

**slump** is a period of low *demand* and investment, and high unemployment. It is a rather vague term used interchangeably with *depression* to mean a severe *recession* within the *business cycle*. It is often used in the context of 'booms and slumps' to indicate the way the economy tends to fluctuate between these two extremes.

**small claims court:** a local court that will hear cases of dispute concerning sums of up to £5,000. A typical problem might concern a householder claiming against an electrician over a £60 job that proved to be faulty. At the small claims court individuals speak for themselves without the use of expensive legal advice.

**small firm:** a phrase that is taken to mean a firm with limited financial resources which has little or no power over its market-place. The government uses the more precise definition of a firm with fewer than 200 employees. This, however, would allow firms with substantial earnings and high *market shares* to be termed small. As with every type of business, the attempt to define or generalise about them usually falls foul of their wide diversity. It is safer to consider the financial position and market strength of each firm individually than to overgeneralise.

**small-medium sized enterprises** are all businesses with fewer than 250 employees, according to the *European Union*'s definition, which has also been adopted by the British government's Office for National Statistics. Small firms are those with fewer than 50 employees; medium-sized have between 50 and 250. In 1998, SMEs contributed over 50 per cent of all jobs in the private sector. This is shown in the table below:

| Size of business (number of employees) | Total employed (000s) | % of workforce |
|---|---|---|
| Up to 49 | 9 652 | 44.7 |
| 50 - 249 | 2 508 | 11.6 |
| 250+ | 9 434 | 43.7 |
| Total | 21 595 | 100 |

Source: DTI Statistical Bulletin August 1999

**SME:** see *small–medium sized enterprises*

**Smith, Adam** (1723–90) was the eighteenth-century author of much of the classical economic theory which still forms the basis of free market economics. His best known book THE WEALTH OF NATIONS (Penguin, 1982) set out, in 1776, his faith in market mechanisms as a means of promoting efficiency and customer satisfaction. The book's key phrase referred to the *invisible hand* that ensures that customer *demand* can be matched by *supply* without needing a planning authority. The invisible hand is the *price mechanism*, which allocates resources amongst alternative uses. Although in using this reasoning, Smith was assuming that markets will be highly competitive, he was well aware of the tendency among producers to collude in order to secure a higher price. In addition to these ideas, Smith's description of the *division of labour* has become a classic way to introduce that concept.

**social audit:** an independent quantification of the elements of a firm's activities that affect society, such as pollution, waste and workforce health and safety. A social audit can be used internally, by managers wanting to measure their degree of success at environmental improvement; or externally, by pressure groups or shareholders concerned about the firm's long-term health and reputation. The potential value of this technique can be seen in the example opposite. It shows how a social audit of two firms might lead to different conclusions about their real efficiency from those which might emerge from a calculation of financial ratios.

**Worked example: bicycle manufacturing firms**

|  | Firm A | Firm B |
|---|---|---|
| *Financial ratios* |  |  |
| **Trading profit margin** | 6.8% | 8.8% |
| **Return on capital** | 18.5% | 19.8% |
| *Social ratios* |  |  |
| **Average lifetime of bike** | 5.5 yrs | 3.0 yrs |
| **% made from recycled material** | 60% | 20% |
| **Industrial accidents per 100 workers per year** | 1.5 | 8.0 |

**social benefits** are all of the benefits from consumption of a particular item, not just those received by the buyer. They therefore include the external benefits which may be obtained by third parties, i.e. people who neither bought nor sold the item. For example, the social benefits of a pretty front garden include the benefits obtained by the owner of it, together with the benefits of any passers-by who happen to enjoy looking at the garden.

FORMULA:    internal benefits + external benefits = social benefits

**social chapter:** that part of the Maastricht treaty which deals with social issues, including working conditions, employment protection and employee participation. Until 1997, the UK chose to opt out of this part of the treaty, but is now fully committed to the implementation of its provisions.

**social charter:** set up in the late 1980s within the *European Union*, this defined a set of objectives towards which all member countries would work. The idea was to harmonise social legislation as well as the economic framework. It covered twelve areas: freedom of movement, social protection, vocational training, health and safety, elderly people, protection of children, disabled people, sexual equality, living and working conditions, employment and remuneration, collective bargaining, information, consultation and participation. Many of its objectives were embodied later in the *social chapter* of the *Maastricht* treaty.

**social cost** measures the cost to the whole of society of a production process or business decision. This means that no only are the firm's *internal costs* accounted for, but also the costs imposed on society as a consequence of the action (such as pollution or unemployment). These latter costs are external to the company.

FORMULA:    internal costs + external costs = social costs

**social grade** is the occupational category that shows the social class to which each household belongs. Interviewers ask respondents for the occupation of the head of the household and the answer is placed into one of the groupings listed below. This categorisation is used in *market research* as evidence has shown that social class has a large effect on people's lifestyle and purchasing habits. The social grade bands are:

Grade A:    top professional (e.g. lawyers) or directors of large companies

Grade B:    senior managerial

Grade C1:    clerical, e.g. secretary

Grade C2:    skilled working class, e.g. welder

Grade D:     semi- or unskilled working class

Grade E:     state dependent, e.g. long-term unemployed

**socialism** is a social and economic system which involves collective ownership of the means of production and a major role for the state in the provision of services which can improve people's welfare. In its extreme form of communism it dominated the centrally planned economies of Eastern Europe until 1989. China and Cuba are still to a large degree governed in this way. In its social democratic form, socialism has been an important underlying principle for a number of left-of-centre political parties in Western Europe.

**social responsibilities** are the duties towards employees, customers, society and the environment that a firm may accept willingly, or may treat as a nuisance. The historical record of firms' acceptance of their responsibilities is patchy. Some religiously motivated firms such as Cadbury's and Rowntree treated their workforce and customers with respect as far back as the nineteenth century. Yet at the same time, a brand of cigarettes called 'Heartsease' was promoted as an aid to recovery from illness. Such deceptions led to the passing of laws to protect consumers, workers and residents from socially irresponsible companies. Today, many firms believe it is in their best interests to behave correctly, since customer image and workforce contentment are important elements in business success. The key to a firm's attitude to its responsibilities is probably the timespan of its company objectives. A get-rich-quick building firm will have a very different approach to an established family business that thinks in terms of generations rather than months.

**social security** is the system by which governments provide for people in need. Unemployment benefits, pensions, income support, and various other income supplements are payable to people in certain circumstances. Payments may be *means-tested*, as with income support, or handed over as of right, as with pensions. Social security payments have increased enormously in all developed countries in recent years, partly because of ageing populations, and partly because *unemployment* has been higher since 1980 than it was before.

Social security is part of what is called the *welfare state*. Increasing numbers of benefits are now being means-tested because of rising expenditure on *universal benefits*.

**social welfare** concerns the well-being of people and how it may be improved. It involves *normative* aspects of economics which are directed towards deciding the way in which resources should be allocated so as to maximise welfare.

**soft currency:** a currency which is not always completely freely convertible. This means that countries will not want to hold the currency as part of their foreign exchange reserves.

**soft loan:** a loan which is made on concessional terms, so that the interest rate is lower than the market rate, or there is a 'holiday' during which no repayments are necessary. Soft loans are made to developing countries as part of their *aid* packages.

**sole trader:** an individual who may or may not employ other people, but who owns and operates the business. Sole traders generally have little *capital* for expansion, and are heavily reliant on their own personal commitment to make the business a success. Should the business be unsuccessful, there is no cushion from *limited liability* as a sole trader is unincorporated; in other words, the firm's finances are inseparable from the proprietor's.

**solvency** is when a firm or individual's *assets* exceed its external debts. Therefore it has the financial stability that comes from positive asset backing. If external debts are greater than the asset values, a state of *insolvency* exists.

**sources of finance:** businesses which are investing need finance, which may be internal or external. *Internal finance* can come from retained profit, working capital or the sale of assets. *External finance* may come from bank loans or from a new issue of shares.

**span of control** is the number of subordinates answerable directly to a manager. It can be described as 'wide' if the manager has many direct subordinates or 'narrow' if there are few. Within an organisation, the span of control bears an inverse relationship to the number of layers of management hierarchy. In other words, if the span is wide, fewer layers would be needed to manage a given workforce. This is illustrated below, where a span of control of three results in five *layers of hierarchy*, while a span of nine requires only three layers (assuming a shop-floor workforce of 81).

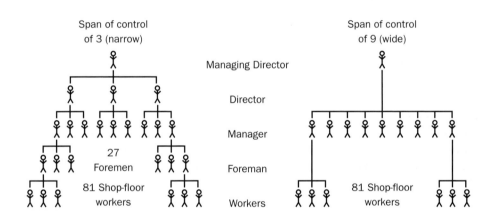

Advantages of a wide span of control include:

- the boss has less time for each subordinate, therefore must delegate effectively
- fewer layers of hierarchy are needed, therefore improving vertical communications (reducing the number of *intermediaries*)
- allows subordinates 'the opportunity to use their ability' which is Professor *Herzberg*'s definition of *job enrichment.*

Advantages of a narrow span of control include:

- tighter management supervision may be necessary in a business where mistakes cannot be allowed (such as the production of components for passenger aircraft)
- less stress involved for each employee, as the scope of each job is limited
- more layers of hierarchy mean more frequent promotion opportunities, i.e. the career ladder has more rungs.

**specialisation:** the division of a work process into separate job functions so that individuals can develop expertise by specialising. This was a vital element in Adam *Smith* and F W *Taylor*'s perception of the benefits of *division of labour*. This has been called into question by the effects of specialisation on *motivation* and the success of the Japanese approach to *multi-skilling*.

**spectrum of competition:** the range of market systems which can be anything between perfect *competition* and *monopoly*. At one extreme there is the situation of many competing producers with easy entry into the market; hairdressing would be one example. At the other extreme there is the single business which dominates the market and cannot be challenged because new entrants to the market have difficulty in getting started. Microsoft is currently the best-known example.

**speculation** involves buying or selling something in the expectation of a price change and so making a profit. Foreign exchange dealers who expect the exchange rate to fall will sell quickly, then when the price has fallen they can buy back the currency at a much lower price than they sold at, so making a profit on the deal.

**sponsorship** is a form of promotion in which funds are provided for a sporting, cultural or social event in return for prominent display of the sponsor's company or brand name.

**spot market:** a term used to describe a commodity or foreign exchange market where the deals are made and completed there and then and delivery is immediate. In contrast, in the *forward market* deals are made in which the price is agreed now, but the delivery of the goods concerned takes place perhaps three months later.

**spreadsheet** is a set of numerical data inputted and displayed on a computer which is connected in such a way, via a number of formulae, that changing one figure will automatically update all the others. In business, spreadsheets are often used to predict events, because it is simple to ask *what if . . . ? questions* and immediately see a result. For instance, if it was suggested that sales might rise by 10 per cent next year, the company could see at a glance what the implications for *sales revenue*, costs and *profits* would be.

**stabilisation policy** aims to keep the economy growing in a sustainable way and prevent a cycle of boom and recession. It uses *fiscal* and *monetary policies* to influence the level of *aggregate demand* and prevent both overheating and rising unemployment. Stabilisation policies are not always successful because the time lags in the economy and weaknesses of some of the data can make it very difficult to predict how much policy change is required. Stabilisation policies can be used for electoral reasons in ways which are ultimately destabilising, but this has been made much less likely since the *Bank of England* became responsible for monetary policy in 1997.

**staff functions** are those of employees who provide advice or assistance to the line managers, who hold responsibility for achieving specific business objectives.

**stagflation** is the economic phenomenon of stagnation and *inflation* happening simultaneously. This had been thought to be impossible, since the effect of stagnation would be to depress wages and hence prices. In practice it was found during the mid-1970s that levels of inflation could rise to the point where people expected it to continue, and acted accordingly. Thus, although unemployment was rising, *trade unions* still negotiated for high pay rises because of the expected levels of prices next year. This led to detailed study of the role of expectations in the determination of inflation, and a fuller appreciation of their impact.

**stagging** is the purchase of shares in a company *flotation* with the sole purpose of selling them quickly on the *Stock Exchange* for a profit. New issues are very often offered at an attractive price in order to ensure that all the shares are sold, thus offering stags a chance to make a quick profit. This was the case with many *privatisation* flotations.

**stagnation:** a situation in which the economy is growing very slowly or not at all.

**stakeholder:** an individual or group with a direct interest in an organisation's performance. The main stakeholders are: employees, shareholders, customers, suppliers, financiers and the local community. Stakeholders may not hold any formal authority over the organisation, but theorists such as Professor Handy believe that a firm's best long-term interests are served by paying close attention to the needs of each of these groups.

**standard cost:** the desired average cost for producing an item. This can be compared with the actual achievement to discover whether the firm is working effectively.

**standard deviation (SD):** a standardised measure of the distribution of data around a *mean* value. Statisticians use the term 'standard deviation' in this precise way, whereas most managers treat it more loosely. In particular, managers often refer to the term standard deviation when the mean the *standard error* from a sample result.

**standard error** estimates the *standard deviation* of sample means around the true population *mean*.

**standardisation** is the production or use of products or components that are identical and thus fully interchangeable. The achievement of standardised parts is a necessary condition for efficient *mass production* to take place. Without it, skilled workers would have to spend time filing down parts to fit them into the right slots. Standardisation is also a key element in *economies of scale*, as modern firms use the same components in different products to enable longer production runs to take place and to save on design costs.

**standard of living** is a rather imprecise term which refers to the ability of people to buy the goods and services they desire. For individuals it can be measured by examining people's real incomes, i.e. wage levels in relation to price levels. For society as a whole, *GNP* or *GDP* may be used as a measure. However money measures of the standard of living cannot take into account non-quantifiable factors such as levels of crime, the time and ease of travelling to work and so on. These are sometimes referred to collectively as the 'quality of life', and some measures of the standard of living include them, for example the *Human Development Index*.

**state-owned enterprises** include all the organisations which sell a good or a service for a price and are in the public sector. This category was large until many such enterprises were privatised from 1981 onwards. The best remaining example is the Post Office.

**statistical process control** is the use of statistical monitoring systems to ensure that production is proceeding efficiently and at high-quality standards. Modern laser scanning-based systems can check production rates and accuracies at various stages in the production process at very low cost. If performance falls outside pre-set standards, an alarm will be sounded or displayed.

**statistical quality control** uses the same approach as above, but focused solely upon product quality.

**statistics:** in a business context, this means the statistical data that firms gather and may try to present in a light that favours themselves. When seeing numerate 'facts' presented, Benjamin Disraeli's famous statement should be borne in mind, that, 'There are lies, damned lies and statistics.'

In an economic context, statistics are the data which record events in the economy and can show trends in a range of important variables. They make it possible to predict likely levels of growth, inflation and unemployment but may be subject to errors and uncertainties, and may only become available with a time lag.

**status:** how highly a person is rated by other members of a group or workforce. This might derive from the individual's own abilities and achievements or from institutional factors such as job title or remuneration. *Maslow* regarded status as an important social need, while *Herzberg* considered it a *hygiene factor*, i.e. a potential source of dissatisfaction.

**statutory requirements** are those that are laid down by law and which every firm has to conform to. Laws are said to be 'in the statutes' or 'on the statute books'.

**sterling** is the name given to the UK's internationally traded currency, the pound sterling, to distinguish it from other countries which also use the word 'pound' for their currencies.

**sterling exchange rate index:** a measure of change in the foreign exchange rate which takes a weighted average of a basket of currencies. These are weighted according to their importance in the pattern of trade.

**stick to the knitting** is a curious phrase that urges firms to concentrate on what they know best, rather than take the risks involved in diversifying into numerous other sectors.

**stock:** materials and goods required in order to produce for, and supply to, the customer. There are three main categories of stock: *raw materials* or components, *work in progress* and finished goods. When aggregated for the whole economy, the level of stocks is important because it may reflect changes in the level of aggregate demand relative to output. Also, changes in stocks may impact upon the level of output. If demand has been falling stocks will rise and de-stocking may become necessary. This means that the level of output will for a while fall below the level of demand, and this may reduce the demand for labour, leading to rising unemployment.

**stock appreciation:** an increase in the value of a company's stocks, generally due to *inflation*. As company *profits* are boosted by increases in stock values, stock appreciation gives a rather artificial boost to profits (causing higher tax and perhaps *dividend* payments).

**stockbroker:** a person who trades in, and can give advice on the buying and selling of, shares.

**stock control** covers the procedures needed to ensure that stock is ordered, delivered and handled with efficiency, so that customer *demand* can be met cost effectively. This may involve a stock reordering system based upon predetermined minimum and maximum stock levels. (see *reorder level*.)

**Stock Exchange** is a market for securities (the collective name for stocks and shares). In the UK, apart from the London Stock Exchange, there are a number of regional ones including Glasgow, Birmingham and Liverpool. The London Stock Exchange is one of the biggest in the world after Tokyo and New York, with an annual *turnover* of over one thousand billion pounds. Its main function is to provide a market in second-hand shares and government stocks.

Stock exchanges create a reliable source of investment funds for businesses. By offering a second-hand market in shares, they encourage people to channel their savings into investment in real resources, and while some contributions may be small, taken together they represent large amounts. The Stock Exchange insists on stringent rules for admittance of firms, and these, along with other legal requirements, offer a degree of protection to buyers of shares. However, recent scandals have suggested that the degree of investor protection is limited, and have called into question the ability of the exchange to regulate itself. Governments as well as business use the Stock Exchange as means of selling large quantities of bonds (*gilt-edged securities*) when there is a need to finance deficit spending.

For firms, there can be disadvantages to being quoted on the Stock Exchange. The share price does not necessarily reflect the true value of a company. It may be the result of rumours, or the overall state of the market. Also being quoted on the Exchange removes some control from the management which may hamper long-term decision-making, as the share price and *dividends* become paramount. The possibility of being taken over can increase, especially if the overall share price falls and a company is known to have attractive *assets*. Predatory companies may then move in and acquire it, only to sell off the valuable assets, in a move known as *asset stripping*.

**stockholding costs** are the *overheads* resulting from the stock levels held by a firm. These include:

- warehouse rental and insurance costs
- energy costs (refrigeration, for example)
- manpower costs, including security guards
- interest charges on the money tied up in the stock.

By moving to a *just in time* system of minimal stock levels, all these costs could be cut dramatically.

**stock market:** see *Stock Exchange*

**stock options:** see *share options*

**stockpiling:** building up stock levels, perhaps in preparation for a seasonal sales peak or before the *advertising* launch of a new product.

**stocks and shares** is a general term for investments that are traded on the *stock market*. In this case, stocks means fixed interest securities such as *debentures* (*loan capital*), while shares give a part-ownership of a company (*equity capital*).

**stocktaking:** a periodical physical count of the items held in stock, usually carried out on the *balance sheet* date at the end of the financial year. This is to ensure accurate stock records and thereby determine the levels of *wastage* and pilfering that are occurring.

**stop–go** was a term used to describe policy measures taken by governments in the 1960s and 1970s. When unemployment became unacceptably high in political terms the government stimulated *demand* through lower taxes (*fiscal policy*) and interest rates (*monetary policy*). This created the 'go' phase of the cycle. Unfortunately, the stimulus eventually resulted in skill shortages and rapid increases in imports and caused *balance of payments* crises. These in turn required the government to bring in the 'stop' phase through higher taxes and interest rates.

**strategic alliance:** see *joint venture*

**strategic decision:** a decision that will have considerable long-term effects on the organisation and therefore requires discussion and approval at a senior managerial level. An example might be whether to sell off a poorly performing division, or to invest sufficient extra *capital* to restore its competitiveness.

**strategic objectives** are wide-ranging, long term goals of significance to the operations of a whole organisation. For example, a firm that has 70 per cent of its sales in Britain might set itself the strategic objective to reduce its dependence upon the home market to below 40 per cent within 5 years.

This might force a rethink about the location of its factories, the type of products it sells, the background or nationality of the staff it employs and so on. Among the most common strategic objectives are:

- to diversify
- to focus (un-diversify or *stick to the knitting*)
- to achieve a dominant market position
- to develop a technological advantage over rivals.

**strategy:** a medium- to long-term plan for how to achieve an *objective*. The plan itself would include not only what is to be done, but also the financial, production and personnel resources required.

**stratified sample:** a research sampling method that draws respondents from a specified subgroup of the population. An example would be a lager producer deciding to research solely among 18–30-year-old men, since they represent the heart of that market-place. Within the chosen group, individuals might be chosen on a random basis, hence the term 'stratified random sample'. (See also *random* and *quota samples*.)

**stress** is often assumed to be a symptom of an over-pressurised working life. Research evidence shows that managers are rather less prone to stress than shop-floor workers with repetitive jobs. This suggests that stress is mainly a function of feeling out of control of one's life. Stress can lead to migraines, high blood pressure and excessive drinking.

**strike:** a situation in which workers stop work in order to exert some power in an industrial dispute. Most often this will be over pay, but it can be about redundancies or unfair dismissal. Strikes may be official, i.e. sanctioned by the trade union, or unofficial. They are much more likely to occur in larger businesses than in smaller ones. In recent years strikes have been fewer in number, partly because of the fear of unemployment and partly because the law now requires a secret ballot of union members as to whether they want to strike.

**strike pay** is a payment by a *trade union* to members who are on an official strike. This is usually of a sum that is far below the striker's regular wage.

**structural adjustment:** a set of policies which has become associated with the International Bank for Reconstruction and Development (the World Bank). The package of policies will depend upon the circumstances of the country concerned, but is likely to include devaluation of the currency, cuts in government expenditure, reduced trade restrictions and the encouragement of market forces in a variety of ways. Often the World Bank is in a position to dictate the policy prescription because of the country's need for development finance.

**structural change** is the process by which resources are reallocated away from the production of items for which demand is falling and towards items for which it is rising. This reallocation of resources leads to changes in the composition of output. It also entails major changes in employment patterns. Where a localised industry declines, it can cause whole communities to be affected by increased unemployment, often for many years. Coal and shipbuilding both provide examples of serious structural problems.

**structure of industry:** the composition of output.

**structural unemployment** occurs when there is a change in *demand* or technology which causes long-term unemployment. Very often this occurs in particular regions which have been heavily dependent on certain industries, such as coal in Wales, and shipbuilding in the North East. The problem is exacerbated by occupational immobilities and by geographical immobilities, which make it difficult for people to find alternative jobs. *Supply side measures* such as training and retraining are needed to deal with these. Regional policy and regeneration measures can be helpful too. There has been a long-term and substantial increase in structural unemployment in many developed countries which governments have had little success in reducing. Unskilled people are particularly vulnerable and the problem remains very grave in many parts of the EU.

**sub-assembly** means putting together a component that will later be part of the final assembly of the finished product. Therefore, on a car *production line*, the assembly of a gearbox would be termed a sub-assembly.

**subcontracting:** finding a supplier to manufacture part or all of your product. The main circumstances in which subcontracting is used are:

- when a firm is already operating at maximum capacity and therefore cannot meet further *demand* in any other way
- when there are elements of a product that you are ill-equipped to manufacture efficiently
- to cope with seasonal peaks in demand.

**subjective decision:** a decision that has been made either without, or in spite of, the evidence of researched data. Such decisions might be made by a lazy or prejudiced manager, or might be the result of an inspired *hunch*. A good example of the latter was the Sony Chairman's support for the 'Walkman', despite research evidence that consumers saw no need for it.

**subjective factors** are those for which personal judgement is necessary since they cannot be quantified effectively. They may be very important in business decisions such as capital investment, though there is a tendency to treat figures as facts and therefore downgrade non-quantifiable issues. Subjective factors include: effect upon morale, expectations of competitors' actions, and the effect on, and importance of, the *corporate image*.

**subsidiarity** is the idea that decisions should be made at the lowest appropriate level. The word has been much used within the context of the *European Union*. UK governments have used it as an argument to prevent what they see as the over-centralisation of power in the hands of the *European Commission*. Local authorities in England and Wales, on the other hand, have used it as an argument against the same UK government whom they see as usurping their traditional role within local communities of looking after such things as education.

**subsidiary:** a business that is owned by another business (the *holding company*). The subsidiary is likely to be trading under its own name, but as the holding company owns more than 51 per cent of its shares, it is the latter that will have effective control. The subsidiary's financial figures will form part of the parent company's *consolidated accounts*.

**subsidy:** a sum of money paid by governments to the producer, so that the price to the customer will be lower than it otherwise would have been. This may be done either for social reasons (e.g. to a railway as a provider of an essential service), or to raise incomes (e.g. hill sheep farmers), or to keep down prices of essential goods.

**subsistence level:** an amount of real income which provides only just enough to keep the person alive in the long run.

**substitutes:** goods and services which are possible alternatives for the consumer, so that a change in the price of one will have some impact on demand for the other.

**suggestion schemes** are formal procedures for collecting ideas from the shop-floor. The suggestions might relate to new products, improved working or cost-cutting measures. Often, such schemes offer financial or promotional bonuses to suggestions that are adopted by the company. Many firms have suggestion boxes for workers to place their ideas, but not many are successful. They lack the personal involvement and group spirit of *quality circles* or *kaizen* (improvement) groups.

**summary dismissal** is the on-the-spot sacking of an individual due to behaviour believed to make his or her *employment contract* invalid. Examples include theft, violence or being offensive to customers. In such circumstances, instant dismissal is not wrongful or *unfair*.

**sunk costs** are costs which have already been paid for and which no longer figure in the decision-taking process. For example, once the product is brought to the market, research and development costs are sunk costs.

**sunrise industry:** one positioned in a rapidly growing market, usually based on new technology and innovation.

**sunset industry:** one believed to be in terminal decline, with obsolete technology and an obsolete product.

**supernormal profit:** profit which is in excess of the amount needed to keep the resources in the industry. When demand is rising, it will often be possible for the firm to make supernormal profit because it can raise the price and still sell the goods. This situation will continue until more firms have moved into the industry, thus competing and driving prices back down to the level where *normal profit* only is made. If there are *barriers to entry*, then the firm may make supernormal profit in the long as well as the short run, because the level of competition is reduced. In fact any kind of market power will allow supernormal profits to be made; for example brand names, such as Levi's create loyalty which reduces the power of competition to force down profits.

**supplier relationships:** businesses which depend on supplies of inputs from other businesses may take their relationships with those businesses very seriously. The quality of the product may depend on being able to negotiate changes in the way the supplier produces. *Just in time* stockholding may require close collaboration to work effectively. The prospect of some security in relation to future orders may encourage suppliers to work in a close partnership with the customer business.

**supply** is a term used in economics to denote a firm's willingness to produce and deliver goods or services demanded by customers. Supply is a key part of the *market mechanism* by which supply and *demand* are kept in balance through the price level. In other words if supply is short (e.g. few tomatoes due to bad weather), the price will rise in order to reduce the quantity demanded to match the available supply. Supply is affected by input costs in general, and by technological change and government policies which affect taxes and subsidies. (See also *supply curve*.)

**supply chain:** the sequence of processes by which a final product is created. For many products, the supply chain takes in many different suppliers, often located in different countries. Many sophisticated manufactured products are built up in developed countries using intermediate products assembled in *developing countries* where wages are lower.

**supply curve:** the curve showing the quantities producers wish to supply at a range of different prices. It is normally shown sloping upwards to the right. This is because a higher price gives a business more of an incentive to produce and indicates possible higher profits (as at $p_2$ and $q_2$ on the diagram).

The supply curve will shift if there is a change in costs, and it may then change its shape as well. For example new technologies will tend to make the supply curve shift down and to the right, reflecting the fact that costs have fallen and possibly also economies of scale have been reaped. Then it may be possible to produce the larger quantity ($q_3$ in the diagram) at the original price.

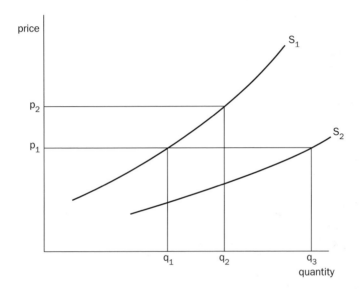

**supply elasticity:** the responsiveness of quantity supplied to a change in price. The formula is:

> FORMULA:  elasticity of supply $= \dfrac{\text{percentage change in quantity supplied}}{\text{percentage change in price}}$

Inelastic supply will be less than one, while elastic supply will be greater than one. Supply may be perfectly inelastic (i.e. equal to 0) in the *market period* simply because there has not been time to mobilise the resources needed to increase supply, or to disband them if the price is falling. In the *short run*, supply can be increased by the addition of *variable factors of production* to the production process. In the *long run*, *fixed factors of production* can also be increased. So supply becomes more and more elastic, the longer the time period. Housing is usually in inelastic supply: it takes time to build more; equally, if demand is falling the existing stock of housing will continue to stand for some time. This means that changes in demand may produce sharp fluctuations in price. Another example of inelastic supply occurs when scarce skills are in demand; it will take time to train more people and in the meantime the supply of the skills will be very inelastic.

If very scarce resources are needed to produce the item, then costs may rise as output increases, thus making supply rather inelastic. As depletable resources of mineral products are exploited, the price will rise and this means that supply is inelastic. In contrast, the supply of most manufactured products in the long run is highly elastic.

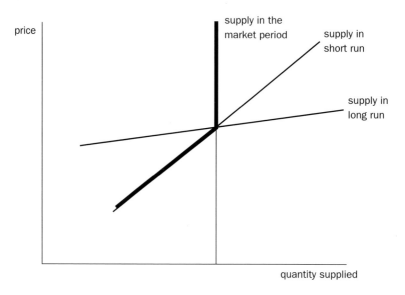

**supply schedule:** the set of prices and quantities which show how much producers are prepared to supply to the market at different prices.

**supply side measures** are those designed to encourage the free working of markets, including that for labour (by restricting *trade union* activities and reducing unemployment benefit, in order to increase the incentive to work), *capital* (by ending *monopoly* controls and *restrictive practices*) and land (by dismantling such things as rent control). The notion of supply side economics was derived from *monetarism*, which argues that government's only two legitimate functions are to ensure that markets are free to operate efficiently and to control the amount of money or *credit* in circulation. Any other government activity, particularly that concerned with manipulating *aggregate demand* (see *Keynesian*), is a waste of time since any increase in demand only bids up prices (see *demand inflation*), and therefore is soon cancelled out.

Many supply side measures have in fact secured widespread support from all political parties, and support is not confined to the original Conservative monetarist enthusiasts. Measures such as improving training and retraining, helping people to find jobs and spending money on research and development can all help to increase productivity and employment, as well as fostering growth.

**surplus:** any excess of revenue over costs earned by *non-profit-making organisations*.

**survey:** another term for *quantitative* market research; in other words, research among a large enough sample of consumers to provide valid data.

**sustainable growth:** growth which can be kept up at a steady rate over the long term. In contrast, unsustainable growth requires resources which will become increasingly scarce as growth proceeds. In particular shortages of scarce skills will develop and when they do, wage rates will be bid up, costs will rise, and inflation will accelerate. This will lead the government to damp down the growth process and the result may be a swing into recession which will last until such time as people's inflationary expectations have adjusted under the impact of the threat of unemployment. (This sequence of events was experienced in the UK between 1987 and 1992). So sustainable growth must be at a rate such that the resources available at the time can meet the aggregate demand without input prices (including wages) being bid up through increasing scarcity.

In the context of the environment, sustainable growth means growth which does not rely on exploiting resources which cannot be replaced. For example, the use of depletable resources such as oil can probably not be sustained indefinitely unless the rate of use can be slowed dramatically. The exploitation of hardwood forests cannot be sustained indefinitely unless the rate of use slows and more attention is given to replanting.

**sweat shop:** a workplace where exploitation is common, with low wages in return for high effort levels. Such a situation is most likely to occur if local unemployment is high and unionisation is low. It can probably be found more often in *developing countries* but there are still instances of such situations in some developed countries.

**sweating your assets** is a commonly used phrase indicating the importance of achieving a high *asset turnover*, in other words, generating a high sales level from the firm's asset base. The higher the asset turnover, the harder the assets are working, therefore the more they are 'sweating'.

**SWOT analysis** is the assessment of a product, division or organisation in terms of its strengths, weaknesses, opportunities and threats.

| Strengths | Weaknesses |
|---|---|
| • expertise at financial services | • short-termist approach partly due to take-over threat |
| • low-cost production due to deregulated labour markets | • poor education and training within workforce |
| • influence of Japanese firms on British management | • capacity cutbacks during the 1980 and 1990 recessions |
| **Opportunities** | **Threats** |
| • to gain market share or develop new markets within Continental Europe | • that foreign firms may prove more competitive, thereby taking a rising share of UK markets |
| • to build Europe-wide brands (such as Kit Kat) thereby enjoying large economies of scale | • that future European laws may restrict business decisions by British firms |

*SWOT analysis of British firms in the single European market*

Its simple, four-box format makes it easy to use as a visual aid in a management meeting or conference. The strengths and weaknesses are the actual position of the product or company, while opportunities and threats represent future potential.

**synergy** occurs when the whole is greater than the sum of the parts, i.e. when $2 + 2 = 5$. This is often anticipated in *take-over bids*, when directors assert that the purchase of a rival will provide such *economies of scale* as to make the combined firm a world-beater. Research evidence suggest that synergy is achieved far less often than it is forecast.

**systems analysis** is the detailed examination of how procedures such as stock control actually work, in order to identify the features required of computer software in order for efficiency to be maximised.

**Do you know we also have A–Zs for:**

- **Accounting**
- **English Literature**
- **Mathematics**
- **Psychology?**

Ask for them in your local bookshop or see the inside back cover for ordering details.

**tacit agreement** between firms meaning *collusion*, perhaps over-pricing or market sharing, but without any kind of personal contact or formal agreement. It is characteristic of oligopolies. The sellers will simply not take action in any way which might increase the level of competition between them. Because there is no actual agreement, this is hard to prevent, even though it may have considerable impact on the buyer. It is possible for a long period of tacit agreement to follow a price war which the participants have found very damaging. They may just set their prices at similar levels and avoid further price competition.

**tactical decisions** are those based on short-term considerations such as meeting this year's budgets or plans. For instance if a product's sales are 4 per cent below the annual forecast with one month until the year end, the sales manager might decide to run a *sales promotion* or cut the price. Usually, tactical decisions are made by middle management, though a decision to start the winter sale before Christmas would be a senior managerial decision for a clothes or jewellery retail chain.

**tactics** are the measures adopted to deal with a short-term opportunity or threat. Although managers would want to adopt tactics that fit in with the long-term strategy, there may be occasions when this is not possible.

**take-over:** obtaining full management control of another firm as a result of purchasing over 50 per cent of its *share capital*. This process is also known as acquisition. Usually, the bidder (*predator*) is sufficiently bigger than the target company to make the acquisition relatively easy to finance. However it is possible for a small firm to raise the finance to buy a larger firm; this is known as a *reverse take-over*.

**take-over bid:** the attempt by a *predator* company to buy a controlling interest in another firm. This is done by offering the target firm's shareholders a significantly higher price for their shares than the prevailing market price. The offer can be made in any of the following ways:

- a cash bid, e.g. 150p per share
- a paper bid or share swap, e.g. three Firm A shares for every two of Firm B's
- a combination of cash and paper, e.g. 50p cash plus two Firm A shares for every two of Firm B's.

**tall hierarchy:** an organisation with many *layers of hierarchy* and a narrow *span of control* (see diagram on the next page).

**tangibles** is a term used to distinguish physical *fixed assets* such as land and machinery from *intangible assets* such as patents and *goodwill*.

**target market:** the precise profile of the customers a firm wishes to sell to. For a new cider, the target market may be working women aged 18–30; for an iced lolly it might be children aged 8–12. A firm will decide on its target market after conducting extensive *market research* including, perhaps, a *market segmentation* analysis. The choice of the target market will then affect every section of the *marketing mix*, including:

- distribution outlets: supermarkets or sweetshops?
- pricing
- style of *advertising* and choice of advertising media
- product characteristics such as sweetness or colour.

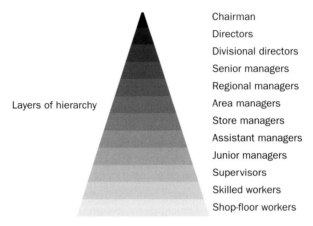

Chairman
Directors
Divisional directors
Senior managers
Regional managers
Layers of hierarchy — Area managers
Store managers
Assistant managers
Junior managers
Supervisors
Skilled workers
Shop-floor workers

*Tall hierarchy*

**target setting:** the process by which an employee agrees performance targets with his or her boss. This gives the individual a clear idea of what to aim for during the year and can form part of an annual *appraisal* interview.

**tariff:** a tax imposed on an imported good. This is likely to reduce demand, and makes the products of domestic competitors more attractive to consumers. The importer may seek to redress the imbalance by cutting *profit margins*, or by becoming more efficient, or in extreme cases by setting up a production plant inside the country itself. Import tariffs are discouraged, and some are banned, under *WTO* agreements.

Tariffs can be levied in one of two ways:

- an 'ad valorem' tax, i.e. a percentage added to the price of the imported good
- a 'specific duty', such as £1 per item, regardless of whether the good is valued at £10 or £100.

The impact of tariffs depends on the *elasticity of demand* for the product. If demand is elastic, this implies that there are competing substitutes available from domestic producers, and the tariff will cut imports considerably, as in diagram (a) overleaf. It may be impossible for the importer even to pass on the full amount of the tariff to the consumer. An example of this might be a tariff on steel products. If, on the other hand, demand is inelastic, as in diagram (b) overleaf, the price increase brought about by the tariff will be quite high but the fall in quantity demanded will be less than proportional because people carry on buying the import as they see few or no satisfactory substitutes. This might happen with a tariff on hi-fi equipment.

The general principle on which tariffs work is the same as that of *tax incidence*.

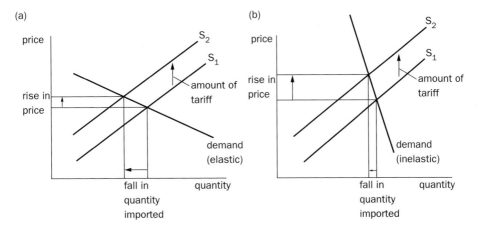

(a) ... (b)

**tax allowance:** a specific amount which may be deducted from income before tax is calculated.

**tax avoidance** is the use of legal measures to minimise personal or corporate tax bills. Typical business examples include the use of *tax havens* and of *transfer pricing*.

**tax base** includes all the sources of tax revenue. For example profits are taxed to provide corporation tax, individuals are taxed to provide income tax and products are taxed to provide VAT revenues. Widening the tax base means devising ways of raising revenue which rely on different sources.

**tax burden** refers to the total amount of tax. When taken as a proportion of GDP it is possible to compare the tax burden in different countries.

**tax evasion** means paying less tax than is legally due. For example a person might not declare all of their income and thus pay less income tax than they should. Or they may claim allowances to which they are not legally entitled.

**tax expenditures** occur when people are allowed to offset some of their income against *tax allowances*, which means that they pay less tax than they otherwise would. This reduces their tax liability and gives them more spending power.

**tax haven:** a country that levies low or no direct taxation, such as the Cayman Islands. British firms may set up *holding companies* based in the tax haven, enabling company profits to attract much lower tax levels.

**tax incidence:** see *incidence of taxation*

**tax relief** is a means by which the government encourages individuals or firms to act in ways thought to be beneficial to the economy. It works by enabling taxpayers to set certain types of expenditure against tax, thereby providing an effective subsidy. For instance, firms may be able to claim tax relief for *capital expenditure* on high technology machinery.

**tax revenue** is the money which is paid to the government in tax. The total is important because it influences both the amount which the government may spend and the amount which has to be borrowed.

The expected revenue from taxation is determined by the policies laid out in the *Budget* each March.

**tax thresholds** are determined by the size of the personal tax allowance, which is the amount of income people are allowed to earn before tax becomes payable. An increase in the personal allowance means that the tax threshold rises. There is another threshold at the point at which the person becomes liable for tax at the 40 per cent rate.

**tax yield:** the revenue raised by a tax, less the cost of collecting it.

**Taylor F W** (1856–1915): an American engineer who invented *work study* and founded the scientific approach to management. He emphasised the duty of management to organise the working methods of shop-floor labour, so as to maximise efficiency. Then, by setting financial incentives that would provide high rewards for hard work, both the worker and the business should benefit. Taylor used work study and *cost accounting* to analyse business efficiency, and advocated high *division of labour*, specialised tools, piece-rate payments and tighter management control as the main methods for productivity improvement. Taylor's most important work with companies was between 1895 and 1905, though his widest contribution to management was through his 1911 book PRINCIPLES OF SCIENTIFIC MANAGE-MENT (W  W NORTON, 1980).

His methods had considerable impact in America and then in Britain, notably through *mass production* at the Ford Motor Company. Taylor's impact on shop-floor labour was equally substantial but far less happy. The alienation caused by *deskilling* and loss of power led to the drive for unionisation that characterised the industrial scene between 1925 and 1975.

A 1977 biography of Taylor captured the essence of the man in its title, THE ONE BEST WAY (Robert Kanigel, Little, Brown & Co, 1997).

**team briefings:** a form of *oral communication* in which supervisors inform the members of their team about production requirements, quality problems or company successes. Such sessions are often held at the start of a working day or week.

**teamwork:** the system by which production is carried out by teams of people who co-operate in order to achieve efficient ways of working. It may be associated with *decentralisation* of decision-taking and multi-skilling, whereby some members of the team can carry out a number of different tasks. (See also *autonomous group working*.)

**teamworking** occurs when production is organised into large units of work, instead of by a high division of labour. The team of people working on the large task (such as making complete shoes, instead of just making the soles) will need to be:

• multi-skilled and therefore well-trained

• motivated by something more than the piece-rate rewards they received while working on the single, repetitive task.

**technical or technological change** refers to the process by which both products and the processes of production are developed and improved, as a result of increased scientific knowledge and the application of that knowledge to production. A technical breakthrough may make a *new product development* possible. Fax machines are a relatively recent new product. Equally, technical change leads to new and cheaper methods of producing, and this leads to costs falling and sometimes also falls in relative prices. Telephone calls have recently become cheaper because of improved equipment. The process of implementing technical change is known as *innovation*. Technical change provides a substantial impetus to the process of *economic growth* because it makes it possible to increase productivity, i.e. to reduce the quantity of real resources needed to produce a particular item. The gains from technical change are most obvious in manufacturing, but there have also been major increases in productivity in the *primary sector* and in the *service sector*, for example as a result of using computer systems.

**technical economies:** see *economies of scale*

**technical efficiency:** a production process is said to be technically efficient if the costs of production have been minimised by economising in the use of real resources. It is one element in *economic efficiency*, and is achieved when average total cost is at its minimum point. *Economies of scale* are often important in achieving technical efficiency. To achieve it, factors of production must be combined in the most effective way.

**technical unemployment** occurs where people have been made redundant as the business invested in labour saving capital equipment. However they will only remain unemployed if they are also affected by *occupational* or *geographical immobility*.

**teleworking** means working at home, though linked to the office by instant communications such as telephone, *fax* and computer *modem*. This can benefit the employer by reducing the *overhead* costs per worker, and provides a route back into work for employees who have been looking after dependent relatives.

**tender:** the closed bid for a contract such as the construction of a building, where firms are asked to submit their price for a job and the lowest is accepted.

**terms of trade:** the price of exports relative to the price of imports. It is measured by the terms of trade index. The formula is:

$$\text{FORMULA:} \quad \text{terms of trade index} = \frac{\text{the index of export prices}}{\text{the index of import prices}} \times 100$$

The terms of trade improve if it becomes possible to buy more imports with the proceeds of a given quantity of exports, i.e. if import prices fall or if export prices rise. For example, if the price of copper rises, Zambian copper producers will receive a higher price for their exports and will be able to buy more imports. Similarly, if the price of copper stays the same but the price of imports rises, Zambia's terms of trade deteriorate.

There will be a change in the terms of trade if there is a change in the exchange rate. A *depreciation* leads to lower export prices and higher import prices. This implies a deterioration in the terms of trade. This leads to confusion. because the terminology suggests that deteriorating terms of trade are a bad thing. In fact a depreciation may have the beneficial effect of making producers more competitive, and lead in time to an improved *balance of trade*.

**tertiary sector** is that part of the economy concerned with *service sector* businesses. It is the largest sector in terms of employment in the UK, accounting for nearly three-quarters of the workforce.

**test market:** the launch of a new or improved product within a tightly defined area, in order to measure actual sales potential. Launching a product nationally is so expensive in production costs, advertising expenditure and *opportunity cost* that many firms will not take the risk of assuming that successful *market research* findings will mean successful sales. They first want to test a promising idea out in an area that may be as small as a town, or as large as the Midlands.

Pros:  • provides more accurate sales forecasts, therefore the right-sized factory can be set up

   • enables lessons to be learnt before the national launch.

Cons:  • gives competitors a chance to evaluate your product and decide how to respond

   • management and *salesforce* focus on a small area, which may cause higher sales than are realistic nationally.

**Thatcherism:** the term given to the range of policies and attitudes developed during Mrs Thatcher's period as Prime Minister (1979–90). The underlying attitudes were based upon her dislike of *public-sector* activities, extreme faith in the effectiveness of the free market and an *authoritarian* approach to leadership in general and unionised labour in particular. The main policies implied by the term Thatcherism include:

• *deregulation* of *private-sector* businesses

• *privatisation* of state- and local-authority-controlled trading organisations

• *centralisation* of control of the remaining *public-sector* activities

• *monetarism*

• switching from *direct* to *indirect taxation*, due to concerns about the effect of direct taxes on work incentives

• income redistribution towards the 'wealth creators' (the better off) as part of her desire to promote an enterprise culture.

**them and us** is a traditional statement of the divide between managers and workers. Managers see the workers as 'them'; workers see the managers as 'them'. This situation is fostered by *separate status*, by the recruitment of graduate trainees who do not start at the factory floor, and perhaps by the very existence of *trade unions*. Many feel it originates in a class-obsessed society or in the school divide between grammar and comprehensive and state versus private education. Whatever its origins, most commentators would agree that its elimination is an important management task.

**theory of the firm:** a branch of economics which seeks to explain price and output decisions. It uses *marginal analysis* to explain the profit maximising output of the firm. It examines the nature of the various market forms, covering *perfect competition*, *monopolisitic competition*, *oligopoly* and *monopoly*. In recent years it has been extended to analyses of relationships between firms through game theory.

**Theory X** is *McGregor's* term for the common management attitude that most workers have an inherent tendency to dislike work. In his own words:

Behind every managerial decision or action are assumptions about human nature and human behaviour. A few of these are remarkably pervasive:

**1** The average human being has an inherent dislike of work and will avoid it if he can.

**2** Because of this human characteristic, most people must be coerced to get them to put forth adequate effort toward the achievement of organisational objectives.

**3** The average human being prefers to be directed, wishes to avoid responsibility, has relatively little ambition, wants security above all. (D McGregor THE HUMAN SIDE OF ENTERPRISE Penguin, 1987; first published 1960)

(See also *Theory Y*.)

**Theory Y** is a managerial approach based on the belief that human beings can be stimulated by and energetic towards work, providing it has the potential to engage their interest. A common mistake is to believe that *McGregor's* theory is about different worker types. It is not. His concern was to examine managerial attitudes and their effects. The main assumptions identified by McGregor as Theory Y were:

The expenditure of physical and mental effort in work is as natural as play or rest . . .

The average human being learns, under proper conditions, not only to accept but to seek responsibility . . .

The capacity to exercise a relatively high degree of imagination, ingenuity, and creativity in the solution of organisational problems is widely, not narrowly, distributed in the population. (D McGregor THE HUMAN SIDE OF ENTERPRISE Penguin, 1987; first published 1960)

It has often been remarked that McGregor's Theory Y anticipated by more than 10 years almost all the management approach known as the *Japanese way.* (See also *Theory X* and *Theory Z.*)

**Theory Z:** the writer Ouchi's term for the Japanese approach to management, which he distinguished from McGregor's *Theory Y* in the following ways:

● the Japanese focus on lifetime employment

● the intense attempt to make the employee conform to company practices and attitudes

● a strong emphasis on *human relations.*

**third parties:** individuals or groups which are not the main parties in a transaction, but are affected by it. For example, if a paint factory is polluting the atmosphere, and people living nearby are affected by the pollution, those people are third parties in the transaction which takes place between the producer and the consumer of the paint.

**third world countries:** another term for *developing countries.*

**tight (fiscal) policy** is a government economic strategy which raises taxes and/or reduces public expenditure. Its purpose is to restrict *aggregate demand*, usually to keep *inflation* in check. It might be combined with a tight *monetary policy.*

**tight monetary policy** involves high interest rates, so that borrowers are trying to keep their loans to a minimum. This is usually associated with *counter-inflation policy.*

**time-and-motion study** is the investigation of the efficiency with which a task is carried out. It is a popular term for *method study.*

**time-based management:** focusing on time as a key business resource. In the 1970s price was the key competitive tool. In the 1980s it was quality. Now, speed of delivery, speed of response and speed of development are all-important. Speed adds value, as you can see in the price list of every photo-processing outlet.

**time lag:** a delay in the reaction of one *variable* to a change in another variable. For example, during the *business cycle*, *unemployment* may start to fall only 12–18 months after output starts to rise at the end of a recession. An increase in *interest rates* will also have a delayed effect, spread over a period of perhaps a year, during which borrowers adjust their plans in response to the change.

**time rate** is payment for the length of time spent working, rather than the quantity of *output* achieved.

**time-series analysis** is the processing of data into sequences of figures over time. Such data can consist of four main elements:

1 the longer-term trend, perhaps growth or decline

2 seasonal or cyclical factors, i.e. ups and downs that occur in a regular pattern

3 erratics: unpredictable fluctuations in the figures, caused by known elements (such as the weather) or by unknown ones (e.g. variations in the trendiness of a particular product)

4 responses: results of specific measures you have taken to affect the series (e.g. advertising spending causing a temporary sales increase).

To analyse this data effectively it is necessary to process it by:

● smoothing out the erratics (by the use of *moving averages*)

● smoothing out the seasonal variations (by *seasonal adjustment*)

● identifying and measuring the responses.

This would make it possible to identify the underlying trend and then extrapolate it forwards in order to forecast the future position.

**top-down management** is a leadership style based on decisions and orders being issued from the top, without *consultation* or *delegation*, i.e. it is autocratic.

**total quality management (TQM):** the attempt to establish a culture of quality affecting the attitudes and actions of every employee. This is usually attempted by trying to get every workgroup (or department) to think of those they work for as customers, even if they are fellow employees. An example would be for the maintenance engineer to treat a shop-floor worker with a defective machine as a valued customer, rather than as a nuisance. Other main features of TQM include:

● the use of *quality circles*

● emphasis upon service and *after-sales service* quality as well as quality manufacture

● the idea that high quality (and low cost) stem from getting things right first time.

American firms with a long experience of TQM have reported that change occurs far more slowly than managers expect, leading to a phase of disenchantment with the whole process. This should not be a surprise because TQM relies on a workforce that wants to improve quality and has the power to achieve it. Giving the workforce that *motivation* is no easy task, especially if the managers' views are rooted in those of F W *Taylor*.

**TQM:** see *total quality management*

**tradeable permits:** these allow certain businesses the right to pollute the atmosphere or water up to a certain point, but no more. If they are able to reduce their polluting activities below that level, they may be able to sell the permit to another business, enabling it to carry on with its polluting activities. Tradeable permits are used to gradually reduce the overall level of pollution by granting fewer each year.

**trade advertising:** messages to retail, wholesale or industrial customers that are placed in trade media such as THE GROCER magazine. Usually, consumer firms place advertisements in trade media in the week or two prior to the start of consumer advertising. This is to achieve retail distribution before consumers come in to search for the product.

**trade association:** an organisation set up to represent the interests of all the firms within an industry, notably for *lobbying* government and sharing information.

**trade barriers** impede the trading process and include *tariffs*, *quotas* and other *non-tariff barriers*. Tariffs tax imports. Quotas place a physical limit on imports. WTO aims to reduce trade barriers over time.

**trade creation** occurs when a new *trading bloc* has been set up and businesses begin to take advantage of the opportunities arising from *free trade* between member countries. Because there are fewer *trade barriers* new markets open up and businesses will try to extend into them. There will be increased *specialisation* and more *trade*.

**trade credit:** providing business customers with time to arrange for the payment of goods they have already received. This period is one of interest-free credit, which helps the customer's *cash flow* at the cost of the supplier's. Although the typical credit period offered to customers is 30 days, the average time the customers take to pay is nearer 75 days.

**trade cycle** is the way the economy moves from boom to slump in a regular fashion over a period. It can also be called the business or the economic cycle. The time taken from boom to boom is controversial; the economist who identified the cycle in the 1860s, Juglar, thought it was 8 to 11 years, whilst others thought it was as little as three and a half years, and *Kondratieff* thought there was a very long cycle of 50 years. Certainly it is possible to identify periods of booms and slumps since the industrial revolution, although they have all been superimposed on an upward trend line. Because of the general trend upwards, output in each successive boom has tended to be higher than in the previous one (see diagram below). (See also *business cycle*.)

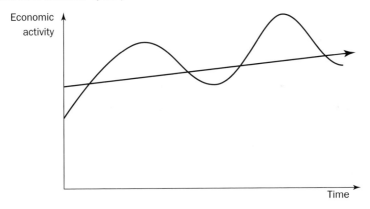

*The trade cycle on an upward growth path*

**trade deficit** occurs when visible *imports* are greater than visible *exports*.

**Trade Descriptions Act 1968** prohibits false or misleading descriptions of a product's contents, effects or price. This affects *packaging*, *advertising* and promotional material. It is one of the key pieces of *consumer protection* legislation.

**trade discount:** the percentage of the consumer selling price being provided as the *gross profit* margin for the retail trade.

**trade diversion:** when a new *trading bloc* is created, trade diversion takes place because some member countries will shift to buying more from other member countries rather than from non-member countries. For example, when the UK joined the European Union, it began to buy more butter from France and less from New Zealand. The absence of *trade barriers* between member countries and the *common external tariff* give people an incentive to switch. NAFTA, the *North American Free Trade Area*, is demonstrating trade diversion at the present time, as people in the USA, Canada and Mexico will tend to buy more from each other and less from outside the area.

**trade exhibition:** an industry market-place, where suppliers in a sector such as fast food can display their products to an audience of fast food restaurateurs or *franchisees*.

**trade gap:** a deficit on the *balance of trade*.

**trade liberalisation:** the process of limiting and reducing *trade barriers*, and drawing closer towards a situation of *free trade*. The impetus for this has come from the *GATT/WTO* and it has been carried out through the *Uruguay Round* of trade negotiations. It has resulted in reduced tariffs on a wide range of goods and services, and restrictions on the use of quotas and other non-tariff barriers.

**trade fair:** see *trade exhibition*

**trade mark:** a *logo* or symbol displayed on a company's products and *advertising* to distinguish the firm's brands from those of the competition. For exclusive use, a trade mark must be registered at the *Patent Office*.

**trade-off:** in making decisions people often have to consider that having more of one thing may mean having less of another. An important trade-off in *macroeconomic policy* is between inflation and unemployment. It is often the case that lower unemployment can be achieved but at the price of accelerating inflation. Another trade-off involves *equity* and *efficiency*. Increased wage *differentials* lead to improved incentives but less *equity* in the *distribution of income*.

In making a decision which involves a trade-off, there will be an opportunity cost. For example, the opportunity cost of reducing the rate of inflation may be the increase in unemployment which results.

**Trades Union Congress (TUC):** the organisation that represents British *trade unions* at a national or international level. The TUC was formed in 1868 and has had periods of considerable influence on government decision-making, notably the 1970s.

Its functions are to:

- be the voice of the union movement as a whole
- prevent or solve inter-union disputes
- promote international labour solidarity, especially within Europe.

**trade surplus** occurs when the value of visible *exports* is greater than the value of visible *imports*.

**trade union:** an organisation representing the interests and goals of working people. Membership involves the payment of subscriptions, usually of about £10–£15 per month. Craft unions represent people with a particular skill. Industrial unions represent employees across an industry (e.g. the Communication Workers Union). General unions represent a wide range of employees (e.g. the Transport and General Workers Union).

Advantages of trade unions, to union members:

- collective bargaining on their behalf
- help in cases of unsafe or unfair practices
- access to free legal advice and support.

Advantages of trade unions to businesses:

- communication link between management and workforce
- avoids the time-consuming need for individual bargaining
- a strong union may encourage managers to take worker needs seriously.

**Trade Union Act 1984:** legislation designed to ensure that *trade unions*

- become liable to be sued by employers if a strike is authorised without a secret ballot of the membership
- elect or re-elect voting members of the union's national executive at least every five years.

**Trade Union Reform and Employment Rights Act 1993:** a further piece of legislation that critics say is designed to weaken trade unions, though the government declared its aims as to increase the rights of individual employees and trade union members, and to improve competitiveness. It extends the changes brought about by previous *Employment Acts*. Among its main provisions were:

- requiring unions to provide employers with at least seven days' notice of official industrial action
- requiring union members to give periodic written agreement to the deduction of union subscriptions from their pay (making it more likely that people will let their union membership lapse)
- creating a new 'citizen's right' to restrain unlawfully organised *industrial action* (making it easier to stop unofficial strikes)
- abolishing the remaining *wages councils* and their statutory minimum pay rates.

**trade war:** a protectionist battle between governments in which *tariff* barriers against a country's imports leads to retaliation. If a trade war becomes serious enough it can cause a widespread downturn in world trade.

**trading bloc:** a group of countries that share *free trade* agreements between each other, but with common *tariffs* that discourage imports from countries outside the bloc. The *European Union* is a good example.

**trading profit** is the difference between the *revenues* and *costs* generated by a firm's ongoing business. As it is not a consequence of one-off items, it can be assumed that current trading profit is likely to recur in the future. Therefore it is regarded as high-quality profit. Another term for trading profit is 'operating profit'. As shown in calculation on the following page, trading profit can be calculated by deducting *overheads* from the company's *gross profit*.

A
B
C
D
E
F
G
H
I
J
K
L
M
N
O
P
Q
R
S
T
U
V
W
X
Y
Z

Worked example:

|  | £000 |
|---|---|
| Revenue | 920 |
| Cost of sales | 420 |
| Gross profit | 500 |
| – Overheads | 280 |
| = Trading profit | 220 |

**training** means developing knowledge and skills of direct relevance in the workplace. The *Learning and Skills Councils* (previously the Training and Enterprise Councils or TECs) organise local provision. The LSCs are run by local business representatives, working in col-laboration with neighbouring further education colleges where off-the-job training will take place. The idea is that the LSCs are able to define local needs and ensure that they are met by a combination of on-the-job training and courses.

**transfer earnings:** the wages which could be earned in the best alternative employment. For example if a teacher was able to earn £20 000 working in a bank, that would be that person's transfer earnings.

**transfer payment** occurs when government revenue from one part of society, e.g. taxpayers, is paid to another part. The best-known transfer payments are pensions and social security payments such as income support.

**transfer pricing** is employed where no external market exists which would set a price. It is often used by large companies for internal purposes to control costs, or, in the case of *multinationals* to reduce taxation. This is achieved by one *cost centre* in a low tax country charging another in a high tax country a high transfer price. The first one will make a large profit on which little tax is paid, whilst the other will make low or no profits and so will also have a low tax liability.

**transitional economies** are those of countries which have previously had *centrally planned* economies and are now allowing *market forces* to operate at least in parts of the economy. Russia, Poland and many other East European countries are currently in transition.

**transmission mechanism:** in business communications, this means the process by which a message or event is transferred from one person or place to another. It is the medium by which a message is conveyed, e.g. telephone or memo.

In economics, the transmission mechanism connects changes in the stock of money in the economy to the level of income and output. It shows how increased bank lending leads to increases in both consumption and investment, then in aggregate demand, and finally in the level of production.

**transnational corporation:** another name for a *multinational*.

**transparency** occurs when a deal or decision is made in an open manner, so that all those affected understand the reasons. Lack of transparency can lead to rumours or ill feeling often directed at particular individuals.

**Treasury:** the UK government department responsible for executing the government's taxation and spending policies. It comes under the direct responsibility of the *Chancellor of the Exchequer*, although the Prime Minister, as First Lord of the Treasury has ultimate control. Because it has the power to withhold or spend money, it is the most influential of all departments. The annual spending round, where Ministers have to bid for money for their departments, can make or break a Minister's political career. The Treasury also operates a complex *macroeconomic* forecasting model which is designed to help decision-making, especially when devising the *Budget*.

**Treasury bills** are short-term (three months) government securities. They are sold in order to make up for any shortfall in government spending in excess of tax revenue. Because they are so short term, they provide a very flexible way for governments to borrow.

**treasury function:** active management of a firm's financial resources, so that cash is earning the highest returns possible, while financial risks such as foreign exchange losses are minimised. Corporate treasurers can generate high profits for a firm, though there have been several cases of major firms losing hundreds of millions of pounds due to treasury errors. In some firms, corporate treasurer has become a new title for the same old financial director.

**Treasury model:** a computerised economic forecasting model used by the government to estimate future economic trends. (See also *economic models*.)

**Treaty of Rome:** the initial agreement between the original six members of the then European Economic Community, Belgium, France, Germany, Italy, Luxembourg and the Netherlands. It came into force in 1958.

**trend:** the underlying pattern of growth or decline within a series of data. This pattern can be projected forward as a prediction of the future in the process known as *extrapolation* of the trend.

**troubleshooter:** originating in the oil industry, this term is used to describe an individual who is asked to sort out a business problem of someone else's making. *Management consultants* may be used in this role, though large firms may have their own head office staff who can troubleshoot.

**true and fair view:** the phrase used by auditors to confirm that a firm's accounts are accurate within the terms of the accounting practices used to draw them up. Occasionally, auditors qualify a set of accounts by stating that they are not happy with one element of the data provided. This occurs if they believe that an aspect of the accounts does not provide a true and fair view of the company's finances.

**TUC:** see *Trades Union Congress*

**turnkey project:** a contract for something as substantial as a whole factory, in which the supplier supplies, installs and tests every aspect of the specification, so that the customer can make it operational at a mere turn of the key.

**turnover** is an abbreviation for sales turnover, which means the same as *sales revenue*.

**two-factor theory:** the view that the factors related to *job satisfaction* can be divided into two: those that only have the potential to provide positive job satisfaction and those that can only cause dissatisfaction. Professor *Herzberg* came to this conclusion in the late 1950s, after conducting research among accountants and engineers in America. The findings of his research are presented below. Many have criticised his research method, but many managers have attempted to put his theory into practice and have enjoyed considerable success. (See diagram below.)

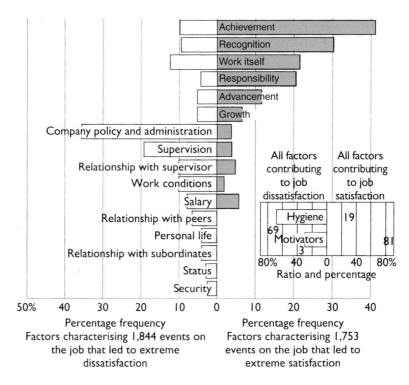

**two-way communication** occurs when instant *feedback* is possible, thereby enabling a proper conversation to take place. This should be far more effective and motivating than *one-way communication*.

**Do you need revision help and advice?**

Go to pages 325–341 for a range of revision appendices that include plenty of exam advice and tips.

**uncertainty** is the situation that underlies every business decision. This is because decision-making concerns changes that will have an effect in the future, and the future can never be predicted with certainty. An important issue that stems from this is that uncertainty increases over time. In other words, a forecast of next year's sales or costs has a lower chance of accuracy than an estimate of the figures for next week. Therefore decisions that rely upon circumstances in the distant future are subject to very great uncertainty. Examples of this include commercial failures such as supersonic aircraft and nuclear power.

**UNCTAD:** see *United Nations Conference on Trade and Development*

**underemployment** occurs where people nominally have jobs, but jobs that do not keep them fully occupied. This often results in very low wages, and is particularly prevalent in the agricultural sectors of underdeveloped countries.

**underdeveloped country:** see *developing country*

**underlying inflation:** the long-term trend rate of *inflation*. In the UK this is usually measured using the *retail price index*, minus the change in mortgage interest rates. This is known as *RPIX*.

**undertrading** happens when a firm is operating at a lower or slower pace than its working capital would allow. By implication, it has plenty of working capital, but is not using it effectively to generate profits and/or growth.

**undervalued exchange rate:** an *exchange rate* which is below its long-term equilibrium value. This means that its exports are very competitive and therefore high, and imports appear relatively dear and will be fairly low. The outcome is a *current account surplus* on the *balance of payments*.

**underwriting** is the acceptance of a business risk in return for a fee. Lloyd's of London has a worldwide reputation for its willingness to underwrite any type of insurance wanted by a client. For a *stock market* new issue, a *merchant bank* will underwrite it by guaranteeing to buy any shares which are not sold in the company *flotation*.

**unearned income:** income derived from interest, dividends and rents, i.e. from assets which are owned, rather than from employment.

**unemployment:** the problem encountered when there are people able and willing to work but unable to find jobs. This leads to a loss of potential output. The two main categories of unemployment are *demand deficiency* (sometimes called *cyclical*) and *structural unemployment*. Since the early 1980s unemployment has been consistently higher than previously. This reflects the rapid structural changes which have taken place, and the fact that counter-inflation policies have kept the level of aggregate demand below the level needed to employ more of the working population.

Policies to deal with unemployment can be varied. When the cause is lack of demand, *expansionary policies* may be appropriate. Structural unemployment requires measures which reduce *immobilities*. Training and retraining help. Regional policy can be used to help areas where major industries are declining.

In recent years attention has been focused on whether employment protection laws reduce the rate at which new jobs are being created, especially for unskilled jobs. Policies have emphasised the need for labour markets to be flexible.

In the USA, unemployment fell steadily during the late 1990s, in contrast to the situation in most of the EU, where unemployment in a number of countries was above 10 per cent for some time. This has been attributed to the very flexible labour market which exists in the USA.

**unemployment benefit** is the social security payment made to people who have become unemployed. It has recently been renamed the *jobseeker's allowance* and is now paid for a maximum of six months. The intention is to create an enhanced incentive to find work.

**unfair dismissal:** terminating the employment contract of a member of staff for a reason that the law regards as unfair. This would include anything other than *gross misconduct*, incapability and genuine *redundancy*. Workers who believe they have been dismissed unfairly must appeal to an *employment tribunal* within three months (see *Employment Relations Act* 1999).

**Uniform Business Rate** is a tax paid by businesses to cover the use of goods and services provided by local government. It was the successor to the local rating system which then applied to businesses. It is set nationally but reflects local property values.

**unincorporated** means a firm which operates as a *sole trader* or partnership which has not applied to the *Registrar of Companies* for incorporation as a *joint-stock company*. Those running an unincorporated business have *unlimited liability* for the firm's debts.

**union:** see *trade union*

**union density** measures the proportion of a workforce that belongs to a *trade union*. This is a major influence upon the effectiveness of union activity.

**union recognition** is the acceptance by an employer that bargaining on wages and conditions will be negotiated with the employees' trade union representatives. Between 1980 and 1999 employers were not obliged to negotiate with unions, even if all staff were union members. This position changed with the Employment Relations Act 1999, which forces employers to recognise a trade union if a majority of staff vote for union representation (as long as 40 per cent of workers cast their vote in favour). Firms with fewer than 20 staff are exempt.

**unique selling point (USP):** the feature of a product that can be focused on in order to differentiate it from all competition. The USP should be based on a real product characteristic, such as the advertising slogan used by Mars for one of their chocolate bars: 'Topic – a hazelnut in every bite'. Stronger still are USPs based on a patented technical advantage. Many firms, however, attempt to create USPs that are based purely on advertising imagery. This can be effective (better to be the sexiest chocolate bar than the hazelnuttiest) but usually at the cost of extensive TV advertising support. (See *product differentiation*.)

**unitary taxation:** an attempt to defeat tax avoidance measures such as *transfer pricing*, by imposing company profit taxes based on a firm's *turnover* within a particular state or country. When introduced in California, unitary taxation caused a storm of protest by *multinational* firms, but it increased sharply that State's revenues from *corporation tax*.

**unit cost** is the average cost of making one item, found by dividing total cost by the number of units produced. This sounds straightforward, but unit (or average) costs are among the trickiest concepts in business. This is because it seems as if you can use unit costs to work out the total cost of producing any specified number of units. In fact, however, unit costs comprise two elements: *variable costs* (which are a true cost per unit) and *fixed costs per unit* (which are only correct at one level of output). Therefore before 'using' unit costs it is necessary to strip out the fixed element.

### Worked example: unit costs

At 400 units of demand, unit costs are £2, half of which are fixed. What are total costs if demand doubles?

Fixed costs stay at £1 × 400 = £400

Variable costs are £1 × 800 = £800

Therefore total costs at 800 units = £1200 (**not** 800 × £2 = £1600)

**United Nations Conference on Trade and Development (UNCTAD):** the organisation within the United Nations framework which enables the developing countries to secure improved trade agreements and aid payments.

**unit of account:** one of the functions of money, by which it allows different values to be added and compared.

**unit trust:** a fund that spreads small savers' investments over a wide portfolio of different *stocks and shares*. This is a popular and relatively inexpensive way of investing on the *Stock Exchange*. Unfortunately the slump in share prices between 2000 and 2003 showed that even unit trust investment is not safe from losses.

**universal benefit:** a *social security* payment which is given to all who qualify regardless of income. The most important example is the old age pension. In contrast, *means-tested benefits* are given only to those whose incomes are below a certain level, e.g. income support.

**unlimited liability** means that because a business is trading without having become incorporated, its owners are liable for all the debts it may incur. If these debts are greater than the personal assets of the proprietors, they may be forced into *bankruptcy*. The main types of unlimited liability business are *sole traders* and *partnerships*.

**unofficial strike:** a refusal to work that has been agreed locally by union members, but has not been approved by the national union. As a result, strikers will not receive any *strike pay* and will have their legal case weakened should the firm dismiss them. Unofficial strikes are sometimes called *wildcats* or walk-outs. Both terms give the correct impression of a dispute that has arisen so suddenly that workers act before getting official union approval.

**unsecured loan:** borrowing that is not backed by any form of security or *collateral*. This would be hard to obtain and would carry relatively high interest charges.

**unsustainable growth:** economic growth which is faster than the long-term trend rate of growth, which reflects the actual increase in the productive capacity of the economy. A period of unsustainable growth is likely to be followed by a period of slower than average growth. The UK is widely believed to have been growing at an unsustainable rate of growth in 1988 and also in 1993, in both cases at an annual rate of more than 4 per cent. In both cases this was not sustained.

An alternative definition of unsustainable growth would emphasise the environmental considerations: it would be growth at a rate which involved the use of depletable resources which could not be continued in the long run because they would become progressively scarcer and therefore more expensive. Sustainable growth involves the management of resources so that they are replaced as they are used. For example, trees are replanted and reliance on fossil fuels is progressively reduced.

**up-market:** a word used commonly in marketing to denote a product that is aimed at wealthier consumers. Its opposite is a *down-market* product.

**upper turning point** is the highest point in the *trade cycle*. It is usually reached where there are shortages of skilled labour and capital goods, and when expectations that the boom will continue begin to fade. The loss of confidence and rising costs reduce levels of investment, and through the *multiplier*, result in a downturn.

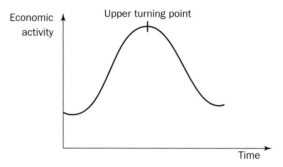

**upstream** activities are those that focus on earlier stages in the *production chain*. Therefore upstream integration is another term for backward *vertical integration*.

**upturn** is that point in the business or *trade cycle* where business confidence returns, investment restarts, unemployment falls and incomes begin to rise.

**URL:** uniform resource locator is the term for the address of a website. This usually begins: http://.

**Uruguay Round:** the trade negotiations which took place under the auspices of *GATT* and were put into effect at the beginning of 1995. (The negotiations originally began in Uruguay). They had the effect of reducing trade barriers for a wide range of goods and services, including some which had previously been strongly protected by *tariffs* and *non-tariff barriers*.

**USP:** see *unique selling point*

**utilities** are industries which provide the most basic services such as water and power. Before *privatisation* it was generally accepted that utilities were state-run, not only because of their importance to the overall economy, but also because they were often *natural monopolies*. Most utilities in the UK are now regulated within the private sector.

**validity:** measuring or judging the reliability of data such as the findings of *market research*. To assess the validity of research findings, the following should be considered:

- whether the questionnaire was biased
- whether the sampling method was appropriate
- whether the sample size was large enough to provide statistically valid data
- whether the interviewing was carried out consistently and without bias (overenthusiastic, for example)
- whether the research results can be related directly to customer actions (people may say they will try a product, but not bother in real life).

**value added** is the difference between the cost of materials and the price customers are prepared to pay for the finished product. It is value added that creates the surplus to pay the wages, *overheads* and *dividends*. A product with high value added is likely to have been produced and/or designed with great skill, though it may also be the result of creating a very desirable brand image.

FORMULA:    selling price   – bought-in goods and services    = value added

£4          –            £0.80              =       £3.20

The diagram below shows how the £3.20 value added is distributed. It also indicates that value added can be expressed as a percentage:

£4.00 selling price

Profit

Finance costs (allocated)

Overheads (per unit)

Wages and salaries

Value added £3.20

£0.80

Cost of bought-in goods and services

$$\% \text{ value added} = \frac{\text{value added}}{\text{materials}} \times 100$$

$$= \frac{£4 - 80p}{80p} \times 100$$

$$= 400\%$$

A business may be very profitable even though little value is added by it. A high turnover combined with a small profit on each item sold, as in the case of some supermarkets, may prove very successful.

**Value Added Tax (VAT)** is a percentage tax added on to the price of a good or service. It was introduced in 1973 to replace purchase tax and to harmonise with the rest of the *European Union*. Since each stage of production adds value (the difference between the cost of its inputs and the revenue gained from its output), the tax is added at each stage, and can be claimed back, until it reaches the final consumer, who cannot reclaim it. The tax is in principle *regressive* in that it takes a higher proportion of a poor person's income than someone who is rich. In the UK this unfairness is overcome to a certain extent by goods which are either exempt or *zero-rated*. These include food, housing and children's clothes which are likely together to account for a large proportion of the spending of the less well-off.

**value analysis:** the study of each aspect of a product to see if it adds sufficient value to justify its cost. Companies conduct value analysis to look at both new and existing products to see whether they are designed in a way that satisfies the consumer in terms of what the product looks like, what it costs and how well it performs its job. Achieving this goal requires a combination of *market research*, cost information and engineering skills.

Generally, the term 'value analysis' is used to mean the identification of costs that could be cut, either by using cheaper materials or by redesigning a product to use fewer components. It is this negative approach that has led to value analysis being blamed for reductions in quality and workmanship, for example, cars being made with thinner body steel and window frames becoming much less ornate than in the earlier part of the century.

**value judgement:** an opinion based on beliefs rather than facts. Although the term could be used to describe decisions taken by *entrepreneurs* in an unscientific manner, it is more commonly used as a criticism of student essays. Students often make the error of stating value judgements as if they are facts (for example, 'All firms profit-maximise').

**values:** ethical principles that guide one's actions, enabling one to identify decisions or actions that are morally unacceptable. (See *ethics*.)

**variable:** a factor that changes and thus causes other changes to occur. This may be in the context of an individual business, or of the economy as a whole. In either case it will affect plans or outcomes. In the case of a firm, some variables are within its influence, such as pricing levels, employee *motivation* and *advertising* effectiveness. An efficient firm will measure and evaluate these variables in order to decide what policies to adopt towards them. Others are wholly outside the firm's control, such as the weather, competitors' actions and consumer confidence. These variables should be measured and anticipated so as to aid the firm's planning process. If a weather forecast predicts a heatwave, for example, a soft drink producer should know whether to expect sales to rise 20 per cent or 200 per cent.

In the macroeconomy, changes in variables may be predicted by economic models. For example, the effect on spending of a tax change can be estimated. Changes in independent variables (such as tax rates) can be fed into the model, to give predictions about the effects on dependent variables (such as incomes and expenditure).

**variable cost:** one that varies in direct proportion to changes in output, such as raw materials, components, *piece-rate* labour and energy used in production. In other words, these are costs that should double if output doubles. Although *break-even charts* require the assumption that some costs vary in direct proportion to changes in *output*, in practice it is unlikely that any costs will be totally variable. For instance, raw materials are likely to cost less per unit when buying in bulk. In this case the materials cost might not quite double when output doubles.

**variable cost per unit:** total variable costs divided by the number of units produced. In the worked example, it is assumed that variable costs per unit will not change as output changes.

Worked example:

|  | Yesterday | Today |
| --- | --- | --- |
| Variable costs | £360 | £720 |
| Output (units) | £240 | £480 |
| Variable cost p.u. | £1.50 | £1.50 |

**variable factors of production** are those factors which can be varied in quantity in the short run. Raw material or component inputs are an example: the amount used will depend on the level of output and can be varied as necessary. Labour may be a variable factor, if the number of people employed or the hours worked can be varied according to the amount of work to be done. This might be the case if overtime was worked in order to increase output. Alternatively, labour may be a fixed factor, if the employees concerned will have to be kept on even if output falls.

**variable overheads** are costs that vary in proportion to changes in demand or output, but are not related directly to the production process. Examples include any commission paid to sales representatives, and any variable costs associated with delivery, such as the cost of postage for a mail-order company. When making profit or break-even calculations, variable overheads should be added to variable costs, **not** to fixed overheads.

**variance:** the amount by which an actual figure differs from a budgeted one.

**VAT:** see *value added tax*

**velocity of circulation:** the ratio of the value of output to a particular measure of the stock of money in circulation in the economy. Over the years this may change, depending on the extent to which idle bank balances are held.

**venture capital** is risk capital, usually in the form of a package of loan and *share capital*, to provide a significant investment in a small or medium-sized business. The need for it arises when a rapidly growing firm requires more capital, but the firm is not yet ready for the *stock market*. In these circumstances, *merchant banks* might provide the funds themselves, or arrange for others to do so. A typical venture capital investment might provide £500 000: half in loans and half in shares.

**VER:** see *voluntary export restraint*

**vertical communication** is the passage of information up and down the management hierarchy. It may be upward, as in a shop-floor complaint to managers about safety conditions, or downward, as in a manager-run team briefing session. Successful vertical

**315**

communication can overcome *them and us* barriers and can enhance the speed and quality of *consultation*. To achieve this, however, requires a clear sense of common purpose and a flat enough hierarchy to minimise the layers through which the communication must pass.

**vertical integration:** occurs when two firms join together that operate in the same industry, but at different stages in the production/supply chain. The integration might come about through *merger* or *take-over*.

Backward (or upstream) vertical integration means buying out a supplier, e.g. a chocolate manufacturer buying a sugar producer.

Forward (or downstream) vertical integration means buying out a customer, e.g. the chocolate firm buying up a chain of newsagents.

**vested interest:** a participant in a decision, action or statement who has a direct interest in the outcome and therefore may prove biased. For example, estate agents have a vested interest in suggesting that the housing market is strong enough for prices to rise.

**video conferencing** is the establishment of a TV and video network that can enable staff working at a distance from each other to 'meet' without travelling.

**virus** (computer): a software program that latches on to other programs with the purpose of disrupting them. This might cause the loss of valuable or even vital data.

**visible balance:** another name for the *balance of trade*, i.e. visible exports minus visible imports.

**visible trade** is concerned with the export and import of goods. The difference between visible exports and visible imports is called the *balance of trade*. (See *balance of payments*.)

**voluntary code of practice** a formal statement by a committee or organisation of the methods of working recommended as good practice for the firms and individuals within the industry. Such codes are often devised by the *employers' association*, which provides a symbol that participants in the scheme can display to potential customers. The code is voluntary if it has no statutory or legal backing. This is usually what employers say they want, though financial scandals within the City of London have led many within the financial sector to call for statutory and therefore legally enforceable codes of behaviour.

**voluntary export restraints:** a *quota* placed on imports from a particular country, with the agreement of that country's government. (See quotas for explanation of the likely impact.) They have been negotiated mainly with Japan, but also with countries such as Taiwan and South Korea. They apply mostly to manufactured goods such as cars and televisions. Their objective is to protect the domestic industry of the importing country. The exporting country may be persuaded to accept them if the alternative is a more damaging trade barrier. They are outside the rules of the *WTO* but nevertheless continue to exist in a number of countries.

**voluntary liquidation:** a decision by the company directors or shareholders to ask *receivers* to liquidate the business in the best interests of the shareholders. *Liquidation* meaning turning *assets* into *cash*. This process of winding up the company's affairs may be due to a financial crisis or simply because a firm's directors wish to retire and have no successors.

**voluntary organisation:** a non-profit-making enterprise such as a charity or a youth group. The special difficulties of managing such organisations have been analysed by Professor C

Handy. Key amongst them is the need for a management style that makes staff feel valued, since there is no financial reason for volunteer staff to work effectively.

**vote of (no) confidence:** this is the way in which shareholders who believe that their company has been mismanaged can demand that the current chairman resigns. A vote can be called at the *annual general meeting* between the directors and the shareholders. Although this procedure is an important aspect of the theoretical *accountability* of company managements to their shareholders, in practice it is extremely rare for a vote of no confidence to succeed.

A vote of no confidence may also be carried out when a government policy has been so seriously called into question that the Speaker of the House of Commons accepts an Opposition call for a no-confidence debate. Should the government lose such a debate, it is accepted parliamentary practice that it resigns from office and a general election is held.

**Vroom V:** a highly influential author on *motivation* and leadership, whose most significant work focused on *expectancy theory*.

**Do you need help with the synoptic element of your Economics and Business course?**

Go to page 335 for tips and advice.

A
B
C
D
E
F
G
H
I
J
K
L
M
N
O
P
Q
R
S
T
U
V
W
X
Y
Z

**wage differentials:** see *differentials*

**wage-price spiral:** a phrase describing a situation in which wages chase prices, in turn causing prices to rise further, and so on. When *inflation* rises to such a level that workers see their *real incomes* falling, they respond by demanding wage increases to compensate. This is also known as *cost-push inflation*. Whether wages follow prices at the start of the cycle, or prices follow wages has been subject to a great deal of political debate in the past.

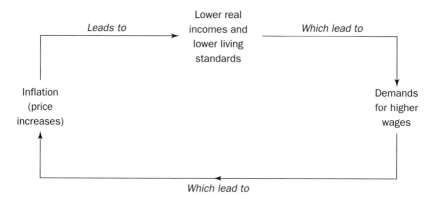

**wage rate:** the price of labour. When wage rates change, the change may be real, or it may be just a change in money wages which maintains their existing purchasing power.

**Wall Street Crash:** the collapse in American share prices that began in 1929 and continued until 1932. It was the result of the American *stock market* rising so far during the 1920s that share prices no longer reflected reality. Investors took risks in highly speculative shares, such as land deals in the Florida Everglades and in Europe. Once rumours of the risks of these shares became common knowledge, the bubble burst and share prices plummeted, helping to bring about the *Great Depression* which continued until the Second World War. The same pattern of share price boom and bust has happened to a rather lesser degree several times since 1929, notably in the 1980s and early 2000s.

**wastage** is the rate of loss of resources within a production or service process, either necessarily (such as the weight loss when filleting a fish) or unnecessarily (such as through sloppy work). Staff effort should be devoted to minimising the wastage that is within their control or influence.

In manufacturing, the main problems are:

- materials wastage

- reworking (due to poor quality first time)

- defective production (with products sold off as 'seconds').

In retailing, the main problems are:

- customer or staff theft and pilfering

- products passing their sell-by date (due to over-ordering or poor stock rotation)

- poor handling, leading to products becoming damaged.

**wastage rate**, in the context of *human resource management*, refers to the loss of employees through labour turnover. This is a waste because of the time and resources involved in recruitment and training.

**waste management:** ensuring that waste materials and emissions are kept within legal limits, at the lowest possible cost to the business. This process might be helped by *environmental auditing*, especially if the audit results were published each year.

**wealth:** the stock of *assets* held by an individual or organisation. These assets can be used to yield a stream of *income* in the future. They may consist of financial assets such as bank balances or shares, or of real assets such as property.

**wealth distribution:** a measurement of the proportion of the nation's total assets held by different sectors of society. For instance it may be that the richest tenth of the population owns 40 per cent of the country's wealth, while the poorest tenth own just 1 per cent. The distribution of wealth is often much more unequal than the distribution of income, because income is to some extent redistributed through the tax and benefit system.

**weighted average:** an average that is weighted in line with the relative importance of its different components. This is necessary to make the final figure a true reflection of the information.

For example, if there are three size categories for British companies – small, medium and large – with sales *turnovers* of £100 000, £5m., and £1bn respectively, what is the average turnover of a British company?

The worked example below shows an unweighted average of this information on the left. It gives a highly misleading answer of £335m. The right-hand column weights the average by the proportion of firms there are in each size category. It takes into account that there are many more small firms than large and therefore results in a more accurate, much lower figure.

| | Simple average | Weighted average | | | | |
|---|---|---|---|---|---|---|
| | | figure | times | weight | = | weighted total |
| Small | £100 000 | £100 000 | × | 80% | | £80 000 |
| Medium | £5 000 000 | £5 000 000 | × | 16% | | £800 000 |
| Large | £1 000 000 000 | £1 000 000 000 | × | 4% | | £40 000 000 |
| Total | £1 005 100 000 | | | | | |
| | 3 | | Addition of weighted totals | = | | |
| | = £335 033 333 | | weighted average | | = | £40 880 000 |

**weighted index:** the calculation of a data series with a base figure equalling 100 within which the principles of *weighted averages* are applied. Among the most widely used weighted indexes in Business and Economics are the *retail prices index (RPI)* and the Financial Times Stock Exchange 100 Index (FT-SE 100, popularly known as *Footsie*).

A problem with weighted indexes is that the weights applied can become out of date as market or consumer habits change. This is why some statisticians prefer current year weighting to the more common base year weighting.

**welfare:** a term usually used to refer to people's well-being. It is hard to measure. *National income* statistics are an imperfect guide. Sometimes, other measures are used, which might include life expectancy, child mortality or the ownership of *consumer durables*.

**welfare state:** the system of social security benefits and health care which was set up in the UK after 1945. It was designed to meet the needs of all those in need, but is constantly threatened by efforts to cut costs and avoid raising taxes. The capacity to provide is affected by the ageing population, which increases demands on the welfare state.

**what if... questions** are hypothetical considerations of:

- what might happen in the future?
- what might result if things are done differently today?

What if . . . ? questions are the essential preliminary stage to *contingency planning*, i.e. to the process of preparing responses to possible opportunities or threats. These questions are made far easier to think through if a firm's sales, production, distribution and financial data is kept on a single computer model.

**whistle blower:** an individual whose sense of moral outrage leads him or her to expose wrongdoing within an organisation, either to the authorities or to the press. Since 1998, the Public Interest Disclosure Act has offered protection to whistleblowers from their employers. This protection only applies if the employee has tried to correct the concern internally before going public.

**white-collar union:** a *trade union* representing clerical, professional or managerial staff.

**white knight:** a company that comes to the rescue of a firm that is facing a *take-over bid* from an unwelcome *predator*. The white knight steps in with a counter-offer for the firm, thereby saving it from the predator. A classic example of this was Waterford's rescue of Wedgwood from the clutches of the London Rubber Company (Durex).

**White paper:** a document setting out proposals for government legislation.

**wholesale price index:** a measure of changes in wholesale prices. It is useful because it may give an advance warning of impending changes in retail price levels.

**wholesaling:** the process of buying large quantities of product from suppliers and selling on in smaller volumes to retailers or business users. This is known as 'breaking bulk'. This traditional role as the middleman is often looked down on because the wholesaler's profit margin appears to make goods more expensive for the consumer. As shown by the diagram on the next page, however, without a wholesaler the number of journeys required for each manufacturer to service each retailer would become prohibitively expensive. Furthermore, there would be serious effects on traffic and the environment from the number of extra journeys necessary.

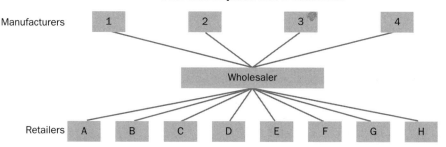

*The role of a wholesaler*

**wildcat strike:** spontaneous unofficial industrial action brought on by the sudden emergence of a major grievance. A typical catalyst might be the sacking of a respected shop steward.

**windfall gain:** a one-off gain that can aid this year's profit or cash position, but cannot be expected to recur in future.

**winding up** is the process of completing the *liquidation* of a business in order for it to cease trading in an orderly manner.

**window-dressing:** presenting the company accounts in such a manner as to flatter the financial position of the firm. This is a form of *creative accounting* in which there is a fine dividing line between flattery and fraud. In the overwhelming number of cases, window-dressing is no more misleading than tidying up before visitors arrive. Among the different ways of window-dressing accounts are:

- Masking a deteriorating *liquidity* position. This is in order to present a *balance sheet* that looks financially sound.

- Massaging the profit figure. Although firms' revenue totals and cost totals sound like facts, there is a great deal of scope for changing the figures. At the end of a poor year's trading, managers may be asked to bring forward as many invoices and deliveries as possible, to, in effect, push two months' revenue into the last month before the year-end.

**withdrawals** occur when money is taken out of the *circular flow of national income*. They are also known as leakages, and consist of taxes, imports and savings. In each case, the withdrawal leads to a lower level of aggregate demand for domestic output, i.e. they reduce spending power. A fall in withdrawals will lead to an increase in spending, as with a tax cut.

**word of mouth:** the spread of information or publicity through individuals' decisions to talk about a product or event. This is an especially important form of free *advertising* for fashion-based and/or children's products. Favourable word of mouth will spread if a product has been particularly well designed and made.

**worker participation** is the active involvement of the workforce in the ideas, decisions and actions of the organisation. It can be encouraged by structures such as *quality circles*, *kaizen* groups and *works councils*. Such structures are only successful, however, if senior management give full support to the suggestions that come up from the factory floor.

**working capital** is the day-to-day finance for running a business. In exam questions, the term means the day-to-day finance available for running a business.

> FORMULA:    current assets − current liabilities  =  working capital

Working capital is used to pay for raw materials and running costs, and also funds the credit offered to customers (*debtors*) when making a sale. If a firm has too little working capital available, it may struggle to finance increased production without straining its *liquidity* position. Yet if a firm has too much capital tied up in the short term, it may not be able to afford the new machinery that could boost efficiency.

**working conditions:** the physical surroundings and atmosphere of a workplace, e.g. state of decoration and amount of pollution. Professor *Herzberg* regards them as *hygiene factors*, for whereas poor working conditions may be demotivating, good conditions become accepted as the norm and therefore give no positive satisfaction.

**Working Families' Tax Credit:** a benefit paid to people with families whose pay is very low. It helps to ensure that people on low pay do have some incentive to work.

**working population:** all those who are working or actively seeking work.

**working time directive:** the legal requirement that employees should work a maximum of 48 hours per week averaged over any 17 week period. Strangely, there is an opt-out from this rule. Any worker can volunteer to waive the right to this working time ceiling. The directive formed part of the social chapter of the *Maastricht* treaty.

**work in progress (WIP):** semi-completed components within the production process, either stockpiled or on the *production line* itself. This is one of the three types of stock: the others are raw materials and finished goods. Although in many factory contexts, WIP is a minor element of stock, in others such as shipbuilding and construction, the long production time makes work in progress a heavy user of the firm's *working capital*.

**works council:** a regular forum for discussion between management and workforce representatives. Excluded from the agenda would be bargaining over wages, terms and productivity levels, as these matters would be left to *trade union* negotiations. The role of the works council is to look ahead at the company's plans and to draw ideas for improvements from the factory floor. A weakness of works councils has always been that because they include representatives from the whole firm, they lack the focus of a localised *quality circle* or improvement group.

The European Works Council Directive revived works councils in the 1990s, as it forced large firms that operate in more than one European country to have regular works council meetings. Compulsion can never be successful, however, while managers see such meetings as disruptive rather than a positive opportunity to consult and learn from the shop floor.

**work study** is the systematic measurement of working processes and timings with the intention of identifying the best available method and realistic *output* targets. Also known as *time-and-motion study*, it was one of the key management tools devised by F W *Taylor* at the end of the nineteenth century.

**World Bank:** see the *International Bank for Reconstruction and Development*

**world-class manufacturing** is a term coined by R *Schonberger* to denote the characteristics of the world's top-performing companies. *Benchmarking* is the technique used most commonly to identify how well a firm's performance stands up against the world's best-performing manufacturers.

**World Development Report:** an annual publication of the World Bank providing extensive data on growth and development issues.

**WTO:** see *World Trade Organisation*

**World Trade Organisation:** oversees and regulates the international trading environment. It replaced *GATT, the General Agreement on Tariffs and Trade*, early in 1995. As with GATT, its objectives are to promote freer trade. In practical terms it aims to reduce *trade barriers*. There have been successive rounds of tariff negotiations which have cut tariffs on a wide range of products, and sought to eliminate quotas and reduce non-tariff barriers. (The last of these, the *Uruguay Round*, was the most far-reaching to date and was implemented from 1995). Most of the world's nations belong to the WTO and participate in its work. In addition to reducing trade barriers, it has mechanisms for resolving international trade disputes. Although *WTO/GATT* has been highly successful in reducing tariff barriers on trade in manufactures, there are still major restraints on trade in agricultural products which are being reduced only very slowly.

At the WTO's Fourth Ministerial Conference in Qatar in November 2001, members committed themselves to the Doha Development Agenda, which is effectively a new round of negotiations. Its work programme is concerned particularly with the needs of developing countries. Agriculture and services figure large, having been rather neglected in previous rounds. There is a strong focus on implementation of past agreements. The completion date is 2005.

China's acceptance as a member in 2002 represented the WTO's biggest ever increase in economic importance world-wide.

**write down:** the decision to cut the *book value* of an *asset* down to a level that is now thought more appropriate. In a sense that is what *depreciation* does each year, but the term 'write down' is usually used to denote any reduction in an asset's book value other than through normal depreciation.

**write off:** the decision to cut the *book value* of an *asset* down to zero (or to a nominal sum such as £1). This would be done if it became clear that a physical asset had become worthless or a *debtor*'s item had become unrecoverable.

**x-inefficiency:** the tendency for costs to rise because the organisation has few or no competitors. This is likely to occur if the producer has a degree of monopoly power, whether in the public or the private sector, which allows management to become careless about keeping costs to a minimum.

**year to date:** accumulated figures for the months of the year so far. The term is used commonly on *spreadsheets* of monthly budgets.

**yield:** another term for *dividend yield*

**yuppie:** a 1980s label describing a supposedly new class of young upwardly mobile professionals devoted to smart but faddish lifestyles.

**zero defects:** the goal of achieving perfect product quality, time after time. Many believe that this could only be feasible at an excessively high design and production cost.

**zero-rated:** products for which VAT declarations must be made, though the rate of tax is 0 per cent.

# ECONOMICS AND BUSINESS REVISION LISTS

The following pages set out lists of terms to revise for examinations. When approaching exams, look up each word in the main text, making sure that you understand it and can memorise the definition.

**1** Economic and business background

**2** Markets and market failure

**3** Business organisation

**4** Decision taking and management accounts

**5** Production

**6** Marketing

**7** Human resource management and the labour market

**8** The macroeconomic framework

**9** The UK economy, the government and the legal framework

**10** International trade

**11** Economic development

**12** Business responsibility and the environment

**13** Accounting and ratios

**14** Statistical terms

# 1 Economic and business background

# 2 Markets and market failure

Perfect competition

Price discrimination

Price elasticity of demand

Price leader

Price maker

Price taker

Price war

Product differentiation

Profit

Profit maximisation

Profit-payoff matrices

Profit-signalling mechanism

Relative price

Slump

Smith, Adam

Substitutes

Super-normal profit

Supply

Supply elasticity

Tacit agreement

Tax incidence

# 3  Business organisation
TOP 30 REVISION TERMS

Bank

Conglomerates

Culture

Diseconomies of scale

Diversification

Economies of scale

Enterprise

Entrepreneur

Equity capital

External financing

Finance

Gearing

Horizontal integration

Institutional investors

Internal financing

Limited liability

Merger

Multinational

Partnership

Private limited company

Public limited company

Share

Sole trader

Strategic objectives

Subsidiary

Tactical decisions

Take-over

The City

Unlimited liability

Vertical integration

# 4 Decision taking and management accounts

TOP 30 REVISION TERMS

Ansoff's box

Appraisal

Average rate of return

Business plan

Cash flow forecast

Change management

Constraint

Contribution costing

Culture

Diversification

Divestment

Focus

Gearing

Investment appraisal

Merger

Mission statement

Payback period

Pricing methods

Receiver

Risk management

Risk:reward ratio

Scientific management

Strategic decision

Supplier relationships

SWOT analysis

Synergy

Tactical decisions

Taylor, F W

Trade-offs

Uncertainty

# 5 Production

TOP 40 REVISION TERMS

Automation

Average total cost

Batch production

Break-even

Buffer stock

Capacity utilisation

Capital-intensive

Cell production

Continuous improvement

Direct cost

Diseconomies of scale

Division of labour

Economies of scale

Factors of production

Financial economies

Fixed costs

Fixed factors

Flow production

Indirect cost

Industrial relations

Innovation

Intermediate goods

Job production

Just-in-time

Labour-intensive

Lean production

Mass production

New technology

Productivity

Quality assurance

Quality circle

Quality control

Reorder level

Retail price index

Standardisation

Stock control

Technology

Total quality management

Variable costs

Variable factors

# 6 Marketing

# 7 Human resource management and the labour market

Single status                    Teamwork
Span of control                  Trade union
Strike                           Trade Union Congress
Structural unemployment          Unemployment
Suggestion schemes               Unfair dismissal
Tall hierarchy                   Wage rate

# 8 The macroeconomic framework

TOP 25 REVISION TERMS

Aggregate demand                 Injections
Aggregate supply                 Interest rates
Business cycle                   Investment
Circular flow of national income Money
Economic growth                  Multiplier
Economic indicators              National income
Expectations                     Recession
Financial intermediaries         Recovery
Full capacity output             Savings ratio
Gross domestic product           Skill shortage
Gross national product           Trade cycle
Growth                           Unemployment
Inflation                        Withdrawals

# 9 The UK economy, the government and the legal framework

TOP 40 REVISION TERMS

Bank of England                  Forecasting
Competition Commission           Income distribution
Corporation tax                  Indirect taxes
Cost-benefit analysis            Keynes, J M
Cyclical unemployment            Local government
Demand deficiency unemployment   Merit goods
Deregulation                     Monetary policy
Direct taxation                  Monetary Policy Committee
Economic planning                Nationalisation
Fiscal policy                    Office of Fair Trading

Private sector
Privatisation
Productivity
Public expenditure
Public goods
Public sector
Real interest rates
Regeneration
Regional multiplier
Regional policy

Regressive tax
Regulator
Self-regulation
Stabilisation policy
Structural unemployment
Subsidy
Supply side measures
Taxes
Tight money
Value added tax

# 10 International trade

TOP 50 REVISION TERMS

Absolute advantage
Appreciation
Balance of payments
Balance of trade
Bilateral trade
Common Agricultural Policy
Common external tariff
Comparative advantage
Competitiveness
Depreciation
Devaluation
Dumping
Economic and monetary union
Emerging markets
European Union
Exchange rate
Export marketing
Export-led growth
Exports
Fixed exchange rate
Floating exchange rate
Import controls
Import penetration
Imports
Interdependence
International Monetary Fund

Invisible trade
Maastricht
Multilateral trade
Multinational
Non-tariff barriers
Open economy
Protectionism
Purchasing power parity
Quotas
Revaluation
Single European market
Specialisation
Sterling exchange rate index
Tariffs
Terms of trade
Trade barriers
Trade deficit
Trade liberalisation
Trade surplus
Trade war
Trading bloc
Transitional economies
Transnational
Voluntary export restraints
World Trade Organisation

# 11 Economic development

Absolute poverty

Aid

Debt problem

Developing country

Equity/efficiency trade-off

Human Development Index

Industrialisation

Infrastructure

Interdependence

Intermediate technology

International Bank for Reconstruction and Development

Inward investment

Less developed countries

Official development assistance

Poverty

Soft loan

Sustainable growth

Third world country

UN Conference on Trade and Development

World Bank

# 12 Business responsibility and the environment

Accountability

Balanced growth

Consumer protection

Corporate responsibility

Environmental audit

Ethical code

Ethical investment

Ethics

Externalities

Finite resources

Lobbying

Negative externalities

Polluter pays principle

Pressure groups

Recycling

Social audit

Social benefit

Social cost

Sustainable growth

Voluntary organisations

# 13 Accounting and ratios
TOP 40 REVISION TERMS

Accounting Standards Board

Acid test ratio

Asset:turnover

Assets

Balance sheet

Bankruptcy

Capital employed

Cash flow

Cash flow forecasts

Cost of sales

Creditors

Current assets

Current liabilities

Debtors

Depreciation

Disclosure of information

Dividends

Fixed assets

Gross profit

Gross profit margin

Insolvency

Intangible assets

Liability

Liquidation

Liquidity

Net current assets

Operating profit

Operating profit margin

Overheads

Profit and loss account

Profit margin

Ratio analysis

Reserves

Return on capital employed

Share capital

Shareholders' funds

Solvency

Statutory disclosure

Working capital

# 14 Statistical terms
TOP 20 REVISION TERMS

Base year

Decile

Extrapolation

Frequency distribution

Index numbers

Median

Moving averages

Primary data

Quartile

Random sample

Retail price index

Return on capital

Sample

Secondary data

Shareholders' funds

Stock turnover

Trend

Trend analysis

Weighted average

Weighted index

# Top 20 terms for A-grade Economics and Business Studies revision

Aggregate demand
Business cycle
Business responsibility
Change
Competition
Competitive advantage
Culture
Economic growth
Elasticity
Exchange rate

Financial disclosure
Innovation
Marketing
Monopoly
Motivation
Opportunity cost
Pricing
Productivity
Profit
Unemployment

REVISION LISTINGS

# SYNOPTIC ASSESSMENT

From September 2000, all A level specifications will include the new phrase: 'synoptic assessment'. This means an examination that tests a candidate's understanding of the subject as a whole; how different subject areas relate to each other. In all subjects, this exam must take place at the end of the course, and must comprise 20% of the total marks for the A level. The government believes that this will be the toughest test within an A level.

To succeed with synoptic questions, candidates need to think in an integrated manner. In economics and business studies, this might mean seeing the financial or personnel implications of a marketing decision; or the effects on marketing and operations of an economic recession; or the impact of new technologies on individual businesses and on the rate of economic growth. This should not be a great problem for economics and business studies students, as teachers have been used to teaching in an integrated manner. Nevertheless, the following section has been devised to help synoptic revision.

## Synoptic revision

Synoptic revision means bringing together the different parts of the two subjects. Examiners will test this by creating situations which demand an integrated solution. For example, a particular business may face greatly intensified competition due to the entry of new businesses in a market where it previously had few competitors. The attempt to cope with the competition will affect all aspects of the business. Candidates will need to explain a range of possible strategies and their implications. They will need to set the issues in the context of a changing world economy.

Candidates will need quickly to plan the likely implications for different parts of the business. A spider diagram is shown on the following page, in which the first arrow shows the broad impact (e.g. impact on staff). Second stage arrows then show the further, more detailed analysis intended.

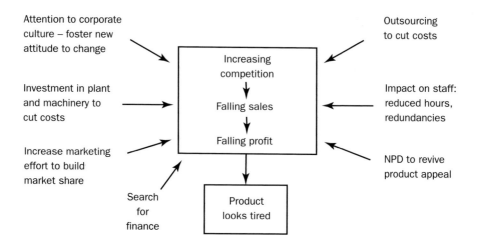

Having completed the spider, it is useful to go to a further stage, which is to organise (and extend) the thoughts further, using a planning hierarchy like the one shown below. Final completion of the process involves looking at how the different elements relate to each other. This is also shown in the second figure. The dotted lines represent connections. For example, falling sales may make it difficult to raise the necessary funds needed for further investment.

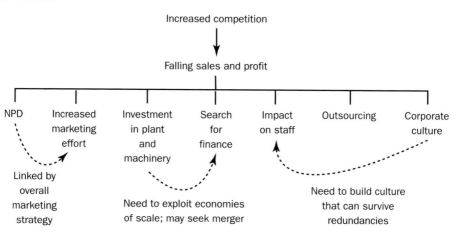

Having looked carefully at these diagrams for responding to competition, try out the other themes listed below. We recommend completing one per day in the lead-up to a synoptic exam.

# Further themes for synoptic assessment thought maps

1  Business planning for uncertainty
2  The growth of multinational businesses
3  The UK joining the Euro
4  The impact of R & D on competitiveness
5  Internet shopping and the High Street
6  The consequences of rapid growth
7  The effects on business and individuals of a sharp recession
8  The impact of globalisation on businesses
9  Business responsibility and the welfare of the individual

SYNOPTIC ASSESSMENT

## **EXAMINERS' TERMS**

## INTRODUCTION

The following entries should help explain what examiners mean by the words they use in exam questions. It is important to remember, though, that the words are only half the story. The other key factor is the mark allocation. This not only gives an indication of the length of answer required, but also the depth. The higher the *mark allocation*, the more likely it is that the examiner is looking for the skills of analysis and, especially, evaluation – and the more likely that the exam question will be marked on the basis of levels of response.

**Analyse:** to break a topic down into its component parts. This should help to identify the causes and effects of the issue and to explain the process whereby the causes bring about the effects. This encourages more depth of study. It implies a writing style that uses continuous prose in fully developed paragraphs. Bear in mind the word 'why?' when analysing.

**Assess:** weigh up and thereby *evaluate* two or more options or arguments.

**Assumptions:** see *state your assumptions*.

**Comment:** draw conclusions from the evidence, possibly in the form of a stated opinion. For example, in the first part of a question you might be required to analyse a company's financial position using ratios; part b) might ask you to comment on your findings. You might reach a conclusion about the firm's profitability and liquidity, then state your opinion about the firm's overall financial health. Also, it is often helpful to comment upon any further information needed.

**Consider:** another term inviting you to weigh up options or arguments in the form of continuous paragraphs of writing.

**Critically analyse** means to look in depth at an issue (analyse) from the perspective of a critic. In other words the examiner is encouraging you not to take the issue at face value; instead you should be questioning the assumptions or evidence involved. However, it is important to remember that film 'critics' may write a favourable review. You, too, should look at the strengths as well as the weaknesses involved.

**Debate:** put both sides of the case as forcefully as you can, then criticise each side from the perspective of the other. Take, for example, the essay title 'Debate the issue of whether cigarette advertising should be banned completely'. You should put forward the views both for and against, then tackle the arguments of those in favour from the point of view of opponents (and vice versa). You may decide, in the end, to 'vote' or abstain, as in a real debate.

**Decide which:** make a choice between the options, supported by your reasoning.

**Define:** explain the meaning of the term as precisely as you can; giving an example can help, but is not a substitute for explanation.

**Discuss:** put forward both sides of a case before coming to a conclusion. Discussion would require continuous writing and would be likely to be marked on a levels of response basis, with a high proportion of marks awarded for *evaluation*.

**Discuss critically:** a little different from 'discuss', though the examiner appears to be hinting that there may be a reason to be sceptical of the theory or question under discussion. Therefore you should look carefully for weaknesses in the logic.

**Distinguish between:** (as in 'distinguish between revenue and profit'). Here, you should explain each of the two terms and then look for the point of difference between them: 'the difference is that costs have been deducted from revenue to find profit'.

**Draw a graph:** it may sound absurd, but many Examiners' Reports state that students drew bar charts or even pie charts when asked to draw a graph. By graph the examiner means line graph.

**Evaluate:** this vital term means weighing up evidence in order to reach a judgement. In the context of an essay, you will have to present that evidence (pros and cons, perhaps) before reaching a conclusion. As the term invites your judgement, do be willing to state your opinion within the conclusion, e.g. 'In my view . . .'. It can be helpful to keep in mind the phrase 'to what extent . . . ?

**Examine** means to look in detail at the argument, evidence or theory presented. It requires continuous writing and should be rounded off with a conclusion.

**Explain:** expand upon in order to show your understanding of the term or theory being tested. The depth of explanation required will be indicated by the *mark allocation*. Giving a well-chosen example will often gain a mark.

**Give:** this means list, as in 'Give two possible reasons for reducing interest rates.' There is no requirement to explain the points you make. Point-form answers are acceptable.

**How might:** this phrase suggests a need to explain a process, as in 'How might a firm choose between two investment options?' You must explain the process with care, then consider the *mark allocation* before deciding whether a conclusion is required. If 5 marks are available, no conclusion would be necessary; with 25 marks, however, you would be wise to *evaluate* your answer.

**Identify:** to name one or more examples of the topic being examined. Usually this would require no more than a list, with one mark awarded per point made.

**Justify your answer:** present an argument in favour of the views you are expressing, for example: 'Should the Post Office be privatised? Justify your answer.' Although the question appears to be expecting a yes or no at the outset, it is better to wait until the end to state your opinion, because you will have given the matter enough thought to be able to justify your decision.

**Levels of response:** a way of marking answers based upon different academic skills rather than the quantity of knowledge shown. This is the way in which most high-mark questions are examined. If ten marks are available for 'Explain the impact of higher interest rates upon firms', a levels of response marking scheme would put a ceiling on the number of marks available for listing points (see diagram on following page). Therefore you are better off writing a full explanation of two or three points.

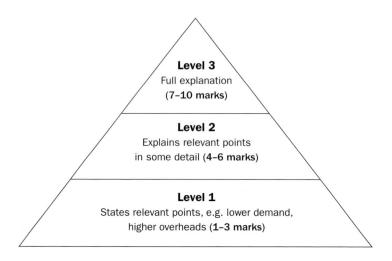

Level 3
Full explanation
(7–10 marks)

Level 2
Explains relevant points
in some detail (4–6 marks)

Level 1
States relevant points, e.g. lower demand,
higher overheads (1–3 marks)

**List:** briefly state, not necessarily in a full sentence (same as give).

**Mark allocation:** the number of marks on offer for each part of a question.

**Name:** same as list or give.

**Outline:** provide a description of an event, theory or method. The length and the level of detail will be governed by the *mark allocation*.

**Report format:** see *Write a report*.

**Show your workings:** this phrase is used often with numerical questions, but should never be ignored. In the pressure of the exam room, almost every candidate will slip up somewhere in a complex calculation. If there are 10 marks on offer for the answer '£24 800', the candidate who gives the answer '£248 000' with no workings will get 0, while a candidate with the same answer will get 9 marks if the workings show where the single slip was made. The secret with numerical questions is not to get 10 out of 10 one time and 0 the next. It is to get 8 or 9 marks every time.

**Sketch a diagram:** this suggests a quick drawing on the ordinary exam writing paper, paying little attention to precision in the lines being drawn. However, to convey any meaning, the sketch will need properly labelled axes and/or lines and a clear title. With sketches, the labelling may carry more marks than the diagram itself.

**State:** means the same as give.

**State and explain:** this should be tackled exactly in this way, i.e. give a reason (in perhaps 4–8 words) then explain it (in perhaps 4–8 lines).

**State your assumptions:** in a numerical question, tell the examiner the decisions you have made when there has been some uncertainty about the correct figures. To gain a mark, your assumption must be based on uncertainty and must be logical. For example, in a recent exam, many students calculating profit assumed that corporation tax would stay unchanged at £40 000 from one year to the next. As corporation tax is charged as a per-centage of pre-tax profit, this was not acceptable. Do not confuse an assumption with a conclusion.

**Suggest** means to put forward an idea. If few marks are allocated, this might require no more than a list of points. The word is used more commonly, though, in the context of higher-mark case study or essay questions. In this case it would require a full explanation and justification for the suggestions made.

**SWOT analysis:** an investigation into an organisation's current strengths and weaknesses and potential opportunities and threats. It is usually presented in report format.

**To what extent:** this commonly used examining phrase requires you to reach a judgement about the degree to which a statement, theory or evidence is true. It is likely that the levels of response marking scheme will reward evaluation especially heavily. So focus on relatively few themes, deal with each in depth and then make a judgement about 'to what extent . . .'.

**What do you understand by?** (or **What is meant by?**): explain the meaning of the term or phrase given. An example may be helpful, but is not a substitute for explanation.

**Why might:** this phrase invites you to suggest possible explanations for why a firm or individual may have chosen a course of action. The use of the word might give you scope to stray outside the confines of, perhaps, a case study text. Any answer will be accepted as long as it is not too far-fetched; but remember that examiners want to reward your business and economics understanding, so try to draw from relevant theories.

**Write a memo:** present your answer to a question in the form of a business memo (memorandum). This requires headings (To, From, Title, Date) and is likely to be a relatively brief statement of (or request for) factual information. The contents can be written in continuous prose or in point form.

**Write a report:** present your answer to a question in the form of a business report. A report is a document that is likely to provide a great deal of information (written and numerical) and is therefore broken down into sections, each of which is split into sub-sections. The users of the report expect to be able to refer to any part of it at any time and in any order. Therefore it has a contents page and frequent cross-referencing. A busy manager may want to do no more than read a summary of the report's findings and recommendations, so most reports start with an 'executive summary'.

In the context of an exam, where only 30 or 45 minutes may be available, little of the above is possible. So the report need only have title headings (To, From, Title, Date) and a structure of numbered sections with numbered sub-sections. If time permits, it is valuable to start with a section on the background to the report and to end with recommendations/points for action.